AF560734

THE DUTCH FACTORIES IN INDIA

A COLLECTION OF DUTCH EAST INDIA COMPANY DOCUMENTS PERTAINING TO INDIA

VOL. II [1624–1627]

This publication has been financially supported by the Delhi University EurIndia Project sponsored by the Economic Cross-Cultural Programme (ECCP) of the European Union. The European Union, however, is in no way responsible for its contents.

THE DUTCH FACTORIES IN INDIA

A Collection of Dutch East India Company Documents Pertaining to India

Vol. II [1624-1627]

Translated, annotated and edited by
OM PRAKASH

With the editorial assistance of
V.B. GUPTA

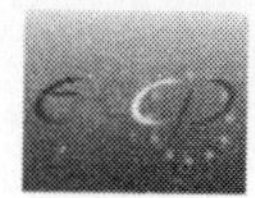

MANOHAR
2007

First published 2007

ISBN 81-7304-739-1

Published by

Ajay Kumar Jain *for*
Manohar Publishers & Distributors
4753/23 Ansari Road, Daryaganj
New Delhi 110 002

Typeset at

Digigrafics
New Delhi 110 049

Printed at

Lordson Publishers Pvt. Ltd.
Delhi 110 007

Contents

Preface

It was way back in 1984 that the first volume in this series covering the years 1617 to 1623 was published. Other more pressing engagements kept me away from getting back to this project. It had, however, been gratifying to note over the years the fairly extensive use to which the 1984 volume had been put by researchers working in diverse fields. So when an opportunity presented itself in the form of an invitation to join the EurIndia project of the University of Delhi, I decided to do another volume. It was, however, quite apparent early on that given the increase in the volume of correspondence, the maximum number of years I could expect to cover in the present volume would be no more than four, namely those between 1624 and 1627.

The overall style followed in the present volume remains similar to that in Volume 1. Basically, the volume contains the extant documents of the Dutch East India Company pertaining to India for the years 1624 to 1627 preserved at the *Nationaal Archief*, The Hague, the Netherlands. All the important information available in a document—whether it be a letter or an enclosure to a letter—has been retained. This applies equally to economic, social, political and religious information. The bits that have been omitted related largely to purely administrative and establishment matters of the Company with little bearing on the Company's trade or the history of the local economy and society. The details of the journeys between Batavia and India have also usually been omitted. Wherever necessary in the interest of clarity and cohesion, the material within a document has been rearranged. For example, references relating to the procurement of textiles occurring in a letter from Batavia to Coromandel at three places have been brought together. Statistical materials have been presented, as far as possible, in a tabular form. The documents have not been translated word for word. For given the archaic character of the seventeenth-century Dutch language, and the limited linguistic competence of an average factor of the Company writing the letter, such a procedure held the prospect of producing rather bleak results. Great care has, however, been taken to capture the intent of the letter writer faithfully.

The system of footnoting adopted is that a proper noun or a term is identified or explained only the first time it occurs. For subsequent references, it would be necessary to refer to the index where the page number for the identification or explanation is provided and indicated in bold print. An asterisk is used whenever an editorial comment on a document is called for.

Documents where complete information regarding the date of origin was not available have been placed at the end of the relevant year. Documents consulted but not included in the present collection either because they did not contain any information pertaining to India (though they originated at Jacatra/Batavia and as such could have contained information on India) or because they did not contain any useful information have been listed in Appendix I. Information regarding the names of the ships that carried the various documents has been tabulated in Appendix II. Letters and other documents in the Company's archives are often available in multiple copies. Appendix III lists the sources where additional copies are available. Finally, Appendix IV lists the corresponding K.A. numbers of the V.O.C. volumes used for the present collection.

A considerable amount of published material both in the English and the Dutch languages has been found useful in the course of annotating the present volume. Special mention must be made in the former category of W. Foster (ed.), *English Factories in India* (Oxford, 1906-27), John Irwin and P.R. Schwartz, *Studies in the Indo-European Textile History* (Ahmedabad, 1966) and T. Raychaudhuri, *Jan Company in Coromandel* (The Hague, 1962). Among the Dutch published sources used are W.Ph. Coolhaas (ed.), *Generale Missiven van Gouverneurs-Generaal en Raden aan Heren XVII Der Verenigde Oostindische Compagnie*, vol. 1, 1610-38 (The Hague, 1960), H.W. Colenbrander et al. (ed.), *Jan Pietersz. Coen, Bescheiden Omtrent Zijn Bedriff in Indie* (7 vols., The Hague, 1925, etc.), W. Ph. Coolhaas (ed.), *Pieter van den Broecke in Azie* (2 vols., The Hague, 1962) and H. Terpstra, *De Opkomst der Wester-*

kwartieren van de Oost Indische Compagnie Suratte, Arabie, Perzie (The Hague, 1918). Whenever a document included in the present collection has earlier been printed in any of these books, this fact has been mentioned in the editorial comments on the document.

I would like to take this opportunity to thank my colleagues in the EurIndia project, Jean-Marie Lafont, Vibha Maurya and TKV Subramanian, for extending whole hearted support to this work. Thanks are also due to the staff of the *Nationaal Archief*, The Hague, for providing all help. The editorial assistance by Mr. V.B. Gupta has been invaluable. Finally, a word of thanks to Mr. Ramesh Jain of Manohar Publishers for producing this volume both efficiently and expeditiously.

Delhi
December 2006

Om Prakash

List of Documents

Introduction

The rise of an early modern world economy, facilitated by the great discoveries of the closing years of the fifteenth century, held important implications for the Indian subcontinent. The availability of an all-water route between Europe and Asia via the Cape of Good Hope, and of a growing amount of American silver for export to Asia, involved a substantial expansion in the volume and the value of Euro-Asian trade. The Portuguese monopoly of the all-water route was challenged at the beginning of the seventeenth century by the English and the Dutch East India companies, who eventually came to dominate this trade. The only other body of any consequence engaged in this enterprise was the French East India Company. The so-called minor companies—the Danish, the Ostend, the Swedish and others—never really accounted for more than an insignificant proportion of the total trade between the two continents. At least one of the corporate enterprises, namely the Dutch East India Company, also carried on a substantial amount of trade within Asia. Employees of corporate enterprises also engaged in intra-Asian trade in their private capacity. By far the most important category of these employees was that in the service of the English East India Company.

India was at the centre of the Europeans' trading activities in respect of both Euro-Asian as well as intra-Asian trade. The Portuguese procured all their pepper for Europe in India: their intra-Asian trading network largely revolved around the Bay of Bengal. When textiles and raw silk dominated Euro-Asian trade from the last quarter of the seventeenth century onward, India also became central to the northern European trading companies' imports into Europe. India similarly dominated the Dutch East India Company's as well as the English private traders' intra-Asian trade.

In the early part of the seventeenth century, India was of critical importance for both the English and the Dutch East India companies, the two principal European corporate enterprises engaged in the Indian Ocean trade. India was important to the English as the provider of goods such as textiles, indigo and saltpetre for Europe besides being the place from which efforts could be made to gain entry into the silk trade of Persia.

The attractions of the Indian trade were even greater for the Dutch. The Dutch East India Company was founded in 1602 by a charter granted by the States-General, the national administrative body of the Dutch Republic. The founding of the Company had been preceded by a number of voyages to the East on the account of the so-called pre-companies. These early adventurers had found that the most important medium used by Asian merchants to procure the Indonesian spices—which had traditionally been at the heart of Euro-Asian trade—was Indian textiles which were in great demand in the region and afforded a high profit. The bulk of these textiles were comparatively cheap and coarse in quality though some, of course, were very expensive. The area where they were produced on a large scale was the south-east coast of India known as the Coromandel coast. It was immediately obvious to the Dutch East India Company that if it invested the precious metals brought from home in Indian textiles and then sold these textiles against Indonesian pepper and other spices, a given amount of precious metals would buy it a much larger amount of spices than if the precious metals were invested directly in the procurement of the spices. Soon after its establishment, therefore, the Company took active steps in this direction and established a factory on the Coromandel coast as early as 1606. Six years later Hendrick Brouwer, a future Governor-General of the Dutch East Indies, described the Coromandel coast as the 'left arm of the Moluccas and the sorrounding islands because without textiles that come from there [the Coromandel coast], the trade in the Moluccas will be dead'.[1] The availability of extensive monopsonistic and monopolistic privileges in the Indonesian archipelago further helped the extension of the Company's trade in Asia. In 1618, Governor-General Coen visualized a situation where eventually the Euro-Asian trade could be financed out of the profits of the intra-Asian trade.[2] The following year Coen sent to the Directors a blue-print of the Company's intra-Asian trade in which the Dutch factories on the Coromandel coast and in Gujarat had a crucial role to play. The point is that even though Indian goods did not figure significantly in the Dutch cargoes to Europe until the second half of the seventeenth century, the Company was nevertheless deeply committed to participation in the trade from India from the very beginning because of the role such participation played in the overall strategy of the Company's intra-Asian trade.

As pointed out above, the Company's participation in the Indian trade started with the establishment of a trading post (called a factory) at Petapuli in north Coromandel in 1606. By 1616, trade relations had also been established with Gujarat, another major textile producing region in the country. The factories in Coromandel and Gujarat were answerable to the Governor-General and the Council at Jacatra (renamed Batavia in 1621) who, in turn, reported to the Central Board of Directors, the so-called Gentlemen XVII who met for six years in succession at the Chamber of Amsterdam followed by two years at the Chamber of Zeeland. The hierarchical structure did not, of course, preclude the possibility of the Directors getting in touch directly with the factors in India or these factors getting in touch directly with the Board. This set-up generated a large amount of written material in the form of correspondence and enclosures thereto.

The papers of the Dutch East India Company covering the period 1607 to 1795 are preserved at the *Nationaal Archief*, The Hague, the Netherlands. The bulk of this extant material consists of correspondence amongst the various agencies of the Company dealing mainly with commercial matters. These included the orders placed by the Board of Directors for various Asian goods, along with complaints regarding under-fulfilment of the earlier orders, the quality of the goods received, their prices and so on. At the other end, the factors in Asia were constantly justifying the shortfalls in supplies, the poorness of the quality and the high prices with reference to the enormity of the competition for limited supplies by rival European companies as well as Asian competitors, the 'villainy' of the merchants dealing with the Company in supplying to third parties goods that they had got prepared against advances taken from the Company, and so forth.

The first link in the chain was that of the Board of Directors sending annually to the Council of the Indies at Batavia a list of goods to be procured in the East Indies. The list specified the exact nature of each item to be procured (in the case of textiles, for example, the length and the width of each piece and the colour combinations, etc. were mentioned) as also the region where it was to be bought. Often, the lists also referred to the performance of the relevant item at the immediately preceding sale in Amsterdam or another chamber of the Company. These lists as well as the other correspondence from the Netherlands to Batavia and the various Asian factories are available in the series designated 'Resolutions of the Gentlemen XVII' and 'Copies of letters from the Gentlemen XVII and the Amsterdam Chamber to the factories in Asia and the Cape'. The relevant extracts from the orders list and other correspondence, if any, were then passed on by Batavia to each of the Asian factories: at the same time Batavia also dispatched a list of its own, consisting of goods to be procured by that factory for the intra-Asian trade of the Company which was co-ordinated from Batavia. These latter lists, as also the correspondence from Batavia to the individual factories, form part of the 'Batavia's outgoing letter-book' beginning in 1621. For the earlier period, this correspondence forms part of the 'Letters and papers received' series to be discussed presently.

Once the orders (and, of course, the wherewithal to buy the ordered goods consisting of both goods and precious metals) had been received at the chief factory of the region concerned (each region had a chief factory where the 'governor' or the 'director' in charge of the Company's trade in the region had his establishment with jurisdiction over a string of subordinate factories), action was initiated to begin the work of procurement almost simultaneously at the chief factory and the subordinate factories. Contracts were put out to merchants, and the mutually negotiated sums of money advanced to them. The correspondence originating at the subordinate factory level would be full of details regarding the factors' assessment of the chances of procurement in the context of the competition that might be put up by the rival

European traders as well as by the Asian merchants. These letters were usually accompanied by various kinds of enclosures which might include: letters received from the indigenous brokers; a copy of the diary that might be kept at the factory; a report about the manufacturing processes involved in the production of an export item, be it a silk textile or indigo or saltpetre; a list of the ships arriving at and departing from the local port on the account of the Asian merchants; a report about the political situation in the area, and so on. Basing themselves upon these letters and reports as well as on their own daily journal and other information, the Council at the chief factory would have a regular series of consultations which, in turn, would constitute the raw material for the letters to the Council at Batavia. There would ordinarily be two to three such letters per annum, one with each shipment. These letters would include details that were likely to be of interest to the Batavia Council. The same principle would ordinarily be followed in deciding what enclosures were to be appended to the letter. Thus, while a shipping list relating to the Asian merchants would normally find a place in the enclosures for the simple reason that the information would have been collected at the behest of Batavia who wanted to keep themselves informed of movements in this trade, a report dealing purely with local issues was unlikely to find its way to the Batavia Council, though on occasions that did happen. Instructions and memoranda left by the outgoing 'governors' or 'directors' for their successors, which ordinarily constitute an important source of information, were usually included in the enclosures.

At Batavia, the Governor-General and the Council wrote a so-called 'general letter' to the Gentlemen XVII which was dispatched with the autumn fleet returning to the Netherlands at the end of the year. This letter reviewed the major developments in the East Indies over the preceding year region by region. In any one year, there could, of course, be more than one such letter. To these letters were appended a large number of enclosures including letters, reports, journals and invoices, etc., originating mainly at the individual Asian factories. While in the early years of the seventeenth century, these documents added up, on an average, to about 3 to 4 rather substantial volumes per annum, the number had gone up to 30 to 40 by the eighteenth century.

This series is called the 'Letters and papers received' and is easily the most voluminous as well as the most important collection in the Dutch records at The Hague. But it nevertheless is only a part of the materials received at Batavia. The Batavia Council evidently engaged in a large-scale weeding out exercise and eliminated items which were not deemed to be of any interest to the authorities at home. The result is that while the bulk of the information—qualitative and quantitative—that a researcher reconstructing the flows of trade within Asia and between Asia and Europe would be interested in would, in fact, be found in the Dutch sources, a good bit of the materials pertaining to the coastal city and the local economy and society would no longer be available. This, of course, is not to suggest that the materials do not contain a great deal of information pertaining to the mechanics of Asian economies and societies. This information might pertain to wage rates, the organization of manufacturing production and procurement, agricultural and mineral products, the political organization and the system of justice, social and religious affairs, and so on.

The present volume contains the extant documents of the Dutch East India Company pertaining to India for the years 1624 to 1627. The years from 1617 to 1623 had been covered in volume I in the present series published in 1984. These documents include first of all the correspondence amongst the various agencies of the Company. Thus there were letters exchanged amongst the factors stationed at different factories within each of the two regions of Coromandel and Gujarat, between the factors at the chief factories of the two regions, between the factors of the chief factory in a region and the Governor-General and the Council at Batavia and between the chief factories and the Board of Directors. The correspondence between Batavia and the Board of Directors also contained references to the Indian factories. The enclosures to the letters included items such as invoices of ships, lists of goods ordered, lists of goods in stock, an estimate of the resources available at a particular factory, lists of factors at a given factory, amounts and prices of goods sold, memoranda relating to outstanding debts and the chances of their recovery, and so on. Another range of documents covered the business activities of the English who were the principal European rivals of the Company at this time. Yet another set of documents pertained to the exploratory material collected by the Company's factors relating to the possibilities of trade in a given area. Other enclosures included copies of passports issued, *farmans* received, inventories of goods taken out of the ships seized by the Dutch, a copy of the memorandum left by the outgoing chief of a factory for his successor, and so on. In brief, one could expect to find a wide range of issues covered in the correspondence and its enclosures.

The Indian factories of the Company during the period covered by the present volume were on the Coromandel coast and in Gujarat. The Coromandel coast denoted the east coast of India south of the Godavari river and extending as far as Nagapattinam or even the island of Manar. The northern part of the coast between the Godavari and the Pennar rivers was then included in the Qutb Shahi kingdom of Golconda, one of the five Deccan sultanates which arose after the disintegration of the Bahmani kingdom. The southern Coromandel was ruled by a number of semi-independent feudatory chiefs who had emerged in the area after the defeat of Vijayanagar in 1564-5. Pre-eminent among these were the *nayaks* of Gingi, Tanjore and Madura, part of whose territories covered a wide tract of southern Coromandel.

The first Dutch factory on the Coromandel coast was established at Petapuli in north Coromandel in 1606 followed by another in neighbouring Masulipatnam the same year. A *farman* granted by the king of Golconda stipulated the payment by the Dutch of a 4 per cent customs duty on their exports and imports. The Company was exempted from the stamp duty on cloth amounting to about 12 per cent. South Coromandel was reached with the establishment of a factory at Tirupapaliyur in 1608. Yet another factory was established at Pulicat in the same region in 1610. Later in the year, the Dutch Council of the Indies at Bantam decided to reorganize the four factories on the Coromandel coast into a directorate with the factory at Pulicat being designated the chief factory of the region. In 1612, the 4 per cent duty at Masulipatnam was commuted into a fixed payment of 3,000 *pagodas* a year. A fort was constructed at Pulicat in 1613 and given the name of Fort Geldria. The Coromandel factories were reconstituted into a 'government' in 1616 with Hans de Haze as the first governor.

As a counter-measure against the local *havaldar's*[3] extortionate demands, the factory at Petapuli was closed in June 1616. The subsequent pleas by the *havaldar* to reopen the factory were turned down. The civil war that engulfed southern Coromandel following the death of king Venkata II of Vijayanagar in 1614 made it impossible to do any profitable trading at the factory at Tirupapaliyur. Therefore, notwithstanding assurances of help given by Itsjapa Nayak who controlled Tirupapaliyur, it was decided in 1618 to abandon the factory. It was argued that the textiles ordinarily bought at Tirupapaliyur could in fact be bought cheaper at Masulipatnam. As for the *balatius* for the Moluccas and the saltpetre for Holland, which were both available only at Tirupapaliyur, it was pointed out that the Company could organize their procurement through Malaya, the chief Indian broker the Dutch had in southern Coromandel.

In June 1619, Governor Hans de Haze ordered a temporary closure of the factory at Masulipatnam as a protest against the orders of the local *havaldar* stipulating that in future, the Company would be obliged to deal with a single merchant, Lingua,[4] nominated by him. The authorities were somewhat surprised at this move since they believed that the Company carried on a large and profitable trade at Masulipatnam. They were also apprehensive that the Dutch might attack the Indian shipping. But the king of Golconda acted promptly and replaced *havaldar* Mir Qasim by one Itimad Khan. The latter brought along a *farman* granted by the king on 25 July 1619 stipulating that the Dutch would be allowed to trade freely. They were also to be exempt from all tolls and imposts at Masulipatnam subject to an annual payment of 3,000 *pagodas*. Following the receipt of the *farman* and the assurances held out by merchant Kamal-al-Din, Van Dyck started out for Masulipatnam on the 2nd of September with a capital of 19,000 *pagodas*. The factory was actually reopened on 23 October 1619. However, the Dutch, having re-established themselves, felt that things were going well at Masulipatnam 'more because of the fear of the Company's power than out of any regard for the *farman* granted by the king of Golconda'.[5]

The correspondence relating to the Coromandel coast brings out in an unambiguous fashion the commercial priorities of the Company at this time. The procurement for the Indonesian archipelago always took precedence over that for Europe. The Governor-General and the Council took great pains to drive this point home to the factors. In the process, they used arguments such as the fact that the profit on Coromandel textiles sold in the archipelago was no less than that earned in Europe while the turnover was much quicker in the former. The prevalent system of procurement in Coromandel obliged the Company to enter into agreements with merchants to whom a part of the total value of the agreement was given in advance. The merchants insisted on this procedure partly because of the relative paucity of resources with them and partly because it guaranteed an assured market for the goods manufactured at the Company's instance. From the point of view of the Company, the system worked satisfactorily as long as care was taken not to advance too large a sum of money to a single merchant.

While the principal commodity the Company procured in Coromandel was textiles, it often also procured some diamonds, among other goods. Indeed, the Directors of the Company, who usually thought only in terms of goods that could be procured in a given region for the European market, often argued that the Company's funds could not find a better investment in Coromandel than in good-quality diamonds. In 1620, a new deposit of diamonds was discovered in a village south-west of Masulipatnam. The new mine was a large one and reportedly employed as many as 20,000 men. It had been leased out by the king of Golconda at 300,000 *pagodas* per annum. The lease-deed stipulated that all diamonds of more than eight carats each extracted from the mine would be given to the king free of charge. In October 1621, the king ordered closure of the mine apparently because it was feared that the Mughal ambassador to Golconda was likely to ask for some of the best diamonds extracted from the mine. But curiously enough, the mine remained closed for quite some time after the departure of the ambassador from

Golconda. It was only in 1623 that the mine was reopened after being farmed out jointly to four merchants at 260,000 *pagodas* per annum. The new lease-deed retained the clause pertaining to the king's right to all diamonds of more than eight carats each.

In pursuance of the Company's general policy to participate extensively in intra-Asian trade, the factors at Coromandel also tried to establish trading links with a number of neighbouring regions around the Bay of Bengal. These included the Orissa coast, Bengal, Pegu and Arakan. In August 1617, the *Der Goes* was sent to the Orissa coast with a capital of 2,000 *pagodas* with instructions to explore the trading opportunities there but with no results. The possibility of opening a factory in Bengal, where the Company was interested in buying textiles, sugar and saltpetre, was explored by Jan Cornelisz. Kunst. A fleet of three ships, the *Schiedam*, the *Muys* and the *Jager*, sent to Bengal in 1622 under his command, returned to Coromandel in January 1623. In April, Batavia informed Van Uffelen that pending the receipt of Kunst's report, a decision regarding the establishment of a factory in Bengal had been postponed.

As early as 1607, the Coromandel factors had deputed Pieter Willemsz. and Jan Gerritsz. Ruyl to Arakan to investigate the trade opportunities there. They managed to persuade the king to allow the Company to trade in his territories without having to pay any duties. The *quid pro quo* asked for was assistance in expelling the Portuguese settlers at Chittagong. A Dutch factory was established at Mrauk U in 1610 by Jacob Dirksz. Cortenhoeff but nothing much happened by way of trade there for several years and the Company's representative was recalled to Pulicat in 1619.

It was Jan Pietersz. Coen's plans to procure a large number of slaves to provide the labour force needed for the nutmeg and mace plantations on Amboina and in Banda and generally to populate and secure the Dutch colonies in the Indonesian archipelago that seriously attracted the Company to Arakan for the first time.[6] The correspondence between Coen and the successive heads of the Company's Coromandel establishment in the early 1620s establishes beyond any doubt Coen's near-obsession with this project. In his letter of 8 May 1622 to Andries

Soury and Abraham van Uffelen at Masulipatnam, for example, Coen wrote:

> The *Muys* is being sent to Coromandel mainly to bring back as many slaves—young males and females—as possible. In spite of the fact that Coromandel textiles were in great demand, the interest of the Company would be served better by the procurement of slaves, who were likely to afford a much higher profit. With the *Gouden Leeuw*, Batavia had expected to get no less than 1,000 slaves but, in fact, we had received only 124. . . . It was a matter of shame that such an important matter had been treated so lightly. A large number of boys and girls from various quarters of Asia were needed to populate Batavia, Amboina, and Banda with servile people. Even hundreds of thousands of such persons would be welcome. It was instructive to consider the Portuguese precedent of how they had populated their possessions. It was also useful to consider how the Muslims had extended their rule over Asia. They had obtained manpower from the enemy and had also purchased it. The Dutch had been so imprudent as to ignore these precedents.[7]

The regular slave-capturing raids made by Arakanese war-fleets into eastern and southern Bengal had turned Arakan into the largest supplier of this human cargo in the Bay of Bengal region.

The Company's attempts to procure slaves (or for that matter, rice or elephants, the other two items the Company was interested in procuring) in Arakan, however, did not meet with a notable success at any point. One major problem was the unacceptably high mortality rate amongst the slaves—in Arakan, on the way to Coromandel, and finally on the trip from Coromandel to Batavia. Thus, of the 400 slaves bought by the *Vrede* and the *Medemblik* in Arakan in 1624, as many as 100 had died, some in Arakan itself and others on the way to Coromandel.[8] The situation was even worse the following year. The Arakanese fleet had brought in as many as 10,000 slaves that year. But an unusually severe epidemic had taken a toll of 4,000 of them soon after. The two Dutch ships, the *Medemblik* and the *Jager*, managed to buy 544 of the surviving slaves of whom, however, as many as 86 died soon after in Arakan itself. Some more died on the way reducing the number reaching Coromandel to 130. Four more deaths reportedly occurred in Coromandel while another twenty-six were reported to be too ill to travel. The result was that the *Delfshaven* had only 100 slaves on board when she left Coromandel for Batavia.[9] This practically spelt the end of the Company's trade in Arakanese slaves. Even Jan Pietersz. Coen, who had relinquished the office of the Governor-General of the East Indies in February 1623 only to return in September 1627 for a second term, had in the meantime lost his enthusiasm about populating Indonesia with slaves. In a letter to Marten Ysbrantz. at Pulicat in June 1628, Coen wrote:

> We ask you to issue strict orders to all places wherever slaves are purchased that only young persons—boys and girls between the ages of eight to twenty years—are to be bought. The old, the unsuitable, and the useless are to be left out. If you cannot get the right ones, do not buy any slaves for a while.[10]

In September 1628, the remaining factors of the Company in Arakan were recalled to Coromandel.

At this time the Dutch East India Company's interest in the Pegu trade was even more marginal. Two galliots, the *Jager* and the *Haas*, had been sent to Pegu from Masulipatnam on 15 April 1619, on an exploratory mission. But the vessels went instead to Arakan.[11] Another two frigates were sent in October 1620 to Tenasserim, Arakan, and Pegu but it is not clear if Pegu was in fact visited.[12] In May 1622, twenty-six free burghers had started out from Batavia for the Bay of Bengal in the yacht *Bonijt* intending to engage in trade in the region as well as to inflict damage on the Portuguese. But a storm forced the vessel into one of the ports of the king of Pegu where it was seized. The Dutch chief at Masulipatnam, Abraham van Uffelen, wrote to the king of Pegu requesting the release of the ship together with its cargo. Masulipatnam merchants engaged in trade with Pegu were warned to stay away from the area because a possible action against the king of Pegu might inflict collateral damage on them.[13] The result was a disruption in these merchants' trade with Pegu, a branch of trade that together with that of Arakan had traditionally been a reasonably important one for them. Information available in the records of the Dutch East India Company enables one to form a broad idea of the magnitude of this trade. In 1617, for example, three to four small yachts were reported to have arrived at Masulipatnam from Pegu on the account of Muslim merchants. Aboard one of these yachts had also travelled the ambassador of the king of Pegu to the king of Golconda with presents of gold and rubies worth 7,000 guilders.[14] In October 1624, six ships owned by Muslim merchants were reported to have left Masulipatnam for Arakan in addition to four for Pegu. Another two had left for Aceh and one for Tenasserim.[15] In September 1625, ten ships were reported to have left Masulipatnam including two each for Pegu and Arakan. Of the remaining six, three each went to Tenasserim and Aceh.[16] The following March, a ship belonging to Mir Kamal-al-Din reached Masulipatnam from Pegu richly laden with tin and costly rubies. It also brought news that another five ships were on the way.[17] In April of the same year, a ship belonging to the *kotwal*[18] of Arakan reached Pulicat (note that the ships recorded as having arrived at Pulicat were most probably on their way to Masulipatnam).[19] It started back from Coromandel for Arakan on 12 August. Later in the month the yacht *Masulipatam* belonging to the Hindu merchant Malaya left Pulicat for Pegu with a cargo worth 15,000 *pagodas*.[20] A small yacht, the *Pagel*, also left Pulicat for Arakan on the account of this merchant on 30 September 1626.[21] Of the nine ships listed as having left Masulipatnam in September 1628, three went to Pegu and four to Arakan. One each went to Tenasserim and Aceh.[22] We next find a ship belonging to Muhammad Taqi, *havaldar* of Masulipatnam, listed as arrived from Pegu in April 1627 with the news that another ship belonging to Mir Murad was on its way.[23] Yet another ship was recorded as having reached Pulicat in April on its way to Masulipatnam, but was then wrecked.[24] A ship belonging to the king of Arakan carrying thirteen elephants (eight on the king's account, three on that of the *kotwal* of Arakan, and two on the account of the 'governor' of Pulicat) also reached Pulicat the same month.[25]

Among the arrivals recorded at Pulicat in March/April 1628 was a yacht belonging to Malaya returning from Pegu with a cargo worth 100,000 *pagodas* in rubies, and two ships from Arakan belonging to the king of Arakan carrying elephants and rice besides forty-eight male slaves on the account of the Company.[26] In September of the same year, two ships were reportedly ready to leave Masulipatnam for Pegu, one belonging to Mir Murad and the other to the *sar-i-khail*[27] of Masulipatnam.[28]

What these scattered references to the shipping between Coromandel and coastal Burma in the 1620s would seem to suggest strongly is the dominant position of the Masulipatnam merchants, many of whom were of Persian origin, in this branch of trade, though the participation by merchants based at the partner ports, including the kings of Pegu and Arakan as well as state officials such as the *kotwal* of Arakan, was by no means altogether insignificant. What the V.O.C. documents of this period also bring out clearly is the disruption that this trade was often subject to because of political circumstances such as the deteriorating relations between the Company and the authorities at Golconda. The events surrounding the arrest of Abraham van Uffelen by the Golconda authorities and the threatened blockade of the port of Masulipatnam by the Dutch in retaliation is a case in point.

Abraham van Uffelen had taken over as the governor of the Coromandel factories in October 1621. This man was somewhat aggressive in his ways and often had skirmishes with the local administration. Matters deteriorated to a point where, in November 1623, Van Uffelen was arrested along with an underfactor and three of the Company's chief merchants in Masulipatnam. The grounds given for this extraordinary action were (a) that Van Uffelen had detained in the Company's factory the *sarraf*[29] to whom the exclusive right to deal in bills of exchange had been farmed out till such time as he had agreed to exchange 5,000 rials into *pagodas* at a favourable rate; (b) that Van Uffelen had violated the ban on the export of tobacco to Arakan, and (c) that Van Uffelen had refused passes to Indian ships for Pegu. The Dutch maintained that the *sarraf* had been detained long before the arrival of the present *havaldar* at Masulipatnam. In the matter of the export of tobacco, it was pointed out that the Dutch had only been advised the postponement of the export until after the arrival of the new *havaldar*. But since the season was running out, it had not been possible to accept this advice. The Dutch maintained that the real reason behind the outrage was the desire of the authorities to wriggle out of the agreement permitting the Company to trade in

Coromandel toll-free subject to an annual payment of 3,000 *pagodas* at Masulipatnam. But whatever the merits of the case, Van Uffelen and the Company's merchants were subjected to severe torture and their release was ordered only after 16,000 *pagodas* had been collected from the Company. The Company claimed that as a result of the bodily injuries suffered while in prison, Van Uffelen died in Masulipatnam in February 1624.[30]

The immediate reaction of the Coromandel factors was to suggest that Batavia take retaliatory action by suspending the Company's trade at Masulipatnam, blockading the port, and seizing Asian shipping returning from Pegu and Arakan, among other places. Batavia, however, counselled patience and asked the factors to carry on as best they could.[31] Efforts to recover the 16,000 *pagodas* extorted from the Company did not bear fruit. Instead, the Company was forced to deal with just three designated merchants and the situation became increasingly tense. In June 1628, Batavia finally decided to take the offensive and in a secret communication asked Marten Ysbrantsz. to organize the seizure of the ships returning from Mocha, Pegu, Arakan, Tenasserim, Aceh and other places in order 'to recover with interest the sums extorted from the Company'. Ysbrantsz. was asked to keep the matter confidential even from the Masulipatnam Council till it was time to begin the preparations for the ships' seizure.[32] After the long-awaited *Cameel* had reached Masulipatnam and the goods in the Company's warehouses had been loaded on it, the factors boarded the vessel on the night of 1 March 1629 and abandoned the Masulipatnam factory.[33] The yachts *Terschelling*, *Vlielandt*, *Bonne Remedie*, and the *Duyve* together with a sloop were drafted for the siege of the port. Unitl 19 April 1629, the only ship to return was one belonging to Mir Kamal-al-Din which had travelled from Aceh. The ship was seized, but since a good part of the cargo belonged to the merchants of Surat and Persia, whom the Company did not wish to alienate, the cargo was released.[34] In September 1629, an accord was reached with the Masulipatnam merchants stipulating that the Company would not hinder the departure of the ships and indeed would itself resume trading at Masulipatnam.[35] The episode finally came to a close on 11 December 1629, when the king of Golconda granted a *farman* assuring the Company that its liability in the matter of tolls at Masulipatnam would continue to be limited to 3,000 *pagodas* per annum.[36]

The Coromandel documents also contain a good deal of information on the activities of the European rivals of the Company as well as its dealings with them. These rivals were the Portuguese, the Danes, the French and the English. The Portuguese were, of course, the sworn enemies of the Company and all ships sent by the Governor-General and Council to the Coromandel coast had instructions to attack and seize whatever Portuguese shipping they could. But the trade carried on by the Portuguese from their settlement at Sao Tome was on the decline and the Dutch faced hardly any competition from them. Similarly, the Danish and the French presence on the coast was extremely marginal and of little consequence to the Company. The Danes no doubt did manage to secure the cession of the Trancquebar port from the *nayak* of Tanjore in 1620 and build a fort there. But the overall resources available to them were extremely scanty: in 1621, they were even forced to dispose of some pepper they had bought earlier. The lot was purchased by the Dutch and sent on to Holland with the *Naarden*. As for the French, the *St. Louis*, one of the two vessels equipped at St. Male by some merchants of Dieppe, Rouen and St. Male constituting the *Compagnie des Moluques* called at Pondicherry in June 1617. Factors Nicolos Trosol and Michiel Heyne wrote to the Dutch at Tirupapaliyur enquiring about trade prospects and requesting that some individuals conversant with Dutch, English, Portuguese and French languages be sent to them to help them in their investigations. But the Dutch provided no such assistance. Since only a few weavers manufactured Guinea-cloth at Pondicherry, the French were not able to get any supplies and decided to leave the Coromandel coast. Another attempt to secure trading rights at Masulipatnam was made in 1621 by a Frenchman sent by Beaulieu, the commander of a French fleet which had sailed from Honfleur. But the attempt again met with failure and it was not until 1670 that the French reappeared on the Coromandel coast.

The story of the English was somewhat more complex. They had established a factory at Masulipatnam in 1611 and a little later had also started trading at Petapuli. But the Dutch factors at

Pulicat had instructions to try and keep them out of the Pulicat trade. If necessary, the factors had authorisation even of making use of the superior power of the Company in the area. But the 1619 Treaty of Defence that terminated the hostilities between the two companies in the Indonesian archipelago contained a clause entitling the English Company to a share in the trade at Pulicat provided they also shared half of the cost of the maintenance of the Dutch fort and the garrison there. In order to overcome the English apprehension that given the presence of the Dutch garrison in Fort Geldria at Pulicat, the Indian merchants might feel constrained to supply to the Dutch alone to the exclusion of the English, an agreement was signed between the two companies at Jacatra on 13 March 1621. The agreement provided that in the event of the two companies wishing to buy identical varieties of textiles, the goods would be bought jointly. The Dutch also undertook to provide accommodation to the English inside the fort itself against the payment of rent at least till such time as alternative arrangements were made for them. The *Globe* arrived at Pulicat on 19 June 1621 and the cooperation between the two companies formally started.

But the accord ran into problems almost from the very beginning. The English complained that the Dutch did not offer them half of the total textiles procured but insisted on dividing the lot in proportion to the capital invested by the two companies respectively. They also complained about the inadequacy of the accommodation provided to them as well as about the procedure adopted to work out their share of the cost of the maintenance of the garrison. The Dutch retorted that the joint procurement of textiles ensured for the English the same price and quality that the Hollanders got for themselves on the basis of the experience acquired by them over a number of years. The English were not convinced and the result was a growing bitterness between the two companies. Coen, who was in any case strongly opposed to any kind of accommodation with the English, wrote the following to the Directors in January 1622, 'It was impossible to deal with the English. They would do as much damage to the Dutch interests as they could, and then claim that it was they who were the aggrieved party. The jeolousy, the distrust and the envy that these people had was unlikely to be neutralized by any regulations, agreements or orders. The more apart the two stayed from each other, the greater were the chances of continued friendliness between the two.'[37] In May of the same year, he wrote to Andries Soury and Van Uffelen at Masulipatnam, 'Regarding the costs at the Moluccas, Amboina, Banda and Pulicat, the English had nothing but complaints to make. Their ambition and greed could never be appeased. In all matters, big and small, they found themselves cheated, sunk, affronted and despised so much so that it appeared that the entire means at the disposal of the Company would not be enough to meet their claims.'[38] The Dutch factors at Coromandel, of course, did not take such an extreme view of the situation at any stage and indeed consciously tried to accommodate the English whenever possible. The latter, however, found the burden of their share of the maintenance costs of the fort and the garrison at Pulicat crippling. In any case, all hopes of any continued cooperation between the two nations were dashed to the ground following the notorious 'massacre of Amboina' in February 1623. The formal termination at Pulicat came with the English withdrawal from that place on 1 July 1623.

The other major consequence of the 1619 Treaty of Defence was the decision to equip a joint defence fleet to blockade the Portuguese possessions on the Malabar coast and to cruise against the Portuguese shipping on the west coast of India. The admiral of the fleet consisting of seven Dutch and four English vessels that left Batavia on 18 October 1621 was Dutchman Jacob Dedel while the vice-admiral was Englishman Humphrey Fitzherbert. But like the planned commercial cooperation at Pulicat, the venture of the defence fleet was also a dismal failure. On 18 November 1621, the fleet was driven by contrary winds to the Nassau islands. The English then wanted to get back to Batavia but were prevented from doing so by Dedel by using his additional vote in the fleet's council. The fleet was unable to inflict any particular damage on the Portuguese and in July 1622, Coen advised Dedel to return to Batavia after leaving the Dutch ships of the fleet at Surat.

That brings us to Gujarat which was the other theatre of the Company's activities in India in the early part of the seventeenth century. Some time before the establishment of the Dutch

Company in 1602, two Dutch factors, Hans de Wolff and Lafer representing the Middelburg Company (one of the so-called pre-companies which were merged in 1602 to form the Dutch East India Company), had travelled from Aceh to Surat with two Indian ships. They were well-received at Surat and provided with a house to operate from. But in the course of a trip to Calicut in April 1603, they fell into Portuguese hands and were killed. The first contacts with Gujarat on behalf of the Company were made by two ships of the fleet of Admiral Matalief that called at Cambay probably in 1606. But David van Deynsen, the Dutch factor, was reportedly harassed so much by the authorities at the instigation of the Portuguese that towards the end of 1607 he committed suicide at Burhanpur.

After this episode, the Company did not have any contacts with Gujarat until 1615 when Pieter Gillisz. van Ravesteyn was sent from Masulipatnam to Surat. The dual aim of the mission was to recover the Company's effects which were in the charge of Van Deynsen at the time of his death and to obtain permission for the Company's trade. The mission was successful only to the extent of retrieving a part of the Company's effects. But on his return to Coromandel in February 1616, Van Ravesteyn confirmed the rich potential of the Surat trade. A few months later, the Council of the Indies at Bantam sent Pieter van den Broecke to Surat with instructions to try and establish a regular factory there. Van den Broecke arrived at Surat in August 1616 via Mocha, but having failed to secure formal permission to trade, left for Bantam the following month. In March 1617, Van den Broecke once again left for Surat via Mocha. But in July 1617, when Surat was only a few days away, both the vessels under Van den Broecke's command, the *Middleburg* and the *Duyve*, were lost near Daman, though the factors managed to salvage the cargo and the guns. After spending a few months in Surat without being able to get formal documents, Van den Broecke left for Bantam after nominating Van Ravesteyn to look after the Company's affairs at Surat.

Early in 1618, Van Ravesteyn took advantage of the presence of Emperor Jahangir at Ahmedabad to seek from him a *farman* for the Company's trade. He succeeded to the extent of persuading Prince Khurram, the *subahdar*, to grant a document which allowed the Dutch factors stationed at Surat to carry on their trade unhindered. The prince also issued a document addressed to the *mutasaddi* of Surat and the *faujdars* of Burhanpur, Ahmedabad and Cambay asking that the Dutch be provided all protection and exempted from tolls on goods transported by them from Burhanpur to Cambay and Ahmedabad.

Around this time, Van Ravesteyn's relations with the other uppermerchant in the region, Adriaen Willemsz. Goeree, had become extremely strained and the two traded charges against each other. In February 1619, Van Ravesteyn wrote to Coen asking to be relieved of his responsibilities. This could be done only in October 1620 when Pieter van den Broecke took over as director. He held this position until his departure from Surat in 1628. In addition to the chief factory at Surat, the Company established a number of subordinate factories in the region. A factory was opened at Cambay late in 1620. The factory at Broach was headed in the initial stages by Goeree. The factory at Agra established in 1621 was under the charge of Wouter Heuten, who held that position until his death in September 1623.

The principal goods procured in Gujarat were textiles and indigo. A superior grade indigo was also procured in Bayana near Agra. While indigo was sent to Holland, the textiles were predominantly for the Indonesian archipelago. The Council of the Indies instructed the factors time and again to first meet the orders from the archipelago before putting out contracts for indigo for Holland. The rationale provided was as follows. If funds were invested in indigo for Holland, the Company could expect to earn a gross profit of approximately 200 per cent. On the other hand, if the same funds were invested in textiles for the archipelago where they were exchanged against pepper for Holland, the Company could eventually hope to earn a gross profit of 500 per cent on the initial investment in Gujarat.

But the shortage of capital with Batavia provided an almost insurmountable stumbling block during these early years. The Surat factors claimed that the Gujarat trade was as valuable as that from Coromandel and that 'once the Directors had tasted the fruits of the Surat trade, they would never let go'. Coen's response was that he was fully aware of the importance of the trade from Surat. He even claimed that in Batavia's view this trade was more important than even the Coromandel trade. Yet it had been necessary to neglect it thus far because of the non-availability of capital. This had caused no less distress at Batavia than it had at Surat. In the words of the Surat factors, 'the situation was one where water was at the factors' lips but they could not drink it'. Out of sheer desperation, they suggested in 1619 that if the Directors planned to abandon the Surat trade, it was best to do that immediately because even when practically no trade was being carried on, the Company was still subject to establishment costs. 'Twenty persons could not live on air alone and provisions were fifty per cent more expensive at Surat than they were in Coromandel.' The situation improved somewhat after 1621, but even during the following three years, the volume of trade from Surat continued to be rather small. The English, of course, were far ahead of the Dutch in this respect. In 1618, for example, the Dutch factors reported that four to six English ships called at Surat each year.

The substantial amount of maritime trade carried on by the Indian merchants from Surat and other ports in Gujarat also had important ramifications for the Dutch. At one end of the spectrum the considerable ship-building activity in the region afforded to the Company an excellent opportunity of buying ships locally. Thus orders were frequently placed for the construction of frigates and other vessels at Gandevi. But more often, the large maritime activity by the Indians only generated 'problems' for the Company. For one thing, refusal to issue passes asked for would frequently lead to trouble for the Company. Also, Batavia's policy of attacking and seizing vessels originating in Indian ports controlled by the Portuguese and operating with their passes also landed the Surat factors into highly embarrassing situations. To take only one example, following the 1621 capture of a ship from Chaul carrying freight cargo belonging in part to Nawab Asaf Khan, the Company was obliged to meet in full the nawab's claim for a sum of Rs.13,225. At times, the Company had to suffer on account of the actions of the English. In 1623, for example, when the English captured some Muslim ships not carrying their passes, Van den Broecke was summoned by the provincial *subahdar* and asked to obtain the release of the ships.

When Van den Broecke regretted his inability to do this, he together with the other factors was house-arrested in the Dutch factory. The Company's goods at Broach were also detained by the Mughal officials. The matter was settled only after the English had reached an accord with the Muslim merchants.

The Company's factory at Surat was also involved in the opening of Dutch trade with Arabia and Persia. Before his arrival at Surat in August 1616, Pieter van den Broecke had carried on a certain amount of trade at Mocha. He returned to Arabia in August 1620, again on his way from Jacatra to Surat. The factors left by him at Aden arrived at Mocha in January 1621, and established a factory there. But following the seizure by the *Samson* and the *Weesp* of two vessels belonging to the Indian port of Dabhol (which was represented in Mocha by a number of influential merchants), the Dutch factor, Willem de Milde, and his assistants were made prisoners early in 1622. Eventually, the Company's goods were also confiscated. Over the following two years, small amounts of cash were recovered by the Company and a Company servant occasionally was released or escaped, but the idea of a factory at Mocha was temporarily abandoned in 1624. De Milde was reported to have been released by the new *badshah* of Yemen later that year. In 1625, the *badshah* sent a letter to Van den Broecke inviting him to reestablish the trade at Mocha.

The chief attraction of the Persian trade was, of course, the raw silk available there. In April 1621, Van den Broecke informed Batavia that he was planning to send some ships to Persia on an exploratory mission. But it was only in January 1623 that the *Heusden* was sent to Persia via Mocha with Huybert Vissnich aboard. Vissnich had instructions to greet the governor of Hormuz and seek his permission to travel inland for an audience with the Shah. The *Heusden* arrived at Gombroon in June 1623 and obtained permission to unload cargo. Almost immediately after, Vissnich set out for Isfahan for an audience with the Shah. The negotiations with the Shah were successful and the Dutch trade with Persia began. The shortage of resources with the Company was, of course, still a problem. In August 1623, for example, Batavia told Surat that they could invest in the Persian trade only after making provision for buying two years' stocks of cloth for the archipelago and indigo for Holland.

This volume contains a total of 130 documents for the four years between 1624 and 1627. Apart from the correspondence between the factories on the Coromandel coast and Gujarat on the one hand and the Governor-General and Council at Batavia on the other, these include a number of miscellaneous documents sent as enclosures to the correspondence. An important component of this category was the invoices of the Company ships arriving at or departing from the Indian factories. Attention might also be drawn to the detailed diaries kept by the factors in the two regions during these years. Three of these diaries relate to the Coromandel coast while the fourth pertains to the Surat factory in Gujarat. Matters ordinarily not covered in the correspondence between these factories and Batavia often find detailed mention in these diaries. Thus the Coromandel diaries often talk about the ship movement in the Bay of Bengal on the account of Indian and other Asian merchants as well as the wars among the various *nayaks* then raging on the coast. The Surat diary kept by Commissioner Dirck van der Lee, sent on an investigative mission from Batavia to the establishments in Gujarat, Hindustan and Persia, similarly contains detailed references, for example, to the events sorrounding the death of Emperor Jahangir and the succession of Shah Jahan to the throne.

NOTES

1. J.E. Heeres (ed.), 'Corpus-Diplomaticum Neerlando-Indicum', *Bijdragen tot de Taal-Land en Volkenkunde van Nederlandsch Indie*, vol. 57, p. 154.
2. H.T. Colenbrander (ed.), *Jan Pietersz. Coen, Beschieden Omtrent Zyn Bedrijf in Indie*, 7 vols., The Hague, 1919-53, vol. 1, p. 348.
3. The *havaldar* was the governor of a designated area.
4. This is clearly a corrupted form of the name. The name might have been Lingayya.
5. General letter from Governor-General Jan Pietersz. Coen at Jacatra to the Directors at Amsterdam, 8 January 1621. V.O.C. 1072, ff.175-80 vo. Printed in H.T. Colenbrander (ed.), *Jan Pietersz. Coen*, vol. 1, pp. 606-22.

6. H.T. Colenbrander (ed.), *Jan Pietersz. Coen*, vol. 1, pp. 75, 177, 180, 209.
7. Letter from Governor-General Coen and Council at Batavia to Andries Soury and Abraham van Uffelen at Masulipatnam, 8 May 1622. V.O.C. 1076, ff. 76-8.
8. Letter from Marten Ysbrantsz. at Pulicat to the Directors at Amsterdam, 28 April 1625. V.O.C. 1084, ff.166-8.
9. Letter from Marten Ysbrantsz. at Pulicat to De Carpentier at Batavia, 5 December 1625, V.O.C.1087, ff.174-7; Journal kept at Fort Geldria at Pulicat between 20 November 1623 and 28 November 1625. V.O.C. 1087, ff. 179-211vo, entry under 28 November 1625.
10. Letter from Governor-General Coen to Ysbrantsz. at Pulicat dated 14 June 1628. V.O.C.1095, f.296.
11. Letter from De Haze aboard the *Zwarte Beer* at Masulipatnam harbour to Coen at Bantam/Jacatra, 21 June 1619. V.O.C. 1069, ff.452-7.
12. Letter from Andries Soury at Masulipatnam to the Directors at Amsterdam, 29 January 1621. V.O.C. 1073, ff.156-9.
13. W. Ph. Coolhaas (ed.), *Generale Missiven van Gouverneurs-Generaal en Raden aan Heren XVII der Verenigde Oostindische Compagnie*, The Hague, 1960, vol. 1, pp. 133-4.
14. Letter from Hans de Haze at Masulipatnam to Coen at Bantam/ Jacatra, 5 June 1617. V.O.C. 1066, ff.113-17 vo.
15. Letter from Goeree and Libenaar at Masulipatnam to the Directors at Amsterdam, 4 October 1624. V.O.C. 1082, ff.50-3.
16. Letter from Ysbrantsz. at Pulicat to Governor-General De Carpentier and Council at Batavia, 16 October 1625. V.O.C. 1087, ff.164-9vo.
17. Masulipatnam *Day Register, 1625-1626*, entry of 4 March 1626. V.O.C. 1095, f.48.
18. The *kotwal* was the person in charge of law and order in a town.
19. Pulicat *Day Register*, *1626-1628*, entry of 23 April 1626. V.O.C. 1095, f.30 vo.
20. Pulicat *Day Register*, *1626-1628*, entry of 29 August 1626. V.O.C. 1095, f.33.
21. Pulicat *Day Register*, *1626-1628*, entry of 2 October 1626. V.O.C. 1095, f.33vo.
22. Masulipatnam *Day Register*, *1626-1628*, entry of 20 September 1628. V.O.C. 1095, f.55 vo.
23. Masulipatnam *Day Register*, *1626-1628*, entry of 8 April 1627. V.O.C. 1095, f.73.

24. Masulipatnam *Day Register, 1626-1628*, entry of 27 April 1627. V.O.C. 1095, f.74.
25. Pulicat *Day Register, 1626-1628*, entry of 14 April 1627. V.O.C. 1095, f.38.
26. Pulicat *Day Register, 1626-1628*, entry of 30 March and 17 April 1628. V.O.C. 1095, ff.43-3vo.
27. A *sar-i-khail* was ordinarily the chief of cavalry, but was also obliged to discharge civil and revenue functions.
28. Letter from Ysbrantsz. at Masulipatnam to Governor-General Coen and Council at Batavia, 24 September 1628. V.O.C. 1095, ff.11-18.
29. *Sarraf* was a general term used for persons dealing in money and bills of exchange.
30. Letter from Van Uffelen in jail at Bondara (situated at a day's journey from Masulipatnam) to the chiefs of the Dutch forts, factories and ships on the Coromandel coast, 28 November 1623. V.O.C. 1083, ff.176-80; Van Uffelen to Ysbrantsz. at Pulicat, 5 December 1623. V.O.C. 1083, ff.185-5vo; Van Uffelen at Golconda to Van den Broecke at Surat, 27 December 1623. V.O.C. 1079, ff.234-5; Ysbrantsz. at Pulicat to Governor-General De Carpentier and Council at Batavia, 24 March 1624. V.O.C. 1083, ff.205-5vo.
31. Letter form Goeree and Libenaar at Masulipatnam to the Directors at Amsterdam, 4 October 1624. V.O.C. 1082, ff.50-3.
32. Secret letter from Governor-General Coen at Batavia to Ysbrantsz. at Pulicat, 14 June 1628. V.O.C. 1095, ff.275-7vo.
33. Letter from Ysbrantsz. at Pulicat to Governor-General Coen at Batavia, 23 May 1629. V.O.C. 1098, ff.488-91; letter from Masulipatnam to Surat, 3 March 1629. V.O.C. 1097, ff.425-6.
34. Resolution adopted at Masulipatnam roadstead in the yacht *Terschelling*, 19 April 1629, V.O.C. 1098, ff.495-5vo; Resolution at Masulipatnam, 12 September 1629. V.O.C. 1097, ff.469-70vo.
35. Masulipatnam Resolution, 15 September 1629. V.O.C. 1097, f.468.
36. *Farman* of the king of Golconda dated 11 December 1629. V.O.C. 1100, ff.90-90vo.
37. General letter from Governor-General Coen at Batavia to the Directors at Amsterdam, 21 January 1622. V.O.C. 1075, ff.2-10vo. Printed in H.T. Colenbrander (ed.), *Jan Pietersz. Coen*, vol. 1, pp. 688-700.
38. Governor-General Coen at Batavia to Andries Soury and Van Uffelen at Masulipatnam, 8 May 1622. V.O.C. 849, ff.82-5vo.

DOCUMENTS

1624

1. Resolution adopted by the Surat Council, 1 January 1624. V.O.C. 1079, f.190 (Copy).

The English chief, Thomas Rastell,[1] had requested that as a safeguard against piracy, one of their ships, the *Dolphin*, might kindly be allowed to travel to Europe with the *Heusden*. The council resolved to accede to the request with the proviso that the departure of the *Heusden* would not be delayed beyond the requested ten days needed to ready the *Dolphin* for sailing.

1. Thomas Rastell came to Surat in 1616 with the fleet of Pepwell. He was promoted second at Surat in 1618, the chief of the factory at Ahmedabad in August 1619 and chief at Surat in April 1621. He held this office until February 1625, when he returned home with the *Blessing*. He came back to Surat for a second time as President in September 1630 and held that office until his death on 7 November 1631.

2. General letter from Governor-General Pieter de Carpentier[1] at Batavia to the Directors[2] at Amsterdam, 3 January 1624. V.O.C. 1079, ff.7-55 (Original; pagination in pencil).*

The *Weesp* had arrived from Surat on 6 March 1623 with a cargo of textiles worth f.73,931. The position regarding the availability of funds at Surat was as follows:

Cash vide Van den Broecke's[3] letter of 16 February 1623[4]	f.250,000
Cash and goods received from Holland including the cargo picked up at the Cape of Good Hope	f.312,667
Cash and goods sent from Batavia with the *Vrede* and the *Weesp* worth an invoice value of f.178,264 and a sale value of	f.280,000
Goods at Mocha worth an invoice value of f.103,802 and a sale value of	f.150,000
Goods sent by Dedel[5] with the *Heusden* from Goa to Mocha worth an invoice value of f.72,938 and a sale value of	f.120,000
Total	f.1,112,667

Of this, a sum of f.430,000 would be invested in the procurement of textiles for two years for the various factories[6] in the East Indies. Textiles worth half this amount had already been procured and were expected at Batavia by February 1624. The lot for 1625 was due to arrive at Batavia by January 1625. Surat would then be left with a capital of about f.670,000 which should be adequate to meet the annual indigo orders from Holland worth f.300,000 for two successive years. Since Gujarat indigo was better in quality than the Coromandel indigo, the procurement of the latter variety ought to be stopped. In future, proceeds from the sale of spices and other goods sent from Batavia to Surat ought to suffice for the procurement of the textiles and other goods for the Indies. The Directors would then need to send funds to Surat only for the procurement of goods for Holland at Surat and Mocha.

In case spices found a reasonable market in the Red Sea, Surat, the Coromandel coast[7] and other factories in the Indies, and the supplies of textiles expected from Surat and Coromandel for 1624 and 1625 were received in full, the Directors would not be obliged to send any funds whatever to Batavia for the purchase of pepper, cloves, nutmeg and mace for Holland. Capital from home would be needed only for the China trade as and when it was reopened. Indeed, in course of time, profits from the intra-

Asian trade, particularly from the Japan branch, might even enable Batavia to meet Holland's orders for the Chinese goods as well without asking for any funds from home.

The Directors had asked Surat to provide indigo Bayana[8] worth f.200,000 and indigo Sarkhej[9] worth f.100,000. In order to enhance the capital available at Surat, 2,000 sacks of pepper had been sent there with instructions to sell it mainly in Persia where the English had made a good profit on it last year. If a good profit could not be made on this item in Persia or Surat, it was to be sent on to Holland.

On 27 January 1623, Admiral Dedel had sent the *Heusden* from Goa to Mocha with a cargo worth f.72,938 including 20,000 rials in cash. Upper-merchants Huybert Vissnich,[10] Francois Lemmens[11] and Albert Becker[12] travelling on this ship were instructed to close the establishment at Mocha. The goods in stock there as well as the ones now sent aboard the *Heusden* were to be sold there to the extent possible. The proceeds from such sale together with the 20,000 rials and remaining goods were to be sent on to Persia with the *Heusden* with a view to investigate the commercial opportunities there. The vessel was to return to Surat by October 1623.

The *Tholen* had arrived from Coromandel on 7 March 1623 with a cargo worth f.224,699 consisting of 716 packets of clothes, 514 slaves and some opium, steel and iron. Between April and September 1623, the following ships had been sent to Coromandel: the *Masulipatam* on 27 April, the *Tholen* on 19 July, the *Wapen van Rotterdam* on 18 August and the *Wapen van Enkhuizen* on 22 September. The *Tholen* came back from Coromandel on 28 November 1623 with a cargo worth f.231,384 consisting of 720 packets of clothes, 200 slaves and 25,000 pieces of steel.

According to Batavia's calculations, the position regarding the availability of funds in Coromandel would be as follows:

Capital available at Masulipatnam and Pulicat on 1 February 1623	f.450,000
Cargo sent with the *Masulipatam* (sale value)	f.60,000
Cargo sent with the *Tholen* (sale value)	f.230,000
Cash sent from Batavia with the *Wapen van Rotterdam* consisting of 40,000 rials	f.100,000
Cash sent from Holland with the *Medemblik*	f.203,000
Total	f.1,043,000

From this amount, Coromandel had sent cargo worth f.136,000 to Holland with the *Schiedam* and worth f.231,000 to Batavia with the *Tholen*, leaving with it capital worth f.676,000. Batavia's annual orders from there were ordinarily for 1,600 packets of clothes costing about f.400,000. In view of the poor harvest there, the sale of the Company's textiles in the Moluccas, Amboina and Banda had been rather poor and they still had stocks of textiles that would last them for another two years. In view of this, Batavia had placed orders for Coromandel textiles only to the extent of f.340,000. Another f.400,000 would be needed for the procurement of the cargo for Holland.

Director Van Uffelen's[13] complaint that Coromandel had not been provided with adequate capital during 1623 was not justified. No capital could be sent with the *Wapen van Enkhuizen* because funds were needed for China and Bantam. Spices were also not sent with this ship because their output had been poor and it was not considered desirable to reduce the supplies for Holland which already were rather insufficient.

Spices had been sold at reasonable prices in Coromandel. While nutmeg had fetched 100 *pagodas*[14] per 480 ponds and cloves 13 *pagodas* per *maund* of 24 ponds, mace had been sold at 11.5 *pagodas* per *maund*. Spices were consumed almost exclusively in the Muslim lands—the kingdom of Golconda, Bijapur, and Ahmadnagar and in Mughal India and Persia. Spices were not carried to Christian lands or to Turkey.

According to Batavia's calculations, a sum of f.392,000 could be raised per annum by the sale of spices as follows:

At Coromandel

S.No.	Item	Quantity	Price (in pagodas)	Value (in florins)
1.	Cloves	50,000 ponds	13 per *maund*	115,000
2.	Nutmeg	60,000 ponds	70 per *bahar*	37,000
3.	Mace	150 bales[15]	–	30,000
			Total	f.182,000

At Surat

S. No.	Item	Quantity	Price (in mahmudis[16])	Value (in florins)
1.	Cloves	30,000 ponds	200 per 30 ponds	100,000
2.	Nutmeg	36,000 ponds	40 per 30 ponds	25,000
3.	Mace	50 bales	–	15,000
			Total	f.140,000

At Mocha (as per the information given by De Milde[17])

S. No.	Item	Quantity		Value (in florins)
1.	Cloves	15,000 ponds		45,000
2.	Nutmeg	15,000 ponds		15,000
3.	Mace	5,000 ponds		10,000
			Total	f.70,000
			Grand Total	f.392,000

The estimated annual cost of textiles in Coromandel and Surat together was approximately f.650,000. They would thus have to raise another approximately f.250,000 by the sale of sandalwood, lead, ivory, tortoise horn, copper, benzoin and camphor and by any additional sale of spices.

Slaves were brought to Masulipatnam not only from Pulicat and Tegenapatam[18] but also from the coast of Malabar and the neighbouring places. Batavia had sent two big ships, the *Wapen van Rotterdam* and the *Wapen van Enkhuizen* to Coromandel to fetch a large number of slaves, but only 700 of them had been received.

Van Uffelen had sent the *Schiedam* together with two frigates, the *Jager* and the *Muys*, to Bengal to explore the trading prospects there. These vessels had come back to Masulipatnam on 29 June with clothes worth about 5,000 rials and some rice and sugar. In pursuance of orders from Batavia, the yacht *Medemblik* and the frigates, the *Muys* and the *Jager*, were sent again to Bengal on 25 September to collect more firm information about the trading possibilities there. The cargo carried by these vessels included 8,000 rials in cash, some spices and lead, etc. to be exchanged against slaves, wax, clothes and other goods.

The *Medemblik* had captured a Portuguese *fust*[19] near Sao Tome and taken some jewels worn by the ladies aboard. The sample of Bengal sugar sent to Holland with the *Schiedam* had cost 6 to 7 rials per 170 Dutch ponds. The Directors' evaluation regarding the prospects of this commodity would be awaited.

The Danish ships, the *Christiaanshaven* and the *Waterhond* had arrived at Tranquebar. The former was ready to return to Denmark with 1,400 *bahars* of pepper bought at 26 rials per *bahar* of 300 ponds and other goods such as coarse textiles, indigo and refined saltpetre to serve as samples. The *Waterhond* had been sent to Tenasserim with a view to establish a factory there.

The English ship, the *Walvisch* of about 700 *lasts*[20] had sunk soon after leaving Surat for England. There were 37 men aboard and it was reportedly carrying 804 bales of Persian silk, a good amount of indigo Sarkhej and fine clothes from Cambay[21] worth a sale price in Europe of 150,000 pounds sterling.

In view of the uprising of Prince Khurram against his father, the Great Mughal, all routes had become unsafe for the merchants. As a result, the sale of spices and other goods had been poor both in Surat and Coromandel.

* Summarized in W.Ph. Coolhaas (ed.), *Generale Missiven van Gouverneurs-Generaal en Raden aan Heren XVII der Verenigde Oostindische Compagnie* (hereafter *Generale Missiven*) vol.1, *1610-1638* (The Hague, 1960), pp. 131-47.

1. Pieter de Carpentier was born at Antwerp in 1588. In 1619, he was appointed to the office of the Director-General and was a member of the Council of the Governor-General. On 23 January 1623, he was

promoted to the position of the Governor-General and took over from Jan Pietersz. Coen on 1 February 1623. He returned to Holland on 12 November 1627 when Coen had again taken over as the Governor-General. He died on 5 September 1659 at Amsterdam.

2. The reference is to the Central Board of Directors of the Company comprising seventeen members and referred to as the Gentlemen XVII. The members represented the six chambers of the Company, each of which had its own body of Directors as well. The chamber of Amsterdam nominated eight members, Zeeland another four while there was one member each from Delft, Rotterdam, Hoorn and Enkhuizen. The seventeenth member was nominated by one of the four smaller chambers by turn except during the two years in the eight-year cycle when the meetings were held at Middelburg (rather than at Amsterdam) and the right to nominate the seventeenth member was vested in the host chamber of Zeeland.
3. Pieter van den Broecke had made several trips to West Africa between 1605 and 1612. He came to the East Indies in 1613 as a merchant with the yacht *Nassau* and was instrumental in the establishment of the Company's trade with Arabia. He arrived at Surat on 2 August 1616 from Mocha. At the time of his departure from Bantam for Mocha, he had been instructed by Coen to try and establish regular trade relations with Gujarat. His attempts to secure a formal permission to trade at Surat, however, did not fructify and he left for Bantam on 8 September. In January 1617, the Council of the Indies resolved to entrust him with the responsibility of looking after the Company's affairs at Surat. He left Bantam on 8 March as the commander of the *Middelburg* and the yacht *Duyve* (which had replaced the original *Zuyder Eendracht* that had been sent instead to Amboina). On 18 July, the *Middelburg* was caught in a heavy storm near Daman and was grounded the following day. A similar fate had met the *Duyve* a day earlier. Van den Broecke reached Surat on 5 August 1617. On 9 September, he nominated Van Ravesteyn to be the head of the Surat factory with Adriaen Goeree under him. Since there was no likelihood of getting a ship at Surat for a journey to Bantam, Van den Broecke decided to travel overland to Masulipatnam and left for that place at the end of October 1617. He eventually reached Jacatra on 7 November 1618. He left for Arabia and Surat again on 16 June 1620. He finally arrived at Surat on 1 October 1620 where he served as director until 23 December 1628. He left the Swally haven on 6 January 1629 and arrived at Batavia on 19 June 1629. He left for home on 18 December 1629 as the commander of a return fleet.

4. This letter is not available in the Company's archives.
5. Jacob Dedel came to the East Indies in 1618-19 as Vice-Admiral in the fleet of Frederick de Houtman. In October 1621, he was sent to the west coast of India as Admiral of the Anglo-Dutch defence fleet consisting of eleven ships aimed at hurting the Portuguese. He returned to Batavia on 13 July 1623 without having much success in his mission. In May 1624, he took over as Director of the coast of Coromandel and died there on 29 August of the same year.
6. A factory, of course, only denoted a trading post.
7. The European accounts of the seventeenth century used the term 'Coromandel coast' somewhat loosely. In its widest sense, it embraced the entire east coast of the Indian peninsula. More specifically, it was taken to mean the part of the coast lying to the south of Godavari river and extending as far as Nagapattinam or even to the island of Manar, which marked the limit of ordinary coastal navigation.
8. Bayana, situated about 50 miles south-west of Agra, was a major centre for the production of indigo.
9. Sarkhej, situated about six to seven miles south-west of Ahmedabad, was another major centre for the production of indigo.
10. In 1620, Huybert Vissnich appears at Aleppo. On 24 June 1621, he reached Coromandel from Holland for the indigo trade. On 24 May 1622, he came overland from Agra to Surat. On 27 January 1623, he left for Hormuz via Mocha with the *Heusden*. He was the person who laid the foundation of the trade with Persia. He made several trips to the capital city of Isfahan and was in good standing with Shah Abbas. But he did not neglect opportunities of his own profit. When his successor arrived at Gombroon on 7 February 1630, Vissnich refused to leave Persia as the commander of the fleet. He instead left secretly for Europe by the land route on 17 December. He was held as a spy at Aleppo and killed.
11. Francois Lemmens was reportedly a *koopman* at Ternate in 1615. The following year, he took part in a mission to Manila. He was repatriated in 1620 but was brought back to Surat in 1622 from where he went to Mocha in 1623. In 1624 he killed a captain in a duel at Batavia. He was pardoned but nothing more is known about him thereafter.
12. Albert Becker left for the west coast of India with Jacob Dedel on 12 October 1621 on the *Wapen van Zeeland*. Thereafter, he went to the Red Sea and from there came back to Surat. On 27 January 1623, Dedel sent him to Persia via Mocha with the *Heusden*. On 8 November 1623 he went from Surat to Persia with the *Vrede* and

the *Weesp*. He came back to Surat on 9 February 1624 and returned to Batavia on 7 July 1624. On 26 July 1624 he left again for Surat and Persia on the *Zuid Holland* in charge of the ships. He was killed in February 1625 at Hormuz in an encounter between four ships commanded by him and four English ships on the one hand and the Portuguese on the other.

13. Abraham van Uffelen came to the East Indies as an under-merchant in 1618. He was soon promoted upper-merchant and worked in that capacity in Bantam and Jacatra. On 3 August 1621, he was appointed an extraordinary member of the Council of the Indies. Soon after, on 16 October 1621, he was appointed an ordinary member of the Council and governor of the coast of Coromandel. He was arrested In Golconda in November 1623 and was released only after a great deal of money had been extorted from him. As a result of the torture inflicted on him during his detention, he died in Masulipatnam in February 1624.
14. The *pagoda* was a gold (sometimes silver) coin long in use in south India. The local name was *varha* or *hun*. The weight was approximately 52 to 53 grains and the fineness about 21¾ carats. On an average, the *pagoda* was worth 4 to 4½ rupees.
15. A bale of mace weighed 154 ponds.
16. The *mahmudi* was a silver coin of Gujarat worth about 4/9 of a rupee.
17. Willem Jacobsz. de Milde had been an upper-merchant aboard the *Sampson* since 30 July 1619. He succeeded Herman van Gil as the head of the factory at Mocha on 15 July 1621. In February 1622, he was arrested by the Turkish authorities for refusing to issue passes for Asian ships which were later captured by the Dutch. Later, he was taken inland by the Arabs where he died some time after 1632.
18. Tegenapatam is situated about 70 miles north of Nagapattinam.
19. The *fust* was a light vessel of the galley type, propelled by oars as well as sails.
20. A *last* denotes a measure of shipping space, representing about 120 cubic feet. The term was also used as a measure of weight and was equivalent of about 3,000 ponds.
21. Cambay is in Gujarat, being its most important port in the sixteenth century.

3. Herman Pietersz. Prins[1] at Bhagnagar[2] in Golconda to Abraham van Uffelen (in jail), 9 January 1624. V.O.C. 1083, ff.191-2 (Copy).

An Englishman accused of killing two persons had been told by the *sar-i-khail*[3] of Golconda that if he gave him 3,000 *pagodas*, he could intercede with the king of Golconda[4] on his behalf and save him from death. Prins wished to be relieved from Bhagnagar since he was feeling very lonely.

1. This man figures in the list of persons married in the church of Batavia between 24 October 1621 and 29 January 1623. He was an under-merchant at Masulipatnam and was sent by Governor Van Uffelen to Golconda, where he was arrested. In April 1626, he was reported to be secretary of the college of shipping.
2. Present Hyderabad was formerly known as Bhagnagar.
3. The *sar-i-khail* was the chief of cavalry, but was also obliged to discharge civil and revenue functions.
4. Muhammad Quli Qutb Shah was the king of Golconda between 1612 and 1626.

4. Jan Libenaar[1] on board the *Wapen van Rotterdam* at Masulipatnam to Governor-General De Carpentier at Batavia, 10 January 1624. V.O.C. 1083, ff.172-5vo (Copy).

Governor Van Uffelen was arrested on 8 November 1623 and taken in chains towards Golconda. He was presently at a place called Bondara which is about 1½ days' journey away from Masulipatnam. Our factory was then attacked and two metal cannons and two cases of gunpowder taken away by force. On 11 November, the English factory was similarly visited by *Shahbandar*[2] Shah Ali, together with the *kotwal*[3] and 1,000 soldiers. The English agent, Mills,[4] gave them presents of porcelain and damasks worth approximately 300 *pagodas*. Mills is widely regarded as the person behind Van Uffelen's arrest and reportedly pays an annual sum of 1,000 *pagodas* to the authorities in an attempt to have the Dutch thrown out of Masulipatnam.

In the meantime, on 30 October 1623, Herman Prins, on his way to Golconda to greet the king and the ambassador of Persia with presents, ran into the army of Prince Khurram,[5] son of the great Mughal. The army consisted of 14,000 horses, 1,500 elephants, 2,500 camels and 36,000 foot-soldiers and was reportedly heading towards Masulipatnam. Such rumours made many of the important Muslim merchants of the town flee it together with their treasures. We also transported our diamonds, cash and goods to the extent possible to our ships. On 13 November, Prince Khurram reached within half a mile of Masulipatnam. Libenaar went to greet him with a present and complained about Van Uffelen's arrest. Around midnight, an emissary of the prince came to see Libenaar and told him that the prince would be willing to hand the Surat castle to the Dutch in return for provisions for his army for a year and war ammunition. Libenaar told him that this matter could be considered only by Governor Van Uffelen.

On the night of 21 November, an agent of the Persian ambassador told Libenaar that Prince Khurram was likely to leave the following morning. The agent also informed him that a *farman*[6] from the king of Golconda had since been received at Masulipatnam that as soon as Prince Khurram's army left, he was to be arrested. The sale of provisions to us was banned. We were obliged to buy these secretly at four times the normal price. On 24 November, we decided to retaliate by capturing a ship that had come to Masulipatnam a few days earlier from Tenasserim. This should either secure us justice or would serve to compensate for our losses.

1. Jan (or Johan) Libenaar was an upper-merchant on a monthly salary of f.90 in October 1621. In November 1622, he sailed with the defence fleet under the command of Jacob Dedel for the coast of Goa, Malabar and Mozambique. The fleet returned to Batavia on 13 July 1623. In November 1623, Libenaar was appointed incharge of the factory at Masulipatnam, but was recalled to Batavia in February 1626 to answer certain charges levied against him.

2. The *shahbandar* was the officer incharge of the port.
3. *Kotwal* was the chief police officer of the town
4. Thomas Mills was the chief of the English factory at Masulipatnam from the beginning of 1624. In January 1626, he went to Armagon to establish a factory there. In May 1626, he recommended the construction of a fort at Armagon. In October 1626, he was recalled to Batavia to answer certain charges preferred against him. In October 1627, he was reported to be very ill at Masulipatnam and had to cancel his trip to Batavia, with the *Abigael*. He died soon after.
5. Prince Khurram, later Mughal Emperor Shah Jahan, was the third son of Emperor Nur-ud-Din Muhammad Jahangir. He had been sent to the Deccan towards the end of November 1616 to organize the Mughal campaign against Malik Ambar. In 1622, Khurram rebelled against the emperor. The rebellion was, however, crushed in 1624.
6. A *farman* was a document ordinarily originating only at the level of the king.

5. Resolution adopted by the Surat Council on board the *Heusden* lying at Swally,[1] 11 January 1624. V.O.C. 1079, f.190vo (Copy).

The English had requested that the departure of the *Heusden* be delayed to enable one of their ships to accompany it. But since the season as well as the provisions were running out, it was resolved to wait for the English ship for not more than a day or two.

1. Swally was a small town situated at the south of the river Tapti at a latitude of 21°.5′N and a longitude of 72°.50′E. Among the Europeans, it was an Englishman, Sir Henry Middleton, who had first discovered the haven at Swally.

6. Pieter van den Broecke at Surat to the Directors at Amsterdam, 11 January 1624. V.O.C. 1079, ff.225-9vo (Original).

The *Schoonhoven* had arrived from Holland on 2 October 1623. This vessel carried a part of the capital that had been salvaged from the *Naarden* which had wrecked on the way. On 8 October, the *Heusden* had arrived from Mocha, followed by the *Vrede* and the *Weesp* from Batavia on 12 October. Van den Broecke had planned to send the two last mentioned ships to Persia, the *Heusden* to Holland and the *Schoonhoven* to Batavia with textiles. But these plans could not be implemented because in the meantime, the English had captured some Muslim ships not carrying their passes.[1] Van den Broecke was summoned by the *subahdar*[2] of Gujarat and asked to recover the ships from the English. When Van den Broecke regretted his inability to do so, he along with other Dutch factors had been house – arrested in the Dutch factory. The Company's goods at Broach were also detained by the Mughal officials. Since the Company had suffered on account of the English action, Van den Broecke wrote a letter of protest to the English chief at Surat.

In the meantime, the English had reached an accord with the Muslims on 22 November.[3] They were given the equivalent of 350,000 guilders for the blood-coral that they had not been allowed to sell over the last three years.[4] Another sum of 100,000 guilders was given to them to compensate them for the losses suffered by them. It was stipulated that they would henceforth pay an annual sum of 40,000 *mahmudis* (20,000 guilders) by way of customs duties, be entitled to transport their goods unmolested and would be exempted from inland tolls (transit duties). They further wanted a magnificent house and permission to have 3 to 4 *fusts* or frigates constructed. In Van den Broecke's opinion, the stipulated fixed annual sum of 20,000 guilders by way of custom duties was weighed more in favour of the English Company's servants in respect of their private trade which they carried on on a large scale rather than in favour of the English Company itself.

Soon after the conclusion of this accord, the English had reopened all their factories in the region that had earlier been closed. The revival of the English trade was bound to push the prices of textiles and indigo up. The factors at Agra had already reported that after they had bought 372 bales of indigo at Rs.25.75, the price had shot up to Rs. 40 per 50 ponds. The English paid no heed to the Dutch proposal to adopt a policy of joint purchase to prevent any further rise in the procurement price.

The English Company had earned a good sum as freight on the Muslim mechants' goods carried to Mocha but they could not conduct much trade on their own there during 1623. They had sent two ships to Persia laden mostly with freight goods. They had also been planning to send one of their ships to England. Last year, they had not received enough capital from England. They, therefore, got minted the entire stock of silver which they had captured in Hormuz into rupees. They had sent these funds to Persia to settle their accounts with the imperial merchants. They were still under debt to the tune of more than 50,000 rials of eight.

Van den Broecke was pleased to learn that the Directors had liked the indigo that had been sent to them from Surat via Batavia. Since the present lot had been bought cheaper, he believed that the Directors would be even more satisfied. It was indeed surprising that in Holland the price difference between indigo Bayana and indigo Sarkhej was very little. In Surat, the Sarkhej variety was 50 per cent cheaper. During the last three years, the English had not bought any indigo Lauro,[5] because it did not give them as much profit as they earned on the Sarkhej variety. Reportedly, they had bought more than 5,000 packets of indigo Sarkhej.

The Directors' evaluation of the Guinea cloth, *montassies*[6] and the samples of broad *baftas*[7] was awaited. In Van den Broecke's opinion, Surat would be able to produce better quality Guinea cloth than was done on the Coromandel coast and at a somewhat lower cost. The blue and black *baftas* were used in Austria to make aprons for women while in France they were used to make clothes for which silk had been used earlier. Saltpetre was more expensive at Surat than on the Coromandel coast. Surat would not be able to procure more than 25,000 to 30,000 ponds of this item annually till such time as the war ended.[8] Some cotton was being sent as a sample. Surat hoped to be able to procure three to four ship-loads of this item per annum.

The *Sampson* and the *Weesp* had arrived at Surat from Mocha with a capital worth f.21,879. It would have been desirable if the Mocha factory could have been continued. Between Mocha, Persia, Surat and Coromandel, enough spices could be sold each year as not to need any funds from Holland at Surat for the procurement of the return cargo for Holland and for the East Indies. But, of course, it was necessary that in all these places, the quantity of the spices imported was regulated so as to prevent a decline in price.

Adequate care would be taken with regard to the quality of the indigo purchased. It was indeed better to pay 1 to 1½ rupees per 30 ponds more than to buy poor quality indigo which would be difficult to sell in Holland as had happened in the case of the indigo exported by the English to England.

Gold was likely to afford a profit of 2 per cent in Surat. Unminted gold also fetched a good profit. The Company was not required to pay customs duties on gold, rose nobels[9] and ducats. This, however, did not apply to silver. The Dutch *daaldars* did much better than the rials. In fact, on the latter, the Company had lost 1½ per cent. In Surat, a rose nobel and an Hungarian ducat could fetch 8 guilders 10 *stuivers* and 4 guilders 7½ *stuivers* respectively. It would be more profitable if gold rather than silver could be sent to Surat. They hoped to receive annually 100,000 guilders worth of gold and some silver from Holland. It would be desirable if each year two big ships and one yacht could reach Surat by the end of September or by early October.

All the goods that had been received from Holland are in good demand, in particular lead, ivory and red broad cloth. Surat was surprised to note that quicksilver, vermilion and raw blood coral had not been sent at all. The following would convey an idea of the price and the likely annual sale at Surat.

S. No.	Item	Quantity	Price in florins (per 100 ponds)		
			florins	*stuivers*	*pennings*
1.	Lead	100,000 ponds	12	10	0
2.	Ivory	10,000 ponds	76	3	0
3.	Quicksilver	900-1,000 ponds	365	0	0
4.	Vermilion	900-1,000 ponds	355	16	0
5.	Red raw blood coral	20,000-25,000 ponds		–	
6.	Fine red broad cloth	18-20 pieces			–
7.	Woollen cloth (red, yellow or green but not blue)	25-30 pieces			
8.	Red copper	15,000-20,000 ponds	42	0	0

The Company's trade had been adversely affected because Prince Khurram's rebellion against his father, Jahangir, had made the transportation of goods unsafe. The Mughal emperor had deputed Prince Parwez[10] to deal with the rebellion. The factors at Surat would be able to sell goods at a profit only after the rebellion had been contained and safety on the routes restored. Prince Khurram had reportedly since taken flight to Patna where also he had been defeated.

Many important people of Gujarat have complained that out of fear of capture by the English and ourselves, Malabar ships had not dared to come to Surat over the last two years. This had resulted in revenue loss of more than f.100,000 a year by way of tolls. In respect of Malabar ships with no Portuguese links, 15 to 16 passes had been given by the Dutch. Van den Broecke hoped that the Directors would approve of this action.

The English had reached an accord with the Shah of Persia. It was stipulated that they would buy all the silk available in Persia which was worth approximately f.3 million per annum.

A few days ago, Van den Broecke had learnt from some Muslims that the Dutch factors at Masulipatnam had been sorrounded. The English at Surat had also received a letter from their factors in Coromandel that the Dutch factors there had been grossly mishandled and that Abraham van Uffelen had been arrested.

1. In his letter of 25 December 1623 to Batavia, Van den Broecke had written that the English had captured Muslim ships even though they were in possession of English passes. For details, see Om Prakash (ed.), *The Dutch Factories in India 1617-1623*, Delhi, 1984, p. 283.
2. The term *subahdar* was used in the Mughal administrative set-up for the provincial governor. Dawar Baksh, also known in popular parlance as Prince Bulaqi, was the *subahdar* of Gujarat during 1623-24. He was the son of Prince Khusrau, the eldest son of Emperor Jahangir.
3. In Van den Broecke's letter of 25 December 1623, the date of this accord is given as 23 November. See Om Prakash (ed.), *The Dutch Factories in India 1617-1623*, p. 284.
4. In his letter of 25 December 1623, Van den Broecke had stated that the English had not been allowed to sell their blood-coral for the last two years. See Om Prakash (ed.), *The Dutch Factories in India 1617-1623*, p. 284.
5. The Bayana indigo was sometimes referred to as indigo Lauro [Lahore].
6. Probably *minatashis*, described as enamelled fabrics, a name given to a cloth of gold with coloured designs on the surface. It was bought in the Cambay area and exported to the Malay archipelago.
7. *Bafta* was a generic term for a plain calico of Gujarat (esp. Broach and Navsari), varying in quality from coarse to fine—the latter costing nearly twice the former. *Baftas* sent to Europe were usually white, but for Asian markets they were more commonly dyed red, blue or black. After the Gujarat famine of 1630, they became scarce and were imitated in many other parts of India, the term thus losing all local significance.
8. The reference would seem to be to the rebellion of Prince Khurram against his father Emperor Jahangir.
9. A gold coin worth ±12 guilders.
10. Parwez was the eldest son of Emperor Jahangir. After his brother, Prince Khusrau, had died in 1622, Parwez was widely recognized as the heir-apparent. He died in October 1626.

7. Van den Broecke at Surat to the Directors at Amsterdam, 15 January 1624. V.O.C. 1079, ff.230-1vo (Original).

Van den Broecke had learnt from some Muslims that Van Uffelen had been arrested at Masulipatnam, together with twenty-three other factors. The reason was the English capture of the ships from Gujarat, Chaul, Diu and other places. When approached for any information that they might have, the English replied that in the presence of their chief at Masulipatnam, Van Uffelen had been brought to the customs house and treated like a dog and put under arrest. The factors with him had been tortured to find out what capital there was in the Dutch factory.

An ambassador of the king of Golconda came to Surat and asked Van den Broecke whether the Dutch were also a party to the capture of the ships from Surat and Chaul, etc. When told that the Dutch had nothing to do with this, the ambassador asked Van den Broecke to obtain a statement to this effect from some important people of the city. This was necessary to effect the release of the Dutch factors. Van den Broecke would try to do the needful.

Van den Broecke was of the opinion that in order to enjoy in full the fruits of the intra-Asian trade, it was necessary that the Directors issued instructions that no Muslim ships were attacked until the Dutch factory in the region concerned had been closed and capital taken out.

As the English President Rastell was leaving for England, he told Van den Broecke that he wished that the English and the Dutch companies had been able to reach an agreement about the trade of Persia. If such an agreement did not materialize, the Dutch Company would never be able to enjoy the fruits of the Persian trade. The Shah of Persia had agreed to sell silk to the English on an exclusive basis.

8. Van Uffelen at Masulipatnam to Marten Ysbrantsz.[1] at Pulicat, 15 January 1624. V.O.C. 1083, f.184 (Copy).

Van Uffelen had earlier asked Marten Ysbrantsz. to postpone the departure of the *Rotterdam* for Batavia till such time that he had received Van Uffelen's letter addressed to the Governor-General. Since Van Uffelen was indisposed and was not in a position to write the letter, Ysbrantsz. was to proceed with the dispatch of the *Rotterdam* to Batavia.

1. Marten Ysbrantsz. had come to the East Indies in 1611. Around 1615, he was sent to the coast of Coromandel where he was promoted to the rank of an upper-merchant in 1619. He was further elevated to the post of governor there in 1624, a position that he held until 1635 with a brief interruption in 1632. He returned to the Netherlands in 1635.

9. Van Uffelen at Masulipatnam to Ysbrantsz. at Pulicat, 16 January 1624. V.O.C. 1083, f.181 (Copy).

The letter of Herman Prins from Golconda[1] that Van Uffelen had sent to Marten Ysbrantsz. was to be sent on to the Governor-General with the *Rotterdam*. The Governor-General was to be informed that the Company would be obliged to pay a toll of 4 per cent on all exports and imports unless it agreed to pay by way of a gift a sum of 4,000 to 5,000 *pagodas* per annum.

1. This letter is not available in the Company's archives.

10. Van den Broecke at Surat to the Directors at Amsterdam, 16 January 1624. V.O.C. 1079, ff.232-2vo (Original).

Since the seizure of the Muslim ships by the *Sampson* and the *Weesp* two years ago,[1] the Company had been facing problems at Surat. If the Directors wanted to continue trading at this place, the Dutch behaviour towards the local people had to be more civil. These people cared little for the Company's trade and could easily do without it. In fact, they declare that they need not even go to the sea and could use the land routes to Persia and Armenia.

1. For details, see Om Prakash (ed.), *The Dutch Factories in India, 1617-1623*, pp. 189-90.

11. Huybert Vissnich at Isfahan to Van den Broecke at Surat, 18 January 1624. V.O.C. 1082, f.101 (Copy).

Huybert Vissnich had received Van den Broecke's letter of 12 November 1623[1] on 14 January. The goods received with the yachts the *Weesp* and the *Vrede* had been sold to the agent of the king. Vissnich had also promised to sell to him the cash specie and silver on the condition that in exchange he would supply fine quality *ardasse* silk at 45 *tomans*[2] per two bales of 36 Persian *maunds* each.

The English had purchased a similar variety of silk at 50 *tomans* from places in the hinterland one month's journey away. If the expenses of transportation, leakages, etc. were added, the cost would come to 55 *tomans*. As against this, Vissnich hoped to get it in Isfahan at 45 *tomans*.

1. This letter is not available in the Company's archives.
2. The *toman*, a Persian unit of account, was worth 39 to 40 guilders. One *toman* was equal to 50 *abbassis* = 80 *laris* = 100 *mahmudis*.

12. Van den Broecke at Surat to Governor-General De Carpentier at Batavia, 19 January 1624. V.O.C. 1082, ff.47vo-48 (Copy).

Surat wanted to send the *Heusden* to Holland as early as possible. But the English chief Rastell asked Van den Broecke to wait for 8 to 10 days by which time their ship, the *Dolphin*, was expected to be ready to leave. The *Heusden* finally left on 19 January.

The English ship had on board 1,200 bales of indigo Sarkhej and 100 to 200 bales of silk. Besides it carried pepper which had been bought at Surat at 15 to 16 *mahmudis* per 30 Dutch ponds.

On 18 January Van den Broecke received a letter from Golconda[1] and learnt that Van Uffelen and two other factors were under detention at the court.

It seemed that following the seizure of the ships from Dabhol, Chaul and other places, the Muslims had become extremely bitter towards the Dutch.[2]

1. This letter is not available in the Company's archives.
2. For details, see Om Prakash (ed.), *The Dutch Factories in India, 1617-1623*, pp.189-90.

13. An extract from the invoice of the *Heusden* that left Surat for Holland on 19 January 1624. V.O.C. 1079, ff.171-80vo (Copy).

S. No.	*Item*	*Quantity*	*Value (in florins)*
1.	*Minatashis*	7,840 pieces (28 packets)	3,875:18:0
2.	Guinea cloth	1,000 pieces (24 packets)	5,705:8:10
3.	Cotton yarn	775 ponds (5 packets)	317:2:8
4.	Fine white broad *baftas*	120 pieces (1 packet)	398:5:0
5.	White broad *baftas*	120 pieces (1 packet)	275:15:0
6.	Black broad *baftas*	120 pieces (1 packet)	441:5:0
7.	White *baftas*	600 pieces (3 packets)	1,160:5:0

8.	Blue broad *baftas*	400 pieces (4 packets)	1,652:14:0
9.	Black broad *baftas*	120 pieces (1 packet)	446:18:2
10.	Alum Socotra	231 ponds (1 case)	115:10:0
11.	Sealing wax	431¼ ponds (2 cases)	285:17:8
12.	Red coral (from Cape Verde)	100,700 pieces (1 packet)	539:4:6
13.	Merk stones[1]	750 ponds	
14.	Servet Werch[1]	200 ponds (1 packet)	385:17:8
15.	Jambusar indigo	2,325 ponds (15 packets)	610:12:13
16.	Bayana indigo	72,150 ponds (346 packets)	40,228:2:0
17.	Spike-nard[2]	1,200 ponds (8 packets)	212:8:0
18.	Borax	450 ponds (2 packets)	219:0:0
19.	Sal-ammoniac	525 ponds (2 packets)	104:8:0
20.	Cotton (as a sample)	232½ ponds (2 packets)	10:0:0
21.	Unrefined saltpetre	6,457½ ponds (5 packets)	302:5:2
22.	Refined saltpetre	1,540 ponds (8 packets)	190:18:4
23.	Small canvas	100 pieces (1 packet)	142:10:0
24.	Ambergris	2 ponds 14 ounces (1 packet)	371:5:0
25.	Sarkhej indigo	82,587½ ponds (628 packets)	35,251:8:0
26.	Refined saltpetre	1,135 ponds (9 bags)	133:7:0
		Total	f.93,376:4:3

Costs

a.	Customs duty on Bayana, Sarkhej and Jambusar indigo worth f.72,657 at the rate of 3.5 per cent plus 1 *paisa*	f. 2,550:0:0
b.	Payment to the clerks and other employees of the customs house as per usage	755:0:0
c.	The cost of transportation from the customs house to the ships and the cost of packing material, etc.	698:15:0
d.	Amount given to the *mutasaddi* of Surat for the speedy dispatch of the goods	345:10:0
	Grand Total	f.97,725:9:13

1. Not identified.
2. An aromatic Indian plant with rose and purple flowers.

14. Prins at Bhagnagar in Golconda to Van Uffelen at Masulipatnam, 25 January 1624. V.O.C. 1083, ff.193-3vo (Copy).

Prins had received Van Uffelen's letter of 17 January[1] and was very sorry to learn of his indisposition. He reiterates his request to be relieved from Golconda.

1. This letter is not available in the Company's archives.

15. Van Uffelen at Masulipatnam to Ysbrantsz. at Pulicat, 27 January 1624. V.O.C. 1083, f.182 (Copy).

Van Uffelen believed that the presence of the *Medemblik* in Pulicat would be a good safeguard against the Portuguese. Ysbrantsz. is, therefore, advised to keep the *Medemblik* and, if necessary, he could also retain the *Enkhuizen*. He is asked to send samples of the newly produced textiles as also those of Guinea cloth so that the difference in the price could be ascertained.

Ysbrantsz. is asked to enter into a contract with Malaya[1] for the supply of saltpetre to an amount of 1,000 *bahars* by October next with the understanding that he would not agree to supply to anyone else.

1. Malaya was reputed to be the richest merchant of south Coromandel region during the first half of the seventeenth century. The port of Tegenapatam was the original base of Malaya's commercial operations. The Dutch probably came in contact with Malaya in 1608 when they established their factory at the coast of Tegenapatam. Over the next decade, Malaya was the chief Dutch broker in southern Coromandel but his influence extended to Masulipatnam where he often lent money to the Company. He died in 1634.

16. Ysbrantsz. at Pulicat to Governor-General De Carpentier at Batavia, 28 January 1624. V.O.C. 1083, ff.169-71 (Copy).

Van Uffelen had been freed only after paying 5,000 *pagodas* and promising to release the captured ship from Tenasserim.[1] Herman Pietersz. Prins was still in detention at Golconda. After all that had happened, Ysbrantsz. believed that it would not be advisable to continue the factory at Masulipatnam. The losses suffered on land could be avenged by attacking their ships on the sea.

The outbreak of some sort of plague had caused large scale mortality among the slaves, 303 of whom had died since February 1623. Slaves could be purchased only in the ratio of 1 male to 6 females however high the price one is willing to pay for the males. Since the price of rice had gone up due to poor rains, Ysbrantsz. hoped to be able to send a good number of slaves soon.

Pulicat could not fully meet the orders for clothes for Java and Malaya because due to the shortage of funds, contracts for these clothes had been put out rather late. The clothes had to be procured entirely against contracts and advances and not one packet could be obtained against ready cash. The weavers had since been persuaded to produce fine *muris*[2] for Holland. Besides clothes and slaves, the cargo of the present shipment included saltpetre. It was not prudent to keep the saltpetre here because in view of the ongoing war,[3] the *nayak* of Tanjore might have forced us to supply it to him.

Trading at Pulicat had been extremely difficult because of the ongoing domestic troubles and the absence of a ruler. The rulers of Bijapur and sorrounding regions had been troubling the factors a great deal. Ysbrantsz. wishes an early end of these troubles so that the Company could conduct its trade in peace.

Jan Oliversz., who had come to Coromandel seven years ago and had served here with honesty as an assistant and as an under-merchant and had since gotten married had been granted his freedom by Van Uffelen and was travelling to Batavia with this shipment.

1. This ship had been captured on 24 November 1623. See document no. 4.
2. *Muri* was one of the categories of staple cotton-cloth woven on the Coromandel coast, usually of superior quality and much in demand in Europe as a substitute for linen cloth. It was also used for chintz-making. The traditional centre of manufacture was Masulipatnam but later it was also woven in the Madras area. The usual dimensions were about 9 yards by 1 yard 8 inches.
3. The reference is evidently to the wars among the *nayaks* of Madurai, Tanjore and Gingi.

17. Van den Broecke at Surat to Governor-General De Carpentier at Batavia, 29 January 1624. V.O.C. 1083, ff.147-8 (Original).

It seemed that ever since the capture of the ships from Dabhol, Chaul and other places by the *Sampson* and the *Weesp*,[1] the Muslims had become extremely bitter towards the Dutch and had been giving them all sorts of troubles. Recently, Adam Claessen Verhoeven,[2] who had been sent to Agra about a year ago, was forcibly fetched from the factory there in connection with some troubles between a Dutch factor and the soldiers at Agra. He had been treated extremely badly.

Van den Broecke had succeeded in obtaining a written declaration from important Muslim residents of Surat to the effect the Dutch had nothing to do in the matter of the capture of the Golconda ships by the English. He had given the declaration to the ambassador of the king of Golconda who had come to Surat specially to determine whether the Dutch or the English had been guilty of the offence.

1. See Om Prakash (ed.), *The Dutch Factories in India, 1617-1623*, pp. 189-90.
2. Adam Claessen Verhoeven came to Surat in 1617 as an assistant aboard the *Middelburg*. He served in the directorate of Surat till 1629 when Coen recalled him to Batavia.

18. General letter from Governor-General De Carpentier at Batavia to the Directors at Amsterdam, 4 March 1624. V.O.C. 1090, ff.61-7 (Original).*

The *Schoonhoven* had arrived from Surat on 3 March 1624 with 499 packets of clothes. Van den Broecke had sent the *Weesp* and the *Vrede* to Persia on 16 November 1623 with a cargo worth f.150,000 (sale value). Holland could expect a good return cargo from Persia.

The *faujdar*[1] of Cambay had extorted from the Dutch factors at Agra a sum of Rs.13,225 (f.16,531) allegedly in compensation for the amount that the *Weesp* had taken in 1621 from a ship from Chaul.[2]

The English had the following four ships at Surat: the *Blessing* (400 *lasts*), the *William* (350 *lasts*), the *Dolphin* (300 *lasts*) and the *Reformation* (150 *lasts*). Since their agreement with the authorities at Surat,[3] they were in the process of re-establishing the factories that they had abandoned. They were also planning to send a ship to Batavia with textiles.

* Summarized in W. Ph. Coolhaas (ed.), *Generale Missiven*, I, pp. 148-51.

1. The *faujdar* of Cambay at this time was one Agha Saleh.
2. For details, see Om Prakash (ed.), *The Dutch Factories in India, 1617-1623*, pp. 191, 222-3.
3. This agreement had been concluded on 22 November 1623. See Om Prakash (ed.), *The Dutch Factories in India, 1617-1623*, p. 284.

19. Van den Broecke at Surat to the Directors at Amsterdam, 12 March 1624. V.O.C. 1082, ff.10-11vo (Original).

The Dutch factors were well received by Shah Abbas[1] of Persia. Several Muslim merchants who had been allowed to travel on the Dutch ships from Hormuz to Surat on payment of freight seemed very happy. If the Directors decided to continue the Surat – Mocha and the Surat – Persia trade, it would be desirable to keep two ships for the purpose at Surat. They could earn twice the cost of their maintenance by carrying freight cargo to these places.

As soon as Van den Broecke's letter together with the declaration given by the principal merchants of Surat to the effect that the Dutch were innocent in the matter of the capture of the Golconda ships by the English[2] had reached Golconda, Van Uffelen had been released honourably and presented with a horse and a gold cloth. Van den Broecke himself had been honoured by the *subahdar* of Gujarat with a letter of appreciation from the Mughal emperor and a respect cloth.

In the same context, the English factors at Surat had been put under arrest. Their factors at Masulipatnam had also been arrested and taken to the king of Golconda.

Van den Broecke hoped to be able to send next year a ship each to Amsterdam and Batavia. He had already sent a *kafila*[3] with cloves and other goods to Agra and another to Burhanpur.[4] He expected a cargo of silk from Persia to reach Surat before the ships would be ready to leave for Holland and Batavia.

1. Shah Abbas, son of Sultan Muhammad Khudaband, was the ruler of Persia from 1587 to 1629.
2. See document numbers 17 and 20.
3. A *kafila* was a caravan or a convoy of merchant travellers.
4. Burhanpur, in the region of Khandeṣh, is now in Madhya Pradesh. It is situated at a latitude of 21°.17′N and longitude of 76°.16′E.

20. Van den Broecke at Surat to Governor-General De Carpentier at Batavia, 24 March 1624. V.O.C. 1083, ff.160-3 (Copy).

Surat would have sent the *Heusden* to Holland on 2 January, but had agreed at the request of the English President[1] to postpone its departure by 10 days to enable the English ship the *Dolphin* to accompany it. But since the *Dolphin* was not ready on time, the *Heusden* left Surat on 20 January for Holland.[2]

An English ship, the *Reformation*, had left Surat for Batavia on 6 February with some clothes and a lot of cash. The English had bought up all the pepper that had been brought to Burhanpur from Malabar. They had also bought more than 4,000 packets of indigo at Ahmedabad for Europe. Two of their ships had arrived from Persia at Surat on 21 March. En route, these ships had captured three Muslim ships on their way to Mocha.

The *Vrede* and the *Weesp* had returned safely from Hormuz with some Persian merchants together with their goods aboard for which they had paid freight.

Upper-merchant Wollenbrandt Gelleynsz[3]. had been sent to Burhanpur on 23 February with a cargo of cloves, sandalwood, tin and other goods worth a total value of f.12,000 because there were no buyers at Surat.

The *kafila* from Ahmedabad with a cargo of 860 packets of indigo Sarkhej had arrived at Surat on 24 February while that from Agra with 408 packets of indigo Bayana arrived on 28 February.

A *farman*, ordering the arrest of all Englishmen throughout the empire till such time as the assets plundered from the Muslims' ships had been returned, reached Surat on 2 March 1624. In consequence, the English President at Surat was arrested together with the members of his council. Iron chains had been put around their ankles. Also their houses had been attacked and goods taken away.

Van den Broecke had received a friendly letter from the *subahdar* of Gujarat on 8 March. He had requested Van den Broecke to provide all possible help to the ships from Mocha. Dabhol had since come under the jurisdiction of the Mughal emperor and it would be desirable, the *subahdar* had suggested, for the Dutch to make peace with the authorities at Dabhol. The king of Bijapur[4] had also sought peace with the Dutch. In Van den Broecke's opinion it would be highly advisable to make such a peace.

Van den Broecke had succeeded in getting a declaration from some important people of Surat to the effect that the Dutch had nothing to do with the seizure of the Muslim ships by the English. The declaration had been sent to Governor Mir Muhammad.

There was a strong rumour at Surat that King Shah Abbas was likely to grant us full liberty of trade in Persia. It was quite clear that he was no longer happy with the English.

A *kafila* had been sent to Agra with cloves and other goods worth f.23,000. The upper-merchant in charge of the *kafila* had been asked to procure there indigo Bayana, Bengal *khasas* and other varieties of cloth for Europe. In Van den Broecke's view, it would be advisable to have a permanent representative at the Mughal court. Adam Claessen Verhoeven had been sent with some cash to Ahmedabad and Cambay to buy clothes for the southern quarters and indigo Sarkhej for Holland.

Upper-merchant Sebalt Wonderaer[5] was being sent with the present shipment. The diamonds and stones left by the late Upper-merchant Wouter Heuten[6] had been sent to Holland.

1. See document no.1.
2. The *Heusden* had actually left Surat on 19 January 1624. See document no.12.
3. Wollenbrandt Gelleynsz. de Jonge had been engaged at Banda and Halmahera between 1615 and 1621 (as an under-merchant towards the end). In Gujarat, he served first at Burhanpur and since April 1624 as the chief factor at Broach. He repatriated in March 1632 but returned to Batavia in June 1635 as commander of a fleet of eight ships. Thereafter he served at Surat and Persia and again repatriated in January 1648 in the rank of extraordinary member of the Council of the Indies. He died in 1674.
4. Ibrahim Adil Shah was king of Bijapur from 1580 to 1627.
5. Sebalt Wonderaer came to the East Indies in 1612 as an assistant. In 1617, he accompanied Van den Broecke as an under-merchant. Between 1620 and 1625, he was an under-merchant at Surat. In August 1626, he was sent as an envoy to Mataram. Thereafter, he became a free burgher. Between 1636 and his death in May 1653, he held various offices at Batavia and elsewhere in the East Indies.
6. Wouter Heuten came to the East Indies with the fleet of Reynst and, thereafter, became an under-merchant. Between January 1616 and July 1616, he was the chief of the factory at Shihir (on the coast of Southern Yemen, Lat.14°.41N, Long.49°.32E). Between August 1616 and 1617, he was at Surat. In December 1618, he was promoted to

the position of an upper-merchant, in which rank he accompanied Jan Pietersz. Coen to Amboina in the beginning of 1619. In July 1620, he left for Coromandel from where he travelled overland to Surat. At the latter factory, he held the rank of second-in-command. In January 1621, he was appointed head of the factory at Agra, where he died on 7 September 1623.

21. Ysbrantsz. at Pulicat to Governor-General De Carpentier at Batavia, 24 March 1624. V.O.C. 1083, ff.205-8vo (Copy).

The *Muys* had arrived from Masulipatnam on 6 March. The trade there was at a standstill. The factors were waiting for a *farman* from the king of Golconda permitting the Company to trade there as before without paying more than the agreed toll of 3,000 *pagodas* per annum. Because of the capture by the *Muys* at Masulipatnam of a ship from Pegu, the clothes coming from Draksharama[1] and Palicol[2] to Masulipatnam had been detained. This ship belonged to a Hindu merchant of Cochin and had left Cochin the previous year for Bengal to fetch rice but had been driven to Pegu by contrary winds. At Pegu, the ship had been freighted by a Muslim merchant of Masulipatnam named Sansa who had shifted to Pegu four years earlier. The Muslims at Masulipatnam made a lot of noise about the capture of the ship, which eventually had to be released together with its cargo. It was only then that the Masulipatnam factors were allowed to resume their trade.

The taste of the 5,000 *pagodas* that the authorities at Masulipatnam had extorted from Van Uffelen and of the further 11,000 *pagodas* extorted from the merchants of the Company was so agreeable to them that they were looking for other similar opportunities.

On 8 March, Ysbrantsz. had sent Marts,[3] an under-merchant on the *Wapen van Enkhuizen*, together with another person with good knowledge of indigo to Mogena to procure 500-600 packets of this commodity.

Since Pulicat had no stock of sulphur to make gunpowder, it

was not possible to send this item. In case sulphur had been available, they could have supplied gunpowder at 3 to 3¼ *stuivers* per pond. Batavia was not to send any ivory or camphor because Pulicat had been able to sell only a small quantity.

A ship from Masulipatnam on its way to Pegu had been driven by winds to Arakan. Since the kings of Pegu[4] and Arakan[5] are enemies, the ship was detained at Arakan. The king of Golconda then sent an ambassador to Arakan to negotiate the release of the ship. The crew were subsequently released but not the ship or its cargo. The king of Golconda then issued a *farman* prohibiting those sending ships to Arakan to put aboard these ships items such as iron, opium and tobacco. The charges levelled against Van Uffelen included one of violating this provision. Another charge against him was that a *shroff*, who had been farmed against 500 *pagodas* per annum the right of changing all rials and gold at Masulipatnam into local coins had been detained by Van Uffelen in the Company's factory and kept without food for ten days till he had agreed to renounce his farming rights.

Ysbrantsz. was of the opinion that the successor of Van Uffelen as governor of Coromandel ought to operate from Pulicat and not from Masulipatnam. The successor was still awaited at Pulicat.

The frigates the *Jager* and the *Muys* had been sent along with the yacht *Medemblik* to Arakan in September 1623. These two frigates had returned to Masulipatnam on 28 January with 88 Arakanese slaves. The king of Arakan had permitted the purchase and transportation of slaves only after securing a promise from the factors that a factory would soon be established at Arakan. Some free Dutch merchants had also gone to Arakan. It was to be seen whether they would be able to bring some slaves from there.

1. Draksharama was in the north-east of Masulipatnam in the Godavari delta.
2. Palicol or Palakollu was a town in the Godavari delta.
3. Not identified.
4. Anankpetlun succeeded to the throne of Pegu in 1605 and was still on the throne in 1624.
5. Thirthundamma was the king of Arakan between 1622 and 1638.

22. Governor-General De Carpentier at Batavia to Van Uffelen at Masulipatnam, 26 March 1624. V.O.C. 1082, ff.207-11vo (Copy).*

The *Tholen* had arrived from Coromandel on 28 November 1623 and the *Wapen van Rotterdam* on 11 March 1624.

According to Batavia's calculations, the position regarding the availability of funds in Coromandel would be as follows:

Capital available in Coromandel as on 31 January 1623	f.450,500[1]
f.18,396 worth of cargo sent with the *Masulipatam* on 27 April whose sale value would be	f.60,000
f.150,326 worth of cargo sent with the *Tholen* on 15 July whose sale value would be	f.240,000[2]
Sent with the *Wapen van Rotterdam* on 18 August in cash	f.101,441[3]
Cargo sent with the *Wapen van Enkhuizen* on 16 October whose sale value would be	f.7,000
Precious metals and goods sent from Holland with the *Medemblik* worth	f.203,208[4]
f.132,311 worth of cargo being presently sent with the *Wapen van Rotterdam* whose sale value would be	f.177,302
Total	f.1,239,453[5]

As against this sum of f.1,239,453, Coromandel had sent out cargo worth f.135,859 with the *Schiedam* to Holland, and worth f.231,384 and f.126,606 with the *Tholen* and the *Wapen van Rotterdam* respectively to Batavia. Besides 10,000 *pagodas* worth f.42,500 had been extorted from the Company's merchants by the king of Golconda. Another f.25,000 were accounted for by bad debts and expenses on provisions and ammunition for war. All these sums together would amount to f.561,350 leaving with Coromandel a net sum worth f.678,103. This should be enough to meet the orders from both Holland and Batavia. Depending upon availability, Batavia would also send one or two shiploads of spices to Coromandel.

Batavia's orders for clothes and slaves were to be met to the extent possible. *Tapichindaes*[6] from Masulipatnam had sold well and matters would improve even further if the red dye used could be made a little brighter without an increase in the cost. One packet of *tapichindaes* containing 15 *corgis*[7] that cost f.239 in Masulipatnam could be sold at Batavia at 15 rials per *corgi*, rendering a good profit. Batavia hoped to sell 20 to 30 packets of this cloth per annum. The orders for rough *tapis*[8] were to be met in full but the more expensive varieties in this category were to be avoided in so far as *tapi sarrasas* were preferred to these. Since Batavia had enough stocks of *taffechelas*[9] Narsapur[10] and Golconda to last two years, these were to be avoided altogether. No more than two to three packets of the best quality shirts for use by officers in Batavia were to be sent. Coromandel was also to send striped *dungarees*[11] for the Company's slaves in Banda and Amboina. The earlier order for 25 to 30 packets of clothes of the Siamese fashion was to be treated as cancelled because the expected profit was not adequate in view of the stiff competition by the Muslims and the Portuguese. Instead of procuring clothes at Masulipatnam, Coromandel was advised to get as many of them produced in and around Pulicat as possible.

It was a pity that no more than 200 slaves had been sent with the *Tholen*. The Governor-General was very unhappy to learn of the large scale mortality among the slaves. Female slaves are in great abundance here. So in future the number of female slaves procured was not to exceed that of male slaves. Among the males, old persons were to be avoided. Young boys above the age of six were similarly to be procured only when adults were not available.

Notwithstanding the fact that the Directors had not specifically asked for sugar, Coromandel was to buy some white sugar and send it to them.

Since sulphur needed for making gunpowder in Coromandel was not available at Batavia, efforts would be made to get it from Aceh. In the meantime, the factors at Coromandel were to try to get it through Muslim ships and send 200 to 300 vats of gunpowder to Batavia.

Since Batavia had no stocks of opium, Coromandel was to send 5 to 6 *piculs*[12] of good quality opium.

Pepper was to be procured at Trancquebar only if it were available at 2 to 3 rials per sack which was unlikely. Efforts were to be made to hinder the procurement of pepper by the Danes and other Europeans which could hurt the Company's sales in Europe. The price paid at Batavia for pepper bought mainly against textiles was 4½ rials per sack.

* An exact copy is also available in the *Bataviaasch Uitgaande Brievenboek*, V.O.C. 851, ff.32vo-35.

1. In document number 2, the value of the capital as on 1 February 1623 is indicated as f.450,000.
2. In document number 2, the sale value of the cargo sent is indicated as f.230,000.
3. In document number 2, the value of the cash sent with the *Wapen van Rotterdam* is indicated as f.100,000.
4. In document number 2, the value of the cargo sent from Holland with the *Medemblik* is indicated as f.203,000.
5. The total in fact should be f.1,239,451. The small excess of 2 guilders in the total as given in the document arises because of the disregard of the fractions in the individual amounts noted there.
6. *Tapichindae* was a cheap painted or printed cloth made especially for the spice islanders. It must have had a distinctive local character, because when Surat piece goods were copied on the Coromandel coast, it was claimed that, apart from *patola*, the *tapichindae* was the only variety which could not be imitated there.
7. A *corgi* consists of 20 pieces.
8. The *tapi* was a general term for coloured piece goods used as skirts by both men and women in many parts of South-East Asia. A well-known variety known as *tapi sarassa* or *sarassa malaya*, was patterned with birds and foliage.
9. *Taffechela* was a cheap striped cloth of mixed silk and cotton, patterned in the loom, much in demand by the slave traders and also in the Malay archipelago.
10. Narsapur, also known as Narsipur, is a town in the district of Ellore, 48 miles north-east of Masulipatnam.
11. *Dungaree* was a strong coarse calico. It was a cloth of very low grade and was often used for packing other goods.
12. 1 *picul* = 133½ lbs. avoirdupois.

23. Private (*particuliere*) letter from Governor-General De Carpentier at Batavia to Van Uffelen at Masulipatnam, 26 March 1624. V.O.C. 1082, ff.212-13vo (Copy).*

De Carpentier had earlier written to Van Uffelen about the poor state of the Company's trade at both Batavia and in Europe. He was very sorry to learn about the scandalous and tyrannical procedures adopted by the *sar-i-khail* and his substitute, the Muslim governor of Masulipatnam[1] against both Van Uffelen and other servants of the Company as well as against its customary merchants. According to rumours in Batavia, these disasters could have been avoided, or at least their intensity reduced, if Van Uffelen had behaved more moderately and desisted from resorting to certain acts. For instance, in a meeting of the principal merchants of the city where the governor of Masulipatnam was also present, Van Uffelen had slighted the *sarchamat*,[2] an officer of the king, by asking him to keep quiet. He had also humiliated Mir Kamal-al-Din.[3] Van Uffelen had also been accused of keeping ivory which he knew to have been stolen as well as organizing an armed break-in at night into the customs-house where the Company's goods had been kept for appraisal and having them removed from there. He had also kept in detention the person to whom the right to deal in bills of exchange had been farmed out till such time as he had paid him 3,000 *pagodas*. Also while the office of the governor of the city was vacant, Van Uffelen had exported tobacco to Arakan in contravention of the king's orders. Thus even if Van Uffelen was not directly responsible for the troubles at Masulipatnam, his actions had certainly helped cause them. All this was being brought to his attention in a private letter in order that he might take corrective steps.

Batavia firmly believed that the authorities' attempt to annul the old contract regarding tolls and to bring about an increase therein coupled with their insatiable craving for money rather than the detention of the farmer of the bills of exchange or the export of tobacco to Arakan was the real reason behind the troubles. Only if Van Uffelen had not precipitated matters by his actions, the full intensity of the injustice by the authorities would have been established.

With a view to prevent the recurrence of such incidents in future, Admiral Dedel, a member of the Batavia Council was being sent to Masulipatnam to conduct an enquiry into the entire affair. While in Coromandel, he would be incharge of the Company's affairs there. He would send an envoy to the king of Golconda asking for the restitution of the money extorted from Van Uffelen, claim compensation for the damage done to the Company and ask for the withdrawal of the increase in the tolls. In the event of these demands not being met, the further course of action would be determined by Dedel in consultation with the Masulipatnam Council. A copy of the instructions given to Dedel was enclosed.[4]

The Muslims captured by the *Rotterdam* were being allowed to stay at Batavia for the time being.

Prince Khurram had been extremely friendly to the Company. Since he was now in exile, Van Uffelen was to retain his favour by giving him small gifts.

Jan Libenaar had informed Batavia that the English President Mills had spoken a great deal against the Dutch to the Muslim governor. Van Uffelen was to collect the necessary details and send them to Batavia so that appropriate steps could be taken in the matter.

On 16 January 1624 had arrived at Batavia under the command of Bruystens[5] two yachts, the *Diamant* and the *Randevous* together with a Portuguese prize of 100 *lasts* captured near Tenasserim. This ship had come from Sao Tome and was carrying a good amount of clothes and salt.

* An exact copy is also available in the *Bataviaasch Uitgaande Brievenboek*, V.O.C. 851, ff.35vo-36vo.

1. For administrative purposes, the districts or *mahals* in Golconda were divided into smaller units, each of which was governed by a *havaldar*. The Dutch described the *sar-samatu* and the *havaldar* as great governor and local governor respectively.
2. It is not quite clear who the official referred to was. It might have been the *sar-samatu*.

3. Mir Kamal-al-Din was a major trader engaged in overseas trade from Coromandel.
4. See document no. 26.
5. Hendrik Bruystens left for the East Indies in April 1613 with the *Aelus* and reached Bantam in November 1614 as an upper-merchant. He left for the coast of Coromandel via Johor on 8 September 1615. He later served as secretary of Laurens Reael. He played an important role in the bombardment of Jacatra on 30 May 1619. Thereafter he became a free merchant and repeatedly took part in trading expeditions. Between 1 July 1620 and 5 October 1621, he was bailiff at Batavia. Between 30 May 1624 and 6 February 1625, he was superintendent (*voorzitter*) of the Company's ships. He was beheaded on 3 July 1629 on a charge of piracy.

24. Governor-General De Carpentier at Batavia to Ysbrantsz. at Pulicat, 26 March 1624. V.O.C. 1082, f.214 (Copy).*

De Carpentier acknowledges receipt of Ysbrantsz.'s letters of December 15, 1623 and January 28, 1624.[1]

Of the 630 slaves sent from Pulicat, 45 had died on the way while another few died soon after arrival at Batavia. The large scale mortality which substantially increased the cost of each surviving slave notwithstanding, Pulicat was to continue the procurement of slaves.

The samples of *balatius*[2] and *muris* received from Pulicat would be sent on to Holland for evaluation. Pulicat was to ensure that the orders of clothes for the southern quarters were met regularly. Particular care was to be taken in respect of the varieties destined for Java because Batavia did not have a sufficient stock of these varieties.

A surgeon was being sent to Pulicat together with a case of medicines.

* An exact copy is available in the *Bataviaasch Uitgaande Brievenboek*, V.O.C. 851, f.36vo.

1. The letter of 15 December 1623 is not available in the Company's archives. For the letter of 28 January 1624, see document no. 16.
2. The *balatiu* was an unbleached cotton cloth, white, black or blue, used for manufacturing sails in Java and elsewhere. The average size was 7 *vadems* (1 *vadem*=2½ cubits) and 5 *span* (1 span=2¼ centimeters).

25. Governor-General De Carpentier at Batavia to Van den Broecke at Surat, 26 March 1624. V.O.C. 1082, ff.214vo-17 (Copy).*

Van den Broecke had done well in sending the *Schoonhoven* directly to Batavia rather than via Aceh. In future, all ships were to be sent directly unless specifically asked to be sent either via Aceh or the west coast of Sumatra.

Surat ought to meet Batavia's orders for clothes properly. Surat had sent with the *Schoonhoven* 14,800 pieces of white and only 8,890 pieces of black *baftas*, whereas the two varieties had been asked for in the proportion of 1:2. Both Jambi and Batavia had large stocks of white *baftas* left. For 1626, therefore, Batavia would like to have more than the usual number of black *baftas* but only a few white *baftas*.

Batavia would be able to sell 40 to 50 packets of *patolas*[1] (or *chindi* Cambay) at 15 rials for 20 pieces. Half of the lot ought to be of 4 *asta*[2] length and the other half of 5 *asta* length. The latter could be sold at 20 rials per 20 pieces. In the case of *tapi sarassas* of 4 to 5 *asta* length, Batavia would be able to sell 10 to 15 packets. The earlier lot received from Surat was all of 4 *asta* length. The *sarassas Malay* were not in demand: hence at most one packet could be sent. 15 to 20 packets of chintz or *pintados*[3] could also be sold annually at Batavia at 25 rials per 20 pieces.

According to Batavia's calculations, the position regarding the availability of funds in Surat would be as follows:

Funds available in Surat as on 10 October 1623	f.312,387
Funds sent with the *Schoonhoven*, the *Weesp* and the *Vrede*	f.490,931
Funds sent with the *Heusden* with Huybert Vissnich	f.73,313
Funds sent to Mocha (9,060¼ rials and 116 gold ducats)	f.22,692
Goods sent with the *Weesp* and the *Heusden* (sale value)	f.170,000
Goods sent to Persia with the *Heusden* (sale value)	f.40,000
Total	f.1,109,323

As against this sum of f.1,109,323, Surat had sent to Batavia with the *Schoonhoven* cargo worth f.155,670 and to Holland with the *Heusden* worth f.90,000. Besides, Surat would have sent funds amounting to f.300,000 to Persia and would soon be sending the *Vrede* to Holland and the *Weesp* to Batavia with a total cargo worth f.200,000. Surat would thus be left with a capital worth f.363,653 to meet orders for the current year from Holland and Batavia. Surat was not to send more than the aforementioned sum to Persia till a more clear picture of the trade possibilities there was available.

The five horses that Surat had sent to Batavia were found to be rather expensive but nevertheless useful for gifts. Another two to four young horses might be sent. Batavia would like to know what kind of horses were available in Persia.

* An exact copy is available in the *Bataviaasch Uitgaande Brievenboek*, V.O.C. 851, ff.37-8vo.

1. *Patola*, Gujarati *patolu*. A well-known type of silk cloth, warp and the weft being tie-dyed before weaving according to the predetermined pattern. *Patolas* were exported mainly to Malay archipelago, the measurements varying according to the needs of different markets. The chief centre of *patola* weaving was Patan, north-east of Ahmedabad.
2. The *asta* was a synonym of the *covid*, a measure equivalent of 18 inches.
3. *Pintados* were painted calicoes where the dyes and mordants were applied to the cloth not with a wood-block but free hand with brush. Thus each painted design had the character of individual drawing with the human and sensuous touch, instead of being limited to the repeat pattern imposed by the print block. Such cotton paintings

were called either *pintados* (Portuguese pintado, 'painting') or *chinetes* (Hindi *chint*, later English chintz). Whereas the former was applied only to painted cottons, the latter term was used for both painted and printed.

26. Some points of consideration for Admiral Jacob Dedel and Van Uffelen and Council at Masulipatnam regarding a new accord with the king of Golconda, Batavia, 26 March 1624. V.O.C. 1082, ff.217-17vo (Copy).*

1. Restitution of the extorted 5,000 *pagodas*.
2. Compensation for the losses suffered as a result of the arrest of Van Uffelen.
3. Compensation for the disrespect shown to the Dutch nation following from the arrest of Van Uffelen.
4. Continuation of the toll arrangement whereby the Company paid 3,000 *pagodas* per annum.
5. The Company would not be obliged to pay any tolls on goods brought into the kingdom of Golconda at Masulipatnam. Lately, the *havaldar* of Masulipatnam had been asking for tolls on clothes brought in from Palicol and thereabouts.
6. The Company's goods would not be molested at the time of loading and unloading.
7. The *havaldar* would not farm out the exchange or any other business which might be detrimental to the Company's general trade.
8. Everyone would be free to buy from the Company and sell to it all goods that the Dutch were allowed to bring in and take out.
9. The Dutch would be free to transport their goods to any place they liked even if the ruling authorities of that place were enemies of the king of Golconda.
10. No one would be banned from fetching water to the Dutch ships or from selling provisions to them.

11. The Dutch would be allowed to attack and confiscate all Portuguese and Spanish ships even if they were in the king's ports. The king would not be entitled to any share in the booty.
12. The Dutch would be free to deal with the Portuguese and the Spanish the way they liked.
13. In case the Dutch factors at Pegu were still under arrest, the authorities in Coromandel would intercede with the king of Pegu for their release.
14. The Dutch would be allowed to send a representative to the Mughal emperor and deal with him directly through an interpreter.
15. All entities of the United Netherlands would be included in the term Dutch East India Company for purposes of tolls.
16. For the safety of the Company's effects, the Dutch would be allowed to build a stone house in Masulipatnam and be provided against payment with the necessary materials and workers for the purpose.

An exact copy is available in the *Bataviaasch Uitgaande Brievenboek*, V.O.C. 851, f.38vo.

27. A memorandum by Governor-General De Carpentier for Dedel, member of the Council of the Indies, on deputation to Coromandel as an inspector of the Company's trade and affairs there, 26 March 1624. V.O.C. 1082, ff.218-21 (Copy).*

Batavia was sorry to learn of the arrest of Van Uffelen on the orders of the *havaldar* of Masulipatnam, the maltreatment of the other Dutch factors and the whipping of the merchants dealing with the Company. Van Uffelen was released only after a sum of 5,000 *pagodas* had been extorted from him by the authorities. The Company's merchants were also forced to part with another large sum of money. One of the charges against Van Uffelen was that he had detained the person to whom the right to deal in bills of exchange had been farmed out till such time as the latter paid the amount he had owed the Company. Another accusation against Van Uffelen was that tobacco had been exported to Arakan in contravention of the king's orders. According to Van Uffelen, the real reason was the desire of the authorities to cancel the toll contract whereby the Company was obliged to pay annually a sum of only 3,000 *pagodas* by way of tolls. The *havaldar* of Masulipatnam wanted that the Company be also obliged to pay the usual 4 per cent toll on all imports and exports.

With a view to redress this situation, it had been decided to ask Dedel to go to Coromandel and review the state of affairs there with special reference to the matter of the treatment accorded to Van Uffelen and the extortion of a large sum of money from him. Dedel would consult the Masulipatnam Council and take necessary steps. These should include sending a special envoy to the king of Golconda with a letter of protest. It was to be made clear that in all probability His Majesty had no knowledge of the affair because it was unthinkable that a king like him would allow such treatment to be meted out to those who were under his shadow and protection and had been his allies for years, without at least informing the Company in advance. His Majesty was then to be requested to redress the injuries inflicted by the *havaldar* of Masulipatnam. In case the Company was not allowed to trade freely, it would be obliged to leave His Majesty's territories.

In the event the mission failed, permission was to be sought from the king to leave his territories with men and materials unmolested as well as the right to return later should the Company so decide. But before a decision to close the factory was taken, its implications for the procurement of the return cargo were to be considered seriously. If it was ultimately decided to close the factory, departing and incoming Muslim ships were to be attacked and seized but they were not to be damaged in any way. At this stage, a final chance was to be given to the authorities to redress our grievances. If still nothing happened, the seized ships were to be retained.

After his release, Van Uffelen was to leave Masulipatnam and go to Pulicat. If he was unable to discharge his duties because of sickness, etc., Dedel was to take over till further orders. The enclosed statement[1] would enable Dedel to see what varieties of clothes and in what quantities were needed for the Indies and Europe.

In case the trade at Bengal and Arakan showed a good potential, it was to be followed up without, however, affecting the trade on the Coromandel coast adversely. The reports available indicated that because of inland wars little profitable trade was possible at Bengal. The king of Arakan had promised to supply a large number of slaves and rice to the Company.

Having finished his work at Coromandel, Dedel would be free to go back to Holland either directly or via Batavia.

Upper-merchant Adriaen Goeree[2] was being sent to assist Dedel. He could also take the assistance of Under-merchant Barent Pietersz.[3] When the latter was no longer needed, he was to be sent back to Batavia.

* An exact copy is available in the *Bataviaasch Uitgaande Brievenboek*, V.O.C. 851, ff.39-40vo.

1. This statement is not available in the Company's archives.
2. Adriaen Willemsz. Goeree arrived at Bantam on 14 November 1616. Thereafter, he served in various capacities, including that of upper-merchant at Surat, Agra and the coast of Coromandel. He died at Masulipatnam on 30 May 1625.
3. Barent Pietersz. was in fact an upper-merchant and from 16 October 1624 onward, the second in command at the Dutch factory in Masulipatnam. He succeeded Van Rossen as the chief of the Masulipatnam factory on 14 May 1629. On 26 December 1632, he was recalled to Batavia under suspicion of engaging in private trade. From 1635 to August 1637, he functioned as the chief factor at Surat and thereafter until 12 April 1640 as the director of the Surat factory. On 9 September 1640, he returned to Batavia with the *Leeuwarden*. In 1641, he commanded the return fleet to Holland but died on the way.

28. Commission for Dedel given at Batavia, 26 March 1624. V.O.C. 1082, ff.221vo-22 (Copy).*

This is essentially a summary of document no. 27.

* An exact copy is available in the *Bataviaasch Uitgaande Brievenboek*, V.O.C. 851, f.41.

29. Ysbrantsz.'s instructions to Dirck van Haps,[1] captain of the frigates, the *Bonne Remedie* and the *Tenasserim*, going from Pulicat to Arakan, 28 April 1624. V.O.C. 1082, ff.64-5vo (Copy).

In several of his letters, the Governor-General had asked to procure as many slaves—both male and female—as possible and send them on to Batavia. Since a lot of slaves were available at Arakan, Dirck van Haps was being sent there with two frigates. He would first call at Masulipatnam and take further instructions from Jan Libenaar, the Dutch chief factor there. He would then go on to Arakan along the coast of Orissa and try to capture Portuguese vessels in the area.

In Arakan, Van Haps was to request an audience with the king and give him Ysbrantsz.'s letter[2] along with presents. The king was to be reminded of the promise he had made the previous year to allow the Dutch to buy slaves in his kingdom. Once such permission had been received, Van Haps was to buy as many slaves as he could. Persons between 12 and 30 years of age were the ones most useful to the Company and the procurement was to be confined to persons in this age group.

At Arakan, Van Haps was also to find out how many slaves could be bought there each year besides other profitable items of trade. Two or three factors were to be left at Arakan to continue the procurement of slaves. In the event he was not allowed to buy slaves or their number was far too small, Van Haps was not to bring any. On his return trip, he would look for Portuguese vessels but would not attack Hindu or Muslim ships unless there were Portuguese men or goods aboard. The captured vessels were to be brought to Pulicat or otherwise dealt with according to circumstances.

In case the king of Arakan asked for a frigate or sailors for use against an enemy, such a request was to be turned down. He could tell the king that in return for the permission to buy slaves, the Company would help him against the Portuguese or any other enemies of the Company.

Van Haps was to remain mostly on his ship and was to have minimum possible contacts with the Hindus and the Muslims at Arakan.

1. Dirck Dircksz. van Haps came to the East Indies in 1611. He was appointed assistant at Pulicat in 1616. In 1624, he served as a soldier both in Coromandel and Arakan. The following year he became a free burgher and engaged in trade in Tenasserim and Pegu. He died on 29 February 1632 while on a trip to Tenasserim.
2. This letter is not available in the Company's archives.

30. Ysbrantsz. at Pulicat to Governor-General De Carpentier at Batavia, 6 June 1624. V.O.C. 1083, ff.213-14vo (Copy).

44 packets of Guinea cloth had been procured at Tegenapatam and sent to Masulipatnam. If these were found to be of a good quality, a large quantity could be purchased. If the bleached *balatius* and fine *muris* were found useful for Holland, these could also be procured in large quantities at Pulicat. Because of the war at Pulicat,[1] the factors were afraid of giving out advances. Goods against quite a few of the contracts that had been given out for the current year had not yet come in. The *chindaes* received had been found to be of such a poor quality that they had to be rejected.

Over the last 5 to 6 months very few slaves could be bought. The governor, under whose jurisdiction Porto Novo and Trancquebar[2] fell, had promised to supply 100 slaves to the Company each month.

Of the three Danish ships currently at Trancquebar, the *Pearl* and the *Jupiter* had arrived last April from Denmark, while the third had arrived from Tenasserim. The ships from Denmark had started out in April 1623 with Roeland Crappe[3] as the commander-general. They are looking for clothes for Java.

The English were thinking of establishing a factory at Karikal[4] which is 2 miles north of Nagapattinam and 1½ miles south of Tranquebar.

1. The reference is evidently to the civil war that followed the death of King Venkat II of Karnataka.
2. Trancquebar is about 12 miles south of Nagapattinam.
3. Roeland Crappe was taken into the service of the Danish East India Company in 1617. In August 1618, he left for the East Indies as leader of a fleet. His ship, however, was captured by the Portuguese on the coast of Coromandel. But he managed to escape and even obtained farming rights over Trancquebar from the *nayak* of Tanjore. He remained at Trancquebar as the head of the factory there till his departure for Denmark in 1621 with a cargo consisting mainly of pepper. In 1623, he was made incharge of all the Danish establishments in the East. In 1624, he acquired the ownership of Trancquebar. He established trade with Makassar and visited Batavia repeatedly. But he did not get any material support from Denmark and was obliged to offer to sell the Tranquebar fort to the Dutch in 1629. He returned to Denmark on 30 November 1636.
4. Karikal is in Pondicherry. Its latitude is 10°.55′N and longitude 79°.52′E.

31. Governor-General De Carpentier at Batavia to Dedel and Van Uffelen at Masulipatnam, 25 June 1624. V.O.C. 1082, ff.272-5vo (Copy).*

Cargo worth f.19,373 consisting of 10,000 ponds cloves, 2,000 ponds nutmeg, 17 sacks of mace, some sandalwood, Japanese camphor, ivory, lead and copper was being sent with the *Schoonhoven*. Another sum of f.25,000 was being sent for the procurement of rice and ropes. More capital was not being sent partly because Masulipatnam was well provided and partly because the trade there was sober due to the local troubles.

Batavia was in desperate need of rice because none had been received from Mataram for a month. Also in view of the naval campaign that Mataram was currently engaged in, no vessels were expected from there for another two or three months. In the event Batavia did not receive supplies of rice soon, a situation of famine and misery might arise. The factors in Japan had also been instructed to send rice but the supplies from there were unlikely to arrive before December. Dedel was, therefore, asked to send 200 *lasts* of rice to Batavia immediately and to build-up a stock of another 200 to 300 *lasts*. Batavia would like to have 500 to 600 *lasts* of rice during the current year. In case enough rice was not available on the Coromandel coast, a ship was to be sent to Arakan to procure rice and slaves there. If enough rice was not available, beans were to be sent as a supplement.

The Directors had complained to Batavia that the length of cotton piece-goods received with the *Dordrecht* fell short by many *ells*[1] when compared with the size given in the invoice. They had also pointed out that, on an average, a bale of cotton yarn was no more than 132 ponds in weight whereas in the invoice the weight mentioned was 150 ponds. Masulipatnam was to be careful that such discrepancies did not occur in the future.

Batavia had received 40 packets of *goulongs*[2] without gold thread whereas the demand there was only for the variety with gold thread. So only pieces with gold thread were to be sent. Batavia had only 4 packets of *tapi sarassas* left in the stock and would like Masulipatnam to meet their orders for 80 packets in full. There were only 2 packets of *sarassa gobars*[3] in stock at Batavia, so the annual order for 8 packets of this variety was also to be met in full. The length of *sarassa gobars* was to be one *asta* longer than ordinary and the flower work was to be small as in the case of the *tapi sarassas*. The annual order for *rambutins*[4] was for 15 packets but Batavia had received only one packet. Since this variety had afforded a good profit, Masulipatnam ought to meet the orders in full. The latest lot received had cost f.411 per 20 pieces in Tegenapatam and was sold in Batavia at 400 rials per 20 pieces. Similarly a packet of *tapi sarassas* from Tegenapatam received with the *Wapen van Rotterdam* was of very fine cloth and beautiful flower-work. It had cost f.674 and was sold at 600 rials. Masulipatnam should supply 40 packets or more of this variety annually.

Since there were large stocks of *taffechelas* from Narsapur and Golconda, further supplies of this item were not to be sent during the current year. Masulipatnam was to meet only a part of the orders for *salalus*,[5] *samundra muris*,[6] *aritchodes*,[7] *patta Malay*,[8] *balatius* and *muris* because the sale of these varieties had been rather poor last year in the Moluccas and Amboina. Against the orders for 40 packets of *chavonis*,[9] Masulipatnam had sent only 2 packets. Mainly white pieces of this variety were sold in the Moluccas, so Masulipatnam was to send primarily the white pieces. Another lot of *bethilles*[10] ought to be sent soon because Batavia had run out of stocks.

The factors at Masulipatnam were advised to keep the price of pepper at a rather high level so as to ensure that the Danes and other Europeans were not able to buy cheap in Coromandel and compete with the Company in the sales in Europe. The Directors wanted this policy followed everywhere in Asia.

The free burghers were to be allowed free trade at Coromandel so long as it could be done without prejudice to the interests of the Company.

* An exact copy is available in the *Bataviaasch Uitgaande Brievenboek*, V.O.C. 851, ff.72vo-75.

1. An *ell* was equal to approximately 18 inches.

2. *Goulong* was a variety patterned in the loom and usually incorporated gold thread. It was intended chiefly for making into Malay *sarongs*.
3. *Sarassa gobar* was a gaily-coloured silk cloth patterned with flowers and birds.
4. *Rambutin* was a white cotton cloth. The average length was 20 cubits.
5. *Salalu* was a dyed cotton cloth, usually striped, but varying in style according to the particular market for which it was intended. They were usually either blue and black or plain black.
6. Evidently a variety of *muris*.
7. Not identified.
8. The *patta* was a cheap dyed cotton cloth, usually striped but varying in style according to the particular local market for which it was intended. For instance, there was *patta chera-Malaya* (*patta* in Malay-style), *patta* Makassar (*patta* in Makassar-style), etc.
9. *Chavoni* was a very light white cotton cloth embroidered with coloured silk.
10. *Bethille* was the Deccanese term for muslin. Coromandel exports came mostly from Golconda, especially the neighbourhood of Warangal. The length varied from 15 to 25 yards while the usual width was 1½ yards. They were sometimes dyed red and were sometimes striped or flowered with embroidery, much in demand in Europe as neck-clothes. The fine grades were sometimes reinforced with thin wire thread.

32. Governor-General De Carpentier at Batavia to Ysbrantsz. at Pulicat, 25 June 1624. V.O.C. 1082, f.276 (Copy).*

Ysbrantsz. was to open the letter addressed to Van Uffelen[1] and do the needful.

* An exact copy is available in the *Bataviaasch Uitgaande Brievenboek*, V.O.C. 851, f.75.

1. See document number 31.

33. Batavia's instructions for the *Schoonhoven* going to Coromandel, 25 June 1624. V.O.C. 1082, f.278 (Copy).*

The *Schoonhoven* was to first call at Pulicat and then proceed to Masulipatnam. At Pulicat, Marten Ysbrantsz. was to be allowed to take out some goods and cash from the ship if he so wished.

* An exact copy is available in the *Bataviaasch Uitgaande Brievenboek*, V.O.C. 851, f.77.

34. Batavia's instructions for free burghers going to Coromandel with the Company's permission whether in the Company's ships or on their own, 25 June 1624. V.O.C. 1082, ff.276-7 (Copy).*

1. In case the Company's ships were used for the transportation of their persons, cash and goods, they would be obliged to pay reasonable freight charges at the point of disembarkation. They would also be obliged to store their goods—those carried from Batavia as well as those procured in Coromandel—at the Company's warehouses.
2. In case these people decided to engage in trade at a place where the Company had a factory, they would be obliged to declare to the director or the head of the factory the varieties of clothes and other goods they planned to invest their funds in.
3. In case they planned to buy varieties of textiles which the Company dealt in, they would be obliged to take the permission of the head of the factory before doing so.
4. In case the head of the factory believed that a direct participation in trade by these people would be prejudicial to the interests of the Company, he would collect funds from them and invest them on their behalf.

5. These people would be permitted by the director or the chief of the factory to buy on their own goods that the Company might not be dealing in.
6. The free burghers will not be allowed to engage in private trade from the coast of Coromandel except with the permission of the director. This is designed to prevent inconvenience and loss to the Company.
7. At all places in the Bay of Bengal, Pegu and Arakan where the Company did not have a factory, it would not be necessary for these people to obtain permission of the Company's factors before engaging in trade. If at any of these places the Company's ships came to trade or establish a factory, the same conditions would be applicable to them as to the other merchants from the coast.
8. Against goods, slaves and other things carried toll-free in the name of the Company, these persons would be obliged to pay the Company a certain amount.
9. In order to reimburse the extraordinary expenses at Pulicat, the director and the Council of the Coromandel coast might impose a reasonable tax on all cash, goods and slaves which these people carried to Pulicat, Tegenapatam and similar places as well as those that they exported from there.
10. They would also be obliged to permit the inspection of their goods by the director or his nominee.

* An exact copy is available in the *Bataviaasch Uitgaande Brievenboek*, V.O.C. 851, ff.75vo-76.

35. Dedel at Masulipatnam to Governor-General De Carpentier at Batavia, 2 July 1624. V.O.C. 1083, ff.215-18 (Copy).

The *Wapen van Enkhuizen* was being sent to Batavia with a cargo worth f.243,919.245 male and female slaves were being sent. The lot was initially larger but 53 of them had died in the meantime. Dedel hoped to send a substantial number of slaves with the next shipment. A letter from Mir Kamal-al-Din addressed to the Governor-General was also being sent.[1]

The big steel pieces that Batavia had asked for were not available in Masulipatnam. A sample of the largest size available was being sent. The English had bought some of these at 32 *pagodas* per 1,000 pieces. Opium was available at Masulipatnam at 15 *pagodas* per *maund*. Dedel believed that it would be cheaper to buy opium at Surat where it was available in a large quantity. Sugar was available in abundance at Balasore and Pipli[2] in Bengal at 5-6 rials per *fardeel*[3] and Dedel could send two shiploads every year.

In future, Masulipatnam would send only refined saltpetre to Batavia. The Danes had not been able to procure any saltpetre. Once the Danes were pushed out of the market, Dedel hoped to be able to have the price reduced. Masulipatnam would not be able to send any gunpowder because sulphur was not available there. Dedel would ask Aceh to supply some, if possible

Camphor was used by both Hindus and Muslims to massage the dead body. A lot of it was imported from Siam via Tenasserim and was sold at 35 *pagodas* per . . .[4] Masulipatnam hoped to sell annually 100,000 to 150,000 ponds of Japanese copper at 45-50 *pagodas* per *bahar*.

In future, Masulipatnam would not have Bengal *taffechelas*, Narsapur sail cloth or the Siamese clothes manufactured locally. The present stocks would, of course, be sent on to Batavia. Masulipatnam had entered into contracts at Draksharama for 6,000 pieces of *dungarees* for the slaves. An attempt would be made to have the quality of the Guinea cloth produced at Tegenapatam improved. If the price could be reduced somewhat, this variety would do better than the one produced at Masulipatnam.

Unminted silver and gold could be sold more profitably at Pulicat than at Masulipatnam where rials of eight did better than gold. There was no demand for lead at Masulipatnam. The English had an unsold stock of 30,000 ponds of lead in their warehouses.

Dedel had received a request from the *faujdar* of Pipli and

Balasore for the release of the *laskars*[5] captured by the *Wapen van Rotterdam* from a Portuguese ship from Cochin and taken to Batavia. In the interest of maintaining the goodwill of this man, it was important to accede to the request.

According to Dedel's estimate, Pulicat was well provided with cash. After deducting the f.36,000 worth of bad debts and the cost of maintaining the fort, etc., Pulicat would still have f.154,000 available for investment. For meeting the orders for 1623 and 1624 for 500 *bahars* of saltpetre and 500 slaves, they would need around f.191,000. Pulicat would thus require only a little additional capital.

The English ship *Unity* had arrived from Batavia on 6 June. The *Heart* which had accompanied the *Unity* had gone to Karikal where the English were planning to establish a factory. They had already taken samples of *goulongs*, *tapi sarassas*, *chindaes*, *tapi grande*, *rambutins*, *balatius* and many other varieties there to see if they could have them manufactured locally. The Danes were trying to prevent this by giving gifts, etc., to the officials. The reaction of the Portuguese and others was not yet clear.

Six frigates, presumably with the new captain of Sao Tome aboard, had arrived at Nagapattinam. Two Portuguese and two black deserters from Sao Tome were being sent to Batavia because Dedel did not want to keep them at Pulicat.

Eti-Raja, the lord of Pulicat who had had the king of Karnataka murdered had long been at war with his son and successor. He had now concluded a treaty with the young king and had agreed to recognise him and pay tribute.[6]

Dedel had received via Aceh a letter addressed to Herman Prins from the factors in detention at Pegu.

It was learnt that Prince Khurram had conquered the whole of Bengal and had captured a large treasure.

1. This letter is not available in the Company's archives.
2. Balasore and Pipli were major ports in Orissa.
3. The *fardeel* was usually a bale of about 80 ponds. But in the text it is stated to be equivalent of 7 Masulipatnam *maunds* which makes it equivalent of 168 ponds.
4. The unit is not specified.

5. The term *laskar* was generally used for a sailor, though it could also refer to a soldier.
6. These troubles continued until 1629. For details, see T. Raychaudhuri, *Jan Company in Coromandel, 1605-1690*, The Hague, 1962, pp. 23, 35-7.

36. Resolutions adopted by the Councils at Pulicat and Masulipatnam on 5 July 1624, 23 September 1624 and 26 September 1624. V.O.C. 1085, ff.222-7vo (Copy).

[Since matters discussed in these resolutions have also been discussed at length in the letters from Coromandel, these resolutions have not been summarized here.]

37. Governor-General De Carpentier at Batavia to Van den Broecke at Surat, 9 August 1624. V.O.C. 1082, ff.294vo-303 (Copy).*

The yacht *Weesp* had arrived safely from Surat on 5 July. Far too many white *baftas* had been sent and they were selling poorly. Only one-sixth of the lot ought to be in white, the remainder in colours such as brown and blue. The orders list from Surat had been updated on the basis of information received from different factories.

Cargo worth f.204,657 consisting of 24,000 rials of eight in cash, 20,000 rials worth of Japanese silver, 4,000 bags of pepper, 37,472 ponds of cloves, 60,043 ponds of nutmeg, 40 sacks of mace, 100 *piculs* of copper and 3,827 ounces of blood-coral was being sent with the *Noord Bantam*, the *Zuid Holland* and the yacht *Weesp*. According to Batavia's calculations, the position regarding the availablilty of funds at Surat would be as under:

Liquid funds		f.363,653
Capital received from Holland with the *Dordrecht*		f.297,885
Cargo worth f.204,657 being sent from Batavia which should fetch		f.400,000
	Total	f.1,061,538

Of this sum, f.300,000 would be needed for meeting the orders from Holland for indigo, saltpetre, textiles and cotton while another f.220,000 would need to be invested in the textiles for Batavia. Cash and goods such as textiles and spices to be sent to Persia would take up another f.350,000 which would be in addition to the f.350,000 worth of capital already available there. The total investment of f.870,000 would, however, still leave f.180,000[1] with Surat with which procurement ought to be started for 1626.

Persia was a profitable market for pepper and other spices. Pepper was being sent specially for Persia because Vissnich had written that it afforded a higher profit in Persia than even in Europe. Surat was to regulate the supply of pepper to Persia on the basis of expected profitability there with surplus stocks, if any, to be diverted to Holland. Cloves similarly rendered a higher profit in Persia than in Holland and as large a lot was to be sent there as could be sold at a good profit. Nutmeg was sold in Persia at one *daaldar* per pond while in Surat it fetched no more than ten stuivers per pond. Gujarat clothes and other goods were also to be sent to Persia to facilitate the procurement of silk for Holland. Surat ought to meet Vissnich's orders of Surat clothes to the maximum extent possible besides sending some gunnies[2] and cotton to facilitate proper packing of the silk. Also the cash received from Batavia was to be diverted mainly to Persia while Surat itself was to try to buy clothes, etc., for the Indies mainly against spices received from Batavia. Surplus space was to be utilized for freighting goods and persons between Surat and Persia as long as that could be done without prejudice to the Company's own trade.

Since slaves could be bought more cheaply on the Coromandel coast and other places, Surat was not to purchase any.

The sample of saltpetre received from Surat with the *Sampson* was found to be of a much better quality than what was available on the Coromandel coast at a comparable price. Surat was, therefore, to buy 300,000 to 400,000 ponds provided arrangements for its transportation could be made. Surat was to send refined saltpetre to Holland if the difference in cost from that of the unrefined variety was no more than 30 per cent.

According to the information from Surat, the Malabar pepper was bought by the English at Burhanpur at 3 rials per Bantam sack. This lot would seem to be for Persia. The Company had to pay 4 rials per sack on the west coast of Sumatra and more than 5 rials per sack at Aceh and Patani. Both the English and the Dutch had to blame themselves for such high prices. No pepper was to be bought at Surat for Europe unless it was available at 1½ to 2 or at the most 2½ rials per . . .[3] inclusive of all costs. English procurement of pepper for Europe was to be hindered because that was likely to glut the European market. The Directors did not want any cloves or pepper from the Indies. In the case of the latter, they had entered into a contract with the buyers to the effect that there would be a moratorium on sale by the Company between 1 November 1623 and 1 November 1625. As for cloves, they had enough stocks for three years. Till such time as the China trade could be opened, the bulk of the return cargo for Holland will have to come from Coromandel, Surat and Persia.

Since the supply of provisions from Mataram had been extremely poor, Batavia was facing a great shortage of rice and supplies had been asked for from Japara, Coromandel and Siam. Surat must also send as much rice and wheat as possible.

Big ships such as the *Noord Bantam*, *Zuid Holland* and *Weesp* were being sent to Surat to guard against Portuguese attacks as also to inflict maximum possible damage on them in the Persian Gulf. This would enhance the stature of the Company in both Persia and Surat. Surat was to send these ships on to Persia at the earliest opportunity with instructions to return to Surat soon. In order to avoid a dispute with the English regarding the tolls at Hormuz, it would be best that the cargo was unloaded at other ports such as Gombroon.

It was important to reduce costs in all directions—buildings, ships, slaves and so on. In Holland, the Company was under debt to the extent of f.8 million. The Directors were trying to pay off f.4.5 million. That was the reason why Batavia had received no funds from Holland this year.

On the question of representation at the Mughal Court, it would be better to send an occasional envoy to be called a factor or solicitor rather than maintain a permanent ambassador there. If the Mughals were interested in painting, Hendrik Arentsz. Vapour,[4] himself a good painter and who was being sent to Surat, could represent the Company.[5]

Since Mocha was under the protection of the great lord of Constantinople where a number of Dutch merchants carried on a large amount of trade, it would be inadvisable to use violence there.

On 18 July 1620, the Batavia Council had declared the merchants of Dabhol as the enemies of the Company with a view to keep them out of the trade of the west coast.[6] It had now been decided to try and reach a settlement with them to trade with all ports not controlled by the Portuguese. They would, however, not be allowed to carry any Portuguese goods or persons. In return, they would be obliged to secure the release of the Dutch factors and goods at Mocha from the *badshah*[7] of Yemen and obtain for the Company permission to trade there freely. If this was not possible, they would secure compensation for the Company for the losses suffered. If Van den Broecke was unable to negotiate such an accord, an emissary was to be sent to the *badshah* of Yemen asking for the return of the Company's factors and goods and to seek permission to trade at Mocha freely. If no agreement could be reached with the *badshah*, the *Weesp* was to attack all incoming and outgoing shipping from the Red Sea except that from Surat and other Mughal Indian ports. Under threat of attack, the ships from Dabhol were not to be allowed to go to Mocha till a settlement had been reached with the *badshah* of Yemen. The vessels from Chaul, Diu, Daman and other Portuguese ports were to be attacked with impunity.

Batavia was surprised that the dispatch of the Company's ships to Europe had been delayed by months in order that an English ship might sail with them.[8] Surat ought to realize that the Company which put its goods on the European market first made the most profit.

* An exact copy is available in the *Bataviaasch Uitgaande Brievenboek*, V.O.C. 851, ff.89vo-95.
1. This amount should in fact be f.191,538.
2. Gunnies were strong coarse calico for sacking and as covering for bales.
3. The unit is not specified.
4. Hendrik Arentsz. Vapour served at Surat in different capacities from 1615 to 1622. In March 1623, he was upper-merchant and a member of the Council at Batavia. In July 1624, he was sent to Surat and from there to Agra, where he was the chief of the factory in 1626. After Van Hazel's death in 1632, he was temporary director at Surat, where he died on 26 October 1632.
5. Vapour was in fact sent as envoy to the Mughal emperor on 30 March 1625.
6. For details, see Om Prakash (ed.), *The Dutch Factories in India 1617-1623*, document no. 134, pp.170-1, document no. 148, pp.183-4, document no. 168, p.204.
7. The English equivalent of the *badshah* is king.
8. See document no.1.

38. Annual orders of textiles from Surat for the southern quarters[1] together with their estimated cost price, 9 August 1624. V.O.C. 1082, ff.305-6 (Copy).*

S. No.	*Item*	*Quantity*	*Price (in mahmudis per 20 pieces unless specified otherwise)*	*Estimated cost (in florins)*	*Remarks regarding orders for 1625*
1.	Coarse *baftas*	30,000 pieces (20,000 black and 10,000 white)	45 to 90	47,000	2/3rds between 45 to 65 *mahmudis* and the remainder between

					70 to 90 *mahmudis* per 20 pieces. No white pieces.
2.	Fine *baftas*	12,000 pieces (8,000 black, 4,000 white)	100 to 180	42,000	2,000 white pieces
3.	Fine broad *baftas*	2,000 pieces (1,000 black, 840 white, 160 light blue)	140 to 200	8,500	–
4.	Broad *baftas*	2,000 pieces (1,200 black, 640 white, 160 light blue)	90 to 120	5,250	200 white pieces
5.	Broach *baftas* with gold and silk threads	200 pieces (100 black, 100 white)	Black 20 per piece, white 40-50 per piece	3,250	200 black pieces and 150 white pieces
6.	*Cangans*[2]	10,000 pieces (6,000 white, 3,800 black, 200 light blue)	The price is higher than in China and if possible, should be reduced. Should not cost more than f.1 per piece	15,000	5,000 white pieces and 5,000 black pieces. The black ones are doing better than those from China.
7.	*Cheri baftas*	100 pieces	–	900	200 pieces (50 white, 50 bright red, 50 bright black, 50 violet and green for

				the Moluccas)
8. *Berams*[3]	12,000 pieces (9,000 black, 3,000 white)	35 to 60 (2/3 rds 35, to 45 1/3rd 50 to 60)	13,500	–
9. Black *chelas*[4]	18,000 pieces (6,000 fine assorted)	–	9,000	–
10. *Caricams* or red *chelas*	30,000 pieces (20,000 from Ahmedabad, 10,000 fine assorted)	–	18,000	12,000 to 15,000 pieces
11. *Canni-kens*[5]	30,000 pieces (2,000 white)	16 to 24	15,000	The sample received from Dedel was of good quality
12. *Asmanis*[6]	6,000 pieces	–	2,250	–
13. *Tircan-dias*[7]	3,000 pieces	–	1,200	–
14. Sail cloth (Dholka)	60,000 *gaz* or *ells*	–	6,000	–
15. *Dhotis*[8]	20,000 *gaz* or *ells* 10,000 *gaz* bleached 10,000 *gaz* Dhotia Dholka	–	1,000	–
16. Negro cloth[9]	16,000 pieces (6000-8,000 from Broach)	–	8,000	–
17. *Dunga-rees*	4,000 pieces	–	2,000	–
18. Silk *patolas*	500 pieces	–	7,500 (items 18–19)	For Java, Moluccas, Amboina and Banda 800 pieces for Aceh, the west
19. Silk *chindaes*	500 pieces red ground with white borders			

				coast of Sumatra and Jambi
20. *Taffechelas platchiado*	500 pieces (300 with blue and white stripes, 200 with other stripes)	–	2,500	None to be sent until further orders
21. Yarn *taffechelas*	1,000 pieces	–	2,250	500 pieces
22. Round woven *taffechelas*	1,000 pieces	–	1,700	400 pieces
23. Blankets	500 pieces	–	750	
24. *Madafons*,[10] or *alachas*[11]	1,000 pieces	–	2,000	1,350-1,700 pieces
New Orders				
25. *Patchery*[12]	6,000 pieces	–	3,900	
26. *Tapi sarassas*	2,000 pieces	–	1,200	
27. *Chintz* or *pintados*	3,000 pieces	–	4,800	From Burhanpur and Ahmedabad
28. Guinea cloth[13]	100 packets	–	2,000	–
29. Flag cloth	2 packets	–	1,000	–
30 Samples of different varieties[14]	2-3 packets	–	600	From Patan
31. *Camelots*[15]	8-10 pieces	–	–	To be used for gifts
		Total	f.246,050	

* An exact copy is available in the *Bataviaasch Uitgaande Brievenboek*, V.O.C. 851, ff.96vo-97vo.

1. The term "southern quarters" was used for the Indonesian archipelago.
2. *Cangan* was a multi-coloured cotton shawl produced mainly on the Coromandel coast.
3. In the sixteenth century and earlier, the *beram* was famous as a superior white calico, which the Portuguese sometimes called *bairam de Roma* on the assumption that they were similar to the fine cloth brought to Europe by the ancient Romans. In the seventeenth-century records, however, *beram* is often a coarse and inferior calico, usually dyed red, blue or black for Asian markets. This was produced mainly in the Burhanpur area.
4. *Chela* was white or yellow cotton cloth with black stripes. It could also be chekered. It was exported mainly to the Malay archipelago.
5. *Canniken* was cheap coarse calico, dyed black or blue. The basic material was probably identical to that in *baftas*. It was woven chiefly at Broach and Navsari and sold in all the main Asian markets.
6. Not identified.
7. This particular variety might perhaps be traced to the Sanskrit and Marathi *trikanda*, meaning 'three sections'. It was made from *dhotis*.
8. *Dhoti* was a strong coarse calico usually sold in lengths of 12 to 15 yards × 1 yard and woven at Dholka. These were used mainly for sails and as packing material.
9. Negro cloth was a generic name for the calico exported to West Africa and Brazil for use by African slaves. It was also referred to as Guinea-cloth.
10. *Madafon* was a striped cloth woven chiefly in Golconda and exported to the Malay archipelago.
11. *Alacha* was an important Gujarat cloth of mixed cotton and silk, usually striped red and white or blue and white, sometimes flowered or embellished with gold and silver thread.
12. Not identified.
13. Guinea cloth was the generic term for a wide range of cheap, brightly coloured Indian calicoes, mostly striped or chequered, which were bought mainly for consumption by African slaves.
14. The varieties are not specified.
15. *Camelot* was a fine cloth woven originally of silk and camel's hair which came from Turkey.

39. Instructions to the Council of the ships the *Vrede* and the *Medemblik* going from Masulipatnam to Arakan, 25 August 1624. V.O.C. 1082, ff.66-6vo (Copy).

These two ships were being sent to Arakan specially for the procurement of rice. In case enough good quality rice was not available, the deficiency was to be made up by the poor variety. In the event of rice not being available in Arakan, it was to be bought in Bengal where a large amount was produced in Pipli and Satgaon[1] and where it was cheaper than in Arakan.

In case slaves had to be procured in Arakan mainly from the king and the numbers available with the private parties was small, there was no need to have a factory there. A suitable factor with two assistants should, however, be left there in case the slaves had to be bought from many sources. Masulipatnam would like to know the approximate number of slaves that could be bought at Arakan annually. Three cases of Japanese unminted silver worth 6,000 rials of eight were being provided to facilitate the procurement of slaves.[2]

1. Satgaon was a port of much trade on the right bank of river Hugli, 30 miles from Calcutta.
2. In the document the term used erroneously is spices.

40. Ysbrantsz. from the *Schoonhoven* at Masulipatnam to Governor-General De Carpentier at Batavia, 2 October 1624. V.O.C. 1082, ff.58-62 (Copy).

Following the death of Jacob Dedel on 29 August at Masulipatnam, Adrian Marten Ysbrantsz. had been called from Pulicat by Adriaen Willemsz. Goeree and Jan Libenaar. He would soon return to Pulicat after leaving the affairs at Masulipatnam in the hands of Goeree and Libenaar. The *Schoonhoven* had come to Pulicat from Batavia on 1 August 1624 and the *Leeuwin* from Holland on 4 August. The latter had brought a cargo worth f.315,908. The *Vrede* which had left Surat for Holland on 12 March 1624,[1] had been damaged by a heavy storm at Madagascar and obliged to come to Pulicat on 12 July 1624. Its cargo had been transferred to the *Schoonhoven* which would be sent to Holland soon. The cargo for the *Leeuwin* was being procured.

The *Vrede* and the *Medemblik* had been sent from Masulipatnam to Arakan on 26 August to bring rice and slaves.[2] Two frigates had been sent there earlier. Hopefully, Batavia should get enough rice. Masulipatnam had already procured 200 *lasts* of rice and if all of it was not needed for Batavia, the surplus amount would be sold at Pulicat at a profit.

It seemed that the sum of *pagodas* 16,000—5,000 from the Company and 11,000 from its merchants—extorted by the king of Golconda could be recovered only if a decision was taken to abandon the factory at Masulipatnam. The business done by the Company at this port could conveniently be carried on at Pulicat and at other ports on the coast.

Goods such as camphor, ivory and sandalwood were lying unsold. Pulicat expected to be able to provide enough gunpowder for the whole of the Indies and it would cost at the most 3½ to 4 *stuivers* per pond. Dedel had earlier informed Batavia of the troubles the Dutch had been facing at Pulicat at the hands of the Hindus. The city had been plundered. The Company, however, had managed to foil their attempts to build a fort on the other side of the river which would not have been too far from the Dutch fort. Eti Raja had since left Pulicat for Tanjore with the young king.[3]

The problems created by the war notwithstanding, Ysbrantsz. hoped to meet all the orders from Pulicat except for *tapi sarassas*. In spite of the factors' best efforts over the preceding three years, it had not been possible to have them produced at Pulicat. The supplies from Puleceri[4] and Tegenapatam were unlikely to exceed about 60 *corgies*. One needed master painters for producing this variety.

The *Heart*, an English ship, was at Karikal between the beginning of June and the middle of August investigating opportunities for trade. Joseph Cockram[5] had gone to the *nayak* of Tanjore but the Danes had spent a lot of money on gifts to the *nayak* to keep the English out of that area. The English hoped to be able to return next year.

1. See document number 19.
2. See document number 39.
3. The young king of Karnataka was Ramadeva, son of King Sriranga II.
4. Puleceri, the modern Pondicherry.
5. Joseph Cockram had come to the East in 1620 with the *Bull* which had brought news of the peace accord between the English and the Dutch in Europe. He had later served on the fleet of defence and had also gone to Japan where he was a party to the closure of the English factory at Firando in mid-1623. Thereafter, he had been active at Tanjore and Batavia. He returned home on 6 February 1626 and died a few days later.

41. Adriaen Willemsz. Goeree and Libenaar at Masulipatnam to the Directors at Amsterdam, 4 October 1624. V.O.C. 1082, ff.50-3 (Original).

In the matter of the arrest of late Van Uffelen, a sum of 11,000 *pagodas* had been extorted from the Company. Jacob Dedel was sent from Batavia to Masulipatnam on 27 March 1624 to sort the matter out. On his arrival here in May, he learnt of the death of Van Uffelen in January 1624 and assumed charge. But Jacob Dedel himself died on 29 August 1624.

Masulipatnam had absolutely no funds and had taken a loan of 5,000 *pagodas* on interest. Besides, the annual tolls amounting to 3,000 *pagodas* were still to be paid. There were also many outstanding debts which, however, the factors hoped to recover. Trade at Masulipatnam had suffered a lot due to the shameful behaviour of the *havaldar* who had been instrumental in alienating the Company's merchants from it by instilling fear in them.

In the event the trade at Masulipatnam was suspended for a period of two to three years, the Company could capture Muslim vessels due to leave for Aceh, Pegu, Arakan and Tenasserim from this month onward and make good the sum extorted from it. On the first of October, six Muslim ships had already left Masulipatnam for Arakan in addition to two for Aceh, four for Pegu and one for Tenasserim. Another two were expected to leave soon for Mocha. All these would come back with rich cargoes. The Governor-General, however, had asked them to carry on the trade under the tyranny of the Muslims as best as they could.

The *Vrede* which had been sent from Surat to Holland on 12 March 1624 with a cargo of f.128,076 had to return to Masulipatnam on 19 July because of contrary winds. Its cargo had been transferred to the *Schoonhoven* which had arrived at Masulipatnam on 9 August 1624 with a cargo worth f.44,372.

Spices such as cloves, nutmeg and mace received with the *Schoonhoven* had afforded a good profit, particularly nutmeg and mace. The cloves could fetch only 11 *pagodas* per. . . .[1] but good quality nutmeg was sold at 95 *pagodas* per *bahar* of 480 ponds, while the poor variety fetched 70 *pagodas* per *bahar*. Mace was sold at 16 *pagodas* per *maund*. All the quicksilver and vermilion had been sold at 16 *pagodas* per *maund*. The profit on these was not large but nevertheless more than had been earned on gold and silver. Gold received with the *Leeuwin* was sold at Pulicat at a profit of 5 per cent while it rendered a loss at Masulipatnam. One *tola* (3/8 ounce) of gold did not fetch more than f.266, 6 *stuivers*, 10 pennings while as per the invoice value it cost the Company f.281. Loss on silver and rials was even greater. At Masulipatnam, a rial could fetch not more than 8 *fanums*[2] while at Pulicat it had never fetched less than 9 *fanums*.

Spelter was sold at 50 *pagodas* per *bahar*. There was little demand for ivory at Masulipatnam. The market for this item was better at Surat. Cochineal[3] was also not in demand. It was sold to a Persian merchant at 90 *pagodas* per *maund* involving a loss of about 45 guilders on the transaction. It would be better to send it to Persia. All four bundles of broad cloth were sold as follows: red at 3 *pagodas* per *gaz* and the other colours at 2 *pagodas* per *gaz*. On this item, a profit at 2,000 guilders had been made.

1. The unit of weight is not specified, but it is likely to have been *maund*.
2. The *fanum* was a subsidiary coin of the gold *pagoda*. The 5-grain *fanum*, heavily alloyed, was one of the smallest gold coins known, and was in general use for ordinary commercial transactions. In the early part of the seventeenth century, the *pagoda* was equal to 15 *fanums* at Masulipatnam.
3. Cochineal was a red dye made from the dried bodies of female cochineal insects.

42. Ysbrantsz. at Pulicat to the Directors at Amsterdam, 12 October 1624. V.O.C. 1082, ff.54-7 (Original).

The Directors would be aware how Van Uffelen was arrested and maltreated by the Muslim authorities at Masulipatnam. An amount of 5,000 *pagodas* was forcibly extorted from him and another 11,000 *pagodas* from the Company's merchants who had been advanced this money for the supply of textiles. A few days later Van Uffelen died partly as a result of the above-mentioned events.[1]

The damage done by the *havaldar* of Masulipatnam to the Company was enormous. In addition to the extortion of the above-mentioned 16,000 *pagodas* (equivalent to f.68,000), it had not been possible to send ships to Holland over the last 1½ years. The *Wapen van Enkhuizen*, *the Rotterdam* and the *Medemblik* had remained in Coromandel for months but could not be equipped for Holland resulting in a considerable loss.

Since the departure of the *Schiedam*, the following ships had left Coromandel for Batavia: in October 1623, the *Tholen* with a cargo worth f.231,384, in January 1624, the *Wapen van Rotterdam* with a cargo worth f.126,606 and on 2 July 1624, the *Wapen van Enkhuizen* with a cargo worth f.243,918. The *Schoonhoven* was being sent to Holland with a cargo worth f.199,099 as follows: cargo transhipped from the *Vrede*: f.128,076, cargo loaded in Masulipatnam worth f.67,788 and that loaded at Pulicat worth f.3,235. Pulicat hoped to send the *Wapen van Rotterdam* to Batavia in December with a good cargo.

In May 1624, the English, in an attempt to establish a factory at Karikal (about one mile south of Tranquebar where the Danes have a fort) got in touch with the *nayak* of Tanjore. They were also interested in building a fort there. The Danes had given many gifts to the *nayak* including two metal canons so as to prevent the English from settling there. The English could not reach an accord with the *nayak* and so went to Puleceri where their plans were foiled by the Dutch. It seemed that they would next try at Armagon. The English found it hard to share the cost of maintaining the fort at Pulicat.[2] All hindrances would be put in their way in procuring textiles that the Company needs for the southern quarters. Ysbrantsz. believed that the English would be given so much trouble by the Hindu authorities that they would regret leaving Pulicat.

The Danes carried on very little trade at Tranquebar. They had reportedly bought 1,500 *bahars* (each of 300 ponds) of pepper. Most of the time they were sitting idle. They were also having problems with the *nayak* of Tanjore. They had sent a ship to Tenasserim. They were keeping great friendship with the Portuguese and were transporting their goods. They were also trying their best to procure saltpetre but Ysbrantsz. would try his best to keep this item exclusively for the Dutch.

The diamond mine was likely to be reopened soon. Pulicat would be able to meet the Directors' orders for diamonds as soon as the mine reopened.

There had been no king at Pulicat for long. Each raja regarded himself as the king. Eti Raja had given a great deal of trouble to the Company and it had been with great difficulty that the factors had managed to keep his forces out of Pulicat. He had since left for Tanjore and things were quiet.

1. Van Uffelen died in January 1624. See document no. 41.
2. For details of the Anglo-Dutch agreement on the sharing of the cost of maintenance of the Fort Geldria at Pulicat, see Om Prakash (ed.), *The Dutch Factories in India, 1617-1623*, pp. 156-7.

43. An extract from the invoice of the *Schoonhoven* that left Pulicat for Holland on 12 October 1624 with goods from Surat, Masulipatnam and Pulicat. V.O.C. 1082, ff.68-88 (Copy).*

(A) *Goods from Surat*

S.No.	*Item*	*Quantity*	*Value (in florins)*
1.	Guinea-cloth	520 pieces (13 packets)	2,642:1:4
2.	Coarse white broad *baftas*	300 pieces (2 packets)	984:7:0
3.	Fine *baftas*	48 pieces	902:4:0
4.	*Alcatifs*[1] (as a sample)	5 pieces (1 packet)	
5.	*Minatashis*	1,400 pieces (95 packets)	1,202:15:0
6.	Black broad *baftas*	320 pieces (1 packet)	1,190:14:0
7.	*Samonas*[2] (as a sample)	200 pieces (1 packet)	480:0:0
8.	Bengai *khasas* (as a sample)	120 pieces (1 packet)	720:0:0
9.	Red lak (as a sample)	125 ponds (1 case)	72:3:8
10.	White incense	1 case	40:0:0
11.	Indigo Sarkhej	135,277¼ ponds (779 packets)	55,107:16:0
12.	Indigo Bayana	78,550½ ponds (374 packets)	56,219:8:8
13.	Sal ammoniac	2,400 ponds (10 packets)	408:6:0
14.	Spiconardy[3]	2,400 ponds (8 packets)	208:10:0
15.	Borax	2,500 ponds (12 packets)	631:7:0
16.	Refined saltpetre	15,774 ponds (59 cases)	1,312:8:8
17.	Diamonds	105 pieces weighting 155-7/8 carats	?[4]
18.	Bezoar stones	21 pieces weighing 12 ounces	?[4]
		Total	122,122:0:12
		Costs	5,954:6:0[5]
		Total	128,076:6:12

(B)	*Goods from Masulipatnam*	67,787:13:6[6]
(C)	*Goods from Pulicat*	3,234:15:5[7]
	Grand Total	199,098:15:7

* The goods from Surat had originally been put aboard the *Vrede* which on its way to Holland had run into contrary winds near Madagascar and was obliged to return to Masulipatnam. Its cargo was then transferred to the *Schoonhoven*.

1. *Alcalif* was a sort of pile carpet.
2. Probably *semiano*, the calico made at Samona in northern India.
3. Perhaps spikenard, an aromatic substance.
4. The value figure is not specified.
5. The details of the costs at Surat are available in V.O.C. 1082, f.70 and are as follows:

a.	toll on indigo Bayana at 3½ plus 2 paise per cent	f.1,800:0:0
b.	toll on indigo Sarkhej at 3½ plus 2 paise per cent	f.1,940:0:0
c.	customary charge of 1 plus 1 paise per cent on indigo	f.1,161:1:0
d.	toll on textiles, saltpetre and other goods	f.394:0:0
e.	given to the man putting the stamp at Surat customs house	f.26:5:0
f.	cost of transport of the above goods to the Company's warehouse	f.380:12:0
g.	cost of loading the goods on the ship	f.105:0:0
h.	cost of gifts given to the governor and other important persons in the city	f.147:15:0
	Total	f.5,954:6:0

6. The details of the cargo from Masulipatnam are available in V.O.C. 1084, f.190 and are as follows:

Cotton yarn	7,050 ponds worth	f.2,426:15:0
Guinea-cloth	3,157 pieces worth	f.14,618:2:10
Muris	3,321 pieces worth	f.15,117:11:0
Gunnies	147 pieces worth	f.195:18:8
Salampuris	204 pieces worth	f.555:12:4
Indigo	57,100 ponds worth	f.27,948:10:15
Refined saltpetre	4,800 ponds worth	f.637:10:0
Parcallas	294 pieces worth	f.1,117:3:1
	Expenses at Masulipatnam	f.5,170:10:0
	Total	f.67,787:13:6

7. The details of the cargo loaded at Pulicat are available in V.O.C. 1084, f.190 and are as follows:

Guinea cloth, 26,025 *ells* worth	f.2,869:3:9
Gunpowder, 488 ponds worth	f.85:8:0
Expenses at Pulicat	f.280:3:12
Total	f.3,234:15:5

44. Libenaar at Masulipatnam to Governor-General De Carpentier at Batavia, 29 December 1624. V.O.C. 1085, ff.218-21vo (Copy).

The affairs at Masulipatnam were in bad shape. The right to trade with the Company there had been farmed out and anyone dealing with it, including even the person who fetched water, was obliged to make a monthly or annual payment to the *havaldar*. Merchants fetching goods from the factory were required to pay each time 5 *pagodas*[1] to the *havaldar*. Contractors who earlier used to accept goods in payment of the return cargo to be supplied by them now insisted on cash payment.

Groa[2] and Gopinath,[3] two old and trustworthy servants and merchants of the Company, had been sent to Petapuli[4] with 15,000 rials of eight to procure within two months 200 packets of cotton yarn, 50 packets of *salampuris*, 5 packets of red and 6 packets of white *parcallas*, 5,000 pieces of Negro cloth, 100 *corgies* of *poulong gobars*[5] and 200 pieces of *dungarees*. Jan Libenaar had managed to persuade the Company's contractor, Lingayya,[6] to prevail upon the *sar-ı-khail* to let Groa and Gopinath carry the Company's cash and goods to Petapuli.

Masulipatnam and other factories had run out of liquid funds. The factors at Palicol and Draksharama, where a large amount of Guinea-cloth and other varieties were procured annually against cash were, therefore, sitting idle. In the absence of dealers willing to change the Company's gold into *pagodas* at Masulipatnam, Libenaar decided to go to Golconda to get more than 200 marks exchanged against *pagodas*. He was secretly followed to Golconda by the *sarraf*[7] to whom the right to buy and sell gold and silver from the Company had been farmed out.

He complained to the *sar-i-khail* that if the Dutch continued to be permitted to carry goods out of and into Masulipatnam unrestrictedly subject only to an annual payment of 3,000 *pagodas* by way of tolls, there would be nothing to prevent them from taking gold and silver out of Masulipatnam making it impossible for him to earn enough business to be able to pay 500 *pagodas* per annum in lieu of his farming rights. The *sar-i-khail* ordered that Groa and Gopinath, who were at Petapuli, be produced before him. But the two went into hiding.

At Golconda, Jan Libenaar was kept under close watch by the king's employees resulting in not a single money changer daring to come to him to buy the gold. As a result, his trip costing the Company about f.3,000 including the costs of the presents, was a waste except for the diamond ring worth f.400-500 presented to him by the *sar-i-khail*. There was thus no alternative but to continue dealing with the merchants who had been farmed the right to trade with the Company.

Apart from engaging in an open conflict with the king of Golconda, the only remedy against the *sar-i-khail's* tyranny was to engage in trade exclusively against cash. That would not only break the monopoly of the merchants to whom the right to trade with the Company had been farmed out but also prevent the *sar-i-khail* from trying to seize money from the Company merchants to whom an advance might have been given as had happened at Petapuli in the case of Groa and Gopinath. Cash transactions would also prevent the use of the Company's advance money by these merchants for their own private trade. Because of the problems created by the farming out of the right to trade with the Company, it had been possible to procure textiles, rice, steel and ropes, etc., worth only f.133,485 which were being dispatched with the *Wapen van Rotterdam*. Extracts from the invoices of the following were enclosed: the *Enkhuizen* to Batavia with a cargo worth f.98,011; the *Schoonhoven* to Holland with a cargo worth f.67,788 and the *Leeuwin* to Holland with a cargo worth f.315,908.

1. The symbol used in the document is 5 p[a]. It is likely to have stood for a *pagoda*, but could also mean per cent.

2. Groa was the Company's interpreter at Pulicat.
3. Gopinath was the Company's broker at Petapuli.
4. Petapuli or Peddapalle, more generally known as Nizampatam, is 40 miles south-west of Masulipatnam.
5. *Poulong gobars* was a specific variety of *poulongs*.
6. Lingayya was an important Muslim merchant to whom the right to trade with the European companies had been farmeded out several times by the government.
7. *Sarraf* was a general term used for money changers.

45. The Directors at Amsterdam to Van den Broecke at Surat, December 1624. V.O.C. 314 (Copy).*

The Directors' last letter to Surat was dated 15 December 1623.[1] The *Heusden* had reached Amsterdam on 24 August 1624 with Surat letters dated 11, 15 and 16 January 1624.[2]

Batavia had informed the Directors that Surat had been provided with as much capital as it had asked for. Additional capital would have been received with the *Dordrecht* from Holland.[3] Batavia would also be sending goods from other parts of the East Indies to Surat. The Governor-General had told the Directors that they needed to send funds to Batavia only for purposes of investment in goods for Holland and that no funds were needed for promoting the intra-Asian trade.

The goods received with the *Heusden* had been sold at a good price, namely *minatashis* at 52 *stuivers* per piece, Guinea cloth at f.12½ per *ell* and cotton yarn at 32 *stuivers* per pond (all against credit of 15 months). Textiles sold against cash included (per piece) fine white broad *baftas* at f.11:11:0, white broad *baftas* at f.7:16:0, three other varieties of white *baftas* at between f.5:15:0 and f.16:10:0, black broad *baftas* at f.10 and blue broad *baftas* at f.9. Indigo Bayana and Sarkhej was sold at 10 stuivers and 8 stuivers 4 pennings per pond respectively at 24 months' credit. Refined and unrefined saltpetre was sold at f.44 and f.30 per 100 ponds respectively against cash.

The *Gouden Leeuw*, the *Walcheren* and the *Heusden* were

being sent to Surat together to be able to jointly face any unexpected attack on them. The *Gouden Leeuw* and the *Walcheren* would return together, the first on the account of the Amsterdam chamber and the second on that of Zeeland chamber with cargo from Persia and Surat. The *Heusden* was to be sent on to Aceh and the west coast of Sumatra where its cargo would be sold against pepper. It would then return to Holland on the account of the Amsterdam chamber. But in case it was not able to procure sufficient cargo at Aceh or the west coast of Sumatra, it would go on to Batavia.

Since the Persian trade was also open to the Company now, a sum of f.400,000 was being sent for investment in Persian goods and of f.200,000 for the procurement of Surat goods for Holland. In the event that the China trade remained closed, Batavia would send on the funds earmarked for that trade to Surat for investment in good quality indigo and in Persian silk. Batavia would also send spices which could be exchanged against Persian silk.

The *Delfshaven* will be sent to Coromandel with f.100,000 in cash besides goods asked for by them.

The following were the orders for Holland which Surat was to supply with the *Gouden Leeuw* and the *Walcheren*.

S.No.	*Item*	*Quantity*	*Remarks*
1.	Indigo Lahore[4]	worth f.200,000	good quality without adulteration.
2.	Indigo Sarkhej	worth f.100,000	only if the quality was good.
3.	Indigo from Jambusar	–	to be sent only if sufficient quantity of Bayana and Sarkhej indigo was not available.
4.	Refined saltpetre	good quantity	the lot received with the *Heusden* was more expensive than the lot from Coromandel. To be sent as ballast.

5.	Guinea cloth	nil	available more cheaply and in proper size in Coromandel.
6.	Cotton yarn	200 bales	the lot received with the *Heusden* was of reasonable quality.
7.	White *baftas*	reasonable quantity	both fine and coarse of proper length and width.
8.	Black *baftas* and blue *baftas*	reasonable amount	not as many as white *baftas*.
9.	Broach black *baftas* and white *baftas*	15 to 20 pieces of each as a sample	best quality with gold and silk polka dots.
10.	Cheri *baftas*	15 to 20 pieces as a sample	best quality.
11.	*Minatashis*	6,000 to 8,000 pieces	–
12.	Sealing wax	30 to 40 cases	–
13.	Red coral	reasonable amount	–
14.	Mark stones	good quantity	–
15.	Spicanardy	reasonable amount	–
16.	Ambergris	good amount	–
17.	Persian carpets	500 pieces plus 100 pieces of carpets if available substantially cheaper than the ones from Persia	to be used as table clothes. 300 pieces of 4 *ells* length, 100 pieces of 5 *ells* length, 60 pieces of 6 *ells* length and 40 pieces of 7 to 8 *ells* length each. The width to be 2½ to 3½ *ells*. Good stuff, thick wool, bright and permanent colours and good designs.
18.	Blankets		best quality. Quantity available per annum to be ascertained.
19.	*Sarassa Malay*	200 pieces	the best quality as a sample.

20.	*Semianoes* from Agra	some	the best quality as a sample.
21.	*Khasas* from Agra	some	good quality as a sample.
22.	Cotton	as much as could be loaded in the ships	good quality.
23.	*Kamkhanis*[5]	500 pieces	the best quality. The lot brought by Dedel to Batavia was found to be of good quality. These had cost 16 to 24 *mahmudis* per 20 pieces.
24.	*Ginghams*[6] white, brown and blue	15 to 20 pieces of each	the best quality as a sample.

The English were doing a lot of damage to the Company throughout the East Indies. But no cause for complaint was to be given and as little contact maintained with them as possible. In terms of the agreement of 1619,[7] there was no obligation to cooperate with them in Surat, much less in Persia.

Two ships and a yacht were being equipped in Denmark, but the destination or the cargo to be carried were not known.

No ships were being equipped in France for a voyage to the East Indies.

No servant of the Company was to be allowed to engage in private trade till such time as he had completed his obligatory period of service with the Company. Any violation must be punished with confiscation of capital and goods.

The exact date of the letter is not given in the document. The volume is not foliated but the document covers 19 single folios.

1. Om Prakash (ed.), *The Dutch Factories in India, 1617-1623*, document 244, p. 282.
2. See documents nos. 6, 7 and 10.
3. As per the Directors' letter of 15 December 1623, a sum of 100,000 rials of eight had been sent to Surat.
4. This term was also used for indigo Bayana.

5. A plain muslin woven near Patna, sometimes compared with *khasas*.
6. The term *gingham* has been assimilated into modern English in the sense defined by the Oxford English Dictionary as 'a kind of cotton or linen cloth, woven of dyed yarn, often in stripes or checks'. It is derived from the Malay *ginggang* 'striped'. It is not certain whether Coromandel *ginghams* were the same as Bengal *ginghams* of mixed cotton and tussur-silk or whether they were of cotton alone. The important feature to traders was that they were woven with double threaded warps and wefts, thus having a distinctive texture. They were sent to the Malay archipelago and after 1640, to Europe. The dimensions were approximately 20 yards by 1 yard.
7. For the agreement, see Om Prakash (ed.), *The Dutch Factories in India 1617-1623*, pp. 156-7.

46. The Directors at Amsterdam to Van Uffelen at Masulipatnam, December 1624. V.O.C. 314 (Copy).*

The Directors' last letter to Masulipatnam was dated 15 December 1623 and had been sent with the *Leeuwin*.[1]

The Directors had learnt from Van Uffelen's letter to Van den Broecke at Surat dated 27 December 1623 about the affronts done to the former at Masulipatnam.[2] They did not know the details but no provocation was to be given for a situation endangering the Company's goods and property to arise. No return cargo had been received from Coromandel in 1624.

The Directors had learnt from Batavia's letter dated 3 January 1624[3] that Coromandel had been provided with adequate funds. These should suffice for buying goods for the Indies; for the procurement of goods for Holland, funds would be sent by them.

Spices had sold reasonably well on the Coromandel coast in 1623. Since the consumption of these spices in the East had no adverse effect on the sales in Europe, Coromandel was to try to sell as much as possible at a good or even a reasonable price.

Since sugar could be sold in Persia, the Governor-General had been asked to arrange for the procurement of Chinese and Bengal sugar to the extent possible. The supplies over and above the requirements of Persia could be sent to Holland where this item was doing well in view of the interruption of the supplies from Brazil. But it was essential to keep the cost price low. The last lot received with the *Schiedam* was of very poor quality and rendered only a small profit.

If a good amount of saltpetre could be bought in Bengal as cheaply as in Coromandel, Van Uffelen was to arrange for a large quantity to be bought there, mainly the refined variety. Unrefined saltpetre was to be bought only if the cost price was particularly low. In that case considering that the labour cost was much lower than in Holland, this lot was to be refined at Coromandel. The lot received with the *Schiedam* was sold at f.46 per 100 ponds on 12 months' credit. If the refined and unrefined varieties had been sold separately, the likely price would have been f.51 and f.41 respectively.

Regarding Batavia's query whether Coromandel indigo should not be dispensed with in favour of Lahore [Bayana] and Sarkhej indigo, the Directors' position was that since the Coromandel variety afforded a good profit, its procurement should be continued.

The goods received with the *Dordrecht* and the *Schiedam* had been sold at the following prices:

		The lot received with the *Dordrecht*	The lot received with the *Schiedam*
S.No.	*Item*	*Price*	*Price*
1.	Indigo	34 *stuivers*, 8 pennings per pond at 24 months' credit	51¼ *stuivers* per pond at 24 months' credit
2.	Guinea-cloth	12⅛ Flemish *groots*[4] per *ell* at 15 months' credit	12¼ Flemish *groots* per *ell* against cash payment
3.	Cotton yarn	31 *stuivers*, 5 *duits* per pond at 24 months' credit	26 *stuivers* per pond against 24 months' credit
4.	*Salampuris*[5]	f.17:5 per piece against 9 months' credit	–

5.	*Parcallas*[6]	f.8:12 per piece against 9 months' credit	f.8:5 per piece against 9 months' credit
6.	Saltpetre	f.46:7½ per 100 ponds at 12 months' credit	
7.	Refined saltpetre	–	f.51 per 100 ponds against 12 months' credit
8.	Unrefined saltpetre	–	f.41 per 100 ponds against 12 months' credit
9.	*Balatius*	–	f.16:7:8[7] per piece against 9 months' credit
10.	Bengal sugar	–	12 *groots* per pond against cash payment

This letter was being sent with the *Delfshaven* on the account of the Delft chamber[8] with f.100,000 in cash in addition to the goods asked for by Coromandel. There will be no direct shipments to Holland any more and all ships, including the *Delfshaven*, would return via Batavia. The following cargo was to be put aboard the *Delfshaven*.

S.No.	*Item*	*Quantity*	*Remarks*
1.	Indigo	worth f.30,000	best quality.
2.	Cotton yarn	worth f.10,000	best quality.
3.	Guinea-cloth	worth f.30,000	best quality. One-third of the lot to be unbleached and the remainder bleached.
4.	*Parcallas*	4,000 pieces	best quality.
5.	*Salampuris*	7,000 to 8,000 pieces	best quality.
6.	*Bethilles*	6,000 pieces	size 24 *asta* each. The lot received with the *Schiedam* was of reasonable quality and rendered a reasonable profit.

7.	*Muris*	2,000 pieces	best quality. The lot received with the *Naarden* was sold at f.10 per piece.
8.	Bengal fine stuffs and fine cotton clothes	15 to 20 pieces of each variety as a sample	the likely number of pieces available per annum to be ascertained.
9.	Refined saltpetre	amount needed to ballast the return ships	–
10.	Unrefined saltpetre	only if adequate refined variety not available	–
11.	Diamonds	a reasonable number	pure and bright quality, provided the cost price was not more than that of the last lot. A good amount of Coromandel diamonds were in the Company's stock in Holland.
12.	Bengal sugar	as much as possible	cash price not to exceed 5 rials per bale of 170 ponds.
13.	Cotton	as a sample	–
14.	Painted cotton blankets	1,000 pieces	best quality.
15.	Painted clothes	a few samples	best quality. To be used as table clothes and wall hangings.
16.	Bengal wax	as much as possible	good quality. Last lot sold well in Holland.

In case an adequate quantity of fine cotton textiles was not available, the surplus funds were to be invested in the procurement of additional quantities of indigo, diamonds and Bengal sugar.

* The exact date of the letter is not given in the document. The volume is not foliated but the document covers 13 single folios.

1. Om Prakash (ed.), *The Dutch Factories in India, 1617-1623*, document no. 243, pp. 279-81.
2. Om Prakash (ed.), *The Dutch Factories in India, 1617-1623*, document no. 250, p. 291.
3. See document no. 2.
4. 1 florin (guilder) = 20 *stuivers* = 320 pennings = 160 *duits* = 40 Flemish *groots*. The *groot* was also a Dutch coin equivalent to half stuiver.
5. *Salampuri* was a variety of white cloth with red borders. Its usual dimensions were 4 yards by 1 yard.
6. *Parcalla* was a closely woven cotton cloth. It was a sort of fine white cambric. Its dimensions were 8 yards by 1 yard.
7. The units are florins:*stuivers*:pennings.
8. The six chambers of the Company were Amsterdam, Zeeland, Rotterdam, Delft, Enkhuizen and Hoorn.

1625

47. Ysbrantsz. at Pulicat to Governor-General De Carpentier at Batavia, 21 January 1625. V.O.C. 1085, ff.209-14vo (Copy).

Marten Ysbrantsz.'s last letter to Batavia dated 2 October 1624 had been sent with the English ship, the *Heart*.

The *Vrede* and the *Medemblik* had returned from Arakan on 16 January 1625 with rice and 300 slaves. Under-merchant Pouwels Cramerheyn together with two assistants had stayed on in Arakan to continue the procurement of slaves. No more than 300 slaves could be procured in Tegenapatam over the last seven months. The promised supply of 100 slaves per month did not materialize.[1] There was a large scale mortality among the slaves from Arakan as a result of some kind of suspected plague. More might die on the trip to Batavia.

Ysbrantsz. had hoped to procure 500 to 600 *bahars* of saltpetre by the end of January, but so far it had been possible to procure only 200 *bahars*. 100 *bahars* of saltpetre which had been bought for the Company had been taken over by the *nayak* of Madura for the preparation of gun-powder. As long as the young king was at war with this *nayak*,[2] it would not be possible for the Company to get much saltpetre. Once peace was restored, the Company ought to be able to get enough saltpetre at Puleceri.

At Puleceri, the Company would be able to get fine *tapis* and *goulongs*. Some pieces of the latter without golden threads were being sent with the present shipment. In future, only pieces with golden threads would be procured. The factors at Tegenapatam would put the available supplies of *rambutins* and sail cloth in this ship[3] together with *chavonis*, *poulong gobars*, blue *balatius* and *chelas*. If these were found to be of as good a quality as those from Masulipatnam, the entire orders could in future be met by supplies from Tegenapatam.

In October, the Danes had sent a ship to the Moluccas with 20-25 packets of textiles painted in Karikal, Trancquebar and Trymelepatnam.[4] At Puleceri, they had managed to buy some textiles directly from the artisans secretly. They were trying to have some clothes for Java manufactured. Their procurement of pepper had been hindered by the war between the young king assisted by the *nayak* of Tanjore on the one hand and the *nayak* of Madura on the other. They were also trying to procure saltpetre. The *nayak* of Madura had, however, told them that if they wanted him to ban the procurement of this item by the Dutch, they would have to give him 800 *pardauws*[5] annually besides other duties and taxes. They were stregthening their fort and it seemed that they had no intention of leaving Trancquebar.

The plentiful presence of rajas around Pulicat was hindering trade. They were ever trying to extort money from anyone they could making trade a very risky business. The *visiadoor*[6] of Pulicat, Pede Raja,[7] had recently been released from prison by Eti Raja against a promise to pay 14,000 *pardauws*. Before having him arrested in May 1624, Eti Raja had taken away all his lands and animals. So it was not quite clear how Pede Raja would raise the necessary funds.

It would indeed be injurious to the Company if the free merchants[8] were allowed to trade in textiles on the Coromandel coast. The weavers and painters were given advances by the Company for the production of the textiles and the free merchants might deal with these artisans clandestinely.

Adriaen Willemsz. Goeree, appointed head of the Masulipatnam factory by Jacob Dedel, had requested to be relieved of his charge and allowed to return to Holland with the *Leeuwin*. Batavia's orders in this behalf were awaited.

The cases of poor quality cinnamon were being returned to Batavia because they could not be sold at Pulicat.

1. See document no. 30.
2. The first phase of the civil war in Karnataka was over in 1619 when the daughter of Eti Raja was married to the young king Ramadeva, but the campaign against the *nayak* of Madura continued even after that.

3. Usually the ships went from Masulipatnam to Pulicat and then on to Tegenapatam.
4. Not identified.
5. The *pardauw* was a gold coin struck by the rajas of Vijayanagar. Its value was about 360 reis or about 58 pence.
6. Local chieftains of Pulicat. The term is also used for the superintendent of the customs-house at Pulicat.
7. Pede Raja was the local chieftain of Pulicat. Since he had rebelled several times against Eti Raja, the latter had put him in prison in May 1624.
8. Dutch residents in Batavia and other places in Asia but not in the employment of the Company were referred to as free burghers or free merchants.

48. General letter from Governor-General De Carpentier at Batavia to the Directors at Amsterdam, 27 January 1625. V.O.C. 1082, ff.129-77 (Original).*

The yacht *Weesp* had arrived from Surat on 5 July 1624 with 263 packets of Gujarat clothes. It was sent back to Surat on 9 August together with the *Nieuw Bantam* and the *Zuid Holland* with a cargo worth f.204,657 consisting of 44,000 rials of eight, 37,472 ponds cloves, 60,043 ponds nutmeg, 40 bales mace, 100 *piculs* sandalwood, 500 *piculs* lead, 20 *piculs* Japanese copper, 4,000 *piculs* pepper and 3,827 ounces of blood coral. Once this cargo reached Surat, they would have enough capital to meet Holland's orders of indigo and Batavia's of clothes and be left with enough funds to engage in the Persian trade. As per Batavia's calculations, Surat would have a capital (sale value) of f.1,000,000. Persia already had a capital of f.350,000. From this total sum of f.1,350,000, Holland could expect Persian silk of the value of f.350,000 and indigo besides other goods from Surat worth another of f.300,000. Batavia was likely to get textiles, etc., worth f.220,000. If Surat sent goods worth another f.350,000 to Persia, it would still be left with f.130,000. In order to ensure that as little cash as possible had to be sent to Surat, more spices had been sent there than what Van den Broecke had asked for. As long as the Chinese trade was not available to the Company, no more highly profitable return cargo could be obtained for Holland than that from Surat and Persia.

Efforts would be made to procure the Surat textiles for the Indies against spices as far as possible. At present, the Company could expect to sell spices annually to the extent of f.150,000 at Surat. Once the Company was fully established at Mocha, a sale of f.70,000 worth can be expected there making a total of f.220,000 worth.

The following spices had been sold in Persia at a good profit: 2,000 sacks of pepper, 20,000 ponds of cloves, 18,000 ponds of nutmeg and 25 bales of mace. More of these spices, particularly pepper, could have been sold there. Van den Broecke had been advised to send to Persia as much of spices as were likely to be sold there. According to the latest information available, spices (except for mace) were selling at a better price in Persia than in the Mughal empire and even in Holland.[1] In Persia, pepper fetched as much as 12 *stuivers* per pond, cloves 89 *stuivers*, nutmeg 32 *stuivers* and mace 41 *stuivers* per pond. The corresponding prices for cloves, nutmeg and mace at Surat were 60 to 66 *stuivers*, 15 to 20 *stuivers* and 60 to 63 *stuivers* per pond.

A limited amount of pepper was available at Surat at 6 rials per Bantam sack. This was brought overland from Malabar to Burhanpur and from there to Surat. Van den Broecke had been asked not to buy it at such a high price for Holland but if it continued to do well in Persia, a certain amount could be bought for Persia.[2]

Vissnich was received by King Shah Abbas of Persia in a friendly manner. The goods taken there were exchanged with the king's factor against silk. Vissnich hoped to be able to collect 350 to 360 bales of silk (1 bale = 204 ponds), which was by far the best return cargo from Persia for Holland by the summer of 1624. If adequate cash, spices and other goods were sent to Persia, the Company would not be short of silk.

Batavia would await the Directors' decision as to how they would want the Persian trade conducted and what ships and goods they were willing to provide for this trade. Batavia itself would be able to send some cash to Persia but only as long as the China trade was not available to the Company.

According to the information received from Van den Broecke, spices were carried from Surat to Agra, from Agra to Bengal and then overland to the border of China. Spices were also taken from Surat to Persia and from there to Turkey via Armenia and Babylon. In course of time, the factories at Coromandel, Surat, Persia and Mocha would probably be among the most profitable the Company had.

Surat had been instructed to buy a large amount of saltpetre. Since the war was over,[3] Van den Broecke hoped to be able to procure a good amount.

Now that the king of Bijapur, under whose jurisdiction Dabhol lay, had become a tributary of the Mughal emperor who earned a considerable amount of revenue at Dabhol, a good deal of pressure was being put on the Company by the king of Bijapur and the *mutasaddi* of Surat besides several notables of Surat and Dabhol to cease hostilities with Dabhol. The Surat factors were of the opinion that in the event the hostilities with Dabhol continued, the Surat merchants who had extensive dealings with the merchants of Dabhol, would stand to lose and were likely to complain to the Mughal emperor who was now Dabhol's protector. That, in turn, might lead to a ban on the Company's trade in the empire, besides harassment of the Company's factors along the lines of the English last year. It had, therefore, been decided to ask Surat to try and reach an accord with Dabhol and not to attack the ships based there unless they were found to be carrying Portuguese cargo. The merchants of Dabhol would, in turn, be required to obtain the release of the Company's goods and factors at Mocha from the *badshah* of Yemen and to obtain trading rights for the Company there. Van den Broecke had also been asked to send an emissary to the *badshah* of Yemen to request the restitution of the Company's goods. In the event of the failure of the mission, the Company's yacht to Mocha was to cruise in the waters around till it was time to return to Surat.

At Hormuz, the English had been asking the Company for half the usual tolls on goods unloaded by the latter there. The English maintained that by virtue of their contract with the Persians, they were entitled to half the income of the port of Hormuz. They argued that the situation was similar to that of the Dutch at Batavia. The English were not ashamed of making such a claim notwithstanding the fact that the Company had been allowed by the Shah to trade in Persia toll-free and was held in greater esteem there than the English. The factors had, therefore, been ordered not to unload any cargo at Hormuz but to go on to Gombroon and other ports from where Isfahan was conveniently accessible.

Because of the seizure of some Muslim ships by them, the President of the English Company at Surat[4] had been arrested together with other factors and their goods sealed.

The *Wapen van Rotterdam* had arrived from Coromandel on 11 March 1624 with the following goods worth f.126,604:179 packets of different kinds of textiles, 1,561 carat diamonds, 230,308 ponds saltpetre and 630 slaves. News had been received regarding the arrest of Van Uffelen and the extortion of 11,000 *pagodas* from the Company's merchants. The charges against Van Uffelen were (a) the export of tobacco to Arakan in contravention of the express orders of the king of Golconda, (b) compelling a *sarraf* who had been farmed the exclusive right to change rials, to change 5,000 rials into *pagodas* at a favourable rate and (c) denial of free access to Pegu to the Muslim merchants from Masulipatnam. He was released only after a sum of 5,000 *pagodas* had been extorted from him.

In order to enquire into the totality of the situation on the Coromandel coast and to look into possible avenues of redress for the injuries suffered there, the Batavia Council sent Jacob Dedel to Coromandel on 26 March 1624 with the *Wapen van Rotterdam*. This ship carried a cargo worth f.132,311 consisting mostly of cash but also some spices.

The *Muys* had arrived from Coromandel on 4 July 1624 bringing the sad news of the death of Van Uffelen on 1 February 1624. Before its departure from the coast, the *Muys* had captured within sight of Masulipatnam a ship based at Cochin and which had been freighted by a Muslim merchant for a trip from Pegu to Masulipatnam.[5] This caused problems for the Company including a ban on its trade. Eventually, it had been necessary to release the ship's cargo and men. The empty ship had to be presented as a gift to the *sar-i-khail*. It was only then that the Company was allowed to engage in trade again.

Following the death of Van Uffelen, Marten Ysbrantsz. had been appointed the provisional chief of the Coromandel factories. After news had been received of the death of Jacob Dedel in Coromandel on 29 August 1624, Ysbrantsz. had been appointed regular director of the Coromandel factories. Adriaen Williemsz. Goeree and Jan Libenaar had been appointed provisional chiefs of the Masulipatnam factory.

The *Wapen van Enkhuizen* had arrived from Coromandel on 20 November 1624 with a cargo worth f.243,919 consisting of 862 packets of textiles, 286,434 ponds of saltpetre, 130 *lasts* of rice and 298 slaves.

Guinea gold had been sold at a profit of 6 to 7 per cent at Pulicat but at Masulipatnam it had rendered a loss. Hungarian ducats and unminted gold ought to be sent preferably to Masulipatnam because the former were in use as currency there and were as profitable as the latter. The rial had fallen at Masulipatnam from 9 to 8 *fanums*. A *bahar* of tin was sold there at 50 to 55 *pagodas*, the *pagoda* being equivalent to 4 guilders and 5 *stuivers*. This price was lower than in Holland. There was little demand for lead on the coast and they had a stock of 15,000 ponds. The price of lead was 12 to 13 *pagodas* per *bahar*. There was no demand for ivory of which there was a stock of 38,000 ponds. Quicksilver could be sold at 16 to 18 *pagodas* per *maund* of 24 ponds. The annual demand was for 10 to 12 *bahars*. The last lot of spelter received with the *Leeuwin* was sold at 40 *pagodas* per *bahar* and vermilion at 16 to 18 *pagodas* per *maund*. The entire lot of red, blue and green broadcloth received with the *Leeuwin* had been sold at the following prices; the red at 12¾ guilders and the others at 8½ guilders per *ell*. Refined sulphur was in great demand and rendered a good profit.

* Summarized in W.Ph. Coolhaas (ed.), *Generale Missiven*, I, pp. 152-71.

1. See document no. 37.
2. See document no. 37.
3. The reference is evidently to the rebellion of Prince Khurram against his father, the Mughal Emperor Jahangir.

4. The English president at Surat was Thomas Rastell.
5. See document no. 21.

49. Van den Broecke at Surat to Governor-General De Carpentier at Batavia, 22 April 1625. V.O.C. 1084, ff.42-51 (Copy).

The *Dordrecht* had arrived from Holland on 15 September 1624 with a large amount of capital and goods. The *Zuid Holland*, the *Nieuw Bantam* and the *Weesp* arrived from Batavia on 5 October 1624. In the context of the strengthened naval capability of the Portuguese in view of the arrival of seven galleons from Portugal, this was a matter for relief. The *Zuid Holland*, the *Nieuw Bantam*, the *Dordrecht* and the *Weesp* had been sent to Persia together for fear of the Portuguese. Spices and cash had been sent there as per Batavia's instructions.

Surat had learnt that de Milde[1] had been freed by the new *badshah*. Since only a small amount of spices had been taken to Mocha over the past three years, they were likely to afford a good profit in Mocha and Van den Broecke hoped that Batavia would send enough spices for that factory.

The English ships, the *William* and the *Blessing* arrived at Surat in October followed by the *Royal and James*, the *Jonas*, the *Star* and the *Eagle*, in addition to the sloops *Look out* and *Take All* under the command of John Woddell[2] who had helped in the conquest of Hormuz two years ago. These vessels were well armed and carried a large amount of capital.

The English factors were extremely friendly. They had written instructions to this effect which they let Van den Broecke read. On the expiry of his term, Thomas Rastell had left for England on 25 February 1625. He had since been succeeded as President by Thomas Kerridge.[3] John Woddell had told Van den Broecke that the English would be happy to form a defence fleet together with the Dutch at Surat. The ships that could be made available for this venture were the *Eagle*, the *James*, the *Jonas* and another one or two. The total fleet, including the Dutch ships, could consist of ten vessels which would be capable of inflicting substantial damage on the enemy. The encounter with the Portuguese had increased the respect for the Company in Surat and Persia tremendously. English President Rastell had told Van den Broecke that in a small Portuguese vessel that they had captured, a letter containing instructions by the king of Spain (and Portugal) to reconquer Hormuz and to drive the English and the Dutch out of Coromandel and conquer the fort at Pulicat had been found. In Van den Broecke's view, it would be advisable to send a strong fleet to Surat to break the power of the Portuguese. The Company's ships had returned from Persia on 25 March 1625 in the company of English ships. They had together fought a furious battle three days earlier with eight Portuguese galleons in which the Dutch commander, Albert Becker, had been killed.

Huybert Vissnich had allowed the Persian ambassador to the States-General passage on the Company's ships from Persia to Surat. After some discussion, the Surat Council allowed the ambassador to proceed to Holland.

The cloves, nutmeg and mace sent to Agra were sold at a good profit. The sales at Surat suffered because of the continuing war in Hindustan[4] which has ruined a number of merchants. Both the Muslim and the Hindu merchants maintain that if the Company wanted to do business with them, it must have an adequate amount of cash available.

Surat would have access to as much capital as had been suggested by De Carpentier.[5] It would be possible to buy the goods in time and cheaper only if enough funds were available. After the arrival of the ships, prices normally went up by 20 to 25 per cent. Van den Broecke believed that there was no harm in borrowing funds on interest and buying the return cargo three to four months before the arrival of the ships. That period was also the best season for the procurement of the goods. The interest cost over a period of four months at 1 per cent per month would be just 4 per cent but the saving in cost would amount to 20 to 25 per cent. It would be even better if the Surat factory could be provided with funds a year in advance so that the goods might be bought in the proper season and be ready when the ships arrived. This would also facilitate the timely departure of the ships for Holland, say by the end of October or the middle of November.

Similarly, if the ships for Batavia left on schedule, the goods would reach the markets on time.

The supply of spices and other goods to Surat ought not to exceed the orders because if the prices fell, it was very difficult to restore them to their earlier level. Also, there was no point in maintaining large stocks of goods because the buyers always preferred fresh goods. The following goods were to be supplied for Surat and Persia annually.

S.No.	*Item*	*For Surat*	*For Persia*
1.	Cloves	25,000 ponds	20,000 ponds
2.	Nutmeg	50,000 ponds	25,000 ponds
3.	Mace	25 to 30 bags	25 bags
4.	Sandalwood	50 *piculs*	50 *piculs*
5.	Radix China	100 *piculs*	100 *piculs*
6.	Benzoin	15 to 20 cases	10 to 15 cases
7.	Camphor	25 cases	a good amount of the white variety from China
8.	Tortoise horn	25 *piculs*	–
9.	Porcelain (fine and ordinary)	some	–
10.	Japanese deer skins	100 to 200	–
11.	Sugar	–	?[6]
12.	Preserved ginger	–	?[6]

Batavia might send as much cash as it wished. In addition to the proceeds from the sale of spices, Surat would require 40,000 rials for the procurement of textiles for the Moluccas, etc. Van den Broecke hoped that the Mocha trade would revive and that Surat would get the necessary liquid funds from Mocha.

Van den Broecke would try his best to provide a large return cargo for Holland provided enough funds were available. The Directors would be able to appreciate the importance of the Surat and the Persia trade when they received the return cargo with the *Heusden*, the *Schoonhoven*, the *Dordrecht* and the *Weesp*. Once they tasted the fruits of the Surat trade, they would revise their intention of not sending more money to Surat than what was needed simply for the ordered return cargo for Holland.

Wollenbrant Geleynsz., Francisco Pelsaert[7] and Adam Claesen Verhoeven had been sent with the necessary goods to Agra, Burhanpur and Ahmedabad—Cambay respectively. The goods were likely to afford a good profit there. While nutmeg was sold at Surat at one *daalder* per pond, at Agra it fetched a price as high as at Isfahan.

It was not necessary to have a permanent agent at the court of the great Mughal. A factor or a solicitor at the court along the lines of the English would be enough to persuade the officials not to give any trouble to the Company. Recently, a *kafila* of the Company on its way from Agra had to pay extraordinarily high and unprecedented tolls at Burhanpur and other places. It had, therefore, been decided by the Surat Council to send upper-merchant Hendrik Arentsz. Vapour to Agra with the next *kafila.* He would present to the emperor a *casuwaris*[8] bird and try to win his support for the Company. Since the last *farman* was four years old, he would request the emperor to grant a new *farman.* Vapour would later return to Agra to gain first hand experience of the trade there before Pelsaert left that factory. For a factor to command respect at the Mughal court, it was necessary to ensure that he was a man of standing.

The red blood coral had been sold at 90 *mahmudis* per *seer* of 120 ounces at two months' credit. A loss of 2,000 guilders had been incurred in the transaction. No female black slaves had been bought because they had become more expensive. Enough indigo Lahore could not be purchased because of the shortage of funds. 65 *lasts* of refined saltpetre were being sent for Holland with the *Dordrecht* and the *Weesp* as ballast. Since the best quality gall-nuts were available in Baghdad and Aleppo, Surat had asked Persia to procure this item for Batavia.

A list of the Muslim merchants' cargo carried on freight by the Company from Surat to Persia was enclosed.[9] The Company not only earned some money in the process but also the goodwill of the merchants.

As ordered by the Directors, Surat would try to obtain some curious birds and animals for the Prince of Orange. Four pigeons received as presents at Agra from Nawab Mukarrab Khan, the head of the royal treasury, were being sent to Batavia.

Quite a lot of shipping materials such as ropes and other things had been lost in the conflict at Hormuz. Five ropes of 14, 15 and 16 thumbs thickness had been bought as a sample for future supplies because the ships were short of them.

The English were distressed to find that the Dutch Company's standing with the Surat authorities was now very good. In the matter of the capture of the Indian ships, they had lost as much as f.300,000 and were now planning to change their strategy in their dealings with the authorities. They were busy reopening their factories with small stocks of goods. The emissary they had sent to the emperor had eventually succeeded after six months and many gifts in obtaining a *farman* addressed to the officials at Surat, Ahmedabad and Broach. The goods confiscated from them will now be returned.

Nawab Safi Khan[10] and other important people of Surat had been urging us to send a ship to Mocha every year. Van den Broecke had so far excused himself from this and was not very hopeful about the restitution of the Company's goods confiscated there.

The merchants of Surat had been requesting that their goods be transported to Batavia on the Company's ships or their ships granted passes for passage there. Instructions in this behalf would be awaited.

Van den Broecke thanks the Governor-General for allowing him to continue at Surat for another year or two and promises to give full satisfaction. He leaves the decision regarding a possible increase in his salary to the Governor-General.

Van den Broecke had reappointed Adam Claesen Verhoeven and Jacob Mahuizen[11] for three years, the former as upper-merchant at Ahmedabad at f.80 per month and the latter as book-keeper at Surat at f.60 per month.

After the defeat at his brother's hands, Prince Khurram was rumoured to have managed to collect a large force and get his women folk into the fort at Kondapili in Golconda. Since Prince Parwiz was in Agra with the royal army, Khurram was planning to take over Surat. On the advice of our friend, Nawab Safi Khan, it had been decided for reasons of safety to send the Company's *kafila* via Ahmedabad rather than via Burhanpur, although the former route takes 14 days longer.

Van den Broecke was distressed to learn from the letter from

Goeree that the Company's trade at Masulipatnam was in a poor state. Gold which could be disposed of there only at a considerable loss, could be sent by Goeree to Surat, if Van den Broecke so wished.

1. Willem de Milde had been arrested at Mocha in February 1622 for refusing to issue passes for Asian ships which had later been captured by the Dutch. For details, see Om Prakash (ed.), *The Dutch Factories in India, 1617-1623,* p. 208.
2. John Woddell had come to the East in 1621 as commander of the English fleet. It was under his command that the English had captured Hormuz in 1622 from the Portuguese. He returned home in 1626 but from the end of 1628 to April 1631 and from 1632 to 1634 he was again in the East. In April 1636, he returned to the East with six ships on the account of the New Company. He died in 1639 on his return voyage to England.
3. Thomas Kerridge had come to Surat in 1611 as an assistant in the service of the English Company. He had been sent as ambassador to the Mughal court in 1613. On 18 February 1616, he became the President of the English Company at Surat and held that position till he left for England in March 1622. He was again President of the Surat factory between 1625 and 1628. Thereafter till 1648, he was in the management of the English Company. He died in 1657.
4. Hindustan was a general term used for Mughal north India.
5. See document no. 48.
6. This entry is left blank in the document.
7. Francisco Pelsaert came to the East Indies in 1618 as an assistant and eventually rose to the position of an upper-merchant. Between 1624 and 1627, he worked mainly at the factory in Agra. He went home in 1627 but returned in October 1628. In August 1629, he was named an extraordinary member of the Council of the Indies. He died in September 1630. *Jahangir's India*, edited by Moreland and Geyl in 1925, is based on an account written by Pelsaert. A recent publication, *De geschriften van Francisco Pelsaert over Mughal Indie, 1627, Kroniek en Remonstratie* edited by D.H.A. Kolff and H.W. van Santen (The Hague, 1979) is an exhaustive account of the writings of Pelsaert.
8. According to W.Ph. Coolhaas, this bird died a few months later. (See his Journal of Van den Broecke.) This bird was found only in Ceram island in the Moluccas. Other species of this bird had been observed in Guinea, Britain and Australia. In the neighbouring islands of the Moluccas, this bird was called emen or eme.

9. This list is not available in the Company's archives.
10. Nawab Safi Khan was later designated Nawab Safi Khan Jahangir Shahi. This man was Nawab Asaf Khan's son-in-law and had been appointed *faujdar* of Cambay by Empress Nur Jahan, the consort of Emperor Jahangir.
11. After serving in Gujarat, Jacob Mahuizen (Mahieusen) served on the Coromandel coast and in Bengal. In the beginning of 1637, he was transferred to the factory at Pipli. In October 1639, he was sent to Batavia at his request. He became a member of the Council of Justice in September 1640. He returned home in November 1640 as second-in-command of the return fleet.

50. Van den Broecke at Surat to Antonio van Diemen,[1] member of the Council of the Indies at Batavia, 23 April 1625. V.O.C. 1085, ff.183-4vo (Copy).

Van den Broecke had received Van Diemen's letters of 26 March and 9 August 1624[2] and was sorry to learn that mistakes had been detected in the copies of the account books of the factories under Van den Broecke's charge.

1. Antonio van Diemen was born in 1593. He reached Bantam on 22 August 1618 and was promoted member of the Council of the Indies in 1625. He became Director-General in 1627 and was the Admiral of the return fleet that left for home in March 1631. He returned to the East Indies the following year and served as Governor-General between 1636 and his death on 19 April 1645. On her arrival in the Netherlands, his widow was presented with a gift of f.20,000 on behalf of the Directors.
2. These letters are not available in the Company's archives.

51. Van den Broecke at Surat to the Directors at Amsterdam, 24 April 1625. V.O.C. 1084, ff.1A-4 (Original).

Van den Broecke's last letter to the Directors[1] would have arrived with the *Schoonhoven* that had left Coromandel together with the cargo of the *Vrede* in November 1624.[2] Soon after the departure of the *Vrede*, Surat had sent the yacht *Weesp* to Batavia with textiles for the southern quarters.

A letter from De Milde[3] had been received at Surat on 16 September 1624 with a ship from Catchini[4] in Arabia Felix. The letter detailed the happenings at Mocha since the take-over by the new *badshah*. Van den Broecke had never been in favour of starting hostilities at Mocha which was one of the best milch-cows that the Company had providing cash against spices for investment in Surat and Persia. The Governor-General had asked Surat to send a ship with a suitable person as ambassador to the king of Arabia Felix if it could be done without much cost. But given the strong Portuguese presence there it was not considered advisable to do this. In case enough ships were provided by Batavia, one would be sent to Mocha next year with spices which were likely to afford a good profit there because practically no spices had been sent there over the last three years.

The *Dordrecht* had arrived from Europe on 18 September 1624 with a rich cargo. Van den Broecke wished that two to three big ships could be sent to Surat each year.

Since the arrival of Van den Broecke at Surat, the price of cotton had gone up from 32 to 112 *mahmudis* per. . .[5] The lot being sent with the present shipment had been bought at 85 *mahmudis*.

The English bought a considerable amount of Malabarese pepper at Surat at 6½ and 7 rials of eight per Bantam sack of 2 Surat *maunds*. They had sent approximately 50,000 guilders worth of pepper to England this year with the *Blessing* and the *William* which had left on 25 February 1625 laden mainly with indigo Sarkhej, pepper and cotton.

Surat had sent a fleet to Persia on 26 November 1624 with a good cargo. Near Daman, it came across the English ship *Eagle* which had captured two small Portuguese ships. The Dutch fleet returned to Surat on 16 March together with the English ships. On their way, they had a furious battle for three days with the Portuguese who had 8 large galleons and 40 frigates. With the help of God, the Dutch vessels succeeded in driving the enemy vessels away but lost Commander Albert Becker in the battle. The enemy lost Captain Nuno Alvares Botelho[6] together with many others. Van den Broecke believed that after this defeat the Portuguese were finished unless they received fresh assistance from Portugal. The Muslims of Persia, together with the passengers on board these ships who witnessed the battle, were struck with awe. This had tremendously improved the stock of the Dutch in the eyes of the people of Surat. The English were terribly jealous as a result. Van den Broecke wished that the Dutch had been able to finish the Portuguese power altogether so that it would no longer have been necessary to deploy ships to protect the Company's goods and trade here.

Surat was left with very little capital to purchase goods with for the next year. The interests of the Company would be best served if the Surat factory was kept well provided with funds all year round. Return cargo could be bought 20 to 25 per cent cheaper before the arrival of the ships. Besides, a better selection of goods was possible if the factors had sufficient time to procure the goods.

Surat ought to be provided with the following funds and goods:

300 to 400 ponds smelted gold of the variety received with the *Dordrecht*, 8,000 Dutch *daalders* and 20,000-25,000 rials of eight, 3,000 ponds of quicksilver, 3,000 ponds of vermilion, 200,000 ponds of lead—the smaller the pieces the better, 25,000 ponds of red copper, 50,000 ponds of spelter, 25,000 to 30,000 ponds of bright red blood coral, 18 to 20 pieces of bright red broadcloth, 20 pieces of corsages—red, yellow and green, 100 to 200 bright chrome swords, 5 to 6 tapestries with female figures, 5 to 6 bright mirrors and 10 to 20 dozen fine knives besides sundry items.

1. See document no. 19.
2. See document nos. 40 and 43.

3. This letter is not available in Company's archives.
4. This is modern Qishn in southern Yemen, Lat.15°.25′N, Long.51°.40′E.
5. The unit is not indicated but is likely to have been a *maund*.
6. Nuno Alvares Botelho was the Commander-in-chief of the Portuguese fleet since 1624. He often had success against the Dutch and the English.

52. Ysbrantsz. at Pulicat to the Directors at Amsterdam, 28 April 1625. V.O.C. 1084, ff.166-8 (Original).

Ysbrantsz.'s last letter to the Directors was dated 12 October 1624.[1] The *Wapen van Rotterdam* had been sent to Batavia on 22 January 1625 with a cargo worth f.235,600.

The Masulipatnam establishment had been facing all kinds of problems at the hands of the Muslim authorities. The right to trade with the Company there had been farmed out and the prices for the goods imported by it were fixed unilaterally by the merchants to whom the farming rights had been granted. The prices of the goods procured by the Company were also subject to these merchants' discretion. The Company's trade had thus become a forced trade. Notwithstanding the fact that the Company was paying 3,000 *pagodas* per annum on account of tolls, it was not allowed to trade peacefully in the surrounding areas which were under the jurisdiction of Golconda.

During his stay on the Coromandel coast, Admiral Dedel had granted free passes to the ships of the Muslims for various destinations. This had made the wicked Muslims even more bold. In Ysbrantsz.'s opinion, Dedel had behaved rather softly in this respect. He should have been more firm with the Muslims and not issued passes to them.

Pulicat had learnt from Goeree at Masulipatnam that there was little chance of their being able to supply a full load for the *Leeuwin* because the contracted goods had not been supplied on time. Also, they had received only a small amount of indigo. A large amount of saltpetre was lying ready in Tegenapatam but could not be transported because of the insecurity on the routes in view of the war in the area.[2] Since time was running out, it was decided to send the *Medemblik* to Masulipatnam on 28 April with instructions to the factors there to put aboard this ship the cargo which they had planned to send to Holland with the *Leeuwin*. Ysbrantsz. had himself planned to travel to Masulipatnam but had not dared leave the fort because the entire area was in a state of turmoil.

The young king and Eti Raja were still in the field against the *nayak* at Madura.[3] Eti Raja was repeatedly trying to garner the support of the *visiadores* of the surrounding areas.

The ships from Batavia which apparently will come to Pulicat first were awaited daily. A Portuguese armada of frigates and fusts with one Diogo de Melo[4] as commander was expected any day from Goa.

Upper-merchant Jan Libenaar had gone to Golconda with one hundred marks of gold to buy diamonds with but returned without buying a single stone because none had been mined so far.[5]

The *Vrede* and *Medemblik* had returned from Arakan on 11 January 1625 with rice. These ships had also bought 400 slaves of which 100 had died, some in Arakan itself and some on the way. Letters from Arakan received with a Muslim ship had brought the news that the king of Arakan had captured 7,000 slaves in Bengal who were expected to arrive in Arakan any day. Hopefully, a good number of these would be bought by the six Dutch factors left there by the *Vrede* and the *Medemblik* mainly to buy slaves. There is not much more to do in Arakan than to buy slaves.

Last month a Danish ship from Tenasserim came to Trancquebar. They had sent some persons from Tenasserim to Siam with textiles mainly to buy Chinese goods with, some of which have been brought by this ship. They were planning to get their factors out of Tenasserim. They have been trying to earn profits on a sector which is thoroughly dominated by the Muslims. The latter can equip their ships much more inexpensively than the Dutch or the Danes and yet they barely manage to cover their costs. The Danes were also reported to have sent a mission to Pipli which in Ysbrantsz.'s view would be as disastrous as the one to Tenasserim involving losses.

Roeland Crappe, the Danish chief on the Coromandel coast, had been placing hindrances in the Company's trade and using all possible means to drive the Dutch out of the saltpetre trade. Puleceri, where the Company had been buying saltpetre and slaves, had been obtained on farm by the Danes from the lord of that place.[6] Because of the Danes, the Company had to pay higher prices. They had also been trying to persuade the lord of the place to grant them exclusive rights to buy saltpetre. If the Danes had not been in the Company's way, Ysbrantsz. would have been able to send over 1,000 *bahars* of saltpetre rather than the present lot of just 400 *bahars*. He would try his best to appropriate the saltpetre trade for the Company.

Once peace returned to the region and the coronation of the young king was accomplished, it would be highly advisable for the Company to farm Tegenapatam and Puleceri from their lords. In addition to saltpetre and slaves, a large amount of textiles such as *balatius*, *rambutins*, *tapi-sarassas* and *goulongs* could be purchased there for the southern quarters. The Danes already had their eyes on these textiles but they had completely run out of capital and were sitting idle. They had received no information about the ship they had sent to the Moluccas last year. Ysbrantsz. thought that the ship had been sent to the Moluccas to buy cloves from the Spaniands or others rather than to Makassar as the Danes claimed.

1. See document no. 42.
2. The reference is evidently to the wars among the local *nayaks* of the region.
3. See document no. 47.
4. In 1625, Diogo de Melo de Castro was sent as Captain-General of Sao Tome. He retained this position until 1634.
5. Jan Libenaar had reported that he had been to Golconda to exchange more than 200 marks of gold against *pagodas* but had not been able to do so because not a single merchant dared to come to him. For further details, see document no. 44.
6. The lord of the place here refers to the *nayak* of Gingi.

53. An extract from the invoice of the *Dordrecht* that left Surat for Holland in April 1625. V.O.C. 1084, ff.52-4 (Copy).

S.No.	*Item*	*Quantity*	*Value (in florins)*
1.	*Minatashis*	6,080 pieces (22 packets)	2,903:12:12
2.	Guinea cloth	1,000 pieces (16 packets)	5,053:10:2
3.	*Chautar*[1] Semiana	200 pieces (2 packets)	545:2:2
4.	*Khasa* de Bengal	600 pieces (6 packets)	4,981:18:0
5.	*Khasa Malseli*[2]	100 pieces (1 packet)	1,496:0:0
6.	Fine berty[2]	100 pieces (1 packet)	745:16:0
7.	Cotton	5,000 ponds (50 packets)	450:0:0
8.	Indigo Bayana brought from Agra	81,967 ponds (400 packets)	59,759:13:0
9.	Indigo Bayana bought at Surat	1,062½ ponds (5 packets)	816:0:0
10.	Indigo Sarkhej	261,247½ ponds (1,369 packets)	116,025:3:13
11.	Refined saltpetre	138,517½ ponds (438 packets)	12,206:3:12 (items 11–13)
12.	Refined saltpetre	8,604 ponds (32 vats)	
13.	Unrefined saltpetre	1,474 ponds (8 vats)	
14.	Red seal lac	793 ponds	461:11:10
15.	Raw silk from Persia	4,453 *maunds* (413 packets)	245,002:9:2
16.	Sal ammoniac	1,234 ponds (6 packets)	144:9:0
17.	Rhubarb	243½ ponds (2 cases)	512:14:0
		Total	f. 451.242:17:13[3]
	Cost by way of tolls, packing charges, freight, gifts etc.		10,301:18:4
		Grand Total	461,544:16:1[4]

1. *Chautar* was a plain white calico, usually of superior quality and much in demand for shirting. It was exported mainly to the Malay archipelago.
2. Not identified.
3. The total should in fact be f.451,104:3:5.
4. Accordingly, the grand total should in fact be f.461,406:1:9.

54. An extract from the invoice of the *Zuid Holland* sent from Surat to Batavia in April 1625. V.O.C. 1084, f.59 (Copy).

S.No.	Item	Quantity	Value (in florins)
1.	Ordinary black *baftas*	7,680 pieces (38 packets)	14,255:14:8
2.	Fine black *baftas*	7,138 pieces (35 packets)	21,445:6:5
3.	Ordinary white *baftas*	4,000 pieces (20 packets)	6,690:2:8
4.	Fine white *baftas*	800 pieces (4 packets)	2,705:0:0
5.	Fine black broad *baftas*	240 pieces (2 packets)	928:0:0
6.	Fine black broad *baftas*	120 pieces (1 packet)	299:5:0
7.	White broad *baftas*	240 pieces (2 packets)	644:14:0
8.	Fine blue *baftas*	160 pieces (1 packet)	706:2:10
9.	Extraordinarily fine black *baftas*	100 pieces (1 packet)	1,075:4:0
10.	Extraordinarily fine white *baftas*	100 pieces (1 packet)	2,425:6:10
11.	Ordinary red *chelas*	5,300 pieces (18 packets)	4,905:18:2
12.	Fine red *chelas*	8,500 pieces (28 packets)	10,395:13:0
13.	Ordinary black *chelas*	3,000 pieces (10 packets)	2,577:0:8
14.	Fine black *chelas*	1,940 pieces (6 packets)	2,332:5:10
15.	White *berams*	360 pieces (1 packet)	316:12:13
16.	Black *berams*	4,120 pieces (14 packets)	5,054:14:14
17.	Fine *cannikens*	7,240 pieces (18 packets)	4,161:17:3
18.	Ordinary *cannikens*	2,400 pieces (6 packets)	1,085:11:10
19.	Blue *cannikens*	400 pieces (1 packet)	184:0:0
20.	Guinea clothes	1,480 pieces (37 packets)	7,474:3:7
21.	Small *dhotis Dholka*	2,800 pieces (28 packets)	2,406:5:0
22.	Broad *dhotis Dholka*	700 pieces (7 packets)	1,098:15:0

23.	*Dhotis* for sails	6,000 *gaz* (5 packets)	349:19:2
24.	*Alcatifs*	19 pieces (1 packet)	421:4:0
25.	*Seribafs*	200 pieces (1 packet)	1,385:15:0
26.	Deccani clothes	200 pieces (5 packets)	446:5:0
27.	*Bethilles* for flags	560 pieces (2 packets)	966:0:0
28.	*Tapichindaes*	8,340 pieces (10 packets)	2,532:17:15
29.	*Chintz*	600 pieces (2 packets)	788:9:11
30.	*Minatashis* as a sample	300 pieces (1 packet)	145:6:4
31.	White *cannikens*	800 pieces (2 packets)	425:5:0
32.	*Alacha madafons*[1]	1,320 pieces (11 packets)	1,807:13:0
33.	*Taffechelas platiados*	250 pieces (1 packet)	1,667:2:3
34.	Black *cangans*	400 pieces (2 packets)	568:19:11
35.	White *cangans*	1,000 pieces (5 packets)	1,200:3:6
36.	*Tricandia*	2,100 pieces (6 packets)	3,471:19:1
37.	*Tapi sarassa*	1,000 pieces (1 packet)	583:2:8
38.	Clothes from Patna as a sample	142 pieces (1 packet)	466:11:4
39.	*Dungarees*	1,500 pieces (6 packets)	1,676:11:4
40.	Negro clothes	420 pieces (2 packets)	314:1:4
41.	*Asmanis*	800 pieces (2 packets)	362:5:0
42.	Red *chelas*	200 pieces	231:11:4
43.	*Tricandia*	100 pieces (1 packet)	
44.	Ropes	3 pieces	726:0:0
45.	Gun-powder	4,269 ponds	711:16:0
46.	Wheat	300 candy	3,843:0:0
47.	Slaves	6	1,276:11:14
48.	Red lac, etc.	–	1,196:19:0
49.	War ammunition	–	5,662:10:0
50.	Stones	8	11:2:0
		Total	f.127,366:5:13[2]

1. *Alachas* and *madafons* are two different varieties of textiles. It is not quite clear why these two appear together.
2. The total should in fact be f.126,416:3:7.

55. An extract from the invoice of the *Nieuw Bantam* sent from Surat to Batavia in April 1625. V.O.C. 1085, f.185 (Copy).

S.No.	*Item*	*Quantity*	*Value (in florins)*
1.	Black *berams*	4,274 pieces (14 packets)	5,305
2.	*Asmanis*	4,000 pieces (10 packets)	1,937
3.	Black *cangans*	3,600 pieces (18 packets)	5,168
4.	Fine black *baftas*	4,440 pieces (22 packets)	13,655
5.	White *cangans*	5,200 pieces (26 packets)	6,335
6.	Ordinary black *baftas*	18,010 pieces (89 packets)	33,935
7.	*Alacha Modafons*	1,380 (11 packets)	2,046
8.	Negro clothes	9,220 (38 packets)	6,187
9.	White *cannikens*	1,200 (3 packets)	667
10.	Broad white *baftas*	560 (4 packets)	1,999
11.	White *berams*	2,700 (9 packets)	3,483
12.	*Tricandia*	1,200 (3 packets)	546
13.	Fine broad white *baftas*	120 (1 packet)	489
14.	Broad black *baftas*	1,920 (17 packets)	7,003
15.	*Dungarees*	2,100 (8 packets)	2,099
16.	*Cannikens*	19,754 (49 packets)	10,758
17.	Guinea cloth	520 (12 packets)	2,604
18.	Chintz	3,035 (9 packets)	4,640
19.	*Minatashis* (as a sample)	300 (1 packet)	145
20.	*Dhotis* for sails	3,000 *gaz* (3 packets)	210
21.	Dholka broad *dhotis*	100 (1 packet)	151
22.	*Tapichindaes*	2,000 (1 packet)	764
23.	*Taffechelas platiados*	250 (1 packet)	1,167
24.	Green *taffechelas*	400 (2 packets)	737
25.	*Patolas*	804 (2 packets)	4,191
26.	Red *chelas*	19,000 (63 packets)	20,583
27.	Fine white *baftas*	1,400 (7 packets)	4,862
28.	Ordinary white *baftas*	3,202 (16 packets)	6,038
29.	Black *chelas*	12,080 (40 packets)	10,211

30.	Persian silk stuffs	75 (1 packet)	610
31.	Horses	3	467
32.	Rose water	-	793
33.	*Alcatifs* from Agra	2 (1 packet)	51
Note: The value of *taffechelas platiados* was underestimated by			500
		Total	f. 160,334[1]

1. The total in fact should be f.160,336.

56. An extract from the invoice of the *Weesp* sent from Surat to Holland in April 1625. V.O.C. 1085, f.188 (Copy).

S.No.	*Item*	*Quantity*	*Value (in florins)*
1.	Indigo Bayana	40,983 ponds (200 packets)	30,024
2.	Indigo Sarkhej	42,336 ponds (224 packets)	23,819
3.	Refined saltpetre	60,000 ponds (264 packets)	3,310
4.	Sal ammoniac	378 ponds (2 packets)	48
5.	Borax	1,638 ponds (8 packets)	257
6.	Persian silk	2,568¼ *shahi maunds* (151 packets)	41,241
7.	Cotton	600 ponds (10 packets)	50
8.	Textiles	46 pieces (1 packet)	1,663
		Total (860 packets)	f. 200,412

57. An extract from the invoice of the *Leeuwin* sent from Masulipatnam to Holland, 23 May 1625. V.O.C. 1084, f.176 (Not stated whether original or copy).*

S.No.	*Item*	*Quantity*	*Value (in florins)*
1.	Cotton yarn	55,349 ponds	25,338:13:4
2.	Guinea cloth bleached	7,929 pieces	37,274:3:4

3.	*Salampuris*	5,072 pieces	20,991:19:4
4.	*Parcallas*	2,797 pieces	5,910:10:12
5.	*Bethilles*	1,831 pieces	10,556:14:2
6.	*Muris*	2,996 pieces	12,351:15:4
7.	White clothes	176 pieces	358:18:8
8.	*Seprados*[1]	100 pieces	546:17:8
9.	*Chelas*	68 pieces	321:2:8
10.	*Dungarees* for packing	2,437 pieces	1,218:10:0
11.	Planks for saltpetre cases	2,407 pieces	566:16:6
12.	Iron for fixing the planks	720 pieces	25:10:6
13.	Cotton	394 ponds	67:10:0
14.	Saltpetre	224,375 ponds	22,114:19:14
15.	Gunpowder	730 ponds	127:15:0
16.	Indigo	21,017 ponds	9,717:2:0
	Costs		8,212:16:3
	Tolls at 4 per cent		3,800:0:0
		Total	f.159,501:14:7

* The details of the cargo are available on ff. 177-89.

1. Not identified.

58. Goeree and Libenaar at Masulipatnam to the Directors at Amsterdam, May 1625. V.O.C. 1084, ff.164-4vo (Original).

A copy of Masulipatnam's last letter to the Directors dated 3 October 1624[1] was enclosed. Cargo worth f.159,502 was being sent with the *Leeuwin*.

The right to trade with the Company had been publicly farmed out to Lingayya, Ramanna and Coutour, each of whom were obliged to pay to the authorities 3,000 *pagodas* per annum for carrying on the bulk of the trade with the Masulipatnam factory. Besides, other small items had also been farmed out. The merchant who supplied gunnies to the Company was obliged to give 300 *pagodas* for the privilege. Similarly, other items such as the right to supply victuals to the factory had also been farmed out. From this one could see in what poor state the trade of the Company at Masulipatnam was.

The financial position of the Masulipatnam factory was as follows:

Liability towards Batavia in the form of capital in hand at the time of the closure of books by Van Uffelen	f.503,387
Goods received with the Wapen van Rotterdam	f.132,311
Goods received with the *Schoonhoven* from Batavia	f.44,373
Goods received with the *Leeuwin* from Holland	f.315,409
Total	f.995,480

As against this, the following entries are on the credit side:

Cargo sent to Batavia with the *Wapen van Enkhuizen*	f.243,919
Cargo sent to Batavia with the *Wapen van Rotterdam*	f.234,049
Cargo sent to Holland with the *Schoonhoven* in addition to the cargo this ship carried from Surat	f.71,022
Non-recoverable bad debts	f.34,569
Annual tolls of 3,000 *pagodas*	f.12,750
The amount owed to the Masulipatnam factory by the merchants Pera, Ramanna, Ayna and Coutour to whom the right to trade with the Company had been farmed out[2]	f.15,483
(There was no chance of recovery of this amount which represents the value of the Company's goods seized by the *havaldar* of Masulipatnam from these merchants in 1624)	
Amount owed to the Company by Mir Kamal-al-Din which is unlikely to be recovered	f.2,520
Value of the cargo being sent to Holland with the *Leeuwin*	f.159,502
Total	f.773,814

Masulipatnam would thus be left with a capital of f.221,666. This amount would be divided among the factories at Pulicat, Petapuli, Palicol, Draksharama and Arakan. The merchants with the right to supply goods at Masulipatnam will also have to be provided funds from this amount. Masulipatnam hoped to receive timely financial assistance from Holland or Batavia.

1. See document no. 41 where the date mentioned is 4 October 1624.
2. Earlier in the document, the names of the merchants mentioned to whom the farming rights had been given were Lingayya, Ramanna and Coutour.

59. Ysbrantsz. at Pulicat to Governor-General De Carpentier at Batavia, 14 June 1625. V.O.C. 1085, ff.205-8 (Copy).

The *Wapen van Rotterdam* had left for Batavia on 21 January 1625. The *Leeuwin* had arrived at Pulicat from Masulipatnam on 29 May 1625 with a cargo worth f.159,502 for Holland.

The procurement of saltpetre at Tegenapatam was proceeding poorly because of the continuing wars among the *nayaks* of the surrounding areas. The Hindus had equipped their forts well with saltpetre and its price had gone up from 12-13 rials per *bahar* in 1621 to 14-15 rials in 1625. Earlier when the Company had a factory at Tirupapaliyur,[1] saltpetre used to be procured there at 6½ to 7 rials per *bahar*. Once peace returned to Tegenapatam, it might be possible to procure this item at the old price. Reportedly, the *nayak* of Tanjore was exhausted and was seeking peace with the *nayak* of Madura. Negotiations were going on at Trichanapali with the young king of Karnataka, Etiraja and others.

Slaves would have to be procured at Arakan because no more of them were available around Tegenapatam and Pulicat. After the departure of the *Vrede* and the *Medemblik* from Arakan, another 100 slaves had been bought there. The king of Arakan was reportedly still in Bengal with his armada and had captured 7,000 slaves there. These were expected to arrive at Arakan soon and the Dutch factors hoped to be able to buy a large number of them. As soon as more ships arrived at Pulicat from Batavia, the *Tenasserim* would be sent to Arakan.

Pulicat had sent the *Vrede* with a cargo worth f.93,122 for Batavia to Masulipatnam to pick-up some more cargo there. Adriaen Goeree died at Masulipatnam on 30 May 1625. There had been a large scale mortality there because of some kind of a plague.

The Portuguese Captain Don Diogo de Melo had arrived at Sao Tome on 18 May with 5 frigates and 14 *thonys*.[2] Captain Manual de Vries[3] had come with de Melo and had been given the title of the Captain of Pulicat by the Viceroy of Goa. Some notable persons of Pulicat had asked Captain de Vries to lay a seige of Pulicat and had offered him 3,000 to 4,000 Hindu soldiers to be used together with the European soldiers both on water and land to accomplish this job. They had further offered to compensate the Portuguese for the cost of the seige. After the fort had been conquered, it was to be handed over to the king with everything in it. In this state of affairs, Ysbrantz. was unable to leave Pulicat and would leave the matters at Masulipatnam to be handled by Libenaar.

The great Aya[4] or general of the *nayak* of Tanjore had looted Tegenapatam and burnt Tirupapaliyur on 20 May 1625. The Company's goods were secured on the *Vrede* which was anchored at the mouth of the river there. The Company only lost 80 bags of saltpetre worth about 500 rials.

The *Tenasserim* and the *Bonne Remedie* together with the sloops had returned from Point Galle where they had been sent for cruising together with the *Medemblik*. They had burnt some *sampans* and brought back a small ship with them which belonged to a Hindu merchant of Nagapattinam and had returned from Aceh. The goods carried by this ship were sold for f.3,750.

In order that the weavers and the painters were kept in continuous employment, it was essential that the factory had adequate funds at all times. Financial assistance was, therefore, needed immediately from Batavia or Holland. Pulicat had about 1,500 rials worth of Japanese silver but in view of its poor quality it will have to be sold at a substantial loss.

The 26 Muslims and *kafirs*[5] who had been captured[6] were being sent to Batavia. Pulicat would like to be provided with two yachts on a permanent basis.

1. See Om Prakash (ed.), *The Dutch Factories in India, 1617-1623*, document no. 40, p. 67.

2. A *thony* was a small boat, sometimes made of a tree stem.
3. Not identified.
4. The *aya* was the chief officer of the *nayak* of Gingi who had allowed the Dutch to settle at Tegenapatam. The *aya* was thought to be even more powerful than the *nayak* himself.
5. A *kafir* was an infidel and a non-believer in Islam.
6. These persons would seem to have been captured from the seized ship.

60. Libenaar at Masulipatnam to Governor-General De Carpentier at Batavia, 26 June 1625. V.O.C. 1085, ff.215-17vo (Copy).

The *Leeuwin* left for Holland on 23 May with a cargo worth f.159,502. The invoice of the ship was enclosed.[1]

On his return to Masulipatnam in April 1625 from a cruising trip, Libenaar found things in great disorder. Adriaen Willemsz. Goeree had been in trouble with the qazi[2] to whose house he had gone in a state of drunkenness inviting the charge of attempted murder. *Kotwal* Lingayya had sent a complaint to the king of Golconda who had ordered the recovery of a sum of 3,000 *pagodas* from the Dutch chief. Goeree was put aboard a ship where he stayed for three weeks. But he kept on drinking there and died three or four days after coming back to the factory.[3]

This letter was being sent with the *Vrede* with a cargo worth f.150,919 of which Pulicat had supplied goods worth f.93,132.[4] The shortage of cash prevented the procurement of more cargo. The *havaldar* of Masulipatnam had been harrassing the suppliers of the Company. He had kept in captivity for 6 to 7 days the three merchants, Lingayya, Ramanna and Coutour to whom the right to trade with the Company had been farmed out. They had been tortured and a sum of 3,000 *pagodas* extorted from them.

Because of the shortage of funds, the factors were obliged to sit idle. If funds had been available, the factors at Draksharama and Palicol could have bought 1,500-2,000 pieces of Guinea cloth each month. Because of the lack of demand from the Company, the weavers had moved to other jobs.

Masulipatnam had sold cloves at 10½ to 11 *pagodas* per *maund*, nutmeg at 80 to 85 *pagodas* per *bahar*, *rompen*[5] at 40 to 45 *pagodas* per *bahar* and mace at 11½ *pagodas* per *maund*. Lead had been sold at 10½ *pagodas* per *bahar* while good quality sandalwood had fetched 85 to 90 *pagodas* per *bahar*. Since stocks of camphor, ivory and benzoin were still available, further supplies of these items were not to be sent.

The rials of eight which used to be sold at 9 *fanums* per piece now fetched only 8 *fanums*. A variety of Japanese silver called berg silver had to be sold at a big loss but most of this was borne by the merchants to whom payment for textiles supplied was made through this medium.

Masulipatnam would not be able to meet the Directors' order for diamonds. The mine was operated directly on the private account of the king and was closed for the merchants.[6] As a result, diamonds were nearly as expensive in Masulipatnam as in Holland. These were bought mainly by the merchants from Aceh and Gujarat.

The ambassador of the great Mughal[7] as well as the factors of Prince Khurram who had stayed in Golconda for some time had left about 4 to 5 weeks ago with a large treasure consisting of diamonds and gold. This was likely to become an annual pattern so that there was little chance of the mine being reopened.

1. See document no. 57.
2. The *qazi* was the dispenser of justice.
3. In document no. 59, the cause of Goeree's death was stated to be some kind of a plague.
4. See document no. 59.
5. *Rompen* was the unripe variety of nutmeg that had fallen off from the trees prematurely.
6. See Om Prakash (ed.), *The Dutch Factories in India, 1617-1623*, p. 239.
7. The Mughal emperor used to send an ambassador to Golconda to claim a share in the income from the diamond mine.

61. Governor-General De Carpentier at Batavia to Ysbrantsz. at Masulipatnam, 26 July 1625. V.O.C. 1085, ff.123-30 (Copy).*

The *Wapen van Enkhuizen* and the *Wapen van Rotterdam* had reached Batavia safely. But the large scale mortality among the slaves in Coromandel had been compounded by the death of another 93 of them on the trip to Batavia further increasing the cost of the surviving slaves per unit.

The Directors had informed Batavia that they intended to send a capital of f.100,000 to Coromandel in gold besides the goods asked for. This amount, together with the cargo worth f.163,449 including 40,000 rials of eight being sent with the *Edam*, ought to suffice for the procurement of goods for Holland and the Indies, particularly if spices and other goods had a good sale in Coromandel.

According to Batavia's calculations, the financial position of the Coromandel factories would be as follows:

Capital in hand as per Van Uffelen's books	f.503,382[1]
Cash and goods sent from Batavia with the *Wapen van Rotterdam*	f.132,311
Cash and goods sent from Batavia with the *Schoonhoven*	f.44,373
Cash and goods sent from Holland with the *Leeuwin*	f.315,908[2]
Value of the jewels from the seized *Don Antonio Manuel*	f.3,705[3]
Value of 299 pieces of lead (57,292 ponds[4]) sent with the *Wapen van Enkhuizen* in 1623	f.3,875
Cash and goods sent with the *Delfshaven* from Holland in1624	f.130,000[5]
Cash and goods being sent from Batavia with the *Edam*	f.163,449
Profit likely to be earned on goods sold in Coromandel	f.250,000
Total	f.1,547,003

The entries on the credit side would be as follows:

Value of goods sent to Batavia with the *Wapen van Enkhuizen*	f.243,919
Value of goods sent to Holland with the *Schoonhoven*	f.71,022
Value of goods sent to Batavia with the *Wapen van Rotterdam*	f.233,601
Value of 5,000 *pagodas* extorted from Van Uffelen, at f.4¼ per *pagoda*	f.21,250
Value of 11,000 *pagodas* extorted from the Company's merchants which were expected to be recovered only slowly	f.46,750
Bad debts at Masulipatnam	f.10,194
War ammunition, etc., in the effects of late Van Uffelen which could not be treated as Company's effects	f.12,591
Bad debts at Pulicat according to Dedel's report	f.36,000
Cost of establishments on the Coromandel coast for 2 years—1 February 1624 to 1 February 1626	f.100,000
Value of the cargo to be sent to Holland with the *Leeuwin*	f.175,000
Total	f.950,327

Coromandel would thus be left with f.596,676 worth of capital which ought to be used as follows: goods worth f.150,000 to be sent to Holland with the *Delfshaven* and worth f.300,000 to Batavia. The remaining sum of f.146,676 was to be invested in the procurement of clothes for the southern quarters unless it was considered necessary to invest some funds in saltpetre to keep the Company's participation in trade in this item alive.

The Directors had agreed to send the necessary amount of capital to Coromandel, Surat and Persia for meeting their orders from these places. Coromandel was, therefore, to procure indigo, cotton textiles, diamonds and other goods for Holland in accordance with the funds received from Holland. The funds received from Batavia were to be invested in procuring goods for the Indies and first priority was to be given to textiles for Java.

Batavia had asked for 450 packets of Guinea cloth but if Coromandel had insufficient funds, only 300 packets might be supplied. The Guinea cloth sent to Holland from Surat with the *Heusden* was sold there at 12½ *groot* per *ell*. It was, therefore, necessary to meet the orders for this item. Till further orders, Coromandel was not to supply *taffechelas* de Golconda, *taffechelas* de Bengale, *taffechelas* de Narsapur, the so-called Siam clothes as well as shirts and trousers. However, the cloth needed to manufacture the last two items at Batavia was to be sent. Varieties such as *patta Malay*, *samudra muris* and black *salalus* sent to the Moluccas and Amboina were also not to be sent because there were adequate stocks. Funds were to be invested in the varieties for Java and in fine *bethilles*, *chavonis*, *salampuris* and *muris*. These were to be provided pro rata to the availability of capital.

The textiles manufactured in Tegenapatam and further south were found to be quite reasonable. The procurement of these varieties as well as those normally manufactured at Masulipatnam was to be continued. If the weavers were instructed properly, the quality of the textiles manufactured in the south could be brought to the level of those manufactured at Masulipatnam. Once this was achieved, it would be possible to abandon Masulipatnam and escape the tyranny the Company was subjected to there. In the meantime, steps justified by the Company's resources were to be taken to obtain redress at Masulipatnam with care being taken to ensure that advance news regarding such steps did not reach the king of Golconda.

In view of the great demand for opium this year, Batavia could have earned a large profit. But none was received from either Coromandel or Surat. If available, Coromandel was to send 300-400 *cattys*[6] of good quality opium.

For populating the Company's territories and for securing them better, a large number of slaves were needed. So if enough slaves were not available in Pulicat and Tegenapatam, they should be procured in Arakan. Batavia's information was that thousands of Bengal slaves could be bought in Dianga[7] if only the king of Arakan would allow them to be carried out of his kingdom.

Batavia was in desperate need of rice which was needed for the ships and the forts. Last year only a small quantity was received from Java and this year none was received. Coromandel was, therefore, to send as much of rice of local, Arakanese or any other origin as the ships could carry (even 1,000 *lasts* if possible). In the past, Jacob Dedel had not sent rice from Coromandel because it was 16 per cent more expensive than usual. But in future rice was to be procured irrespective of the cost.

On being asked if they could not make do with the indigo sent from Surat, the Directors had replied that since the best quality Coromandel indigo rendered a good profit in Holland,[8] its procurement was not to be neglected either, particularly because one never knew when the Company's trade at Surat might be interrupted the way that at Masulipatnam had been.

Sugar had afforded a good profit in both Holland and Persia. The Directors had, therefore, recommended that a good amount of this item be procured in Bengal and China. The Bengal sugar could be collected by a ship sent from Coromandel. It was learnt that a large quantity of sugar could be bought at Balasore and Pipli at 5 to 6 rials of eight per 170 Dutch ponds working out at 1-2/3 *stuivers* per pond. The Directors had complained about the dampness in the Bengali and the Chinese sugar.[9] Care must be taken to pack it properly to prevent this.

Regarding the pepper trade at Trancquebar and the surrounding areas, steps were to be taken to ensure that the Danes and other Europeans were not able to buy this spice there cheaply and compete with the Company in Europe.

The Danes had equipped a big ship and a yacht in Denmark to be sent to the Indies. The French had asked the Directors to carry their goods and men to the Indies on freight and might try to get there on their own. As far as the English were concerned, only one big ship and a yacht had come to Batavia. Another four English ships had gone to Surat. The massacre at Amboina[10] had caused great discontent and bitterness in England. The English left Batavia in December 1624 and went over to an island in the Sunda strait. But in view of the large scale mortality there, they asked for help and were allowed to return to Batavia in June.

Ysbrantsz. is appointed the new chief of the Coromandel establishment for a period of three years at a salary of 200 guilders per month. It would be best for him to stay in Pulicat and let another factor look after the factory at Masulipatnam.

The *Nieuw Bantam* and the *Zuid Holland* had arrived from Surat at Batavia in June 1625 with 829 packets of textiles.[11] The *Dordrecht* and the *Weesp* had been sent from Surat to Holland with 412 bales of Persian silk together with a good amount of indigo, saltpetre and cotton.[12] The Company's affairs were in an extremely good state both in the Mughal empire and in Persia.

Batavia was very short of gunpowder both on land and on the ships. Some sulphur was being sent to Coromandel for making gunpowder with.

The English Company factors at Batavia had provided an attestation (copy enclosed)[13] by Thomas Mills and other English factors at Masulipatnam regarding the murder of an Englishman Arthur Baker by Jacob Coper,[14] the ex-captain of the *Wapen van Rotterdam*. Ysbrantsz. was to find out the true facts.

The free merchants at Batavia had complained that they had not been allowed to buy textiles from the indigenous merchants nor had they been supplied from the Company's warehouses. They ought to be allowed to deal with the indigeneous merchants directly and whenever possible also supplied goods from the Company's warehouses.

Batavia would like to know what success Libenaar had at Point de Galle in capturing Portuguese vessels. If he could be spared, he was to be sent to Batavia to make his report to the Governor-General personally.

* An exact copy is available in the *Bataviaasch Uitgaande Brievenboek*, V.O.C. 852, ff.97vo-105vo.

1. See document no. 58 where the value indicated is f.503,387.
2. In document no. 58, the value of the cargo given is f.315,409.
3. In document no. 59, this value is given as f.3,750.
4. De Carpentier's letter of 21 September 1623 to Masulipatnam had noted that Batavia had sent 70,113 ponds of lead with the *Wapen van Enkhuizen* (see Om Prakash (ed.), *Dutch Factories in India, 1617-1623,* p. 273).
5. In document no. 46, the cash component of this was said to have been f.100,000.
6. The *catty* was a weight used in China and was introduced by the Chinese into the archipelago. The Chinese name is *kin* or *chin*. The word kate is Malayo-Javanese. It is equal to 16 taels, i.e. 1-2/3 lbs. avoirdupois or 625 grammes. One hundred *cattys* made a *picul*.
7. Before the rise of Chittagong, Dianga was the chief port of north Arakan. Its latitude is 22°.50'N and longitude 92°E.
8. See document no. 46.
9. See document no. 46.

10. In this notorious episode, which became something of a landmark in Anglo-Dutch relations for a long time, the English factors resident in the Dutch fort at Amboina under the agreement of 1619, were charged with conspiracy to seize it. They were convicted on the basis of confessions obtained by torture and many of them were executed.
11. The *Zuid Holland* and the *Nieuw Bantam* had sailed from Surat for Batavia on 22 April 1625. See document nos. 54 and 55.
12. The *Dordrecht* and the *Weesp* had left Surat for Holland on 28 April 1625. See document nos. 53 and 56.
13. This document is not available in the Company's archives.
14. Jacob Gerritsz. Coper (or Cooper) came to the East Indies in 1618 and played an active role in the conquest of Banda in 1620. In May 1621, he was the skipper of the *Amsterdam* and in March 1623 involved in the Amboina affair. He came to Masulipatnam some time after 1623 with the *Wapen van Rotterdam*. Shortly thereafter, he repatriated to Holland. In March 1633, he returned as skipper of the *Nassau*. Between August 1636 and June 1637, he took part in the blockade of Goa with fifteen ships. In January 1638, he went to Amboina and in mid-1638 to Batavia. He took part as commander in the siege of Malacca from 15 November 1640. He died there on 3 January 1641.

62. Commission given by Governor-General De Carpentier at Batavia to Ysbrantsz., the new head of the Coromandel factories, on 28 July 1625. V.O.C. 1085, f.130 (Copy).*

Since both Van Uffelen and Jacob Dedel had died, Marten Ysbrantsz. had been appointed the Director of the Coromandel coast factories. He would be in-charge of the Company's forts, offices, ships and personnel in the area and be responsible for the conduct of the Company's trade there.

* A copy, though not exact, is available in the *Bataviaasch Uitgaande Brievenboek*, V.O.C. 852, f.106.

63. Commission given by Governor-General De Carpentier at Batavia to Commander Frederik Kistjens[1] going to Surat and Persia with three ships, 13 August 1625. V.O.C. 1085, ff.150-50vo. (Not stated whether original or copy.)*

[This is a usual appointment letter instructing Kistjens to call at various ports].

* An exact copy is available in the *Bataviaasch Uitgaande Brievenboek*, V.O.C. 852, ff.131vo-2. The date mentioned in this document, however, is 14 August 1625.

1. Frederik Kistjens came to the Indies as an under-merchant in 1612 and was sent to Johor on 4 May 1613. On 22 September 1621, he went as an upper-merchant on the fleet of defence to Malabar. In April 1624, he commanded the *Haerlem* to Aceh and Malacca. During the first half of 1625, he commanded some ships to Bantam. He returned from the trip to Surat and Persia on 25 June 1626. He was sent on a similar trip again between 6 August 1626 and 6 June 1627. During the siege of Batavia in 1628, he commanded troops. He was chosen as a free burgher in May 1629. In September 1630, he held the rank of treasurer-general. He died in 1631 or 1632.

64. Governor-General De Carpentier at Batavia to Van den Broecke at Surat, 14 August 1625. V.O.C.1085, ff.135-9vo (Copy).*

The quality of the textiles received with the *Nieuw Bantam* and the *Zuid Holland* which had arrived at Batavia on 26 and 28 June respectively was very good. This ought to be kept up for the current year as well. The coir ropes sent from Surat were also found to be of good quality but were somewhat more expensive than those from Coromandel.

Three properly armed and well provisioned big ships—the *Goede Fortuin*, the *Nieuw Bantam* and the *Bear*[1]—were being sent with cash and goods including the amount of spices asked for by Van den Broecke. In addition, Surat would get three ships from Holland.

The Directors desired that the Surat factors maintained cordial relations with their English counterparts without compromising the Company's interests in any way. The possibility of co-operation was also to be explored in the matter of the procurement of indigo, in resisting the authorities' attempts at imposing monopolies in various items and in other areas. Care was to be taken that the Company did not get involved in any way in any problems the English might have had with the authorities.

Notwithstanding the fact that the proceeds from the sale of the spices and other goods being sent were likely to be adequate to buy textiles for the southern quarters, cash was also being sent so that procurement was not hindered in any way.

According to Batavia's calculations, the financial position at Surat would be as follows:

Sale Value of the goods at Surat and Agra	f.120,000
Value of the effects in Persia	f.355,000
Surat would be getting with the three ships from Holland a capital of f.600,000 in gold and silver in addition to the goods asked for by Surat	f.635,000
Cash, spices and other goods worth f.148,905 being sent from Batavia with three ships would fetch at Surat at least	f.390,000
Total	f.1,500,000
As against this, textiles orders from Batavia would need	f.230,000
The orders from Holland for goods from Surat and Persia would need	f.770,000
Total	f.1,000,000

Surat would thus be left with f.500,000 which could be used for meeting the establishment costs for the current year and for the procurement of goods at Persia and Surat for next year till such time as more capital arrived there from Holland. Persia must be provided with at least as much capital as last year and somewhat more if that could be done without injuring the Surat trade too much.

In view of the fact that Batavia did not have a large stock of pepper and would need a good part of it for the autumn shipment to Holland, only 90 *lasts* of pepper were being sent to Surat, all of which was to be sent on to Persia.

If enough spices could be sold at a good profit in Surat and Persia, Van den Broecke was not to bother about the Mocha trade for the time being. But if for some reason Surat was not able to sell spices profitably, a ship was to be sent to Mocha with spices. The ship could also carry as much freight cargo as possible both on its outward as well as return voyages. Safi Khan and other notable persons of Surat were to be requested to get the Company's goods and factors at Mocha released by the *badshah* of Yemen and the Company granted permission to trade there without hindrance. If the people of Dabhol were of no help in the matter of the Mocha trade, an emissary was to be sent to Mocha to bring back the Company's factors and goods. However, should the *badshah* so insist, a few factors of a low rank could be left there with resources just adequate to maintain themselves there. In case the *badshah* referred the emissary to Constantinople (as had been done in the case of De Milde), the representative of the States-General at Constantinople should be approached to assist in securing restitution of the Company's goods and securing permission for trade at Mocha.

The request by the merchants of Surat to be permitted to send their goods to Batavia in the Company's or in their own ships could not be acceded to because it would be prejudicial to the interests of the Company besides being unfair to the free merchants of Batavia who are not permitted to go to Surat for trade.

Spices were not to be sold at an unusually low price simply to raise capital for the procurement of textiles. In the event of a shortage of funds, local borrowing at 1 per cent per month ought to be resorted to. Such borrowing was to be done three to four months prior to the arrival of the ships because while the additional costs of interest would only amount to 3 to 4 per cent, the saving in cost might be as much as 25 per cent.

Batavia was surprised that the factors at Persia had allowed the Persian ambassador to go to Holland in one of the Company's ships with a large amount of silk. Prior permission of Batavia ought to have been obtained in this behalf.

The outcome of the visit of upper-merchant Vapour to the court of the Mughal emperor was awaited.

25 to 30 *lasts* of good quality wheat and as much of rice as could be carried by the ships without adversely affecting the transportation of the important return cargo were to be sent to Batavia.

* An exact copy is available in the *Bataviaasch Uitgaande Brievenboek*, V.O.C. 852, ff.112-17.

1. The *Bear* had been captured by the Dutch from the English at Tiku in 1619. See Om Prakash (ed.), *The Dutch Factories in India, 1617-1623*, p. 162, note 2.

65. Instructions by Governor-General De Carpentier at Batavia for the Commander and the Council of the ships the *Goede Fortuin, Nieuw Bantam* and the *Bear* going to Surat and Persia, 14 August 1625. V.O.C. 1085, ff.147vo-50 (Copy).

The commander of these three ships would be Frederik Kistjens. The coast of Surat was not to be reached until after the full moon of September because it was dangerous to do so before that.

The English factors at Batavia had been discussing with De Carpentier and the Batavia Council the possibility of making a joint voyage from Surat to Persia. Batavia's willingness in this regard had been mentioned in detail in De Carpentier's letter to Van den Broecke.

In order to avoid any dispute with the English at Hormuz over the question of tolls (from which the Company had been exempted by Shah Abbas but which the English were insisting on charging from the Company at half the usual rate), no cargo was to be unloaded there but taken on to Gombroon or to any other safe port. At the time of unloading the cargo, proper care was to be taken that no damage was inflicted by a Portuguese vessel.

In order to increase the Company's profits and to improve its image in both Surat and Persia, Batavia approved of the transportation of the personnel and goods of the merchants of these two places by the Company's vessels.

66. Governor-General De Carpentier at Batavia to Van den Broecke at Surat, 12 September 1625. V.O.C. 1085, ff.153-3vo (Copy).*

Cargo of the total value of f.55,519 consisting of 16,000 rials of eight in cash, 20,000 ponds cloves, 20,000 ponds nutmeg, 30 bags of mace and 14 cases of camphor was being sent with the *Hollandia*, the *Oranje* and the *Mauritius*. These ships together with the *Gouden Leeuw* and the *Walcheren* were to be sent on to Holland with the return cargo and any excess spices. In view of the large availability of indigo and cotton at Surat, there ought to be no problem in finding an adequate cargo for these ships.

If a ship could be spared, it should be sent to Mocha with spices and freight cargo. It could also try to inflict damage on the Portuguese.

Herman van Speult,[1] a member of the Batavia Council was being sent with the present shipment. He would be the in-charge of the Company's affairs at Surat during his stay there. He would also inspect the factories there and would return to Holland with these ships.

* An exact copy is available in the *Bataviaasch Uitgaande Brievenboek*, V.O.C. 852, ff.135-6.

1. Herman van Speult came to the East Indies with the fleet of Gerard Reynst. He was an upper-merchant at Amboina in 1615 and director in 1617 and later lieutenant-governor. He succeeded Steven van den Haghen as governor of Amboina on 4 April 1619. He became a member of the Batavia Council on 23 March 1620.

67. Governor-General De Carpentier at Batavia to Commander Kistjens at Surat, 12 September 1625. V.O.C. 1085, f.153vo. (Not stated whether original or copy.)*

The *Oranje*, the *Mauritius* and the *Hollandia* were being sent to Surat with a view to augment the Dutch power there. Governor Herman van Speult was travelling with these ships.

* An exact copy is available in the *Bataviaasch Uitgaande Brievenboek*, V.O.C. 852, ff.136-6vo.

68. Governor-General De Carpentier at Batavia to Ysbrantsz. at Masulipatnam, 24 September 1625. V.O.C. 1085, ff.159vo-62 (Copy).*

Batavia had sent a cargo worth f.163,449 with the *Edam* to Coromandel on 26 June 1625. The *Coningh David* was now carrying a cargo worth f.70,923 consisting of 20,000 rials of eight in cash, 15,000 ponds cloves, 20,000 ponds nutmeg and 100 bags of mace. Batavia hoped that this capital, in addition to what Coromandel would be receiving from Holland with the *Delfshaven*, would be enough to meet the orders from Holland and Batavia, particularly if the spices sold well.

The Directors had decided that partly for reasons of safety, return cargo to Holland will all be sent via Batavia. Goods for Holland ought, therefore, to be sent to Batavia in time for the homeward bound ships leaving in November and December.

Since the departure of the *Edam* from Batavia, the *Vrede* had arrived from Coromandel on 6 September with Ysbrantsz'.s letter of 14 June 1625[1] and Libenaar's of 26 July. The cargo received with the *Vrede* was found in good condition.

Coromandel's orders for spices had already been dispatched with the *Edam*. If the lot being sent currently was considered excessive, it could be sent on to Holland.

Since it was unlikely that Coromandel would have been able to send more than one ship to Arakan to fetch rice, it was decided to send the indigenously built *Arend* of 120 *lasts* directly to Arakan from here with instructions to buy rice and slaves and return directly to Batavia. Merchant Cramerheijn[2] had been provided with 40,000 rials in cash which would be debited to the account of the Coromandel establishment.

If possible, a ship or a yacht ought to be sent to the Bay of Bengal for procuring sugar and textiles. Sugar was useful for both Persia and Holland. Saltpetre could also be bought in Bengal which could render a good profit.

On the recommendation of the Council of Church, the Batavia Council had decided to depute Jan Harmansz. Folynius[3] to Coromandel as priest. He is travelling on the *Coningh David* and will succeed Gerrit Servaes.[4]

Libenaar might be sent to Batavia to make an oral report regarding the state of affairs at Coromandel.

* This is not an exact copy in so far as the last paragraph of the letter is missing in the *Bataviaasch Uitgaande Brievenboek*, V.O.C. 852, ff.143-6. The date is erroneously given in this volume as 24 September 1624.

1. See document no. 59.
2. Not identified.
3. Jan Harmansz. Folynius arrived at Pulicat on 5 December 1625. He died there on 15 November 1626.
4. Gerrit Servaes had died at Pulicat on 26 October 1625.

69. Ysbrantsz. at Pulicat to Governor-General De Carpentier at Batavia, 16 October 1625. V.O.C. 1087, ff.164-9vo (Copy).

Ysbrantsz.'s last letter to Batavia was dated 14 June 1625.[1] Since then, the frigate *Edam* had arrived from Batavia on 28 August. On 9 September, the *Delfshaven* arrived from Holland with a cargo worth f.117,817.

Of the figure of f.36,000 as the amount of the bad debts and the cost of the maintenance of the fort at Pulicat as reported by Jacob Dedel,[2] the figure of bad debts alone was f.7,317. The details were as follows:

Name of the merchant	*Amount (in florins)*
Sarepa (under debt since 1618)	1,656
Cheny Chetty and others (under debt since the time of Adolf Thomasz.[3])	149
Interpreter Naldamby (when asked to pay, he said the Company could take away his wife and children but he had no money. At most, half of the sum could be recovered)	959
Ex-*shahbandar* Shambhu Nelle Mudaliar (no hope of recovery)	64
The *shahbandar* at Pulicat (under debt since the time of De Haze[4] and no hope of recovery)	569
Pancka Pillay (under debt since the time of Thomasz. (some chance of recovery when the situation improves)	549
Chinappa (under debt since the time of Van der Meer[5]) (some hope of recovery)	3,372
Total	f. 7,317[6]

Pulicat would try its best to meet Batavia's orders for the southern quarters in full subject to the availability of capital in time. One could never be certain that the contracts undertaken by the farmers of the Company's trade at Masulipatnam would in fact be honoured. The Company was obliged to dance to the tune of these merchants.

Good quality opium was not available at Masulipatnam. At the most 3 to 4 *maunds* of poor quality opium could be procured at a relatively high price. The present shipment was not carrying any but some opium would be sent with the *Delfshaven*.

Of the spices received with the *Edam*, the entire lot of mace and nutmeg had been sold at Masulipatnam. Mace was sold at 16 *pagodas* per *maund*, nutmeg at 95 *pagodas* per *bahar* and the broken nutmeg (*rompen*) at 67 *pagodas* per *bahar*. Cloves could not be sold yet but were likely to fetch around 11 to 12 *pagodas* per *maund*.

The situation of monopoly continued at Masulipatnam and no improvement was expected. No violent step was being contemplated by the Company. On his last visit to Masulipatnam,[7] Ysbrantsz. found the situation there under control. He was planning to write to the king of Golconda in this connection. Malaya thought that Mansur Khan[8] – an important noble – could be of help in this regard. Masulipatnam was indeed a very good place to trade at but only if one could do that in peace. The Company could always take revenge by capturing Muslim ships because Masulipatnam could not do without seafaring. In September 1625, 10 ships had left Masulipatnam – 3 for Aceh, 3 for Tenasserim, 2 for Pegu and 2 for Arakan. They were due to return in March next year. The Company's trade at Tegenapatam and surrounding areas was in a bad way during 1624. If the Masulipatnam factory had been closed, the supply of the return cargo would have been adversely affected.

The *nayak* of Tanjore had reportedly handed Tegenapatam over to the mother of the wife of the young king[9] for betel money.[10] This increases the Company's chances of resuming trade there. Efforts would be made to have textiles produced there in a good quantity.

Since slaves could not be bought at Tegenapatam or Pulicat, the *Medemblik* and the yacht *Jager* had been sent to Arakan on 23 September to buy slaves. A few hundred were expected from there.

If price was not a constraint and if ship space was available, Coromandel would be able to provide a large amount of rice. Two ships had been sent to Arakan specially to fetch rice. It would probably be cheaper if rice were bought at Pulicat from Muslim ships returning from Arakan because sending the Company's ships there involved a lot of costs. 70 *lasts* of rice (each *last* of 3,600 ponds) were being sent with the present shipment. This ship was carrying a cargo worth f.73,467, of which the cargo put in Masulipatnam was worth f.45,549 and that in Pulicat worth f.27,918.

Ysbrantsz. did not consider it advisable to send a ship to Bengal at the moment for the procurement of sugar because the country was full of wars.[11] Besides, a large amount of sugar could not be bought there immediately. Some factors would be sent there in advance to procure this item.

800 *bahars* of saltpetre had been collected by the factors at Tegenapatam and surrounding places but the *nayak* of Madura did not allow its transportation. He initially wanted a sum of 5,000 *pardauws* to release it but with the help of the brother of Malaya, it was brought down to 1,000 *pardauws*. Pulicat hoped to ship it with the *Delfshaven*. Ysbrantsz. suspected that the detention of the Company's saltpetre had been instigated by the Danes. As reported earlier, Tegenapatam had been plundered and set on fire forcing the inhabitants, including weavers and painters, to flee to Puleceri. The Danes controlled Puleceri and as soon as they came to know that these artisans did business with the Dutch Company, they threw them out of Puleceri. They then moved together with their families to a place called Counimeer which was about 3 miles from Puleceri. The Hindu authorities there received them well.

The Danes were thinking of establishing a factory at Masulipatnam. They had also sent factors to Pipli. One of their ships on its way back to Trancquebar from Makassar had strayed into Bengal. Since Admiral Crappe himself went to Bengal with two ships, it was likely that they were planning something big there. At Trancquebar, they were reported to have purchased 70 to 80 *bahars* of saltpetre and 120 *bahars* of pepper. The *nayak* of Tanjore also extorted money from them because this was the usual custom. Thus though the Danes found Trancquebar a good place, it turned out rather expensive for them.

The Danes had reportedly purchased 500 to 600 *bahars* of pepper at 32 rials per 460 ponds. Last year they were believed to have paid as much as 36 rials but not much reliance was to be put on this figure. The Danes were very close to the source of pepper, a place called Peta near Trancquebar. The Company would be subject to a lot of costs if it tried to buy pepper there. When Ysbrantsz. was at Masulipatnam, he had bought 80 *bahars* of pepper from Mir Kamal-al-Din at 18 Masulipatnam *pagodas* per 480 ponds. Till his departure from there,[12] it had not been delivered. This pepper had come from Aceh with the Muslim ships. Ysbrantsz. bought it simply to prevent the English and the Danes from getting hold of it.

In an effort to get the Dutch factors at Pegu released, Jan Libenaar had sent a present of f.212½ along with a letter to the king of Pegu. As requested by the Governor-General, Jan Libenaar was being sent with the present shipment. Maerten van Rossen[13] and Barent Pietersz. had provisionally succeeded him as the chief factors at Masulipatnam.

A memorandum of the goods that the free merchants had shipped on the *Edam* was enclosed.[14] At Pulicat, the factors had charged them a 2 per cent duty on their exports and a 1½ per cent duty on their imports – the same that the Company used to pay at Pulicat. Goods were not allowed to enter the city till the duty had been paid. From the city, the goods were allowed to be taken to the hinterland only through the gates controlled by the authorities. The authority of the Company was defined by the reach of its guns. The free merchants had been allowed to deal with the suppliers directly. As far as possible, care had been taken to ensure that these merchants were not able to get hold of the textiles manufactured for the Company. They had bought the pieces rejected by the Company.

Raw Chinese silk was sold at 50 Masulipatnam *pagodas* per *maund*. Since the quality of the Japanese copper was poor, it was not likely to fetch more than 48 to 50 *pagodas*. No more gold thread was to be sent because it could not be sold in Pulicat. The lot sent earlier from Batavia would be enough to meet the gold thread needed for use in the *goulongs*. The following items were to be sent to Pulicat in the quantities specified: cloves – 40 to 50 *bahars*, nutmeg – 100 *bahars*, broken nutmeg – 50 *bahars*, tortoise horn – 4 to 5 *bahars*, some Chinese clothes, mainly velvets, light colours but no heavy clothes. Camphor and ivory were not to be sent. The last lot of camphor was sold at 25 *pagodas*[15] and some was still lying unsold.

1. See document no. 59.
2. See document no. 35.
3. Adolff Thomasz. came to the East Indies as an assistant. From 1608 onwards, he served at Masulipatnam and Pulicat as an under-merchant. He was captured by the Portuguese on 12 June 1612, but

was released in September 1613. On 30 March 1615, he was promoted to the rank of upper-merchant. On the eve of his departure in 1619, De Haze named him his provisional successor. But Thomasz. left for Batavia on 23 November 1619 and on 8 July 1620, he was made a free burgher. He returned to Coromandel in this capacity for some time. He died in January 1631.

4. Hans de Haze came to the East Indies as an upper-merchant in 1611. Shortly thereafter, he was appointed a member of the Council of the Indies. In July 1612, he was appointed director of the trade in the Moluccas. In August 1613, he left as Visitor-General for the western factories. At the end of 1615, he was appointed governor of the coast of Coromandel. He returned home in July 1619 and in April 1628 became a Director of the Company in the chamber of Zeeland.
5. Franco van der Meer came to the East Indies on 28 December 1610 on the *Leeuw* as an uper-merchant. In 1612, he became chief of the factory at Tegenapatam. He returned to Holland on 26 February with the *Zwarte Beer* but came out again as an upper-merchant on the *Delft* in the autumn of 1617. He arrived at Jacatra in October 1618, went to Amboina and Banda and was back in Jacatra in May 1619. On 9 July 1619, he went to Coromandel as second-in-command and succeeded Adolff Thomasz. as the head of the factory at Pulicat and the governor of Fort Geldria. He returned to Holland in October 1621 with the *Woerden*.
6. All figures have been rounded off. Hence the total in fact is f.7,318 but in the document given as f.7,317.
7. Ysbrantsz. was at Masulipatnam between 19 September and 4 October 1625.
8. Mansur Khan, an Abyssinian, was Mir Jumla of Golconda and held farming rights over Masulipatnam and Petapuli. In 1628, he was poisoned because of his attempted take-over of Golconda.
9. The young king of Karnataka referred to was Ramadeva.
10. This term is now used colloqually as money used to meet sundry expenses. The usage then might have been different.
11. It is not quite clear what 'wars' are being alluded to.
12. Ysbrantsz. had left Masulipatnam on 4 October 1625.
13. Maerten van Rossen came to Masulipatnam in the beginning of 1624 and was promoted as the chief of the Masulipatnam factory on 16 October 1625. He held this position until 14 May 1629. In the middle of 1629, he left for Batavia from where he repatriated on 15 December 1629 as vice-commander under Pieter van den Broecke.

14. This memorandum is not available in the Company's archives.
15. The unit of weight is not specified but is likely to have been the *maund*.

70. General letter from Governor-General De Carpentier at Batavia to the Directors at Amsterdam, 27 October 1625. V.O.C. 1085, ff.11-31vo (Original).*

Since the Company had already started trading in Persia and its Mocha trade was also likely to be re-established soon, Batavia hoped that spices worth about f.350,000 to f.400,000 would be sold in these places annually. Of this amount, Batavia would need annually about f.200,000 worth of Gujarat textiles for the East Indies. A sum of f.150,000 to f.200,000 would then be available for the procurement of goods for Holland. But additional funds would, of course, have to be sent by the Directors failing which the procurement of textiles for the return cargo for Holland would suffer. If that happened, the Company's rivals, the English, the French and the Danes and even its enemy, the Portuguese, would take advantage of the situation. The sum needed for the procurement of Coromandel textiles for the Indies would be about f.200,000 per annum.

In their letter of 27 January 1625,[1] Batavia had informed the Directors that they had 500,000 rials in capital left with them. To this, a sum of 20,000 rials had since been added by the sale of a house at Batavia to the English and another 50,000 rials had been called in. The total stock of capital thus available was 570,000 rials. As against this, the amounts disbursed were as follows:

a. Amount sent for the pepper trade	64,000 rials
b. Amount sent to Taiwan for the Chinese trade	248,000 rials
c. Amount sent to Siam for the purchase of hides, sappanwood and other goods	20,000 rials
d. Amount sent to Coromandel besides spices, for the purchase of textile and slaves	60,000 rials

e. Amount sent to Surat, besides spices, for the procurement of goods for Holland	36,000 rials
f. Amount sent to the Moluccas for the purchase of slaves	5,000 rials
g. Amount sent to Amboina for the purchase of cloves	24,000 rials
Total	457,000 rials

Batavia was thus left with only 113,000 rials in stock. The sum needed annually for the procurement of the return cargo for Holland was 160,000 rials not including the procurement in China. If only the English were not in the way, pepper and other spices could be bought without any cash being needed from Holland.

* An exact copy is available in the *Bataviaasch Uitgaande Brievenboek*, V.O.C. 852, ff.158-82. Also summarized in W.Ph. Coolhaas (ed.), *Gererale Missiven*, I, pp.174-83.

1. See document no. 48.

71. Current prices of goods at Masulipatnam, 20 November 1625. V.O.C. 1087, ff.403-3vo. (Not stated whether original or copy).

S.No.	*Item*	*Price (in pagodas unless specified otherwise)*	*Remarks*
1.	Cloves	10-11 per *maund*	
2.	Nutmeg	110-130 per *bahar*	Since a large lot was received, it had to be sold at 95 *pagodas* per *bahar*
3.	Mace	20 per *maund*	Since a large lot was received, it had to be sold at 16 *pagodas* per *maund*

4.	Pepper	18 per *bahar*	
5.	Benzoin (fine quality)	4 per *maund*	
6.	Benzoin (poor quality)	1½-1¾ per *maund*	
7.	Alum	18 per *bahar*	If received in large quantity, price would fall
8.	Raw Chinese silk	45-50 per *maund*	
9.	Winded silk	3½-4 rials per *catty*	
10.	Floss silk	40 per *maund*	Good quality
11.	Tortoise horn	15-17 per *maund*	
12.	Spelter	50 per *bahar*	A large amount could be sold
13.	Tin	55 per *bahar*	200 *bahars* could be sold
14.	Lead	13-13½ per[1]	A large amount could be sold
15.	Vermilion	15-20 per *maund*	5,000 ponds could be sent
16.	Quicksilver	18-20 per *maund*	5,000 ponds could be sent
17.	Sulphur	15 per *bahar*	
18.	Sandalwood	100 per *bahar*	Provided the quality was good
19.	Radix China	100 per *bahar*	
20.	Eaglewood (from Cochin)	10 per *bahar*	
21.	Red cloth	3-3½ per *gaz*	10-12 cases could be sold annually
22.	Camphor (from Borneo and China)	–	Remained unsold
23.	Musk	–	Little demand for this item
24.	Chinese wares	–	Little demand for this item
25.	Ivory	–	Not to be sent

1. The unit is not indicated.

72. Van den Broecke at Surat to the Directors at Amsterdam, 28 November 1625. V.O.C. 1090, ff.93-4 (Original).

English ships the *Jonas*, the *Anne* and a small yacht, all from Mocha, had arrived at Surat on 28 September 1625. Then on 2 October, the *Gouden Leeuw*, the *Walcheren* and the *Heusden* had arrived without meeting any Portuguese ships on the way.[1] Four Portuguese galleons together with 14 frigates arrived at the roadstead of Swally on 11 October. On 14 October, Van den Broecke received the news that another three foreign ships were present in the river at Bulsar.[2] On 19 October these three vessels were sighted at Navsari[3] and were reported to have shot at the aforesaid four Portuguese galleons. The same day, the English President came to Van den Broecke with a proposal that the two companies sent out ships to help the three foreign ships and attack the Portuguese.

The *Goede Fortuin*, the *Nieuw Bantam* and the *Coningh David* had arrived at Surat from Batavia on 6 November with a good cargo.

One could buy a good amount of pepper annually at Surat at 6½ to 6¾ rials of eight per bag. Van den Broecke considered this price to be somewhat high and the funds could preferably be invested in textiles.

The *badshah* of Mocha had sent a letter to Van den Broecke and to the English President with a Turkish servant. A copy of the letter was enclosed.[4] In case everything went well, Van den Broecke would send some spices to Mocha with a suitable factor aboard the *Heusden*.

1. These ships had been sent from Holland to Surat on 24 December 1624. See document no. 45.
2. Bulsar is a town about 40 miles south of Surat, at a latitude of 20°.35′N and longitude of 72°.5′E.
3. Navsari is 18 miles south of Surat at a latitude of 21°.07′N and longitude of 73°.40′E.
4. This letter is not available in the Company's archives.

73. Van den Broecke at Surat to Governor-General De Carpentier at Batavia, 4 December 1625. V.O.C. 1090, ff.287-9vo (Copy).

Two Portuguese galleons were sunk near Bombay on 16 September.

Since the arrival of the ships,[1] the price of indigo Sarkhej had gone up by 25 to 30 per cent and was still going up. The price of textiles had also gone up by 10 to 11 per cent as compared to last year. This was because the price of cotton had gone up from 40 *mahmudis* to 140 *mahmudis* per *kandi*.[2]

Francisco Pelsaert had written from Agra that spices worth about 80,000 rupees had been sold there. Surat had sent there another 40,000 rupees so that a large amount of indigo and saltpetre would be expected from there for Europe. The price of indigo there had gone up from 22 to 27 rupees per 50 ponds and had then surged further up to between 30 and 34 rupees. Van den Broecke had suggested to the English President at Surat to have a joint strategy to check the rise in the price of indigo and textiles in Agra. But nothing had come of the proposal.

After the Company's ships to Persia were ready to sail, Van den Broecke asked the English President on 18 November if they were interested in sending any of their ships with ours. If yes, an arrangement could be worked out regarding how to deal with any Portuguese ships on the way. They expressed interest but said that there was no need for a written agreement. The ships of the two companies left for Persia together on 3 December 1625.

A cargo worth f.304,159 consisting of 76,000 rials in cash, 25,000 ponds of cloves, 50,000 ponds of nutmeg and 30 bags of mace besides other goods had been sent to Persia. These goods should afford a profit of about f.200,000, so that the factors in Persia would have about f.500,000 to invest in the return cargo for next year. If more cash had been sent to Persia, an adequate amount would not have been left at Surat.

It would have been advantageous if the *Heusden* had been sent to Mocha with spices which, considering that no spices had been sent there over the last three years, were likely to have afforded a good profit.

During the current year, the English had bought 80,000 rupees worth of pepper at Surat at 6½ rials per sack. At Ahmedabad, they had bought 1,400 packets of indigo and 1,000 *maunds* of saltpetre. At Broach and Cambay, they had bought textiles. All these were expected to be dispatched to England with the *James* and the *Jonas* on 1 January 1626.

Surat had no knowledge of Vapour's performance at the royal court. According to the English, the emperor had liked the bird presented to him by Vapour. Surat would know the details after the return of the *kafila* from Agra.

1. The reference is evidently to the arrival of the English ships on 28 September and that of the Dutch ships on 2 October and 6 November. See document no. 72.
2. The *kandi* was a weight with local variations ranging from 460 to 500 Dutch ponds. It would thus correspond to a *bahar*.

74. Ysbrantsz. at Pulicat to Governor-General De Carpentier at Batavia, 5 December 1625. V.O.C. 1087, ff. 174-7vo (Copy).

Ysbrantsz.'s last letter to Batavia was dated 16 October 1625.[1] This letter was being sent with the *Delfshaven* with a cargo worth f.76,452. The Directors would have liked this ship to be sent directly to them but it would have been May or June 1626 before enough cargo would have been available for it. Since in the meantime Batavia was hard pressed for rice, it had been decided to send the ship to Batavia.

In view of the rainy season, only a limited amount of Masulipatnam textiles could be procured. Poor quality opium was selling at Masulipatnam between 15 and 19 *pagodas* per *maund*. It was, therefore, not purchased.

The *Medemblik* and the frigate *Jager* had been sent to Arakan on 23 September 1625 to fetch slaves from there. The vessels returned to Masulipatnam on 16 November with 130 slaves who were the only ones to survive at Arakan of the total lot of 544 bought. While none died on the way, 4 died at Pulicat within six days of arrival while another 26 were too seriously ill to travel. So only 100 slaves were aboard the *Delfshaven* and there is a possibility that some more might die on the way. If there had not been a terrible famine and pestilence in Arakan this year, as many as 1,000 to 1,500 slaves could have been bought. The king of Arakan had received 10,000 slaves from Bengal. Since the unsold ones would have to be maintained, the king had ordered suspension of further procurement. If enough slaves could not be bought in Arakan, efforts would be made to buy some in Bengal. However, in view of the resentment it causes here, it might be desirable to stop the procurement of slaves.

Pepper had been bought at 18 *pagodas* per *bahar*. 25,200 ponds of this lot was being sent with the *Delfshaven*. Ysbrantsz. was planning to sell the remainder at 28 *pagodas* per *bahar* which was the price the Danes and others paid for it.

On 28 October, Malaya had written a letter to Mansur Khan who was expected to help in sorting out the problems at Masulipatnam by bringing them to the attention of the king of Golconda. There was a rumour at Masulipatnam to the effect that the new *havaldar* of Masulipatnam, Jannat Khan, had been recalled to Golconda because of his mismanagement and tyranny. Each succeeding *havaldar* was interested in filling his own coffers. The Company's affairs at Masulipatnam were in a reasonable shape.

Since the demand for mace and nutmeg had gone up, Pulicat's orders for these items might be treated as augmented by 33 to 50 per cent. Of the other items, Pulicat could expect to sell annually 8 to 10 cases of raw silk, 4,000 to 5,000 ponds of quicksilver, 4,000 to 5,000 ponds of vermilion, 50 to 60 *bahars* of spelter, 250 to 300 *bahars* of lead, 80 to 100 *bahars* of good quality copper and 10 to 12 cases of broad cloth from Holland, mainly red in colour but some pieces also of parrot green, orange, yellow and green colours. The last lot of copper received was of very poor quality. The gold received with the *Delfshaven* was minted into *pagodas* at Pulicat rendering an extra profit of 11 to 12 per cent than if it had been sold at Masulipatnam. Since rials fetched a very low price at Masulipatnam – only 8 *fanums* per piece – Pulicat would provide Masulipatnam with enough goods, the sales proceeds of which could be used to buy return goods.

A Danish ship, the *Jupiter*, reportedly carrying a cargo worth 5,000 rials, had been lost on its way back from Makassar when it strayed on to the Orrisa coast and ran aground there. Their director, Christopher van der Molen,[2] had come to Masulipatnam where they had hired a house and reached an agreement with the *havaldar* that they would pay an export and import duty of 3½ per cent. They had brought only three cases[3] of rials with them but were making a lot of noise as if 'they were going to buy the whole world'. They were getting their textiles painted at both Puleceri and Porto Novo. These included rough *tapi-sarassas*, *sarassas*, *telpucans*,[4] *girdles*,[5] chintz – 6 *covido*[6] in length and 2 *spans*[7] in width and *bethilles* of 25 to 30 *asta* each. They were trying to get hold of as many pieces as possible from the lots that had been contracted for by the Company. It seemed that they had received funds from Makassar. Reportedly, they were thinking of establishing a factory at Aceh for which they were trying to get textiles manufactured. Nothing was known of the ships that they had sent to Bengal.

Ysbrantsz. still had very limited information regarding Bengal. Van Rossen and Barent Pietersz. had written from Masulipatnam about a local Muslim whose brother, Mohammad Kasim, was the governor of Balasore. This man had told them that the Company could carry on a good amount of trade at Balasore in sugar, saltpetre, slaves and Bengal textiles. Some spices could also be sold there. After collecting more information regarding the activities of the Danes there, a small yacht would be sent to Balasore.

A ship of the king of Golconda that had gone to Mocha in 1624 had been attacked there. A small replacement vessel provided to transport the persons aboard to Masulipatnam was captured on its return voyage by the Portuguese at Dabhol together with the people aboard. This news was brought to Masulipatnam by one of the persons who had managed to escape.

Enclosed is the list[8] of the goods put in the ship of free and private merchants for which a sum of 7 per cent by way of freight and convoy charges had been collected.

The carpenter and the cook who had also brought along their wives from Holland were being sent back with this ship because there was not enough work for them here commensurate with their large salaries. They could be occupied more usefully at Batavia.

1. See document no. 69.
2. Christopher van der Molen had come to the East Indies in 1620 as an under-merchant with the *Wapen van Hoorn*. He had repatriated on 24 December 1620 with the same ship. In 1622, he had left for Trancquebar with the *Vandhund* in the service of the Danish East India Company. He was first the chief of the Danish factory at Masulipatnam and later the President at Trancquebar.
3. A case ordinarily contained 4,000 rials.
4. Not identified.
5. A silk textile.
6. The *covid* was an indigenous measure with considerable regional variations. In Gujarat and Bengal, it was equivalent of 18 inches.
7. *Span* is a measure of length, equal to nine inches, based on the distance between the top of the extended thumb and that of the little finger.
8. The enclosure is not available in the Company's archives.

75. Extracts from three letters from the Directors at Amsterdam to Governor-General De Carpentier at Batavia forwarded to Surat in 1625. V.O.C. 1085, ff.139vo-42vo (Copy).*

Extract from the letter dated 17 October 1624

It had been learnt from a personal letter from Isfahan to a friend of one of the Directors dated 18 January 1624 and sent overland that the Dutch factors had been received by the Shah very cordially. The spices and other goods brought there by the *Vrede* and the *Weesp* had been sold to the Shah's factor at a very good price in return for which a large amount of silk had been bought at a reasonable price. The Directors were thinking of sending a good amount of capital to Persia. Batavia was to send as much of spices and other goods as could be sold there at a good profit and exchanged against silk. It was not advisable to keep capital locked up for the China trade to which the Company was unlikely to gain entry. Batavia ought to send this capital at the first opportunity to Surat and Persia for investment in indigo and silk respectively.

The indigo received with the *Heusden* had been sold in Holland at a good profit. The price fetched by indigo Bayana was approximately 50 *stuivers* per pond and that by indigo Sarkhej about 40 *stuivers* per pond.

The Directors were not surprised that Willem de Milde had been treated harshly by the *badshah* of Yemen because he had given him enough cause to do that. The capture of the Muslim ships sailing from Mocha by the *Sampson* and the *Weesp* in contravention of promises given earlier had been a very wrong action.[1] The Directors were given to understand that not only had the *badshah* refused to provide compensation of 63,235 rials of eight for the goods taken from De Milde, but had indeed demanded a large sum of money besides persons of some Dutch factors as a security.

If the Muslim shipping to Mocha was to be intercepted as suggested by Van den Broecke, three ships and a yacht would be needed for the purpose which would be a rather expensive proposition. Batavia should advise whether permitting Muslim ships to go freely to Mocha from Dabhol, Chaul and other places was likely to help reach a suitable accord with the new *badshah* of Yemen. Van den Broecke was of the opinion that permitting the Muslim merchants to trade freely with Mocha, and particularly with Aceh, was likely to hurt the Company. Indeed, the Portuguese might even take advantage of this by trading to Aceh under the cover of the Muslim merchants.

Extract from the letter dated 1 November 1624

The Directors had sent f.600,000 to Surat in gold and silver as follows: f.240,000 in Hungarian ducats, f.160,000 in *ryx-dollars*, f.100,000 in rials of eight and f.100,000 in Dutch *daaldars*. Indigo Lahore had been sold at 10 *stuivers*, 1 penning per pond and the indigo Sarkhej at 8 *stuivers*, 4 penning per pond both on condition that no more supplies would be released for a period of 24 months.[2]

Extract from the letter dated 19 November 1624

[This extract does not contain information of any importance.]

* These letters had been received at Batavia on 4 June 1625 and were forwarded to Surat with the yacht *De Haze*. An exact copy is available in the *Bataviaasch Uitgaande Brievenboek*, V.O.C. 852, ff.118-22.

1. For details of the ships captured by the *Weesp* and the *Sampson*, see Om Prakash (ed.), *The Dutch Factories in India, 1617-1623*, pp. 190-3, 215 and 218.
2. Earlier in this document, the sale price of indigo Bayana and Sarkhej was given respectively as approximately 50 and 40 *stuivers* per pond.

76. Journal kept at Fort Geldria at Pulicat between 20 November 1623 and 28 November 1625. V.O.C. 1087, ff.179-211vo (Copy).*

1623

20 November

We learnt from a ship from Masulipatnam of the problems created there for the Company by the new *havaldar* of Masulipatnam, Muhammad Taqi, who was under the *sar-i-khail*.

A letter from Abraham van Uffelen dated 8 November[1] mentioned that Sultan Khurram, one of the sons of the great Mughal had reached a place three days' journey away from Masulipatnam with an army of 12,000 men. The army of the king of Golconda was chasing him. With a view to safeguarding them, the Company's goods were loaded on the *Wapen van Rotterdam* which was lying in the harbour there.

21 November

Jan Libenaar had written from Masulipatnam that on 9 November, Abraham van Uffelen was summoned to the court of the *havaldar*, subjected to violence there and taken out of the city. The crew on the *Wapen van Rotterdam* were detained and instructions issued that no further goods could be put aboard the ship.

25 November

Another letter from Libenaar mentioned that Van Uffelen was taken inland on the 13th of November under the pretence that he was being taken to the king of Golconda. He was reported to have been asked to hand the Portuguese vessel captured by the *Wapen van Rotterdam* near Narsapur over to the authorities failing which the king would be told of the Company's export of tobacco to Arakan in contravention of his *farman*. There were problems going on between the kings of Golconda and Arakan. Van Uffelen was also threatened that the king would be told of the detention by the Company of the person to whom the right to change money had been farmed out. He was asked for a sum of 10,000 *pagodas* before he was released.

The *havaldar* of Masulipatnam had put under arrest nearly all the *komati*[2] merchants doing business with the Company. Attempts were being made to extract money from them. A sum of 6,000 *pagodas* was extracted from one of them called Pera. Another 1,800 *pagodas* had been taken away from the Company's factory.

Prince Khurram was said to be only 3 days' journey away from Masulipatnam with an army of 10,000 cavalry, 19,000 foot-soldiers, 1,000 elephants and 4,000 camels. As a result, the entire region had been ruined and most of the notable Muslims of Masulipatnam had fled from town. The king of Golconda was chasing Khurram with an army of about 20,000 men.

2 December

The yacht *Masulipatam* sent on October 28 to Tegenapatam to fetch slaves was attacked on 13 November when it was lying just outside Sao Tome by a gallion. The gallion had 4 dead and 7 to 8 injured while four of our men sustained burn injuries. On the 25th of November, the yacht went back to Tegenapatam with all the slaves on board.

5 December

It was learnt from a letter from Masulipatnam that Prince

Khurram had arrived there with an army of 20,000 cavalry, 2,000 elephants, 4,000 camels and 15,000 – 16,000 foot soldiers. The prince was reported to have fled from his father because he had killed his own brother in a dispute over a whore. The prince is carrying a large treasure with him and was visited daily by our factors till he left Masulipatnam. The prince was accompanied by the captain of the *Wapen van Rotterdam,*[3] Assistant Daniel van der Hagen and the indigo expert Gerrit Jansz.[4] On their way back to Masulipatnam, these three persons were arrested by the Muslim authorities. Herman Prins, the under-merchant on the *Wapen van Rotterdam*, who had earlier been sent to Golconda by Van Uffelen, had since been put under arrest there.

Van Uffelen continued to be under arrest. The factors were not allowed to go aboard the *Wapen van Rotterdam*. Most of the spices such as cloves, nutmeg and mace together with items such as sandalwood and copper besides two cases of ivory had been detained. 280 packets of goods lying in the factory had not been permitted to be put aboard the *Wapen van Rotterdam*.

A ship coming from Tenasserim had been captured by the *Wapen van Rotterdam* in the harbour of Masulipatnam. When Van Uffelen was asked to arrange for the release of the captured vessel, he refused to do so till such time as he himself had been freed. Van Uffelen had been treated extremely badly. Both his legs were kept in chains for 24 days and he was told that he could be released only if he agreed to give a present of 3,000 *pagodas*.

26 December

The *Medemblik* had arrived at Masulipatnam from Arakan. The yachts *Jager* and the *Muys* had been left behind in Arakan to fetch the 150 to 200 slaves who were likely to be procured there. Van Uffelen had since been taken to Golconda and Captain Jacob Geritsz. Coper released from detention.

1624

2 January

It was learnt that the *nayak* of Gingi had died last month. 263 of his women are reported to have thrown themselves into the cremation pyre and burnt themselves to death.

22 January

The *Wapen van Rotterdam* arrived here today from Masulipatnam from where it had sailed on 11 January. Van Uffelen was still under detention.

25 January

Learnt from Masulipatnam that Van Uffelen had been released after he had paid 5,000 *pagodas*. Since the cargo lying ready there was still not being permitted to be put aboard the *Wapen van Rotterdam*, it was decided to send the ship to Batavia via Pulicat where it will pick-up 500 *bahars* of saltpetre together with textiles and about 700 slaves.

26-31 January

A number of ships arrived daily from the Orissa coast with rice, oil, butter and other provisions.

2 February

The *Wapen van Rotterdam* left Pulicat with 330 slaves, 62 packets of fine textiles and 136 *bahars* of saltpetre for Batavia via Tegenapatam where it will pick-up 400 slaves, 300 *bahars* of saltpetre and some packets of textiles. The captain of the ship is Jacob Coper.

5 February

The *Medemblik* arrived from Masulipatnam.

6 February

The fluit, the *Muys* arrived from Masulipatnam with the body of Van Uffelen who had died there on 1 February and wished to be buried in the Fort Geldria here. This vessel had arrived at Masulipatnam from Arakan on 28 January with 88 slaves aboard.

19 February

Ysbrantsz. left for Masulipatnam to try and reach an agreement with the authorities there.

23 February

Libenaar came on board together with Lingayya with a *kaul* from the *havaldar* permitting Ysbrantsz. to come to town. According to Lingayya, the *havaldar* was anxious to reach a mutually satisfactory accord.

24 February

Libenaar had discussed the matter of the captured ship with the *havaldar* who had requested the release of one Samsa, a Muslim merchant who had gone to Pegu from Masulipatnam four years ago and was coming back to Masulipatnam with the aforementioned ship. This ship had been freighted at Masulipatnam. Samsa together with his goods worth approximately 200 *pagodas* was then released. Libenaar then communicated to the *havaldar* that we were willing to release the ship minus its goods to the *sar-i-khail*. The *havaldar* seemed satisfied with this and gave Libenaar a statement signed by all the notable Muslims of the port of Masulipatnam that they would not stake a claim to the ship. Later the *havaldar* also asked for the release of the goods belonging to Agha Rasaer, the governor of Dabhol, besides a present for himself.

Mir Kamal-al-Din also came on board today. He maintained that we would eventually be required to release the ship or asked to leave Masulipatnam. It simply could not be tolerated that a ship belonging to Agha Rasaer be captured in a port of the king of Golconda. The king of Bijapur (whose jurisdiction included Dabhol) was likely to have contacted the king of Golconda. If we did not agree to restitute the goods of Agha Rasaer, we had better leave Masulipatnam. But in case the goods were returned, matters would return to normal because the people of Masulipatnam also realized that they had to trade on the sea. Mir Kamal-al-Din was requested to ask the *havaldar* to allow Ysbrantsz. to come ashore with the goods of the governor of Dabhol.

A letter was received from Herman Prins from Golconda saying that since the sum of 5,000 *pagodas* paid by Van Uffelen had reached Golconda, he (Prins) was told that he could be released if he paid 300-400 *pagodas*. When Prins pointed out that he had been detained simply as a surety to ensure the payment of 5,000 *pagodas*, he was also told that the old contract regarding the payment of tolls by the Dutch was no longer valid and that we would henceforth be obliged to pay at the same rate at which the English paid. When the contract was first made with us we brought in just one or two ships into Masulipatnam each year but the number had since gone up substantially. When the *sar-i-khail* was told by Prins that no alteration in the contract could be made without the consent of the Governor-General, he was told that the Dutch chief could get in touch with the Governor-General. Prins also warned that an attack on the Masulipatnam factory was possible and all effects should be transferred to the ship.

26 February

Libenaar again came on board and said that if Mir Kamal-al-Din had not interfered, the matter would have been sorted out by now. The *sar-i-khail* was under arrest at Golconda and the *havaldar* was likely to be replaced within eight days by one Mir Kasim.[5] It was, therefore, resolved not to restitute the goods belonging to the governor of Dabhol.

27 February

Received news that fine quality indigo was available at Mogena and that the merchants would hold it for us for eight days. The price had come down from 37-38 *pagodas* per 288 ponds last year to 28-30 *pagodas* this year.

6 March

English merchant Futter[6] was summoned to the court and was arrested again on the charge that the 400 *pagodas* had not been paid on time. The English President promised to pay this sum in silver or in rials.

10 March

Ysbrantsz. sailed from Masulipatnam for Pulicat in the evening with the frigate *Jager* and the sloop *Onrust*.

12-24 March

[Contains a description of the trip from Masulipatnam to Pulicat.]

25 March

Ysbrantsz. reached Pulicat. The *Muys* was sent to Batavia with letters to the Governor-General containing news of Van Uffelen's death.

Two ships arrived from Arakan, one with rice and the other with four elephants which were in good demand at Masulipatnam.

29 March

The *Medemblik* together with the sloops, the *Kleindort* and the *Onrust*, left for Sao Tome and Tegenapatam from where they would fetch textiles, saltpetre and slaves.

31 March

A ship of the *kotwal* of Arakan arrived with rice. Another ship from Tenasserim also arrived with tin, rice and silk. This vessel also brought gifts for the new king of Karnataka, Ram Raya[7] together with a letter from the king of Siam written on a gold leaf. This vessel had been attacked by three Portuguese galleons at Sao Tome involving a loss of three dead and fifteen injured.

3 April

Learnt of the arrival of some Portuguese fusts at Nagapattinam. They were said to be planning to burn the Muslim ships lying in the Pulicat port—one from Tenasserim, two from Arakan and one from Orissa. In view of this, Ysbrantsz. had increased the number of men on the Company's yachts, the *Jager* and the *Tenasserim.*

5 April

Five Portuguese *fusts* were reported to have arrived at Nagapattinam.

6 April

Learnt from a Company spy at Sao Tome that three fusts and three galleons were ready to arrive at Pulicat tonight. It was, therefore, decided to send some more soldiers from the fort to man the *Jager* and the *Tenasserim.*

7 April

Three Portuguese *fusts* and two galleons arrived at Sao Tome this morning with orders to burn the ships lying in the roadstead.

11 April

Three Dutchmen arrested by the Portuguese in November 1621 from the *Sampson* and kept in the prison at Goa arrived from Sao Tome. In all, eight persons had been arrested at that time. The three who arrived here had been released in exchange of two priests and two women together with their children captured by the *Medemblik* near Sao Tome. The remainder of the Dutch prisoners in Goa had since died. This was in pursuance of an agreement between Van Uffelen and Manuel Mascaynsach[8] that the prisoners of the two sides be exchanged.[9]

12 April

The ship of the king of Siam left Pulicat for Masulipatnam.

13 April

The ship of *Qazi* Bauwe arrived at Pulicat from Arakan and then left for Masulipatnam. Pulicat decided to send the *Medemblik* and the *Jager* together with some sloops southwards to see if they could capture something from the enemy.

19 April

The ship of the *kotwal* of Arakan left for Masulipatnam on its way back to Arakan. Some Dutch free merchants went with this ship looking for opportunities of profit at Arakan.

20 April

The *Medemblik*, the *Jager* and the sloops *Onrust* and the *Cleyn Dort* left for Tegenapatam to fetch the goods lying ready there. On their way, they would try to capture something from the Portuguese. Several *sampans* arrived at Sao Tome from Nagapattinam everyday.

25 April

Received information from Trancquebar about the arrival of two Danish ships – the *Pearl* and the *Jupiter* – from Denmark from where they had sailed in April 1623 under the command of Roeland Crappe.

3 May

The *Tenasserim* was sent to Arakan via Masulipatnam to pick-up some cargo there. It will take with it the captured frigate *Antonio*. A sum of 4,000 *pagodas* was provided for the purchase of slaves at Arakan.

15 May

Admiral Jacob Dedel arrived from Batavia on board the *Wapen van Rotterdam* to visit the coast factories and to sort out the problems with the authorities at Masulipatnam.

21 May

Eti Raja has written to the Company that he had put Pede Raja, the *visiadoor* (local chieftain) of Pulicat under arrest. He has also written to one Ranganath Raja and some merchants to get hold of Pede Raja's goods and women. He also asked us for help. Dedel's reply to Eti Raja is included in the copy book.[10]

22 May

The *Wapen van Rotterdam* left for Masulipatnam after leaving 12 cases of Japanese silver and some gold at Pulicat.

26 May

The *Medemblik* carrying 500 *bahars* of saltpetre and some textiles arrived from Tegenapatam together with the yacht *Jager* and two sloops.

1 June

Learnt from Masulipatnam that the frigates *Tenasserim* and *Bonne Remedie* had gone to Arakan with a cargo worth f.17,000 to procure slaves. The English ship the *Unity* arrived from Batavia and will leave for Masulipatnam within two to three days to investigate the state of affairs there. It had started from Batavia in the company of the *Heart* which parted from it at Ceylon and went on to Karikal where the English were thinking of establishing a factory.

13 June

Tyapa Raja[11] came to Pulicat with 1,000 men. He hoped that with the assistance of another 1,000 men provided by Ponke Pillai, he would be able to conquer the entire area to the north of Pulicat on the other side of the river. Raghu Reddy was forced to retire to Counam[12] but at that point, these men were stopped by the forces of Peda Raja. The aforementioned Tyapa Raja and Ponke Pillai were planning to become the masters of the entire region bordered by the river which flows near the Dutch fort. They were even thinking of building a fort near the river so as to be able to control us. But the forces of Pede Raja arrested Tyapa Raja living in Counam.

14 June

Malaya informed Ysbrantsz. that one of the two persons who had come to Pulicat to collect revenues on behalf of Eti Raja had been advised by friends (including Ranganath Raja and the Company's interpreter Groa) to go back to Eti Raja.

18 June

A young brahmin came to the factory with an anonymous letter that he had been asked by Pede Raja to deliver to Ysbrantsz. or Malaya. In the letter the Company was urged to protect the city against attacks by Eti Raja, Tyapa Raja and Ponke Pillai who were likely to ask for assistance from the Portuguese at Sao Tome. It was learnt from our spies at Sao Tome that the bishop had sent one Manuel Mancedo[13] to the young king with gifts worth about 300 *pagodas*.

21 June

Two ambassadors of Eti Raja came to the city. They wanted the Company to hand over to them the women belonging to Pede Raja together with his goods as well as those of his people. They were told that the Company had no knowledge of the goods. As far as the women were concerned, they were under our protection at the fort. In any event, the 300 or so of Pede Raja's men in the fort would never permit the abduction of the women. After deliberations amongst themselves lasting for four days, the ambassadors left town on 26 June for Pomery.[14] We gave them a gift of 50 ponds of sandalwood. We later learnt that they had instructions to follow our advice and to take no hostile action in relation to ourselves.

6 July

The *Medemblik* arrived from Masulipatnam laden with some lead besides rice and other provisions for the fort. It was learnt that from the *Heart* lying at Karikal, the English had sent a boat with 10 persons offering their services to the local chieftain. They had succeeded in capturing a Portuguese vessel from which they got a good booty which was shared with the chieftain. It was also learnt that the incharge of the *Heart* had gone to Tanjore to negotiate an accord with the *nayak* there to build a fort at Karikal.

Malaya and the brahmin clerk of the Company communicated to Ysbrantsz. that they had firm information from one Penunaja, the brahmin of Ranganath Raja, that when Ysbrantsz. was away to Masulipatnam in March last, the Company's interpreter Groa and Raghna Chetty had sent a clerk Malay Purmael to Venkata Raja,[15] a subordinate of Ranganath Raja informing him that if Pede Raja was captured, a booty worth no less than 30,000 *pardauws* could be expected. Everybody knew that Pede Raja had lots of jewels, etc. Ysbrantsz. also learnt that day before yesterday, Groa had sent a brahmin to Venkata Raja to bring him uptodate about the developments here.

9 July

Three Portuguese *gelias*[16] arrived at Pulicat.

10 July

400 to 500 men of Venkata Raja came to the city and engaged in disruptive activities. After killing two of them, the local people drove them out and they returned to Tierepalveron.

12 July

About 1,000 men of Venkata Raja and Sacckemoelle[17] returned to the city. After a skirmish, they were again pushed out.

The *Vrede* which had left Surat for Holland on 12 March

returned to Pulicat after running into a storm near Mozambique rendering it incapable of continuing the trip to Holland.

14 July

The intruders numbering about 1,200 returned to Pulicat yet once again. The skirmishes with the local people continued between the morning and 2 p.m. with only slight damage on either side. Eventually, they returned to Tierepalveron.

15 July

The *Vrede* left for Masulipatnam. The chieftain of Catour[18] sent us an *ola*[19] offering friendship and assistance. We thanked him as per the letter enclosed.[20]

19 July

Venkata Raja again came to the city with his people. Several houses were put on fire. He then returned with 2 dead and 20 injured.

20 July

Learnt that Venkata Raja and his allies had resolved to send some persons to Carimanel.

21-24 July

Venkata Raja stayed at Tierepalveron.

25 July

Ysbrantsz. was thinking of sending the brahmin clerk to Venkata Raja offering to mediate between him and Pede Raja. But these plans were abandoned when it seemed that the people of Pede Raja might interpret them as a suggestion of their weakness. Some of the natives of Pulicat had already fled out of fear. It was also learnt that Venkata Raja was unlikely to be able to bear the cost of maintaining his troops for long.

Reijer Pietersen[21] has written from Tegenapatam that the Englishmen from the *Heart* were still in Tanjore. They had an audience with the *nayak* to whom they had presented two iron canons, 5 Japanese casgiens,[22] 2 pieces of sandalwood and some spices. These presents were regarded as inadequate by the *nayak*.

He has asked the Englishmen to give him annually 7,000 *pardauws* for farming the city of Karikal to them. The English had replied that they had no authorization from their superiors to do this and that they would look for alternative places to trade from.

The Danes were trying their best to keep the English out of Karikal. They presented the *nayak* with 500 rials and two pieces of red broad cloth and promised two metal canons if he denied the English permission to trade. They also promised to compensate for any of his subjects' ships that might be captured by the English. They were planning to send a ship with textiles to Tenasserim and another to Bengal.

26 July

Received a letter from Reijer Pietersen from Tegenapatam stating that the *nayak* of Tanjore had refused the English permission to trade at Karikal. The Danes had presented the *nayak* with two metal cannons. The English were expected to return to Tegenapatam soon hoping to be allowed to trade there.

28 July

In response to Malaya's letter acquainting him of the actions of Venkata Raja at Pulicat, Chumeobal Raja has suggested that the Dutch ought to protect the place for Eti Raja and not allow the government of this place to fall into someone else's hands. He has also written to Pede Raja to hold his ground and not be worried about doing damage to Venkata Raja. He was himself unhappy with Venkata Raja because he had burnt two villages which were under Chumeobal Raja's governorship and under the overall charge of Pede Raja.

29 July

On his return from the camp of Venkata Raja, one brahmin Muntter told us that Venkata Raja had asked for help from Sao Tome.

1 August

The *Schoonhoven* which had sailed from Batavia on 26 June reached Pulicat this evening with silver, camphor, lead and ivory, etc.

4 August

The *Leeuwin* which had sailed from Holland on 9 January reached Pulicat with a cargo worth f.316,000 mostly in gold.

6 August

The *Schoonhoven* and *Medemblik* left for Masulipatnam with about half the cargo brought to Pulicat by the *Schoonhoven* and the *Leeuwin*.

12 August

The people of Pulicat have reached an accord with Venkata Raja agreeing to pay him a sum of 300 *pardauws* annually. The regular income from the city would continue to accrue to Eti Raja. Venkata Raja left today for Tierepalveron leaving behind 10 men to man the gates.

19 August

On 16 August, a brother of interpreter Padmanabh brahmin went to Tierepalveron together with one of the rajas of Pede Raja. From there, these two persons together with Capour and Venkata Dere[23] proceeded to Outhecoute[23] to see if they could secure the release of Pede Raja. With the brother of Padmanabh brahmin, Ysbrantsz. had sent an *ola* addressed to the wife and children of Eti Raja together with a small Japanese case as a present. The *ola* contained an account of the molestations that Venkata Raja had subjected Pulicat to.

21 August

The brother of Padmanabh brahmin and the raja returned to Pulicat today. They said that they had been warned by a brahmin in the service of a brother-in-law of Eti Raja that Venkata Raja might have them arrested. This surprised us because ambassadors were normally not subject to arrest. The sloop *Onrust* left for Masulipatnam with letters for Jacob Dedel.

26 August

The *Leeuwin* left for Tegenapatam with gold, silver and goods to buy saltpetre, slaves and textiles there and bring them to Pulicat.

The Portuguese Manuel Mancedo had travelled from Sao Tome to Pomery to try and reach an accord with Venkata Raja regarding the requested assistance in the attack on Pulicat.

7 September

The sloop *Onrust* arrived with letters from Masulipatnam. Learnt that on 26 August the *Vrede* and the *Medemblik* had been sent to Arakan to fetch rice.

8 September

Learnt from letters from Masulipatnam received overland that Jacob Dedel had died there on 29 August.

14 September

The *Leeuwin* arrived from Tegenapatam with 172,745 ponds of saltpetre, together with some textiles and slaves.

15 September

In view of Dedel's death, Ysbrantsz. left for Masulipatnam to attend to the affairs there.

19 September

Reached Masulipatnam and found the factory in a reasonably good condition.

4 October

Ysbrantsz. left Masulipatnam for Pulicat with the *Schoonhoven* which would proceed on to Holland. The Masulipatnam factory was left in charge of Adriaen Willemsz. Goeree and Jan Libenaar.

10 October

Ysbrantsz. reached Pulicat.

13 October

The *Schoonhoven* was sent to Holland with indigo, Guinea cloth, fine textiles and other Surat goods.[24]

29 October

Received letters from Reijer Pietersen from Tegenapatam saying that the lands around Gingi were being plundered. Since the Company had quite a few effects in that area, Pietersen has requested for a yacht to be able to secure these effects. The frigate *Jager* would be sent there for the purpose.

31 October

The *Jager* was sent to Tegenapatam to take in the Company's goods lying there because that area was in disarray and the local chieftains were looting everything they could lay their hands on.

Received news from Trancquebar that on 7 September a ship had been sent by the Danes to the Moluccas with about 20 packets of textiles, painted as well as woven. Another ship had left on the 9th of the same month for Denmark with Christopher van der Molen on board. This ship was laden with pepper, indigo and saltpetre.

Received news from Nagapattinam that two ships had left that port for Aceh, five frigates for Malacca and one frigate each for Kedah, Martaban and Manila. No vessels had left Nagapattinam this year for Bengal, Pegu or Tenasserim.

Six galleons and two ships had reportedly arrived at Goa from Portugal. Another gallion was awaited.

15 November

Received news from Pieter van den Broecke at Surat that on the 25th of September had arrived there from Holland the *Dordrecht* and from Batavia the *Nieuw Bantam*, the *Zuid Holland* and the *Weesp* with a total cargo worth f.500,000 in cash and goods.

27 November

Received letters from Venkata Raja written to the Company and to the people of Pede Raja that all the soldiers in the city should be sent to him because he was having troubles with the people of Tyma *Nayak* and Sackemoeleware.[25] They were plundering and burning his lands. He has asked for Dutch assistance in the form of gunpowder and lead along with the soldiers from the city. Ysbrantsz. replied that in these troubled times it was entirely unadvisable to demand soldiers form Pulicat because it was sorrounded by enemies. Besides, Sackemoeleware had never shown any enmity towards the Company and Ysbrantsz. did not want to make fresh enemies. It was not possible to send any gunpowder because the Company was in great need of it for its own protection.

27 December

The sloop *Leeuw Jonge* was sent from Pulicat to Armagon to cruise there because a ship of Karjera[26] with the captain of Manar was expected there soon.

1625

1 January

Arrived two sloops the *Jonge Leeuwin* and *Leeuw Jonge*.

4 January

The ship *Wapen van Rotterdam* came from Masulipatnam to pick-up the goods for Java and go on to Batavia.

11 January

Arrived from Arakan with rice and slaves the ships the *Vrede* and the *Medemblik* together with the yachts the *Tenasserim* and the *Bonne Remedie*.

16 January

The following vessels under the command of Jan Libenaar left Pulicat for the Point de Galle to cruise there looking for Portuguese ships as long as the northern monsoon lasted: the ship *Medemblik*, the yachts *Tenasserim* and *Bonne Remedie* and the sloops *Jonge Leeuwin* and *Leeuw Jonge*. 130 men were aboard these vessels.

22 January

The *Wapen van Rotterdam* left Pulicat for Tegenapatam to pick-up 50 to 60 packets of cloth and 100 slaves. In the month of January, 20 big ships arrived at Pulicat from Orissa, all laden with rice, butter, oil and other provisions.

1 February

Ranganath Raja left Pulicat with his wife and children. He was worried that Pede Raja might take revenge from him for his part in the revolt of July last at the behest of Eti Raja.

11 February

Letters received from Tegenapatam suggested that through a chieftain of his, the *nayak* of Madril had plundered and burnt the city of Peta. This city was about 1½ days' journey from Nagapattinam and the chief trading centre in Tanjore. Peta was under the jurisdiction of the *nayak* of Tanjore who was at war with the *nayak* of Madril. Peta was and continued to be an important trading city. All the pepper that was brought from Malabar into Tanjore was brought to the market at Peta. As a result, the *nayak* of Tanjore earned an income of 5,000 rials in 8 days through tolls at Peta. The Danes procured a lot of pepper at Peta each year and carried it to Trancquebar where they had a fort and which was two days' journey away. The *Wapen van Rotterdam* had left Tegenapatam for Batavia on 27 January.

20 February

The sloop *Cleyn Dort* left for Petapuli to pick up the clothes and cotton yarn lying ready there.

12 March

Learnt from the letters from Adriaen Willemsz. Goeree at Masulipatnam that Prince Khurram had arrived at Ibrahimpatnam[27] on 1 March with his forces. He was planning to march on to Bijapur which had been as good as conquered by Malik Ambar.[28] There was also a rumour that Parwiz, the eldest brother of Prince Khurram, was hotly following him with a cavalry of about 10,000 horses. He was reported to have reached Caraparra (the outermost frontier of Golconda). Prince Parwiz had reportedly been asked by the Emperor to ask the king of Golconda to hand Khurram over to him. If he did not agree to do so, force was to be used. As a result, the people of Golconda were very perplexed. The Muslim lands may all rise in revolt which would have an adverse effect on the Company's trade.

19 March

The *Vrede* left Pulicat for Sao Tome to cruise against possible

Portuguese action against the ships which were expected any day from Arakan with slaves for the Company.

25 March

Learnt from letters from Reijer Pietersen van der Wiel at Tegenapatam that a Danish ship had come back from Tenasserim on 12 March after unloading at Puleceri 100 *bahars* of lead, some benzoin, raw silk and silk textiles. Roeland Crappe had also reached Puleceri which they had taken on farm. The Danes had been trying to bring the Dutch into disrepute by claiming that they did not have a king and that a woman ruled them. Also, that the king of Denmark could indeed prevent the Dutch from going to the East Indies and so on.

5 April

The *Vrede* would be kept at Sao Tome for some more time because some Portuguese fusts were awaited there as also to protect the ships expected from Arakan carrying slaves for the Company.

12 April

Arrived a ship from Arakan with 2,000 *carras* of rice and some Arakanese silk and wax. This ship belonged to the *kotwal* of Arakan.

14 April

Another two ships arrived from Arakan. One of these had brought 1,500 *carras* of rice, some silk and wax while the other had carried six elephants. The latter had brought letters from Pauwels Cramerheijn, the Dutch factor at Arakan, saying that since the departure of the *Vrede* and the *Medemblik*, he had bought another 100 slaves and that the king of Arakan had captured about 7,000 of them in Bengal. The king was expected back in Arakan any day so that it was possible that the Company might get a large supply of slaves from Arakan this year.

21 April

Arrived at Pulicat the yachts the *Jager*, the *Tenasserim* and the *Bonne Remedie* together with the sloops the *Jonge Leeuwin* and the *Leeuw Jonge* which had been sent on 16 January to Point de Galle along with the *Medemblik* in order to cruise there. These vessels parted company with the *Medemblik* at Tegenapatam eight days ago. The latter stayed on there to collect the saltpetre and clothes that were awaited any day. At the Point de Galle, the fleet had burnt two sloops. In addition, it had captured and brought to Pulicat two *thonys* and a small ship owned by some Hindus of Tegenapatam on their way back from Aceh. The total value of the ships was around. . . .[29]

25 April

Learnt that Condelrey[30] and Venkata Raja had sent some spies to Carmenel on the other side of the river. There was a rumour that these two wanted to become the masters of Pulicat and then take the Dutch on. With this end, they had won over to their side the chieftains Ranganath Raja, Tyapa Raja and Krishnam Raja.[31]

26 April

In the evening arrived the *Medemblik* from Tegenapatam. It brought fine textiles and Guinea-cloth worth about f.30,000.

28 April

The *Medemblik* was sent to Masulipatnam.

2 May

Learnt from letters from Adriaen Willemsz. Goeree at Masulipatnam that there had been some trouble with a Muslim waterman of the factory. What had happened was that a street that the Dutch factors had always used was blocked by this man for his private use. When we removed the barrier, he complained against us to the *qazi* and the *havaldar* of Masulipatnam who, in turn, complained against us to Golconda. As a result, a *farman* arrived from Golconda that a sum of 3,000 *pagodas* was to be collected from Goeree as fine. In the event of refusal, he was to be brought over to Golconda. Having been secretly informed of this, Goeree went aboard a Dutch ship without the knowledge of the *havaldar*. Only time will tell what the authorities would do about it. They simply wanted to extort money from the Company.

5 May

Krishnam Raja, who had married the daughter of the sister of Pede Raja only a few days ago, left the city without the knowledge of Pede Raja and even his wife. This had annoyed Pede Raja a great deal. Pede Raja also had troubles with chieftains Ranganath Raja and others and had come to us to seek our help to take revenge on them. We advised him to be patient and said that we would write to these chieftains and after acquainting ourselves with the situation, we would assist him.

6 May

Received a letter from chieftains Ranganath Raja and Tyapa Raja in reply to ours of yesterday in which we had reminded them of the promises they had made to us and to Pede Raja before they had left Pulicat. The chieftains only replied that Pede Raja was trying to bring the territory of Krishnam Raja under his jurisdiction. It seemed that there had been some misunderstanding between the soldiers of the chieftains and those of Pede Raja.

16 May

The sloops *Jonge Leeuwin* and the *Leeuw Jong* left here with about 60 men to strengthen the *Vrede* which was at Tegenapatam with another 30 to 40 men. This was done because the Portuguese were reported to be planning to attack the *Vrede*. Since the *Vrede* was to be sent to Batavia next month, it had been instructed to come to Pulicat soon. Since it was not safe to leave the Company's goods at Tegenapatam, we had instructed one of the sloops to remain in the river there to guard the goods against robbers.

20 May

5 frigates of war and 13 *sampans* had arrived at Sao Tome from Ceylon with rice and other provisions. The frigates had travelled from Goa with an important man named Don Diogo de Mello aboard who will be the Captain General of Sao Tome on the Coromandel coast. It was said that he had brought 150 soldiers along. This armada had been sighted on the 18th of the month by the two sloops that we had sent to Tegenapatam from Pulicat on

the 16th of this month. After the armada had passed, the sloops captured a *sampan* laden with 500 *ammanams* of areca-nuts.

28 May

Received letters from Tegenapatam that the great Ava or the commander-in-chief of the *nayak* of Gingi had reached the city on 20 May with 400 men and had plundered it. Besides, Tirupapaliyur[32] had been burnt and the fort there laid seige of, which was likely to give in any day. All the routes were closed and the saltpetre and textiles lying ready there could not be sent to Pulicat. Malaya had lost about 500 *pardauws* because his house had been looted. If the *Vrede* had not been lying in the harbour there, the Company too would have suffered a lot of damage. However, the only loss we suffered was that our trade in saltpetre had been hindered.

29 May

Having left Masulipatnam on the 24th of this month, the *Leeuwin* reached Pulicat today on its way to Holland. This vessel was laden with the following:

55,349 ponds cotton yarn, 7,929 pieces Guinea-cloth; 5,072 pieces *salampuris*, 2,797 pieces *parcallas*, 1,831 pieces *bethilles*, 21,017 ponds indigo, 2,996 pieces fine *muris*, 224,375 ponds saltpetre together with other sundry items. The ship sailed out of this harbour on the 31st of May. The captain of this ship was Jan Willemsz. and it was manned by 75 persons, all in good health.

30 May

The *Vrede* arrived from Tegenapatam with about 200,000 ponds of saltpetre. This ship will be sent to Batavia next month.

4 June

Learnt from a letter from Tegapa[33] at Sao Tome that 3 *gelias* and a *thony* had left that place on 3 June for the south full of soldiers. We suspect that these would have gone to Tegenapatam. The Pulicat factors had written to Pietersen there that, if necessary, he was to go under the protection of the Danes at Pulceri.

7 June

The *Vrede*, together with the sloops the *Leeuw Jonge* and the *Cleyn Dort*, a gallion and a *prauw* had been sent to Sao Tome with orders to go on to Tegenapatam to see if something could be gotten out of the Portuguese *gelias* and *thonis* there. The fleet was manned by 120 men under the charge of Captain Cornelis van Suylensteyn.[34]

8 June

Ysbrantsz. learnt from a letter from Jan Libenaar, upper-merchant at Masulipatnam, that upper-merchant Adriaen Willemsz. Goeree died there on the 30th of May at about 10 p.m.

10 June

Ysbrantsz. learnt from Kanjiwaram[35] that a Hindu named. . .[36] had arrived there from Sao Tome as an ambassador of the Portuguese with presents to request the chief priest to tell the *nayak* that they planned to take a force of 3,000-4,000 soldiers together with some frigates and ships to Pulicat. If the *nayak* would assist them in this project they would be glad to conquer the fort at Pulicat jointly. The *nayak* could then keep the fort along with everything it contained. They were also willing to meet all the costs of the seige.

13 June

The *Vrede* together with the two sloops that had sailed from Pulicat on the 7th of June returned today. The sloops had had an encounter with the Portuguese galleons in which we had 2 dead and 5 injured. The Portuguese reportedly had 14 dead and some injured.

15 June

The *Vrede* left for Masulipatnam to pick-up the cargo lying ready there for Java and the Moluccas and go on from there to Batavia. This ship had taken at Pulicat 255 packets of clothes, some rice, 5,000 ponds of gunpowder together with 80 slaves and captured men. The aforementioned textiles had cost more than 90,000 guilders.

20 June

Learnt from letters from Reijer Pietersen van der Wiel at Comunoer[37] that he had left Tegenapatam along with the brother of Malaya and had fled to Comunoer. According to him, Tegenapatam had been completely robbed and plundered. We also learnt that the Portuguese had captured from the harbour of Puleceri a *sampan* carrying areca-nuts and belonging to the residents of Puleceri and had burnt it. This was notwithstanding the fact that the Danes had farmed out Puleceri. Only time will tell if the Danes whose reputation had suffered considerably, would take revenge.

23 June

The citizens who had fled to Puleceri from Tegenapatam had to sit idle there because Puleceri had been farmed out by the Danes. The Danes then ordered them to leave the place which forced a number of poor weavers and painters to go to Comunoer. The Danes did this simply because the people of Tegenapatam had carried on trade with the Dutch. The Dutch factor, Pietersen van der Wiel, and the brother of Malaya, who had gone first to Puleceri were obliged to move to Comunoer because of the hurdles placed in their way by the Danes at Puleceri.

28 June

The *Vrede* left Masulipatnam for Batavia with over f.150,000 worth of clothes for Java, Amboina and the Moluccas, etc.

18 July

The *Medemblik* arrived from Masulipatnam with some provisions for the fort at Pulicat.

21 July

The *Medemblik* left for Sao Tome along with the frigates the *Bonne Remedie* and the *Valck* to see what could be taken from the enemy and then to sail on to Comunoer and Tegenapatam to pick up the saltpetre and clothes lying there.

25 July

The aforementioned frigates captured between Sao Tome and

Cattelon[38] a Portugese fust with 30 soldiers and 29 sailors. This fust had left Sao Tome with a view to capture one of our sloops lying near Tegenapatam but was itself captured.

5 August

Learnt that Sangama *Nayak*,[39] Kasturangappa[39] and Karichumappa[39] passed Sao Tome yesterday with a force of 10,000 to 12,000 men on their way to Pulicat. The *Medemblik* and the frigate had, therefore, been recalled to Pulicat.

7 August

This evening, we received two *olas*, one addressed to Pede Raja and the other to Malaya, sent by . . .,[40] captain of the fort Nandjambuk (one mile from Pulicat). Pede Raja had been requested to send him 300 to 400 soldiers tomorrow because he had to visit Sangama *Nayak* and was obliged to present to him all his people.[41] He had written to Malaya to try to persuade Pede Raja to accede to this request. It was also learnt that Sangama *Nayak* was trying to get Pede Raja on to his side.

10 August

The frigates the *Bonne Remedie* and the *Valck* arrived at Pulicat. They had brought along with them the Portuguese frigate captured on the 25th of July.

11 August

It was decided to bring the aforementioned frigates in the river here and their crew into the fort because Sangama *Nayak* had reached within ¾ miles of Pulicat. His intentions were not yet clear.

17 August

The *Medemblik* arrived at Pulicat. The army of Sangama *Nayak* is reported to be 15,000 strong and continued to stay ¾ miles from here. It was, therefore, absolutely essential to have the *Medemblik* on the harbour at Pulicat.

20 August

It was learnt that Sangama *Nayak*, Kasturangappa and Karichumappa left Pulicat on the 17th of August with their armies for their respective places. It was, therefore, decided to send the *Medemblik* to Porto Novo to pick up the 90 *lasts* of saltpetre lying ready there.

21 August

Sangama *Nayak* sent us an ambassador named. . . .[42] This man said that his master was proposing to beseige Sao Tome and was closing all land routes to that place. He wanted us to intercept all water traffic to Sao Tome. He further informed us that the *Nayak* had arrived with his army at Sangelepotte which was his chief fort.

28 August

The *Edam* arrived at Pulicat from Batavia after a 32-day journey. It brought a cargo worth f.163,000 consisting of 40,000 rials, some gold, spices, copper and alum, etc.

1 September

The *Edam* left Pulicat after unloading cash worth f.90,000.

4 September

Learnt from letters from Pietersen at Comunoer that the *nayak* of Madril had detained all of the saltpetre, around 700 *bahars*. 5,000 *pardauws* were being asked for before its release. A gift of 1,000 *pardauws* had been sent. It seemed that the Danes were responsible for this.

6 September

Received letters from Puleceri written by Maerten van Rossen aboard the *Medemblik* in the harbour. He and the other factors had gone on land at the invitation of the Danes who had taken the city on farm. But later the Danes said that they were afraid of the lord of the land, so our people came back to the ship.

Received a letter from Jan Libenaar at Masulipatnam that he had secret information that Mir Kamal-al-Din had written to Jannat Khan in Golconda (who had been appointed *havaldar* of Masulipatnam and was due to arrive there soon) requesting him to obtain a *farman* prohibiting the Dutch from buying textiles or any other commodity in Golconda and be allowed to do so only at Masulipatnam. Alternatively, they ought to be required to pay the same tolls as others namely 4 per cent and not just 3,000 *pagodas* annually in lieu thereof. If a fixed amount had to be kept, it ought to be increased to 10,000 *pagodas* per annum. Besides, the Dutch ought not to be allowed to deal with anyone other than Mir Kamal-al-Din together with three or four others to be appointed for the purpose. It was rumoured that Jannat Khan had already obtained a *farman* from the king along these lines.

8 September

Pietersen had written from Comunoer that from now onwards, the Danes would have to pay only 1,500 *pardauws* at Porto Novo per annum for their exports and imports. The merchants dealing with them would be obliged to pay another 1,000 *pardauws*. These merchants had already contracted for the supply of 500 *bahars* of saltpetre to the Danes within a period of 11 months.

9 September

The *Delfshaven* arrived from Holland with 140 men and 10 women. 3 men had been lost on the way. The upper-merchant on this ship was Cornelis van der Hoeff[43] and the Captain Jacob Pietersz. Heyn.[44]

11 September

Ysbrantsz. left Pulicat for Masulipatnam with the *Delfshaven*.

22 September

Ysbrantsz. reached Masulipatnam.

23 September

The *Medemblik* and the frigate *Jager* were sent from Masulipatnam to Arakan with a cargo of the value of f....[45] to fetch the slaves bought there and to buy some rice there. They have been ordered to return latest by 10 November.

3 October

Ysbrantsz. left Masulipatnam for Pulicat with the *Edam* and the

Jonge Leeuwin to arrange for the departure of the *Edam* from Pulicat to Batavia. Near Masulipatnam, Ysbrantsz. found a Danish yacht, the *Nachtegael*, lying there. On board was Christoffel van der Molen, the Danish director at Tranquebar. This vessel was on its way to Bengal. The Danes were planning to establish a factory at Masulipatnam. Ysbrantsz. had also learnt that last month the Danes had sent from Trancquebar the *Waterhond* to Bengal. Only time will tell what the Danes did there.

8 October

Ysbrantsz. arrived at Pulicat. He found everything in good order there.

17 October

The fluit *Edam* and the yacht *Tenasserim* left Pulicat for Batavia laden with 287 packets of clothes together with yarn, and some iron, steel and rice.

24 October

Ysbrantsz. had learnt from Masulipatnam that the Danes had hired a house there with a view to establish a factory. They had reached an agreement with the Muslim authorities regarding the rate of the export and import duties at 3½ per cent. Their yacht, the *Nachtegael*, had gone to Bengal. They had four ships at Masulipatnam, namely the *Christiaanshaven*, the *Hondt*, the yacht the *Nachtegael* and the ship *Jupiter*, that had come from Makassar. It was also learnt that the *Jupiter* had run aground on the coast of Orissa. Most of the cargo of the value of 50,000 rials had been lost and only 8 men could be saved.

5 November

Pietersen had written from Tegenapatam that the Danes had contracted for 750 *bahars* of saltpetre there. This contract had been concluded with some Chetty merchants of Porto Novo at 16½ rials per *bahar*. The stipulation was that the lot was to be delivered within a year. The Danes clearly had an eye on our saltpetre that had been detained. The chetty merchants had been given advances by them and the merchants had gone to the areas where saltpetre was available. They had tried to get hold of the 800 *bahars* of our saltpetre which had been in detention for the last five months. The Danes were thus trying to fish in troubled waters. Until now, the Danes had contracted for 50 *corgies* of *balatius*, 6 *corgies* of *sarassa* turbans, 30 *corgies* of *Chindes de Bengripatnam* as well as other clothes useful for Aceh where they wanted to establish a factory.

20 November

The Danes had contracted for the following varieties of clothes at Puleceri with the intention of sending them to Aceh and Makassar:

chelas of 8 *covids* at 9¼ rials per *corgie*, rough *sarassa* turbans at 35 rials per *corgie*, *chindes* 6 *covids* long and 2 spans wide as used by the Malays for a head-dress at 9 rials per *corgie*, some rough *tapi sarassas* at 14 rials per *corgie*, some *bethilles* of 25-28 *asta* length and 4½ span width at 11 to 15 *fanums* [10 *fanums*= 1 rial].[46] They had also been trying to get from the weavers as many of the clothes that the Dutch had contracted for with the weavers as they could.

The following ships had left Nagapattinam in September 1625:

1 galliot belonging to Manuel de Conje[47] and Jan Patchieco[47] for Tiraange[47]
1 galliot belonging to Captain Manuel Patchieco[47] for Susalen[47]
1 galliot belonging to Cosinoledo[47] for Malacca
1 galliot belonging to Anthony de Fygeroda[47] for Malacca
1 galliot belonging to a *casado*[48] of Cochin which he had hired on freight for Malacca
1 galliot belonging to Hector de Celes[49] for Bengaryn[49]
1 ship belonging a Muslim merchant Kunjali with goods worth 80,000 *pardauws* for Pegu
1 ship belonging to a Muslim merchant Beridengan[49] for Aceh
1 ship belonging to a Pathan merchant for Aceh
1 ship belonging to a Muslim merchant Fammanoda[49] for Kedah
1 galliot from Goa on freight for Bengal
2 galliots belonging to Rona Matchiado[49] for Bengal

1 galliot had left in May for Manila. This vessel had belonged to Manuel de Barks.[49]

November 28

The *Delfshaven* arrived at Pulicat from Masulipatnam with 318 packets of cloth and cotton yarn, 305 *kandis* of rice, some iron and steel, etc., and 130 slaves.

Of the 544 slaves that had been bought in Arakan during the current year, 386 had died in Arakan while some died on the way so that no more than 130 reached Pulicat. Most of these were also sick. The king of Arakan had brought 10,000 slaves from Bengal. Of these, 4,000 had already died. The king of Arakan has banned the transportation of slaves out of Arakan saying that he would keep all the slaves himself. Therefore, Under-merchant Pouwels Cramerheyn had come back from Arakan leaving only two assistants there.

* This journal was sent as an enclosure to Marten Ysbrantsz.'s letter to De Carpentier at Batavia dated 5 December 1625 (document no. 74).

1. This letter is not available in the Company's archives.
2. The term *komati* or *comati* was used chiefly for a trader in the north of Madras and corresponded to *chetty*.
3. The captain of the *Wapen van Rotterdam* was one Jacob Geritsz. Coper (see document no. 61)
4. Gerrit Jansz. was of Polish origin.
5. Mir Kasim had been the *havaldar* of Masulipatnam several times. In 1619, he was arrested on the orders of the king of Golconda. He was reinstated in this office in 1621 and again in 1624. He also happened to be a rich merchant.
6. Francis Futter held second position at the English factory at Masulipatnam in 1624 when the factory was under the charge of Thomas Mills. He had to face trial at Masulipatnam in connection with a dispute with the *havaldar* of Masulipatnam. He went back to England at the end of 1625.
7. Probably king Ramadeva is intended.
8. Not identified.
9. It is not known when precisely such an agreement was made but such exchange of captured persons among the European companies was a common practice. See William Foster (ed.), *The English*

Factories in India 1624-1629, Oxford, 1906-1927, vol. III, p. 9, note 1.

10. This document does not form part of the journal and is not available in the Company's archives.
11. Tyapa Raja, Ponke Pillai and Raghu Reddy were local chieftains in the kingdom of Karnataka who had been fighting to acquire power. It was only by the end of 1629 that King Ramadeva was able to bring the situation fully under control.
12. Not identified.
13. Not identified.
14. Pomery, probably Ponneri. Its latitude is 13°.21′N and longitude 80°.10′E.
15. Venkata Raja, also known as Venkata *nayak*, came up as a friend of Eti Raja in 1624 when he made an unsuccessful attempt to become the master of Pulicat. He got the farming of Pulicat with difficulty at 300 *pagodas* per annum. He often tried to show as if he was the king of Karnataka. The territories under his rule were to the east of Armagon and a part of north east of Karnataka. In 1629, he submitted to the king of Karnataka.
16. The *gelia* was a small and fast sailing vessel.
17. Not identified.
18. Katur is in the south of river Pennar and to the north east of Pulicat.
19. The term *ola* generally means a letter, often a written order. In Malyalam, *ola* means a palm-leaf. *Ola* was thus probably an order or grant written on a palm-leaf.
20. Ysbrantsz.'s reply is not available in the Company's archives.
21. Reijer Pietersen van der Wiel, an under-merchant at Tegenapatam in 1624, had fled the town together with the brother of Malay at the time of its plunder to a place called Conimoer. He had later become a free burgher and in 1634 had applied for the position of a notary at Batavia.
22. It is not clear what this word means. In the English records, the presents given to the *nayak* of Tanjore are reported to have included two demiculverins. See Foster, *The English Factories in India 1624-1629*, p. 15.
23. Not identified.
24. The *Schoonhoven* had carried Surat goods which had earlier been sent from Surat to Holland with the *Vrede* which, however, had been driven to Coromandel by contrary winds.
25. Not identified.
26. Not identified.

27. Ibrahimpatnam was a village close to Kondapalli, now in the Kistna district, and Bezwada to the north-west of Masulipatnam. Its latitude is 16°.75'N and longitude 80°.75'E.
28. Malik Ambar was an Abyssinian slave who rose to be the chief minister of Ahmadnagar and was in charge of its adminstration for many years. He first rose to prominence in 1601 by defeating a Mughal army in south-eastern Berar. He was distinguished alike as a general and as a statesman and it was his strategy that foiled all the efforts of Emperor Jahangir to conquer Ahmadnagar. He gave to the state of Ahmadnagar not only a good and efficient administration but also a very sound system of land revenue. He died at an advanced age in 1626. It was only after this that the Ahmadnagar kingdom could be annexed to the Mughal empire.
29. The amount is not filled in.
30. Probably Kundal Raja or Kundal Rao.
31. Krishnam Raja was the son-in-law of Pede Raja's sister.
32. Tirupapaliyur is a short distance away from Tegenapatam, now known as Fort St. David in the South Arcot district. In 1608, the Dutch factors were granted the use of an old fort at Tegenapatam, but it proved to be uninhabitable, and they were allowed to occupy instead a smaller fort at Tirupapaliyur. In the Dutch records, the factory is spoken of variously as Tegenapatam or Tirupapaliyur and is situated about 70 miles north of Nagapattinam.
33. Probably a spy of the Company at Sao Tome.
34. Cornelis van Suylensteyn came to the East Indies in 1614 as a lieutenant. In May 1622, he was sent to Pulicat, where he had also served earlier. He was relieved of his duties at Coromandel in 1632 at his own request.
35. Kanjivaram is a town to the south-west of Madras.
36. The name of the person is not filled in.
37. This is Conimoer near Pondicherry.
38. Not identified.
39. These were all local chieftains in Karnataka. Kasturangappa is known to have been punished by the *nayak* of Gingi in 1629.
40. The name of the person is not filled in.
41. This could be something similar to the Mughal *mansabdari* system under which the holders of the *mansab* (cavalry as well as personal rank) were obliged to maintain and provide troops on demand.
42. The name of this person is not mentioned.
43. Cornelis van der Hoeff came as upper-merchant with the *Delfshaven* to Batavia via the Coromandel coast in March 1626 in the capacity

of the head of the factory at Jambi. He was allowed to return to Batavia in May 1629 at his own request. He repatriated at the end of 1629.

44. Jacob Pietersz. Heyn sailed from Holland on 5 January 1625 as the captain of the *Delfshaven*. He reached Pulicat on 9 September and left for Batavia on 5 December. He left for Taiwan in mid-1628.
45. The amount is not filled in.
46. This rate would seem to be per piece, though it is not specified.
47. Not identified.
48. A *casado* was a private Portuguese merchant, usually a New Christian and operating under the jurisdiction and protection of the *Estado da India*.
49. Not identified.

1626

77. Ysbrantsz. at Pulicat to Governor-General De Carpentier at Batavia, 27 January 1626. V.O.C. 1090, ff.216-19vo (Copy).

Conditions at Masulipatnam had not improved since Pulicat's letter of 5 December 1625.[1] As per Batavia's orders, the Masulipatnam factory would not be closed. The *havaldars* there are changed frequently and their sole interest was to make money. The factors had to be on their guard against situations such as the one faced by Van Uffelen. There had been no news from Mansur Khan and they had no option but to have patience.

The spices received with the *Coningh David* at Masulipatnam could not be sold because *havaldar* Jannat Khan still had a large stock of nutmeg and mace which he was trying to force on merchants from outside Masulipatnam before they could reach our factors there. This had made the merchants leave the town but the *havaldar* had since persuaded them to come back giving our factors there hope of being able to sell our supplies soon. Nutmeg was likely to fetch 110-15 *pagodas* per *bahar* and mace 18 *pagodas* per *maund*. Some cloves had been sold at 11¼ *pagodas* per *maund*.

Indigo was high in price and poor in quality but in order to ensure that the entire supply was not diverted to the Danes, it was decided to buy a small quantity of 150-60 *littels*.[2] Surat was likely to send a large amount of indigo to Batavia.

A sack of cotton was being sent as a sample. It is available in plenty at 13 to 14 *pagodas* per *bahar* (= 480 ponds). The 800 *bahars* of saltpetre bought for us by Malaya had been detained. Of this amount, only 500 bales of unrefined saltpetre had since been released. The Danes had taken Puleceri and Porto Novo on farm and had spoiled the saltpetre market. Gunpowder was available in Masulipatnam in abundance.

This letter was being sent with the *Arend* with a cargo worth f.66,848 including 463 lbs. of rather poor quality and expensive opium.

Ysbrantsz. was planning to send a vessel to Bengal. Two Danish vessels, the *Christiaanshaven* and the *Waterhond* had reportedly returned to Masulipatnam with rice and textiles on the 14th of January 1626 after spending several months at Pipli and Balasore. The *Waterhond* had initially been earmarked for Tenasserim but since that voyage could not materialize, it had instead been sent to Bengal. They had reportedly left behind 30 persons in Bengal. At Balasore, they had bought a ship of 150 *lasts* which was expected to reach Trancquebar any day with more rice. They were planning to send a ship to Makassar and another to Tiku and Priaman. At Masulipatnam, the Danes had bought only 100 littels of indigo.

It was decided not to appoint Laurens Rysenbeeck, the Church reader to succeed the late Priest Servaas as the clergyman partly because of the dreadful temper of Rysenbeeck's wife. He was, therefore, being repatriated to Batavia together with his family. Orders regarding clergyman Jan Harmansz. Follium who arrived at Pulicat with the *Coningh David* were awaited. If he was not to stay on in Pulicat as clergyman, another person should be sent for the purpose.

One of our *gelias* had captured two *sampans* about 4 miles from Pulicat. They belonged to Nagapattinam and were laden with coarse rice, 10 to 11 packets of *dungarees*, and 30 to 35 packets of oil worth a total of f.2,500-3,000. This would partly pay for the cost of maintaining our small ships. While the crew of one of the *sampans* had escaped, twenty black individuals, some Christians and some Muslims, were captured from the other. Ten of these were rather old: the other ten were being sent to Batavia.

The proposed cruise against the Portuguese in Ceylon was cancelled partly because the ships were needed for guarding against assaults by Sao Tome and the local rajas and partly because reports had been received from our spies that the Portuguese had been ordered to avoid Point de Galle and to reach Jaffanapatnam via Point de Pedro. The Portuguese had two fusts and four *thonys* at Manar[3] and three galliots and two *thonys* at Trincomalee.[4]

1. See document no. 74.
2. A *littel* contained 12 Masulipatnam *maunds* or 314 lbs. avoirdupois.
3. Manar is in Sri Lanka. Its latitude is 8°.59′N and longitude 79°.55′E.
4. Trincomalee is in Sri Lanka. Its latitude is 8°.33′N and longitude 81°.15′E.

78. General letter from Governor-General De Carpentier at Batavia to the Directors at Amsterdam, 3 February 1626. V.O.C. 1086, ff.1-38 (Original).*

On the 16th of November and the 31st of December, 1625 had arrived from Coromandel the fluit *Edam*, the frigate *Tenasserim* and the ship *Delfshaven* with a cargo worth around f.150,000 consisting of 657 packets of clothes, cotton yarn and Guinea cloth for the Indics and the Netherlands, 22,000 ponds of saltpetre, 25,000 ponds of pepper, 200 *lasts* of rice, some steel, iron and sundry items besides 200 slaves.

Because of the loss of control of the *nayak* of Gingi over Tegenapatam, Tirupapaliyur and the sorrounding areas, our trade there had been adversely affected. Once our trade at Tegenapatnam is restored, the Company can have textiles manufactured there in addition to Masulipatnam.

* Summarized in W.Ph. Coolhaas (ed.), *Generale Missiven*, I, pp. 184-202.

79. Daily register maintained at Masulipatnam between 1 March 1626 and 13 September 1628. V.O.C. 1095, ff.48-77vo. (Not stated whether original or copy.)*

1626

1 March

A Muslim ship arrived from Orissa laden with *nelly*.[1]

4 March

A ship from Pegu belonging to the Muslim merchant Mir Kamal-al-Din arrived at Masulipatnam with the news that another five ships were on their way. We were informed that the king of Pegu was willing to release the free-merchants who had now been in detention for over three years. Mir Kamal-al-Din's ship came richly laden with tin and costly rubies.

5 March

Yet another Muslim ship belonging to Mir Murad arrived from Pegu. A free-merchant travelled aboard this ship.

6 March

We were warned by Mir Kamal-al-Din that a lot of thieves had been operating in and around Masulipatnam and that we ought to be careful. A watchman had, therefore, been appointed.

7 March

Marten Ysbrantsz. left for Pulicat. The *Coningh David* scheduled to go to Holland was sent to Pulicat with a cargo worth f.128,150 for the Delft chamber.

12 March

News was received from our merchants that the castle at Kondapilly[2] had been taken over with a force of 10,000 men. The intention behind this action was not entirely clear. Peace had not yet returned to this area following the death of the old king.[3]

Sent the brahmin to Petapuli to put out contracts for painted clothes and collect from Groa and Gopinath the clothes for which contracts had been given out of them.

17 March

Ysbrantsz. was obliged to return because due to contrary winds and a hard storm, he could not proceed towards Pulicat.

21 March

Ysbrantsz. was obliged to return yet once again after two of the masts of his vessel had been torn to pieces and the sailors refused to proceed further because of contrary winds and storms.

25 March

Ysbrantsz. again left for Pulicat with the yacht the *Medemblik*.

3 April

The son of Aga Baba came here with two of his ships from Arakan. These ships were laden with elephants and some rice. With these ships we received a letter from our factor in Arakan, Jan Pepper, which said that the king of Arakan had maintained that he had never banned us from purchasing slaves in Arakan or in Bengal. He had only banned the purchase of those slaves who were Maghs in origin or spoke the Magh language. It seemed, therefore, that we would again be able to procure slaves there. Pepper had also written that the king had obtained a large booty from Bengal and had conquered two cities. The booty included fine clothes, silk wares and jewels. The value of this booty was being assessed as high as the one that his father had gotten from Bengal a few years ago.

8 April

A messenger arrived from Golconda with a *farman* from the king addressed to Mir Kamal-al-Din, the *shahbandar* and some other important Muslims ordering them to arrest *Havaldar* Jannat Khan in view of his bad government and the bad treatment of his subjects. The *havaldar* was accordingly taken into custody.

10 April

Learnt from Mir Kamal-al-Din that Jannat Khan would be replaced as *havaldar* by Muhammad Taqi who had been *havaldar* here earlier. This man had taken the assignment on farm for five years. Taqi was said to be already on his way. He would ask for the accounts from Jannat Khan and force him to restitute to him whatever he had extorted from his poor subjects.

The ship of Mir Kamal-al-Din arrived from Aceh with elephants and some pepper, tin, camphor and raw silk. 30 elephants had died on the way.

12 April

A richly laden ship belonging to the king of Siam arrived with many silk wares, alum, camphor, *poutchina*, sappanwood and wax. It had encountered a Portuguese fust near Sao Tome bravely. Midway between Sao Tome and Pulicat when the Portuguese fust was still after this ship, two of the Dutch fusts in the area went to the assistance of the ship. This persuaded the Portuguese fust to flee. It was given a chase by the Dutch fusts and forced to the beach where its crew was captured by the men of the master of that area and the fust together with its goods confiscated. The Siamese vessel had one dead and four injured. The Dutch had only one injured. The Portuguese had some dead but the precise number was not known. The captain and the merchants aboard the ship had declared at Masulipatnam that but for the Dutch assistance, their ship would have been captured. Another small ship had come from Aceh laden with 30 elephants.

18 April

A ship belonging to Aga Baba arrived from Tenasserim richly laden with all kinds of goods from Siam and Tenasserim.

20 April

Another richly laden ship arrived from Tenasserim with all kinds of goods from Siam and Tenasserim. On this ship was a Dutch pilot and free merchant named Zijs Stalknecht.

24 April

The new *havaldar*, Muhammad Taqi, arrived at Masulipatnam.

He was received with great ceremony by the important Muslims of the city as also by the English, the Danish and the Dutch. After reaching his house, he announced that he had been given the government of Masulipatnam for five years. He then had some food which had been brought by Mir Kamal-al-Din. This was followed by a performance by the dancing girls. The *havaldar* then got busy with getting charge of the affairs from Jannat Khan who was asked to have the accounts ready.

11 May

An English ship arrived empty from Surat with a view to take in the goods that had been lying at Masulipatnam for a long time.

16 May

There was a heat wave which killed many people.

17 May

The heat wave continued.

22 May

The yacht of Aga Baba left for Arakan mainly with tobacco and iron.

26 May

A ship belonging to the *kotwal* of Arakan arrived at Masulipatnam. On the way, it had unloaded rice at Pulicat. It had brought for the Company 600 *carras* of rice and 6 slaves.

27 May

With the sighting of the new moon, the Muslim days of fasting began.[4] They do not eat during the day but fill their bellies properly in the evening.

1 June

The loading of the *Medemblik* which had arrived from Pulicat yesterday was begun. When the factors objected to the officials' demand for opening the cases, they were told that this was to prevent the loading of saltpetre which we were not allowed to carry.

4 June

Barent Pietersz. returned from Petapuli where he had gone to pick-up the clothes.

5 June

The factors learnt that Malik Ambar had died 15 to 20 days ago. He had fought a continuous war with the king of Bijapur and also against the Mughal emperor. The king of Bijapur was now reported to be preparing to fight the king of Golconda.

14 June

The *Medemblik* left Masulipatnam with a cargo of the value of f.178,756.

15 June

It had been learnt that the son-in-law of Khoja Hasan[5] had come from Surat with a *farman* from the king of Golconda authorising him to prevent any ship from sailing to Pegu till such time as his father-in-law, kept in custody in Pegu for many years, was released by the king of Pegu. The *farman* also provided that no ship was to be allowed to go from Masulipatnam to Arakan. Also that the king wanted the son of Aga Baba to be kept under detention at Masulipatnam. All this was in the context of Prince Khurram writing to the king of Golconda not to permit ships to go from Masulipatnam to Arakan in view of a major victory that the king of Arakan had gained against the king of Pegu.

21 June

The *Medemblik* sailed for Batavia.[6]

29 June

Van Rossen was summoned by Mir Kamal-al-Din to his house where the *havaldar*, the *shahbandar*, the *qazi* and all the important Muslims of the city were gathered. They had granted a *kaul*[7] to the merchants permitting them to freely trade with Pegu again. The *havaldar* announced that he intended to send his ship to Pegu within two months. He also asked Van Rossen to allow a small ship of Mansur Khan lying at Bimilipatnam to go to Jaffanapatnam with provisions, etc. This could not be refused because Mansur Khan was the Mir Jumla of the king of Golconda and his closest counsel. So a pass was issued on the condition that the vessel would not carry any Portuguese men or goods.

16 July

Jannat Khan left for Golconda.

20 July

Both the Dutch and the English were summoned by *Havaldar* Muhammad Taqi and told that he had received a *farman* from the king of Golconda requiring the two companies to compensate for a ship of his which had been captured by the Portuguese last year. He also said that in accordance with the contract with the king they were obliged to do this. The Dutch asked to be shown the *farman* which the *havaldar* said was not necessary. He said that since the Dutch and the English were the ones required by agreement to drive the Portuguese away from Masulipatnam, they were obliged to pay for any ship that the Portuguese might capture. The Dutch factors pointed out that they were not aware of any such agreement. The *havaldar* then asked them to do their best to secure the release of his men in captivity at Goa.

21 July

Havaldar Muhammad Taqi left for Petapuli to see what was there for him to fish and scrub there.

2 August

The Danish yacht, the *Nightingale*, had come to Masulipatnam from Trancquebar where it had arrived recently from Makassar in the company of the *Christaanshaven* under the command of Admiral Crappe. At Makassar, they had bought cloves and sandalwood. The cloves had been bought at 254 to 256 rials per *bahar* of 600 ponds.

4 August

Muhammad Taqi returned from Petapuli after exercising tyranny over the merchants there. He had forced Groa and Gopinath, merchants dealing with the Dutch, to give him 1,000 *pagodas*.

He had extracted about 2,500 *pagodas* from that area. From this one could see what kind of justice prevailed in this land.

6 August

The Danish yacht, the *Nightingale*, had left for Bengal. It had carried only 8,000 ponds of cloves and 8,000 ponds of sandalwood for Pipli.

23 August

The factors were summoned by *Havaldar* Muhammad Taqi and told that he had received a new *farman* from the king of Golconda regarding the capture by the Portuguese of a Muslim ship returning from Mocha. The *farman* had instructed him to collect damages from the Dutch and the English. Eventually, he asked the factors for 200 to 300 *pagodas* to help him finance the release of the persons in the ship. He was told that nothing could be done without the permission of Governor Ysbrantsz.

30 August

Muhammad Taqi summoned under-merchant Meerwyck. He demanded 3,000 *pagodas* from him on account of the tolls. He was told that not a single *pagoda* was available in the factory and that he must be patient till our goods were sold. Meerwyck was then told that he (Meerwyck) would not be allowed to leave till such time as the payment had been made. The factors then went to Mir Kamal-al-Din for intervention which obtained the release of Meerwyck.

4 September

Ysbrantsz. was summoned by the *havaldar* about the 3,000 *pagodas* on account of the tolls. He was told that no merchant had come to the factory asking for goods and so no goods had yet been sold. When asked for the reason behind this, he was told that the reason was the merchants who had been farmed the right to trade with the Dutch. The *havaldar* said that everyone was free to go to the Dutch factory to buy and sell whatever he wanted which Ysbrantsz. contradicted in the presence of many important Muslims. The *havaldar* was told that no cash was available and that the factors would be obliged to sell the goods at a low price.

9 September

Ysbrantsz. was again summoned by Muhammed Taqi and told that he did not want to wait any longer for the 3,000 *pagodas*. If it was not possible to pay in cash, we could pay in spices. Ysbrantsz. was perfectly willing to do so but the *havaldar* wanted them at a very low price. He wanted nutmeg at 100 *pagodas*, mace at 12 *pagodas* and cloves at 10 *pagodas*.[8] Ysbrantsz. was allowed to leave only after he had promised to make the payment within two days.

10 September

Ysbrantsz. had to give 15 *bahars* of nutmeg to the *havaldar* at 105 *pagodas* per *bahar* in part payment of the 3,000 *pagodas* due on account of the tolls. He wanted the rest in the form of cloves and mace. Till such time as that was done, no merchants would be allowed to come to the factory.

18 September

Ysbrantsz. and the factors deliberated on a suggestion made by some merchants from outside whether it would not be desirable to sell the spices in a village outside the jurisdiction of the government of Masulipatnam. Barent Pietersz. was asked to go to Gandesael to talk this over with some merchants there. He returned on the 19th after he had arranged for the sale of spices worth 4,000-5,000 *pagodas* at the following prices: nutmeg – 120 *pagodas* per *bahar*, mace – 13¼ *pagodas* per *maund* and cloves at 10¾ *pagodas* per *maund*. Copper was to be sold at 50 *pagodas* per *bahar*.

20 September

Last week the following ships left Masulipatnam: 3 for Pegu, 4 for Arakan, 1 for Tenasserim, and 1 for Aceh. All these ships were richly laden. The Danish *Christiaanshaven* arrived from Trancquebar on the way to Bengal. It carried 50 *lasts* of saltpetre and 24 *lasts* of indigo which had been loaded at Trancquebar,

Porto Novo and Puleceri. It had brought the news that no ships had arrived at Trancquebar from Denmark.

23 September

Ysbrantsz. went to Muhammad Taqi with Mir Kamal-al-Din to ask for permission to sell the Dutch goods elsewhere. This was not allowed because on goods that the merchants from outside bought from us at Masulipatnam they were obliged to give something to the *havaldar* in the form of betel-money. Eventually, he allowed us to send our goods out but said that we would find ourselves cheated in the process.

24 September

We waited for the brahmin incharge of the warehouse to weigh our goods to enable us to send them out, but he did not turn up.

25 September

The brahmin told us that he had had no permission from the *kotwal* to weigh our goods. When the *kotwal* was approached, we were told that he had had no permission from the *havaldar*.

26 and 27 September

We were still waiting for the *havaldar's* permission. It was resolved to go to the *havaldar* with Mir Kamal-al-Din to ask him why he had gone back on his word.

28 September

When Ysbrantsz. went with Mir Kamal-al-Din to the *havaldar*, he was told that it was not customary for the Dutch to send out their goods themselves. He replied that it had not been customary either for the right to trade with them to be farmed out to three private merchants as had been done now. Muhammad Taqi then asked him how many goods we had in the factory and what the value of these goods would be. The *havaldar* offered to buy the goods but this was politely dclined on the plea that he had orders from the Governor-General not to do any business with officials. The *havaldar* eventually offered to permit us to send our goods out provided one paid all the customary dues paid by the local and the outside merchants. These amounted to 5 *pagodas* per *bahar* of goods carried out. Clearly, he was preventing us from sending the goods out so that his own profit was not adversely affected. Ysbrantsz. then said that he would think about this and asked for permission to leave. He was offered betel leaves[9] and told that he would be allowed to deal with whichever merchants he wanted to. Ysbrantsz. then asked him to make a public announcement that all merchants would be free to deal with the Dutch. The announcement was then made throughout the city.

29 September

It was resolved to sell the goods locally to the merchants to whom the right to trade with the Company had been farmed out as being the most profitable course.

1 October

Havaldar Muhammad Taqi summoned some local officials from the area of Petapuli on the basis of a *kaul* promising not to mistreat them in any way. But in fact they were put in iron chains as soon as they arrived.

8 October

These persons had been kept without food ever since and not yet charged with anything. Subsequently, they were charged with rebellion against the *havaldar* last year and told that a *farman* (not shown to them) had been received from the king of Golconda obliging them to pay a fine of 10,000 *pagodas*. These people claimed that they could not raise such an amount. Two of these persons were then beaten up mercilessly till the nails of their hands and feet came out. All this was the result of these persons championing the cause of their people against the high-handedness of *Havaldar* Jannat Khan the previous year. Muhammad Taqi had not dared to attack these persons in their own lands because they were capable of putting together 5,000-6,000 men within three days.

18 October

Mir Kamal-al-Din told us that he had received a letter from Golconda that 4 Portuguese galleons had attacked 4 English ships in the Red Sea and burnt them down. We doubted the veracity of the news.

25 October

Muhammad Taqi asked Ysbrantsz. for passes for two ships scheduled to go to the Red Sea. One of these was from Chaul and the other from Dharmapuri. Since these places were in alliance with the Portuguese, the passes were politely refused.

30 October

Pietersz. left for Petapuli to collect the goods lying ready there.

2 November

One Ariaal Reddy who had been in captivity for long and had been without food or water for the last 6 to 8 days died during the night. He had left behind him four wives and two small children. As soon as the wives learnt of his death, they all jumped into the cremation fire together. The effects left by this man were confiscated by Muhammad Taqi.

8 November

It was learnt that our merchants Ramanna and Coutour were obliged to sell to Muhammad Taqi goods worth 3,200 *pagodas* because they had not been allowed to sell them to anyone else. The merchants from Petapuli who had bought spices worth 3,500 *pagodas* from us were obliged to give one *bahar* of cloves to the *havaldar*.

14 November

The Danish *Christiaanshaven* arrived from Pipli. It was learnt that their yacht, the *Nightingale*, had been wrecked at Balasore. There was a war going on there and nothing was available in and around Pipli. It was, therefore, presumed that the Danes could not have brought much cargo from Pipli. It was learnt that *Havaldar* Muhammad Taqi had summoned our merchants, Ramanna, Lingayya and Coutour, and reminded them about the 200 *pagodas* demanded from each one of them a few days earlier. Ramanna answered that he and Lingayya had brought 150 *pagodas* each. Coutour, however, said that he had not brought anything. He was beaten so mercilessly that his foot swelled up. Ysbrantsz. went to Mir Kamal-al-Din and asked for his advice. He said that this man had promised to give money to Taqi and was daily postponing the payment. When he registered a protest with Muhammad Taqi, he said that the men had not been kept in custody and that as soon as they settled their accounts, they would be allowed to leave. He was told that every *pagoda* he extorted from them eventually came from the Company's treasury. This way the Company paid annually not just 3,000 *pagodas* but in fact 20,000 *pagodas*. When asked to elaborate, the extortions from the Company's merchants was cited as the reason. Ysbrantsz. was then told to either kill or expel these merchants from the Company's service and deal with others.

16 November

Mir Kamal-al-Din informed Ysbrantsz. that his earlier news regarding the capture of English ships in the Red Sea was incorrect and that all ships had arrived safely at Surat on 3 or 4 October.

19 December

The Danish *Christiaanshaven* left for Trancquebar. Its intention of going from there to Denmark had since been dropped. It took in many variety of textiles worth 24,000 rials at Masulipatnam.

30 December

The English yacht, the *Abigael*, arrived from Batavia. It had brought for the English Company 35¾ *bahars* of cloves, 18,000-20,000 rials of eight in cash mainly on private account, 36 *bahars* of lead, 10 *bahars* of nutmeg and some other goods. It would leave in 15-20 days time for Armagon where the English planned to build a fort subject to permission by the *nayak*.

1627

10 January

The old man who had served as the *shahbandar* at Masulipatnam for many years died today. He was probably about one hundred years old. It was believed that he would be succeeded by his son.

23 January

Arrived from Arakan the *Pagel* belonging to Malaya and a yacht of Aga Baba which had been freighted by our factors there from him.

1 December

The yacht *Medemblik* arrived from Batavia. It brought for Masulipatnam and Pulicat together a cargo of f.120,886 consisting of gold coins, rials, nutmeg, cloves, mace, sandalwood and other goods.

2 December

Ysbrantsz., Van Rossen and Pietersz. went aboard the *Medemblik* to greet and escort the Persian ambassador who had travelled on this ship. He was greeted by the *havaldar*, the *qazi*, the *kotwal* and other important officials and merchants and taken in state to his lodging which had been arranged by the *havaldar*.

8 December

The *Brouwershaven* arrived from Arakan with 400 male and female slaves and 700 *carras* of rice. Given the very high price of rice at Masulipatnam, it was planned to unload the ship here itself.

16 December

The Danish ship, the *Waterhond* arrived from Pipli without any cargo. It left for Trancquebar on 20 December.

23 December

It was learnt that the great Mughal had died. It was rumoured that he had expressed a wish to be succeeded by his grandson. Some people thought that Prince Khurram would succeed to the throne.

1628

1 January

The Danish chief Christoffel van der Molen went along with his staff aboard the *Christiaanshaven* and abandoned their factory at Maṣulipaṭnam. This vessel then captured a ship belonging to the king of Golconda which was then being loaded for Mecca. The Danish flag was flown on it. This had been done as a protest against the *havaldar* having refused to allow them to load their ship pending the payment of the tolls which the Danes claimed had already been done. At this stage, the *havaldar* arranged for their goods to be loaded aboard their vessel through the *kotwal*. The inventory of the goods had been prepared with Mir Kamal-al-Din as a witness. Once all the goods had been received aboard, the king's ship was released.

? January

The Danes sent messages to Lingayya, Ramanna and Coutour to obtain a *kaul* from the *havaldar* allowing them to return to Masulipatnam and engage in trade as before.

? January

The *havaldar* sent Ramanna to the Danish ship with a *kaul* saying that they would enjoy the same freedom of trade as before. The Danes then sent an under-merchant together with an assistant with two *bahars* of cloves and some sandalwood but no cash.

? January

The Danish *Christiaanshaven* left for Trancquebar with Christoffel van der Molen aboard.

22 January

A ship from Vishakapatnam belonging to the *kotwal* of Arakan had arrived at Masulipatnam. It had sailed from Aceh but could not continue the journey to Arakan because of the death of the captain. It brought from Aceh 120 *bahars* of pepper and some sulphur. At Vishakapatnam, it had picked up some provisions.

10-12 February

Many small vessels had arrived from Bengal and Orissa with provisions, sugar and slaves. Besides, they had brought a few *taffechelas de Bengale*, some *chautars* and other Bengal textiles.

28 February

Ysbrantsz. had been summoned by the *havaldar* to his house. He was asked about the goods brought in by the *Duyf* and those lying in our factory. As for the prices, he was quoted 110 *pagodas* for nutmeg and 75 *pagodas* per *bahar* for *rompen*. We offered to sell mace to him at 12 *pagodas* and quicksilver and vermilion at 20 *pagodas* and 18 *pagodas* per *maund* respectively.

30 March

Van Rossen had gone to the *havaldar* to ask why the lifting of the nutmeg sold to Sarwa and Narayan Dev at 115 *pagodas* per *bahar* against the delivery of *taffechelas de Narsapur*, *madops*, *madafons* and red cotton yarn had been banned. The cost of lifting the cargo was to be met by the merchants while the Company was to pay the duties and other customary charges. On 20 March, the *havaldar* had promised that the goods would be allowed to be lifted freely. When the *havaldar* replied that he was interested in buying everything, he was told that the Company would be happy to sell to him if he offered to buy at the market price. Van Rossen was afraid that since the merchants were no longer coming to the factory even to make enquiries, they would be forced to sell to the *havaldar* at whatever price he would agree to pay.

Ramanna and Coutour owed the Company 23,000 *pagodas* and Lingayya 4,000 *pagodas*. When Van Rossen complained to the *havaldar* about this, these merchants to whom the right to trade with the Company had been farmed were summoned by him and told to settle their accounts by the time the ships were due to depart. But this was unlikely because these merchants were already burdened with goods forced upon them by the *havaldar* which he had bought from us but had been unable to sell against cash. Things were likely to get worse in the future and sweet talk was not going to take the Company anywhere.

8 April

A ship from Pegu belonging to Muhammad Taqi had arrived at Masulipatnam with a large lot of rubies and a small amount of tin, rice, long pepper and other goods. It had brought the news that another ship belonging to Mir Murad would soon follow.

10 April

The English 'merchant' and the 'under-merchant' had been arrested and fetched by force from their factory by the peons of the *kotwal*. The alleged offence committed was the beating up of Ganga – the *arrak*-maker. It was through the intervention of the Persian ambassador that these men had been released.

9-11 April

The *havaldar* had detained the merchants to whom the right to trade with the Company had been farmed out because they had refused to take from him the goods that he had bought from the Company. The *havaldar* had asked them to pay him 2,000 *pagodas* by way of his profit. On the basis of threats, he succeeded in getting from them a sum of 1,500 *pagodas* after which they had been released.

13 April

The *havaldar* had two persons beaten to death this week. One of these was a brahmin bania[10] who was a broker of diamonds. This man had been accused of having bought a stolen diamond a year ago which was nothing but a trumped-up charge. When this man had been beaten to death, a gold smith who had levelled the charge against him, had been asked to pay compensation of 100 *pagodas*. The other person beaten to death was the servant of a Muslim named Nasir Khan. This man had died and had left some effects behind him. The *havaldar* had wanted some of these and had accused the servant of having stolen some jewels and cash. The servant, however, had disclaimed all knowledge of jewels. He was beaten up so hard that he had died. Thus two innocent persons has lost their lives in torment and pain.

16 April

A Gujarati ship on its way back from Aceh and captured by the Dutch cruising fleet near Galle and bought to Pulicat had since arrived at Masulipatnam. It had, however, been released by Ysbrantsz. because it was not found carrying any unauthorized goods. It was carrying pepper, sulphur, silk, tin and other goods.

17 April

A ship belonging to Mir Murad had arrived from Pegu. It had brought a large amount of rubies, some tin, gumlac, long pepper and some rice. This was the last ship awaited from Pegu this year. Between themselves, the three ships from Pegu had brought rubies worth more than 200,000 *pagodas*.

24 April

A ship from Pegu belonging to Mulla Muhammad Taqi had arrived at Masulipatnam. It had carried six elephants, one of which had died on the way.

27 April

The ship of Mir Akbar Ali had arrived at Pulicat from Pegu and had unloaded some elephants and other goods there. But then it had run into an easterly wind and had been wrecked near Peru.[11]

29 April

A ship belonging to the king of Siam had arrived at Masulipatnam from Tenasserim. It had unloaded some cargo at Pulicat on the way.

3 May

The former *havaldar* Muhammad Taqi had arrived from Golconda to see how things were going and if he could lay his hands on something. He was greeted at his house. He planned to stay for about a month.

7 May

All the men of Lingayya had left town today. He himself had been thinking of leaving town tonight along with his family but had been taken in custody in the mean time by the *kotwal*. Ramanna and Coutour had also been arrested. Barent Pietersz. had gone to the *havaldar* and informed him that Lingayya owed the Company 14,000 *pagodas*, while Ramanna and Coutour owed us as much as 12,000 *pagodas*.

13 May

Lingayya was summoned by the *havaldar* and honoured with a

tashrif.[12] There was an agreement that no creditor of his would ask for his money back for a period of six months. He owed about 5,000-6,000 *pagodas* to the Muslims which he had taken on interest besides the 4,000 *pagodas* that he owed the Company and the 3,000 *pagodas* that he owed to the English. It would be very difficult to recover this money.

10 June

Havaldar Muhammad Taqi left for Golconda. Many Muslims were doubtful if Taqi would again be given this government on farm next year because he had left his brother in charge here for so long.

11 June

It was learnt that the *kafila* of Muhammad Taqi had been looted near Condipilla.[13] It had been carrying a cargo worth 12,000 *pagodas* besides some goods belonging to other merchants.

29 June

The yacht of Malaya which he had bought at Masulipatnam from Mir Kamal-al-Din had been sent to Pulicat. We had provided him with seven men and a cable.

13 September

It was learnt from a letter from Mir Kamal-al-Din from Golconda that Mir Jumla Mansur Khan, the principal aide of the king, had died. The king had secured his house and goods. The *havaldar* of Masulipatnam, Muhammad Taqi, who had looked after the affairs of Mansur Khan, had been taken in custody.

* The entries for the period 28 January 1627 to 12 November 1627 covered in document no. 102 have not been included in this document. The daily register was maintained at Masulipatnam while Governor Marten Ysbrantsz. was at that factory and at Pulicat when he was there.

1. *Nelly* was a variety of grain.
2. Kondapilly is to the north of Kistna. Its latitude is 16°.38′N and the longitude 80°.36′E.

3. The king of Golconda had died towards the end of 1625 and had been succeeded by a minor.
4. *Ramadan* is an important Islamic practice when day long fasting is observed for almost a month.
5. Not identified.
6. The entry of 14 June had already recorded the departure of the *Medemblik* on that date.
7. A *kaul* was a lease or grant in writing or, in fact, any written engagement.
8. The unit of weight is not specified but evidently it was the *bahar* in respect of nutmeg and the *maund* for cloves and mace.
9. This was a gesture indicating a friendly leave-taking.
10. In terms of caste, one could not be both a brahmin and a bania at the same time, so evidently the term bania is used here simply to denote a trader.
11. Not identified.
12. This is an Arabic term meaning conferring honour upon someone by presenting him with a dress of honour or a donation.
13. This was probably Kondapilly.

80. Daily register maintained at Pulicat between 9 April 1626 and 17 September 1628. V.O.C. 1095, ff.28-47. (Not stated whether original or copy.)*

1626

23 April

A ship arrived here at Pulicat from Arakan belonging to the *kotwal* there. This vessel had brought on our account 1,000 *carras* of rice.

[The arrival and departure of Dutch ships has not been recorded.]

27 May

News had been received from Masulipatnam that the Mughal emperor had asked the king of Golconda[1] not to allow any ships to go from Masulipatnam to Arakan because the king of Arakan[2] had been waging a war against him in Bengal. Further news had been received from Masulipatnam that Malik Ambar had died which could cause travails in the kingdom of Golconda. The king of Bijapur[3] had already begun arming himself in order to be able to put the brother of the present king on the throne of Golconda. This was because the present king was born of a slave woman while the brother (who was in custody) was the son of the daughter of the king of Bijapur.

[Other news received from Masulipatnam and already recorded in the daily register of that city have been ignored.]

8 August

It had been learnt from Tegenapatam that two Danish ships had arrived in Trancquebar from Makassar with 150 *bahars* of cloves and 240 *bahars* of sandalwood.

29 August

The yacht *Masulipatam* belonging to Malaya and laden with 156 packets of clothes, red cotton yarn and some pepper and nutmeg had left Pulicat for Pegu. The ballast was provided by coconuts. The total cargo was worth over 15,000 *pagodas* or f.75,000. Five free Dutch mercants had travelled with this ship to trade in Pegu on their private accounts. On the 17th of August, under-merchant Cornelis van Houten left Masulipatnam for Arakan aboard the yacht of the *kotwal* of Arakan. He had been expressly sent there with a cargo worth f.5,071 and 1,000 rials worth of bills bought from the *kotwal* at Pulicat in order to buy slaves. In case slaves were not available, he was to invest the money in rice and elephants.

2 October

A frigate belonging to Malaya left Pulicat for Tenasserim with some very fine clothes made here for the king of Siam. Other wares on the ship included salt, pots and pans.

Two days prior to that, Malaya had sent a small yacht, the *Pegal,* to Arakan. An assistant had been sent on this ship to bring slaves back with him on this vessel.

16 November

It had been learnt from Nagapattinam that 3 galleons had arrived at Goa with the news that the king of Spain had died.

[The arrival and departure of Dutch ships to and from Masulipatnam and other places has not been recorded.]

1627

21 January

It had been learnt from Teganapatam that they had received definite news that 5 galleons and 2 big ships had arrived in Colombo with a large number of men and soldiers. Their intention seemed to be to take a fort in Matacaloa. These were probably the same galleons which the Dutch and the English had scared away at Daman.

2 February

Two *sampans* had arrived at Pulicat from Arakan. One of these was the *Pegal* belonging to Malaya while the other belonged to a Muslim merchant of Arakan. These vessels had brought for us 3,080 slaves – male and female – who had been bought there by the Company's servants. 17 of these slaves had died in Arakan while another 12 had died on the way. Three of these had been killed by our factors and the steersman because they had tried to take over one of the *sampans*.

Since the 25th of January, 8 ships had arrived at Pulicat from Orissa with provisions.

5 February

Another three ships had arrived at Pulicat from Orissa.

8 February

A small ship belonging to a Muslim merchant of Arakan had arrived at Pulicat with slaves for the Company.

25 February

News had been received from Colombo that the Viceroy of Goa had ordered the governor of Colombo that by May next he was to arrange to have 4,000 cows and 3,000 pigs salted. The intention behind this order was not yet clear.

News had been received from Teganapatam that on 25 February, a small yacht had arrived at Trancquebar from Denmark. It had brought no cash or goods.

14 March

It had been learnt from letters from Petapuli that three *sampans* laden with *nelly* had been wrecked there and everything lost.

1 April

A big ship from Tenasserim belonging to the king of Siam and laden with tin and Chinese goods had arrived at Pulicat. An ambassador of the king of Siam sent to the king of Karnataka had arrived on this vessel.

14 April

A ship from Arakan sent by the king there had arrived at Pulicat. It had brought 13 elephants, 8 of which belonged to the king of Arakan, 3 to the *kotwal* of Arakan and 2 to the *havaldar* of Pulicat. It was a very big ship and had taken 33 days for the voyage.

18 April

A small ship from Tenasserim belonging to Malaya had arrived at Pulicat with 150 *bahars* of tin, some Chinese goods, 2 horses and an elephant. It had left Pulicat in October last.

25 April

A ship from Arakan laden with rice arrived at Pulicat.

19 May

Learnt from a letter from Pietersen at Puleceri that after a long seige, the *nayak* of Gingi had finally taken the fort of Baldover on the 8th of this month. From the same letter, it had been learnt that 4 *patalgos*[4] and 14 frigates had come to Galle from Goa and that another 3 galleons were expected under the command of Simon Delivero[5] who had been honoured at Goa with the robes of Jesus Christ. There were various rumours about the intentions of this man. The Portuguese at Nagapattinam were awaiting three ships from Manila.

5 July

It had been learnt from Ponnery that Venkata Raja had extorted a sum of 1,000 *pagodas* from the artisans who painted clothes for the Company there. He had also given them other troubles. As a result, many of them had run away. The factors had, therefore, written about it to Venkata Raja and to Truangelnath Raja[6] who governed that place. It had been pointed out that this would be injurious to his own interests. The trade was at a standstill there. The money extorted from the painters was that given to them as advance by the Company which had no option but to have patience.

18 August

News had been received from Goa that Don Alvero de Bothela[7] had left Goa with a strong fleet for Muscat to rescue it because it had been beseiged by the Arabs. The Portuguese were also worried that the Dutch and the English might try to conquer Muscat.

13 September

[On a visit to Masulipatnam.]

Ysbrantsz. visited Palicol and Narsapur. He found that in and around Palicol, all the weavers had been sitting still because no yarn was to be had. Because of a poor crop, the cotton yarn had gone up in price by 1/3 or even by ½ in comparison to the preceding year.

1628

12 January

The yacht *Kemphaen* had been sent to Tegenapatam with some gold and goods for the purchase of saltpetre, clothes and slaves, etc., which had been brought there.

10 February

Definite news had been received that the great Mughal, Shah Salim, was dead and that the country was in a state of great turmoil.

14 February

The *Kemphaen* had returned from Teganapatam with saltpetre and clothes which the *Medemblik* had not been able to pick-up from there. The Danish ships, the *Waterhond* and the *Christiaanshaven* had sailed from Tegenapatam on 6 January for Makassar with only about 23,000 rials worth of poor quality clothes. Both Admiral Crappe and their director, Van der Molen, had travelled with this ship. They had left a lieutenant as incharge of the fort of Trancquebar with 25 *bahars* of sandalwood and 1½ *bahars* of cloves to meet the cost of maintenance. One of the two aforementioned ships might be sent from Makassar to Denmark. The following cargo had been put aboard the two ships:

Textile variety	*Quantity (in scores of pieces)*
[Put aboard the ships in Puleceri]	
Gobars	25
Tapis	30
Çomitars[8]	25
Chelas of 9 *asta*	30
Chelas of 30 covids	10
Rough black *salalus*	20
Black *salalus* of 14 *asta*	20
Bethilles of 24 *asta*	30
Bethilles of 40 *asta*	40
[Put aboard the ships in Trancquebar]	
Comitars[8]	50
Tapi sarassas	30
Gobars	30
Balatius	60
Rambutins	20
Negro clothes	100
Black *salalus*	30
Chelas of 9 *asta*	45
Bethilles of 26 *asta*	20
Sail cloth	60

These textiles had cost about 23,000 rials of eight.

22 February

The yacht *Kemphaen* had left Pulicat for Sao Tome with a *prauw* to cruise there and to protect the ships expected from Arakan, Pegu and Tenasserim from the Portuguese.

23 February

A letter had been received from Venkata Raja sent through the brother of the *havaldar* of Armagon. The *Nayak* had invited us to trade in his lands. He had written that we would be free to choose where we wanted to trade in his territories—either at Armagon or at Cottepatnam or elsewhere. He is a very mighty prince and we did not want to turn down the friendship offered by him. The white clothes and the cotton yarn came mainly from the area under his jurisdiction. Our clothes were also painted there. The English had done everything to turn him against us. They had not only obtained permission to establish a factory at Armagon but had also been trying to have us excluded from trading at that place. In view of these considerations, it was decided to send our brahmin clerk to Venkata Raja to see what could be done further. The clerk had been instructed to ask for a *kaul* permitting the Company to operate in his lands freely in the matter of trade, and the loading and unloading of goods. He had also been asked to reach an accord with him regarding tolls so that no problems arose on that account later.

14 March

Our clerk returned after visiting Venkata Raja. He had obtained a *kaul* from him permitting the Dutch to operate freely throughout his lands. He had also obtained a letter to that effect addressed to officials of the various places under his jurisdiction. The raja had also given a *kaul* that on all goods loaded and unloaded in his ports, the Dutch would have to pay only half the usual tolls. Goods brought to his lands but not sold there could be taken away without the payment of any tolls whatever. These *kauls* had been addressed to our Malaya in order that the English had no cause to feel unhappy.

30 March

A yacht belonging to Malaya had come from Pegu. Many

Muslim, Hindu and bania merchants together with a cargo of rubies worth f.300,000 or 100,000 *pagodas* had also travelled aboard this vessel.

13 April

A ship from Aceh had arrived at Pulicat after having sailed for 28 days. It was laden with 24 elephants of which four had died on the way. This ship belonged to a Muslim merchant of Masulipatnam named Mir Kamal-al-Din. Another vessel belonging to Muhammad Taqi, the *havaldar* of Masulipatnam, had also sailed from Aceh with this ship. After Mir Kamal-al-Din's ship had unloaded elephants at Pulicat belonging to various merchants, it had sailed for Masulipatnam.

17 April

Two ships belonging to the king of Arakan arrived from there at Pulicat. One of these had brought 19 elephants and the other rice. It had also brought for us 48 male slaves.

19 April

A large ship belonging to the king of Siam had arrived at Pulicat from Tenasserim. It was laden with some tin, Japanese copper, benzoin, raw silk, radix China and silk clothes, etc.

29 April

The *Leeuwin* had arrived at Pulicat from Nagapattinam where it had been cruising since 4 February. The only prize it had managed to get was a frigate coming from Manila. The crew, except for 7 persons, had jumped into the sea and swam ashore. The vessel had come to Pulicat to load saltpetre, slaves and some iron for Manila. The captured Portuguese aboard had declared that the Danes at Trancquebar had promised to supply them as much of refined saltpetre as they wanted. That meant that the Danes helped our enemy with war materials. Besides, they carried Portuguese men and materials in their ships to and from Bengal and Tenasserim, etc.

4 May

A Danish ship had arrived at Trancquebar from Tenasserim. It had brought nothing on the Danes' account because it had been freighted by a number of residents of Nagapattinam and some other Muslims and Hindus, etc.

The yacht, the *Kemphaen*, had gone to Teganapatam to fetch from there saltpetre, clothes and slaves. One of our *gelias* had gone with this yacht with a view to inflict as much damage on the enemy as possible.[9] A number of *sampans* from Ceylon were expected at Sao Tome.

10 May

It had been learnt from Draksharama that all the places around were full of trouble-makers who were daily engaged in robbing and burning. According to the information provided by Hendrick de Witt,[10] the *havaldar* of Draksharama had had an engagement along with 700 to 800 of his men on the first of May with the opposite party. Many had died on both the sides. Three of the principal chiefs of the rebels had been beheaded. The weavers had run away from Draksharama in all directions. The Dutch factors were, therefore, afraid of putting out fresh contracts.

It had been learnt from Masulipatnam that an ambassador of the king of Persia had come there from Hormuz to request the kings of Bijapur and Golconda for help to drive the Portuguese out of Hormuz and to conquer it so that the trade at that place could be taken over by the king of Persia. He had been given an audience by the king of Bijapur and a suitable reply given. He could not get an audience with the king of Golconda because he had somewhat badly treated Mansur Khan, the closest counsel of the king. The envoy had then come to Masulipatnam hoping to board an English or Dutch ship to return to Hormuz or Persia.

Definite news had been received that Prince Khurram, the son of the late Mughal emperor, had succeeded him. He had arranged to have killed all his brothers and their sons as well as some other important personalities.

2 June

The yacht *Kemphaen* together with the *gelia* had returned from Teganapatam. They had brought along with them a *thony* and a *sampan* which had been captured near Porto Novo.

26 June

Ten of our Bengali slaves had fled from Pulicat in a *gelia*. They could not be found in spite of a chase. The factors guessed that they would go to Bengal.

15 August

News had been received from Teganapatam that the king of Kandi was in the field along with his son and the whole of his forces against the Portuguese. The son had sworn to drive the Portuguese out of Ceylon or die.

10 September

The yacht, *Terschelling*, had returned from Nagapattinam where it had been sent on the 17th of last month. At Nagapattinam, it had captured a frigate with 30 packets of clothes. It had been ballasted with salt, pots and pans.

* The daily register was maintained at Pulicat when Governor Marten Ysbrantsz. was at that factory and at Masulipatnam when he was there. The information in the Pulicat register which duplicates that in the Masulipatnam register covered in the preceding document has been ignored.

1. This was Mohammad Quli Qutb Shah who reigned from 1612 to 1629.
2. Thirthundamma was the king of Arakan from 1622 to 1638.
3. Adil Shah Ibrahim was the king of Bijapur from 1580 to 1627.
4. It is not clear what kind of a vessel this was.
5. Not identified.
6. Not identified.
7. This was probably Nuno Alvarez Bothelo.
8. Not identified.
9. The enemy, of course, referred to the Portuguese.
10. Hendrick de Witt was an assistant at Masulipatnam in 1619. He had subsequently become an upper-merchant in Coromandel. He had made a trip to Bengal in 1629 as an indigo expert. He died at Palicol in June 1632.

81. Ysbrantsz. on board the *Medemblik* at Masulipatnam to the Directors at Amsterdam, 8 March 1626. V.O.C. 1087, ff.1-5 (Copy).

Ysbrantsz.'s last letter to the Directors was dated 5 December 1625 sent with the *Delfshaven* via Batavia.[1] The *Coningh David* had reached Masulipatnam from Batavia on 11 December 1625 with a cargo worth f.70,923 consisting of 20,000 rials, 15,000 ponds cloves, 20,000 ponds nutmeg and 100 bags of mace. The *Coningh David* was now being sent with a cargo worth f.128,150 for the Chamber of Delft consisting of the following: . . . ponds of indigo,[2] 9,495 pieces of Guinea cloth, 26,775 ponds of cotton yarn, 4,165 pieces of *parcallas*, 2,050 pieces of *bethilles*, 3,152 pieces of *salampuris*, 200 pieces of *taffechelas de Bengale*, 160 pieces of *taffechelas de Golconda*, 1,310 pieces of *muris*, 79 pieces of cotton clothes, 35 pieces of painted *pardas*, 6,318 ponds of cotton, 20 pieces of bezoar stones and 260,147 ponds of saltpetre.

The Danes had been trying their best to hinder the procurement of saltpetre by the Company and paid as much as 15 rials per *bahar* for poor quality saltpetre. Unrefined saltpetre afforded the highest profit. The Company also had gunpowder made at Pulicat from refined saltpetre at a cost of 3¼ to 3½ *stuivers* per pond. Enough gunpowder could be made at Pulicat to meet the requirement of the whole of the East Indies.

The *taffechelas de Bengale* and the *taffechelas de Golconda* would afford little profit because of their poor quality. Better quality *taffechelas* were not brought to Coromandel by the merchants of Bengal. Other varieties of Bengal textiles brought were also poor in quality and high in price. These were, therefore, not being sent.

The *Schiedam* and then the *Medemblik* together with some frigates had been sent to Bengal but no evidence suggesting that the Bengal trade would be profitable could be obtained. For the last few years that region had been full of wars which were still continuing. Besides, it was full of the Portuguese. Ysbrantsz. would not be lacking in endeavour whenever an opportunity of making a profit there seemed to arise. Since the export of slaves from Arakan had been banned, Coromandel would try to get some from Bengal.

With regard to the Directors' demand for wax, sugar and Bengal clothes, the position was that wax was available locally only in small quantities and at no less than 3 rials per 24 ponds. Currently, it was not available in Bengal either. Sugar too was available locally only in small quantities and at 1¾ to 2 rials per 24 ponds. If the Muslims brought Bengal goods to Coromandel, they could do it at a much smaller cost than the Dutch with their costly ships. Recently, the Muslim ships had brought nothing but rice and some poor quality clothes from Bengal. Once peace returned to that region, the Company could expect to make some profit there.

In 1625, the Danes sent two ships, the *Christiaanshaven* and the *Waterhond* to Bengal together with their chief, Roeland Crappe. These ships returned on 23 January 1626 with some Bengal clothes, rice and 120 bales of sugar. The Danes left behind some factors at Pipli where the Portuguese had an important presence. They also bought a large indigenous ship there which was on its way to Masulipatnam with rice. At Masulipatnam, they had bought only 80 *littels* of indigo. They were planning to send a ship to Makassar and another to Tiku and Priaman.

It would be preferable if the Directors sent gold rather than rials to Coromandel. Some ducats could also be sent. The rials sold at Masulipatnam at 7½ to 8 *fanums* per piece involving a big loss while on gold, a profit of 11 per cent was made at Pulicat.

The Coromandel factories made a gross profit of f.225,681 in one year. The cost of maintaining the garrison, the fortifications, and the ships, etc., amounted to a total of f.58,762. The net profit of the factories was thus f.166,919.

The following ships had been sent from Coromandel on the account of the Company between January 1625 and March 1626:

On 26 January 1625, the *Wapen van Rotterdam* to Batavia with a cargo worth	f.233,601
In May 1625, the *Leeuwin* to Holland with a cargo worth	f.159,502
In June 1625, the *Vrede* to Batavia with a cargo worth	f.150,920

In October 1625, the fluit *Edam* to Batavia with a cargo worth	f.73,865
In December 1625, the *Delfshaven* to Batavia with a cargo worth	f.75,452
In January 1626, the *Arend* to Batavia with a cargo worth	f.66,848
On 8 March 1626, the *Coningh David* to Holland with a cargo worth	f.128,150
Total	f.888,338[3]

The entire amount of spices received from Batavia had been sold as follows: nutmeg at 110 *pagodas* per *bahar* of 480 ponds, mace at 17½ *pagodas* per 24 ponds and cloves at 11 *pagodas* per 24 ponds. The price of cloves had come down because the English had also brought in some.

Things were going reasonably well at Masulipatnam. Of course, the Company still had to deal with the merchants appointed for the purpose by the Muslim authorities. Nothing of the 16,000 *pagodas* extorted from the Company had been received back. There was not much point in reviving this issue because the English and the Danes were trying to fish in the troubled waters. The *havaldars*, always subject to frequent transfers, were only interested in making money for themselves without giving any thought to the future. The factors were waiting for an opportunity to demonstrate to the authorities that the affronts the Company had been subjected to had not been forgotten.

The rajas around Pulicat had been giving the Company a lot of trouble but it was well armed in Fort Geldria. It was not getting clothes to its satisfaction from outside Pulicat.

In March 1625, the English President, Thomas Mills, had left Masulipatnam for Armagon to consider shifting to that place. He had carried with him some cash and spices to purchase textiles with for Java. Armagon was about 8 to 9 miles north of Pulicat. Should the English shift there, it would be extremely injurious for the Company because currently the Pulicat varieties of textiles afforded the highest profit in Java and its hinterland. Their intention was that they would then be able to procure the Pulicat varieties of textiles without sharing the cost of the maintenance of the Fort Geldria with us. Ysbrantsz. had already issued orders that as far as possible the Dutch factors were to prevent the transportation of the Pulicat clothes to Armagon. The Company could, however, do little to prevent the transportation of these clothes by land.

On 16 February, it was learnt that the king of Golconda had died and that there were differences among the important people as to who should succeed him. It had since been learnt that the 13-year old son of the late king had succeeded him. He had, however, been opposed by most of the important people.

Diamonds were not being sent because these were now mined only for the king and in any case the price was almost as high as that in Europe. Holland could hope to receive any only when the mine was again farmed out as before and the price came down. Merchants were afraid of bringing any diamonds for fear of the *havaldar* who kept a constant vigil on the diamonds brought to Masulipatnam.

Ten to twelve cases of broad clothes, mostly red, could be sold at Masulipatnam annually. Some could also be yellow, brown, parrot green and pear red. 130 to 150 *bahars* of spelter could be sold at 50 *pagodas* per *bahar* and 200 to 300 *bahars* of lead could be sold at 12 to 13 *pagodas* per *bahar*. The tin from Holland received with the *Leeuwin* did not fetch any profit.

1. Ysbrantsz.'s letter dated 5 December 1625 had been sent to Batavia. See document no. 74.
2. The amount of indigo is not filled in.
3. The figure of the total is left blank in the document.

82. An extract from the invoice of the *Coningh David* sent from Coromandel to Holland on 8 March 1626. V.O.C. 1090, ff.222-36 (Copy).*

The merchant on board was Daniel van der Hagen.
The captain on board was Edert Geurtssen Visscher.[1]

S.No.	Item	Quantity	Value (in florins)
	Goods shipped in at Masulipatnam		
1.	Bleached and raw Guinea cloth	9,495 pieces	43,966:3:11
2.	Bleached *bethilles* of 24 *asta*	2,050 pieces	11,251:6:2
3.	*Salampuris*	3,152 pieces	12,951:9:12
4.	Bleached *parcallas*	4,156 pieces	9,450:8:0
5.	*Taffechelas* de Golconda	160 pieces	297:10:0
6.	*Taffechelas* de Bengale	200 pieces	850:0:0
7.	Painted *verhemlte*[2]	35 pieces	656:12:8
8.	Blankets	79 pieces	454:1:9
9.	*Dungarees* for packing	3,188 pieces	1,354:18:0
10.	Bezoar stones	20 *ceer*[3]	1,277:0:0
11.	Cotton yarn	26,775 ponds	10,841:15:0
12.	Saltpetre	6,632 ponds	880:16:4
	Tolls at 4 per cent		3,880:0:0
		Total	98,112:0:14
	Costs incurred		4,143:0:14
	Total value of the goods shipped in at Masulipatnam		102,255:8:12
	Goods shipped in at Pulicat		
1.	Bleached *muris*:		
	a. of 18 *asta*	1,061 pieces	
	b. of 16 *asta*	249 pieces	5,649:0:0
2.	Saltpetre:		
	a. refined	2,632 ponds	
	b. unrefined	250,883 ponds	19,374:3:0
3.	Cotton	6,315 ponds	659:8:0
4.	*Dungarees* for packing	20 pieces	20:0:0
5.	Planks for saltpetre cases	94 pieces	50:0:0
6.	Gunnies and ropes for packing	–	15:10:0
	Costs incurred		126:10:8
	Total value of goods shipped in at Pulicat		25,894:11:8
	Grand Total		128,150:0:4

* Only the summary statement given on folio 235vo has been used here. The invoice is signed by Barent Pietersen and Jan van Moorwyck.

1. Not identified.
2. Not identified.
3. *Ceer* or *seer* or *ser* was one of the most common of Indian denominations of weight, varying widely in different parts of the country. On the Coromandel coast, it was equivalent to about 1.7 ponds.

83. Governor Herman van Speult on board the *Gouden Leeuw* at Surat to Governor-General De Carpentier at Batavia, 5 April 1626. V.O.C. 1090, ff.297-308 (Copy).*

When Van Speult reached Calicut on his way from Batavia to Surat, he was met by an emissary of the *zamorin*[1] of Calicut. The *zamorin* came to the beach with 10,000 armed men and received us very cordially. He invited us to set-up a factory and offered to supply us the entire amount of pepper and ginger produced in his kingdom. He offered to provide us annually 3,000 *kandis* (=510 Dutch ponds) of pepper at 28 rials per *kandi*. For ginger, he asked for 12 rials per *kandi*. Within 10 days' time, we were offered 1,000 *kandis* of pepper at the aforementioned price. But since Van Speult did not know what the price of pepper in Surat, Persia or the Red Sea was and because the funds available were limited, the offer was declined. On arrival at Surat, however, it was discovered that a profit of 100 per cent could have been earned on pepper there. Pepper and ginger could also be sold in Mocha and Persia at a good profit. Also, some varieties of Surat textiles together with some cloves, nutmeg and mace could be sold at Calicut. The establishment of a factory there, therefore, seemed highly desirable. Jan Cremier Papas[2] would make a good chief there.

A Portuguese galleon, the *St. Jacinto*, coming from Muscat, was captured by us on 16 January about 8 miles south of Chaul and brought to Surat. From letters found in this vessel, Van Speult learnt that Nuno Alvarez Botelho was lying in Bombay with four galleons. Another letter, however, suggested that he was to leave Bombay with his vessels on the 15th of January. The idea of capturing these vessels was, therefore, given up. But after arrival at Surat, on the presumption that these vessels might still be in Bombay, a plan was made to attack them. The English agreed to provide two vessels for the purpose but on learning that the Portuguese vessels had actually left Bombay, the mission was cancelled.

Before Van Speult's arrival at Surat, Commander Kistjens had burnt a small Malabarese vessel which had been abandoned out of the fear of Dutch ships. Some opium and other commodities were found in this vessel which belonged to some banias of Cambay. The repurcussions of this episode were so serious that the Company's goods at Ahmedabad and Cambay were confiscated. The merchants demanded a large sum as compensation. Van Speult, therefore, decided to go to Ahmedabad and Cambay personally where he was received cordially by the officials, particularly by Safi Khan who is married to the emperor's daughter.[3] He was also cordially received by Mir Musa, the brother of the governor of Cambay, who promised all help and favours which he indeed made available. At Cambay, the owners of the Malabarese vessel asked for compensation. They knew that some of the packets of opium taken from their vessel had been brought by the Dutch to the Surat customs house, a fact that Director Van den Broecke did not seem to be aware of. Van Speult maintained that since they had only captured an abandoned ship they were not obliged to return the goods. The opium cases lying at the Surat customs house were, however, offered to the owners which failed to satisfy them.

In Van Speult's opinion, it was quite certain that if the Directors' instructions to attack ships from Chaul, Dabhol, Daman and other places under the jurisdiction of Emperor Jahangir were followed, the Company would be subjected to considerable losses.

Hendrick Arentsz. Vapour was received cordially by the emperor, his nobles and Safi Khan. The emperor presented him with one of his horses, which was being sent to Batavia. Vapour also received a *farman* granted by the emperor and the queen.[4] This *farman* proved very useful in the course of his journey to Surat with a *kafila* of 680 camels. The Surat Council had decided to renew Vapour's engagement by three years and he would be stationed at Agra as upper-merchant. It was useful to have some one at the court who had access to important people. Francisco Pelsaert's term had expired more than a year ago and he was on his way to Batavia.

Director Van den Broecke's term of two years was due to expire in October 1626. Since he was a sincere and energetic person, his term had been extended by two years at a salary of 200 guilders per month.

The following cargoes had been sent from Surat:

a. The *Gouden Leeuw*, the *Oranje*, the *Mauritius* and the *Hollandia* to Holland (including 352 bales of silk costing f.311,437) worth	f.875,365
b. The cargo sent to Persia with Commander Kistjens was worth	f.304,000
c. The cargo being sent with the *Bantam*, the *Heusden* and the galleon *St. Jacinto* to Batavia was worth	f.220,000
d. The cargo being sent to Agra was worth a sale value of	f.150,000
e. The cargo being sent to Mocha was worth a sale value of	f.50,000
Total	f.1,599,365

* Folios 302 and 303 are illegible because the ink has come out on both the sides.

1. *Zamorin* was the title of the Hindu king of Calicut.
2. Not identified.
3. Safi Khan was in fact the son-in-law of Asaf Khan, the brother of Empress Nur Jahan.
4. This *farman* is not available in the Company's archives.

84. Van den Broecke on board the *Gouden Leeuw* at Surat to Governor-General De Carpentier at Batavia, 6 April 1626. V.O.C. 1090, ff.289vo-94 (Original).

Governor Herman van Speult had arrived at Surat on 2 February 1626 with the *Mauritius*, the *Oranje* and the *Hollandia* along with a Portuguese ship captured near Goa.[1] These vessels had brought a cargo worth f.55,518. Several Dutch ships had also arrived from Hormuz on 8 February in the company of English ships.

The Surat Council resolved on 10 February that Governor Van Speult would go to Bombay with force to inflict as much damage as possible on the Portuguese who were understood to be lying there with 7 galleons. The English had also agreed to provide two vessels, the *Anne* and the *Falcon*, for the mission. But since news had been received shortly thereafter that the Portuguese had left Bombay for Muscat, the mission was cancelled. The ships were then repaired to prepare them for the voyages to Europe and Batavia.

Unless Batavia provided Surat with cash one year in advance, it would not be possible to send the return cargo earlier than April. Also, if goods were not bought and sold at the proper time, the Company lost 25 to 30 per cent in the process.

The English were selling their goods cheaper than before. They had brought 16,000 ponds of cloves, nutmeg and mace with the *James*. This was likely to prove very injurious to the Company's trade because once the price went down, the Muslim and the bania merchants would not easily pay a higher price at a later stage. A few days ago, a factor had been sent to the English President to ask if he would be willing to enter into an agreement with the Dutch for the sale of cloves and the purchase of indigo. The President replied, as he had done on several occasions earlier, that such agreements were never actually implemented.

After the dispatch of the ships for Europe and Batavia, Surat would not be left with enough cash even to meet the costs of maintaining the factory. It had borrowed 50,000 rupees on interest to be able to dispatch the ships to Holland. It had provided the factory at Persia with goods worth f.304,059 whose sale value there would approximate f.500,000.

A letter had been received from the *badshah* of Yemen (copy enclosed[2]). It had, therefore, been decided to send upper-merchant Van der Lee[3] to Mocha, with the *Walcheren* with some spices. Van den Broecke was hopeful of restoring good relations with Mocha. Since spices had not been sent there for quite sometime, they were likely to fetch a good price.

The merchants of Dabhol were avoiding Surat because of the war with the Deccanese.[4] Dabhol had been taken over by Malik Ambar. Van den Broecke had written to him requesting the release of the Dutch factors in custody there. Malik Ambar had replied that he had no knowledge of such detention and that if the Company was interested in establishing a factory in Dabhol, he would provide a good site with complete freedom to trade there.

It seemed that the English were planning to send some factors to Dabhol to buy pepper and clothes for England as well as Mocha. One could buy a large amount of pepper there annually about 50 per cent cheaper than at Surat. Besides, a large quantity of textiles could be bought there for Mocha and Persia which were likely to afford a good profit. The English ships, the *James* and the *Jonas*, had been sent to England on the 18th of March. The *Jonas* carried pepper and clothes bought at Broach while the *James* carried 100 packets of indigo Sarkhej, 220 packets of indigo Bayana, 80 packets of saltpetre, 250 packets of Broach clothes besides a large amount of pepper bought at 15½ to 15¾ *mahmudis* per 31½ Dutch ponds which (including costs) worked out to about 7 rials per Bantam sack. They had borrowed 150,000 rupees on interest.

It would not be possible to generate sufficient funds at Surat for the purchase of textiles by the sale of spices there. The bulk of the spices would be sent to Agra because they fetched the highest price there and the sale proceeds could be utilized for the purchase of indigo Bayana.

If Batavia decided to resume the trade at Mocha and Persia, the following quantities of spices could be sent to Surat. The exact requirement of Persia could not be ascertained because the chief factor there had not considered Van den Broecke worthy of writing a letter to.

S.No.	Item	For Surat	For Mocha
1.	Cloves	25,000 ponds	15,000 ponds
2.	Nutmeg	50,000 ponds	–
3.	Unripe nutmeg	–	20,000 ponds
4.	Pepper	–	40,000-50,000 ponds
5.	Mace	25-30 bags	20 bags
6.	Radix China	100 *piculs*	25-30 *piculs*
7.	Benzoin	15-20 cases	10-12 cases
8.	Lead	200,000 ponds	–
9.	Camphor	25-30 cases	–
10.	Sandalwood	50 *piculs*	–
11.	Japanese deer skins	50-100	–
12.	Porcelain	Some	Some rough and some fine
13.	Cash	As much as possible	–

It would not be possible for Surat to procure textiles in the near future or to buy indigo for the next year soon.

Van den Broecke found it absurd that the factor in Persia had allowed the ambassador of the Shah of Persia to travel to Holland with a lot of silk in the Company's ship. The great Mughal[5] had also requested that a servant of his, a painter, be allowed to travel to Europe in one of the Company's ships together with 5 or 6 other persons to enable them to buy curiosities for him there. The request had been declined politely saying that only the Governor-General at Batavia was competent to accede to such a request. The matter had not been taken up again since.

The bird presented by Hendrick Arentsz. Vapour at the Mughal court was well received but died soon after. He was honoured by the great Mughal with a respect cloth and a horse which was being sent to Batavia. Copies of the two *farmans*, one of which was from the great Mughal, were enclosed.[6]

Surat was given to understand from the commission given to Commander Kistjens[7] that he had been authorized to capture ships from Chaul, Dabhol and other places outside the jurisdiction of the great Mughal. In Van den Broecke's opinion, if the Company wanted to continue operating in Gujarat, this order needed to be withdrawn. The small Malabarese vessel captured and burnt by Kistjens near Goa had caused, and was still causing, a great deal of trouble at Surat.[8]

We had been requested to provide an escort to the Mughal emperor's ship which he intended to send to Mocha against the Portuguese lying at Bombay.

Van den Broecke had no doubt that the Company's ship would be welcomed at Mocha and that it would be possible to reach a good understanding with the Turks.

Governor Van Speult left Surat with his fleet on 6 April 1626.

1. The Portuguese galleon had been captured about 8 miles south of Chaul. See document no. 83.
2. This document is not available in the Company's archives.
3. Dirck van der Lee came to Batavia as an under-merchant in 1621 and was promoted to the rank of upper-merchant in 1623. He was in service in the western quarters between July 1624 and August 1625 and again between August 1627 and June 1628 as a controller of accounts. In July 1628 he was deputed for similar work to the eastern quarters. In 1629 he was the commander of the guard-ship at Bantam. At the end of 1629, he was secretary to the Governor-General and the Council. On 8 May 1630, he became member of the Council of the Indies. In January 1632, he repatriated as commander of the return fleet. But he returned to the Indies and eventually left for home on 6 January 1638 aboard the *Nassau* as the commander of the return fleet.
4. The reference is evidently to the wars between the kingdoms of Bijapur and Ahmadnagar. The term Deccanese is often used to denote the kingdom of Ahmadnagar though in its wider application after the disintegration of the Bahmani kingdom, the five southern sultanates were known as Deccan Sultanates—Bijapur, Golconda, Ahmadnagar, Bidar and Berar.
5. In the text the term erroneously used is 'the great Mongol'.
6. The copies of these *farmans* are not available in the Company's archives.
7. Commander Kistjens was sent on 13 August 1625. See document no. 63.
8. See document no. 83.

85. An extract from the invoice of the *Hollandia* sent from Surat to Holland in April 1626. V.O.C. 1090, ff.253-9. (Not stated whether original or copy.)*

S.No.	Item	Quantity	Value (in florins)
1.	Cotton yarn	4,380 ponds (in 55 packets)	3,978:13:6
2.	*Minatashis*	1,680 pieces (in 6 packets)	982:10:0
3.	Blankets	100 pieces (in 2 packets)	475:9:6
4.	*Cannikens*	400 pieces (in 1 packet)	259:4:6
5.	*Baftas*	1,200 pieces (in 6 packets)	2,549:6:10
6.	White broad *baftas* (coarse)	140 pieces (in 2 packets)	656:0:0
7.	White broad *baftas* (fine)	140 pieces (in 2 packets)	848:0:0
8.	Black broad *baftas* (coarse)	360 pieces (in 3 packets)	1308:16:0
9.	*Alcatifs*	18 pieces (in 2 packets)	393:2:8
10.	*Khasas* de Bengale	100 pieces (in 1 packet)	705:18:12
11.	Spikenard	150 ponds (in 1 packet)	27:10:0
12.	Borax	300 ponds (in 3 boxes)	72:8:0
13.	Dry ginger	2,170 ponds (in 10 boxes)	150:0:0
14.	Red sealing wax	405 ponds (in 1 case)	231:14:0
15.	Refined saltpetre	57,042 ponds (in 185 packets)	5,536:13:15
16.	Indigo Bayana	32,317½ ponds (in 160 packets)	25,421:0:0
17.	Indigo Sarkhej	75,670 ponds (in 469 packets)	37,677:13:2
18.	Gumlak	1,240 ponds (in 5 packets)	183:5:10
19.	Persian raw silk	77 bales[1]	
20.	Blue *baftas* (fine)	600 pieces (in 5 packets)	2,376:0:0
21.	*Cangans* for a sample	75 pieces (in 1 packet)	123:6:11
22.	White *baftas* (fine)	200 pieces (in 1 packet)	522:12:5
		Total	84,479:4:11

* Only the summary on folio 259 has been used.

1. The value of the Persian raw silk sent is not indicated.

86. An extract from the invoice of the *Oranje* that was sent from Surat to Holland in April 1626. V.O.C. 1090, ff.260-8. (Not stated whether original or copy.)*

S.No.	*Item*	*Quantity*	*Value (in florins)*
1.	Cotton yarn	12,200 ponds (in 80 packets)	5,940:13:6
2.	*Minatashis*	2,240 pieces (in 8 packets)	1,310:0:0
3.	Blankets	150 pieces (in 3 packets)	713:4:1
4.	*Cannikens*	800 pieces (in 2 packets)	525:17:11
5.	White broad *baftas* (fine)	480 pieces (in 4 packets)	1,702:8:0
6.	White broad *baftas* (coarse)	600 pieces (in 5 packets)	1,600:0:0
7.	Small length pleated white *baftas* (coarse)	1,200 pieces (in 6 packets)	2,549:6:11
8.	Long *baftas* (fine)	200 pieces (in 1 packet)	520:0:0
9.	Black broad *baftas* (coarse)	1,720 pieces (in 11 packets)	4,780:16:0
10.	*Khasas* de Bengale	200 pieces (in 2 packets)	2,173:2:8
11.	*Ambertis*	200 pieces (in 1 packet)	605:0:0
12.	*Alcatifs*	46 pieces (in 5 packets)	970:15:10
13.	Red sealing wax	600 ponds (in 4 cases)	339:0:0
14.	Borax	300 ponds (in 2 bales)	38:6:4
15.	Spikenard	600 ponds (in 1 packet)	110:12:8
16.	Dried ginger	3,055 ponds (in 14 packets)	210:0:0
17.	Gumlak	1,240 ponds (in 5 packets)	183:5:10
18.	Indigo Bayana	50,387½ ponds (in 250 packets)	39,607:1:0
19.	Indigo Sarkhej	178,489¾ ponds (in 710 packets)	74,907:4:1
20.	Refined saltpetre	55,122 ponds (in 200 packets)	5,285:0:0
21.	Black *baftas* (fine)	120 pieces (in 1 packet)	476:16:0
22.	Persian raw silk	100 bales[1]	
23.	Cloves	15,470 ponds (in 150 sacks)	7,735:0:0
		Total	152,283:9:6

* Only the summary on folio 268 has been used.

1. The value of the Persian raw silk sent is not indicated.

87. An extract from the invoice of the *Gouden Leeuw* sent from Surat to Holland in April 1626. V.O.C. 1090, ff.269-79. (Not stated whether original or copy.)*

S.No.	*Item*	*Quantity*	*Value (in florins)*
1.	Cotton yarn	17,537½ ponds (in 115 packets)	8,160:13:4
2.	*Minatashis*	2,520 pieces (in 9 packets)	1,473:15:0
3.	*Sarrasas* Malay	200 pieces (in 1 packet)	415:0:0
4.	Blankets	200 pieces (in 4 packets)	950:18:12
5.	*Cannikens*	800 pieces (in 2 packets)	518:8:12
6.	Small length pleated white coarse *baftas*	2,200 pieces (in 11 packets)	4,549:6:11
7.	Broad white *baftas* (coarse)	840 pieces (in 7 packets)	2,288:0:0
8.	Broad white *baftas* (fine)	240 pieces (in 2 packets)	870:8:0
9.	Broad black *baftas* (coarse)	2,000 pieces (in 14 packets)	5,704:0:0
10.	Bengal *khasas* (coarse)	200 pieces (in 2 packets)	1,247:10:0
11.	*Chautars senuknes*	126 pieces (in 1 packet)	375:0:0
12.	*Ambertis*	100 pieces (in 1 packet)	418:15:0
13.	*Alcatifs*	58 pieces (in 6 packets)	1,205;18:12
14.	Borax	750 ponds (in 5 boxes)	95:0:0
15.	Spike-nard	1,200 ponds (in 8 packets)	220:0:0
16.	Gumlac	942 ponds (in 4 packets)	146:10:0
17.	Red sealing wax	994 ponds (in 10 cases)	556:13:0
18.	Dry ginger	2,604 ponds (in 12 packets)	180:0:0
19.	Agate markstones	11,725 pieces (in 1 canassar)	434:10:10
20.	Persian raw silk	125 bales[1]	
21.	Indigo Bayana	80,500 ponds (in 400 packets)	63,252:2:0
22.	Indigo Sarkhej	148,242¾ ponds (in 950 packets)	83,764:14:1
23.	Refined saltpetre	82,066 ponds (in 274 packets)	7,353:4:0
24.	Blood coral for a sample	63,000 pieces (in 1 packet)	326:8:2
25.	Cash	200 rials	510:0:0
26.	Small fine *baftas* as a sample	50 pieces (in 1 packet)	721:9:5
		Total	185,748:5:5

Expenses by way of tolls in Broach, as also on the carts for transporting the goods from Ahmedabad, Cambay and Broach plus other expenses such as on the warehouses, payment to peons, etc.	9,057:8:0
Tolls at Surat on goods worth f.185,748:5:5 at 3½ per cent	6,541:12:0
Grand Total	201,347:5:5

* Only the summary on folio 279 has been used.
1. The value of Persian raw silk sent is not indicated.

88. An extract from the invoice of the *Mauritius* sent from Surat to Holland in April 1626. V.O.C. 1090, ff.280-6. (Not stated whether original or copy.)*

S.No.	*Item*	*Quantity*	*Value (in florins)*
1.	Cotton yarn	7,625 ponds (in 50 packets)	3,558:13:5
2.	*Minatashis*	1,680 pieces (in 6 packets)	982:10:0
3.	Blankets	150 pieces (in 3 packets)	713:4:1
4.	*Cannikens*	400 pieces (in 1 packet)	259:4:6
5.	White *baftas* small length pleated (coarse)	800 pieces (in 4 packets)	1,557:6:11
6.	White broad *baftas* (coarse)	360 pieces (in 3 packets)	1,024:0:0
7.	White broad *baftas* (fine)	360 pieces (in 3 packets)	1,280:0:0
8.	Black broad *baftas* (coarse)	600 pieces (in 5 packets)	2,012:16:0
9.	White *baftas*, small length pleated (fine)	200 pieces (in 1 packet)	496:0:0
10.	*Khasas* de Bengal	100 pieces (in 1 packet)	568:15:0
11.	*Alcatifs*	20 pieces (in 3 packets)	540:0:0
12.	Spikenard	300 pieces (in 2 packets)	55:0:0
13.	Borax	300 ponds (in 2 boxes)	38:0:0

14.	Persian raw silk	40 bales[1]	
15.	Dry ginger	2,821 ponds (in 13 packets)	195:0:0
16.	Red sealing wax	201 ponds (in 2 cases)	116:19:0
17.	Gumlac	922 ponds (in 4 packets)	146:10:0
18.	Indigo Bayana	35,420 ponds (in 176 packets)	27,853:2:0
19.	Indigo Sarkhej	93,000 ponds (in 500 packets)	52,257:3:2
20.	Refined saltpetre	57,204 ponds (in 261 packets)	4,664:6:4
		Total	98,318:9:13

* Only the summary on folio 286 has been used.

1. The value of the Persian raw silk sent is not indicated.

89. Ysbrantsz. at Pulicat to Governor-General De Carpentier at Batavia, 4 June 1626. V.O.C. 1090, ff.245-8vo (Copy).

This letter was being sent with the *Medemblik* with a cargo worth f.178,756. The *Coningh David* was sent from Pulicat to the Chamber of Delft on 8 March 1626 with a cargo worth f.128,150.[1] 280 pieces of fine *rambutins* were being sent with the present shipment. In fact, some of these were to be sent to Holland as samples but they came in too late and the cost was too high. Ysbrantsz. would like to know if Batavia could make a profit on these and whether they would be useful for Holland. The Danes had sent some coarse pieces of these to Denmark.

Pulicat had intended to send some pepper to be sent to Holland with the *Coningh David*. But since it could not be carried by that ship, it was being sent to Batavia. Since March last, a good deal of pepper had been brought to Pulicat by the indigenous merchants from Aceh and the Malabar coast. This, coupled with the fact that the Danes and the English were not buying much pepper now, had resulted in a decline in the price of pepper to 27-28 rials per *bahar* of 480 ponds.

Ysbrantsz. had hoped to be able to send more painted textiles to Batavia but that could not be done partly because Pulicat had run out of cash to be able to honour all the contracts. This also led to the weavers and the painters sitting idle. The Company was short of cash at Masulipatnam also. The orders, therefore, could not be met in full. After the departure of the *Medemblik*, the factors would be sitting idle at Masulipatnam, Palicol as well as at Petapuli. The best time to procure painted textiles was the months of April to June and these were precisely the months when the factors had to sit idle on account of the non-availability of funds. Ysbrantsz. hoped to receive funds from Batavia soon.

Only 64 slaves bought at Tegenapatam were being sent with the *Medemblik*. The procurement of slaves was a difficult task and they were very costly. Pulicat had sent 1,000 rials with the ship of the *kotwal* of Arakan who would pay 2,650 *tangas*[2] to the Dutch factors there. The king of Arakan seemed to be well disposed towards the Company. The factors at Arakan had been told that if they were not able to send slaves, they ought to send rice and one or two elephants to Pulicat. Elephants were in great demand in Pulicat and 18 of them had been brought there with two indigenous ships. The Dutch factors, however, had not been able to send any elephants and had sent only 600 *carras* of rice which had cost the Company f.2,224 including freight.

The English had left three factors at Armagon and were building a house there. They had reached an accord with the lord of Armagon, Tyma Nayak, that they would build a fort and keep 200 black soldiers there at their own cost. The English would be obliged to pay 1 per cent on their imports into Armagon and 3 per cent on their exports from there. Besides, the Dutch would not be allowed to trade at Armagon and Cottepatan.[3] The English had not yet succeeded in having a large quantity of textiles manufactured there. It seemed that they were trying to get there the varieties ordinarily procured at Pulicat. Ysbrantsz. would try his best to make sure that textiles did not reach Armagon from Pulicat and the sorrounding areas. These routes had already been occupied by Pede Raja. The English were always well provided with cash. As a result, the suppliers would try their best to get the textiles to the English.

The spices received with the *Coningh David* were lying unsold at Masulipatnam for reasons mentioned in Ysbrantsz.'s last letter.[4] Only merchants to whom the right to trade with the Company had been farmed out had been asking for the spices.

The death of the aged king of Golconda had created a good deal of uncertainty.[5] A 13-year old son had since been crowned king. Mansur Khan had been appointed the most senior counsellor of the young king and the Mir Jumla. Mansur Khan had sent an emissary on 1 April 1626 ordering the *shahbandar*, the *kotwal* and Mir Kamal-al-Din to arrest the *havaldar* of Masulipatnam, Jannat Khan. He had sent one Muhammad Taqi to take charge. Muhammad Taqi had reportedly taken on farm the *havaldarship* of Masulipatnam and Petapuli for five years. It seemed that Mansur Khan would get annually 140,000 *pagodas* for Masulipatnam and 27,000 *pagodas* for Petapuli. This was the same Muhammad Taqi who had had Van Uffelen arrested and inflicted so much of damage on the Company. In sum, Ysbrantsz. had no hope of the recovery of the 16,000 *pagodas* extorted—11,000 from the Company's merchants and 5,000 from Van Uffelen. In Ysbrantsz.'s opinion, it was time for revenge when Muhammad Taqi was *havaldar* of Masulipatnam for a second time. He would await Batavia's instructions in this regard.

During March 1626, the following ships had come to Masulipatnam: 4 from Pegu reportedly with rubies worth more than 200,000 *pagodas*, 3 from Arakan, 2 from Aceh and 2 from Tenasserim. The ones from Arakan and Aceh had brought mainly elephants. It seemed that this year the Muslims would send out ships in strength because all their ships had returned safely after earning a good profit. The yacht of Malaya had also returned safely from Pegu after having earned a reasonable amount of profit but it had not been able to secure the release of the Dutch factors under arrest at Pegu.

The Danish Admiral Roeland Crappe had left Trancquebar for Makassar on the 1st of April with the *Christiaanshaven* and the *Nachtegaal*. They had sent the *Waterhond* to Bengal. The indigenous ship that they had bought had been sent to Tenasserim. They had not sent any return cargo to Denmark claiming that they were waiting to collect enough cargo to fill two ships. Since the departure of their Admiral, they had been having a lot of troubles at Puleceri and Porto Novo. The issue was a Muslim ship that had been captured by the Danes. The *nayak* of Tanjore had put forward a claim that the ship belonged to him. On their refusal to provide compensation, the factors had been put under arrest by the *nayak*.

The Portuguese had accused the Danes of having captured one of their frigates near Bangeri[6] laden with tin. The Danes had claimed that they had not done it.

Rice was not being sent with the present shipment because it could have been put into the ship only at the expense of other goods. Also, free Dutch merchants had told Ysbrantsz. that a considerable amount of rice had already been carried from Siam to Batavia.

The diamond mine had again been farmed by the same person who had farmed it earlier. Diamonds were thus likely to be available again at a reasonable price.

1. See document no. 82.
2. 1 *tanga* was equal to 1 rupee.
3. This was Kottapatnam which is still a chief port in Nellore district.
4. See document no. 77.
5. Pulicat had learnt of the death of the king of Golconda on 16 February 1626. See document no. 81.
6. Bangeri is on the upper Malay peninsula opposite Ujang Salang.

90. Maerten van Rossen and Barent Pietersz. at Masulipatnam to Governor-General De Carpentier at Batavia, 15 June 1626. V.O.C. 1090, ff.249-51vo (Copy).

This letter was being sent with the *Medemblik* with a cargo worth f.178,756, of which Pulicat had contributed cargo worth f.81,036, and Masulipatnam the remainder. The shortfall was because of the failure of the merchants at Masulipatnam to whom the right to trade with us had been farmed out to fulfil their contracts.

Some cleaned cotton costing 16 *pagodas* per *bahar* was being sent as a sample. If it had been bought at the proper time, it would have cost only 10 to 12 *pagodas* per *bahar*.

The spices received with the *Coningh David* could not be disposed off for a long time. This was not because there was no demand for them but because the *havaldar* of Masulipatnam, Jannat Khan, had not permitted the merchants to buy anything from the Company before they had bought from him 5 *bahars* of nutmeg and 7 *bahars* of mace. These had earlier been bought by him by force from the Company's merchants at a low price which he was now trying to sell back to them at a much higher price. He had also been demanding money from the merchants to whom the right to trade with the Company had been farmed out before he allowed them to sell their goods. Eventually, he managed to sell to these merchants cloves at 11 *pagoda*s per. . .[1], mace at 17½ *pagodas* per. . .[2] and nutmeg at 110 *pagodas* per *bahar*. Nutmeg are in a great demand at the moment and a large amount can be sold at a good profit. As for cloves, they are not available in Masulipatnam at the moment and the price is likely to go up. We should be able to sell a fair amount. Around 200 *bahars* of pepper could be bought at Masulipatnam at 17 to 18 *pagodas* per *bahar*. However, the pepper available at Aceh, Tiku and Priaman is of better quality.

The death of the king of Golconda had resulted in a state of great disorder. The routes had become completely unsafe and the merchants were extremely concerned about the transportation of their goods. The new king and his counsel Mansur Khan had sent Muhammad Taqi to replace Jannat Khan as the *havaldar* of Masulipatnam. Taqi had already prevented the factors from procuring saltpetre claiming that it was a banned item.

Because of the shortage of funds, the factors at Masulipatnam, Pulicat as well as Palicol would have to remain idle once the present shipment had left. If funds had been available, Palicol could have provided 3,000 pieces of Guinea cloth and a large amount of *salampuris*. The latter are distinctly superior in quality and cheaper in price there.

There were enough stocks of alum at Masulipatnam to last three to four years so no more was to be sent for the moment. The sale of ivory was poor. Some sandalwood would be welcome and it could be sold at Masulipatnam at 95 to 100 *pagodas* per *bahar*. Masulipatnam would be able to sell tortoise horn at 15 to 16 *pagodas* per *bahar* provided the quantity sent was not large and the quality was good. They would also be able to sell as much as 200 to 300 *bahars* of lead.

Malik Ambar had died about 20 to 30 days back but his death had not caused any disturbances in Golconda.

During the current year, the Muslim merchants had brought in a large quantity of goods from Pegu, Tenasserim, Arakan, Aceh and Bengal. It was understood that they planned to send out a great many ships this year as well.

The English had established a factory at Armagon. The Danes carried on little trade at Masulipatnam. They had bought only 70 *littels* of indigo at a high price.

In one of the chests received with the *Coningh David*, the rials were found to have been packed loose rather than in sacks and the number was short by 264 pieces of the stipulated 8,000 pieces. It was not clear who was responsible for this. Merchant De Vries declared that he had not counted the coins because he did not have the keys to the chest. Van Rossen and Barent Pietersz. had the lock broken in De Vries's presence.

1. The unit is not specified in the document.
2. The unit is not specified in the document.

91. Governor-General De Carpentier at Batavia to Ysbrantsz. at Pulicat, 27 June 1626. V.O.C. 1089, ff.80-4vo (Copy).

Since the departure of the *Coningh David* from Batavia on 24 September 1625, the following vessels had arrived from Coromandel: the *Edam* on 16 November 1625, the *Delfshaven* on 31 December 1625 and the *Arend* on 8 March 1626. The quality of the opium received was very poor and the rice aboard the *Edam* was found to be exceedingly short-weight.

Given the current prices and the sale of spices on the Coromandel coast, the maximum proceeds that could be expected in a year would be between f.180,000 and f.200,000. Batavia's revised orders for textiles for the Indies would require an annual investment of around f.400,000. The gap of around f.200,000 would be provided in terms of goods from Holland, Japan and China or in rials, silver or gold bullion. The latter could be done only on the receipt of fresh supplies from Holland. The Japanese silver will have to be obtained only through the Chinese trade. The small amount of Japanese silver obtained so far had been invested in the procurement of the Chinese goods at Taiwan.

This letter was being sent with the *Mauritius* carrying the following cargo: 16,612 ponds of cloves, 70,478 ponds of nutmeg, 18,987 ponds of mace, 90,000 *cattys* of Japanese copper, 619 pieces of heavy rials worth of gold and 20,000 rials. The sale value of this cargo was likely to be around f.250,000.

Batavia had intended to send about 30,000 ponds of cloves to Coromandel but the *Mauritius* had brought from the Moluccas only the amount it was now carrying. The English, the Danes and the Portuguese had been buying cloves in Makassar at the high price of 230 to 250 rials per Portuguese *bahar*. They were likely to flood the Coromandel coast with these cloves leading to a fall in its price there.

While a generally helpful attitude was to be adopted towards the free merchants, it was not to be done at the expense of the Company's interests. Some free merchants were being allowed to travel aboard the *Mauritius* together with their goods. But if any one of them was found carrying spices without special permission, they were to be confiscated. Some of them had been permitted to carry cloves, nutmeg and mace amounting to a total of about . . . *piculs*.[1] These would be handed over to Ysbrantsz. by the captain of the ship and would be sold along with the spices of the Company. This would prevent the flooding of the market. The procurement of slaves in Coromandel, Arakan and Bengal was to continue even at the cost of the procurement of textiles for the Indies.

As much rice (even 300 *lasts* and more) was to be sent aboard the *Mauritius* as possible provided this could be done without cutting into the space for other goods. 200 new cases were being sent to facilitate the dispatch of gunpowder from Coromandel to Batavia.

A detailed list of textiles required from Coromandel for the Indies was enclosed.[2] This was a revised version of the list sent in 1623.[3] The manufacturing of textiles at Tegenapatam and the south of Pulicat was to be encouraged so that the dependence on Masulipatnam could be minimized.

The procurement of pepper at Coromandel was not a priority item in so far as other more profitable goods could be obtained there. But in order to discourage the Danes from buying cheap and competing with the Company in Europe, some pepper was to be bought to keep the price at a reasonably high level.

The English were badly off at Surat and were not expecting any textiles from there. According to the information received from Van den Broecke, they were under heavy debts there. The *Jonas* and the *James* had been sent fully laden from Surat to England while the yacht *Valck* had been sent to the Coromandel coast. It was not clear when the English would be able to send a ship from Batavia to Coromandel. They were trying to send a ship to Aceh with some cloves to be sold to the Indian merchants coming there from Coromandel and other places. This ship would fetch from Aceh their pepper lying there.

Ysbrantsz. was being promoted to the membership of the Council of the Indies on the condition that he would first complete his three years as director at Coromandel at a salary of f.200 per month. A nephew of Governor-General De Carpentier, named Roelandt de Carpentier,[4] was being sent as assistant. Ysbrantsz. was requested to keep a fatherly eye on him for which the Governor-General would be grateful.

1. The quantity is not specified in the document.
2. See document no. 92.
3. See Om Prakash (ed.), *The Dutch Factories in India, 1617-1623*, document no. 218, pp. 251-5.
4. Roelandt de Carpentier was born in Dordrecht on 18 July 1603. He left from Vlissingen for the East Indies on the ship *Mauritius* in January 1625. His salary was f.22 per month. He was sent to Pulicat in 1627 and figured in the list of the employees at Palicol in 1630. He returned to Holland in November 1668 and died on 30 September 1673.

92. An estimate of Coromandel clothes that could be sold in a year in the Moluccas, Amboina, Banda, Java, Jambi, Patani and other southern quarters. Prepared at Batavia, 27 June 1626. V.O.C. 1089, ff.84vo-88 and ff.105-5vo (Copy).*

S. No.	*Item*	*Quantity*	*Each packet containing (pieces)*	*Price per packet (florins)*	*Cost Price (florins)*	*Remarks*
1.	*Sarassa gobar*	1,200 pieces (12 packets)	100	500	6,000	All with small flower work
2.	*Sarassa Malay*	2,400 pieces (12 packets)	200	1,100	13,200	8 packets with small flower work and 4 packets with patterns in *daalders* and chains.
3.	*Tapi sarassas*	19,200 pieces (80 packets)	240	460	36,800	The borders to be bright red. Small flower work in lively colours.
4.	*Sarassas de Cochin*	800 pieces (4 packets)	200	800	3,200	2 packets with big flower work and 2 packets with small flower work.

5.	*Tapi sarassas de Cochin*	400 pieces (4 packets)	100	400	1,600	–
6.	*Committers*[1]	700 pieces (7 packets)	100	600	4,200	2 packets each of red, black, white and salpicado[2] colours
7.	Guinea cloth	9,450 pieces (450 packets)	21	100	45,000	400 packets bleached and the remaining unbleached.
8.	*Tapi chindaes of 4 asta*	1,800 pieces (8 packets)	300	300	1,800	Although the demand for this variety has increased, for the present 6 packets are enough
9.	*Tapi chindaes of 5 asta*	1,920 pieces (8 packets)	240	300	2,400	At present these are not in demand
10.	*Caingoulongs*[3]	(120 packets)		300	36,000	–
11.	*Tapi grandes*	(50 packets)		300	15,000	The pieces with gold thread are much appreciated
12.	*Tapi kitchul*	(50 packets)		240	12,000	50 packets and not less

13. *Madafons*	1,800 pieces (12 packets)	150	300	3,600	–
14. *Chelas*	2,400 pieces (15 packets)	160	300	4,500	5 packets of very fine variety with narrow stripes and the remaining of ordinary quality
15. *Madops*[4]	1,600 pieces (10 packets)	160	300	3,000	–
16. Negro cloth	7,500 pieces (50 packets)	150	100	5,000	–
17. Sail cloth	10,000 pieces (100 packets)	100	90	9,000	Half from Masulipatnam
18. Cloth for shirts and trousers	(36 packets)		270	9,720	–
19. *Taffechelas de Bengal*	600 pieces (6 packets)	100	500	3,000	–
20. *Taffechelas de Narsapur*	8,000 pieces (50 packets)	160	200	10,000	–
21. *Tapi* grosses	9,000 pieces (30 packets)	300	170	5,100	–

22. *Dung-arees*	5,000 pieces (25 packets)	200	110	2,750	20 packets bleached, 5 packets unbleached
23. Blue *bolo-nos*[5]	6,000 pieces (30 packets)	200	170	5,100	–
24. *Palang gobars*	6,400 pieces (40 packets)	160	200	8,000	All bleached
25. *Chautars*	500 pieces (5 packets)	100	250	1,250	–
26. *Bethilles*	8,700 pieces (90 packets)	80 to 200	500	45,000	40 packets of 40 *asta* each – 20 white, 12 red, 5 brown-blue and 3 raw. 45 packets of 30 to 32 *asta* each – 15 red, 18 white, 10 brown blue and 2 raw. 5 packets from Tanjore. No *bethilles* of 24 *asta* as also of any other colour were to be sent
27. *Chavonis*	6,000 pieces (30 packets)	200	300	9,000	20 packets white, 6 packets brown-blue and 4 packets red

28. *Salampuris*	3,500 pieces (35 packets)	100	350	12,250	20 packets white, 10 packets brown-blue, 3 packets raw, 2 packets red for Jambi
29. Fine *muris*	2,000 pieces (20 packets)	100	460	9,200	14 packets bleached and 6 packets red. No unbleached
30. *Rambutins*	1,000 pieces (10 packets)	100	400	4,000	Not more than 10 packets. At present enough in stock for 2 years
31. *Balatius*	2,000 pieces (25 packets)	80	280	7,000	–
32. *Patta* Malay	1,600 pieces (10 packets)	160	340	3,400	–
33. *Aritchiodes*[6]	960 pieces (6 packets)	160	400	2,400	–
34. *Red chavonis*	400 pieces (5 packets)	80	360	1,800	Same as were sent last with the *Vrede* and the *Arend*
35. *Samudra muris*	2,400 pieces (15 packets)	160	300	4,500	–
36. *Parcallas*	4,800 pieces (30 packets)	160	400	12,000	20 packets white and 10 packets red.

37. Red *salalus*	(10 packets)				
38. Black *salalus* fine	1,280 pieces (8 packets)	160		8,500	–
39. *Eragams*[7] for Solor	800 pieces (5 packets)	160	320	1,600	–
40. *Eragams* for Patani	(6 packets)		320	1,920	–
41. Cotton blankets	600 pieces (15 packets)	40	90	1,350	–
42. Bengal *ginghams*	200 pieces (2 packets)	100	500	1,000	–
43. Turbans and Bengal silk *khasas*	(3 packets)			2,000	–
44. Salpicado *ginghams*	400 pieces (4 packets)	100	800	3,200	–
45. Red Siamese *badjous*[8]	1,800 pieces (6 packets)	300	400	2,400	For Siam
46. *Talous*[9]	6 packets		320	1,920	For Siam
47. *Goya geyts*[10]	4 packets		600	2,400	For Siam
48. *Pintados*	3 packets		700	2,100	For Siam
49. *Socke Tockes*[11]	40 packets		273	10,920	For Siam

50.	Masulipatnam's *tapi chindaes*	25 packets	280	7,000	Oridinary variety for Java and surrounding areas
51.	Timor's clothes	15 packets	80	1,200	For Solor and Timor
	Total	1,660 packets		f. 416,280	

* This is a revised version of the list sent by Batavia to Coromandel in 1623 (see Om Prakash, (ed.), *The Dutch Factories in India 1617-1623*, document no. 218, pp. 251-5). Both the detailed list available on ff.84vo-88 and the summary statements available on f.89 and ff.105-5vo have been used. An exact copy is available in the *Bataviaasch Uitgaande Brievenboek*, V.O.C. 853, ff.89vo-91vo.

1. Not identified.
2. It is not clear what the word salpicado means.
3. *Caingoulong* was derived from Malay *kain*, 'cloth' and goulong 'rolled'. The term implies that they were exported in rolls. Clothes named thus were apparently patterned in the loom and usually incorporated gold thread. They were woven in Tanjore area and perhaps intended chiefly for making into Malay *sarongs*.
4. *Madop*, probably *madapollam*, was a particular kind of cotton cloth named after a place on the southern delta branch of the Godavari, Madhavapalam.
5. Not identified.
6. Not identified.
7. Not identified.
8. Probably badjoe, the Malay jacket.
9. Not identified.
10. Not identified.
11. Not identified.

93. Governor-General De Carpentier at Batavia to Van den Broecke at Surat, 5 August 1626. V.O.C. 1089, ff.121-7 (Copy).*

De Carpentier had received Van den Broecke's letters of 4 December 1625, 8 March 1626 and 6 April 1626.[1] The captured ship *Jacinto* was still awaited at Batavia.

This letter was being sent with the *Wapen van Zeeland* and the *Zierikzee* together with a cargo worth f.177, 348 consisting of 4,000 bags of pepper, 60,000 ponds of cloves, 90,000 ponds of nutmeg, 60 sacks of mace, 950 *piculs* of Japanese copper, 12,000 ponds of Chinese powder sugar in 217 cases, 10 *piculs* of preserved ginger, 12,000 pieces of Coromandel steel, 2 packets of pickled nuts, 36,000 *pampiers* Chinese beaten gold thread and some fine and rough porcelain. The sale value of this cargo should be around f.600,000.

Of this cargo, the following was to be sent on to Persia: the entire amount of pepper, 20,000 ponds of cloves, 25,000 ponds of nutmeg, 10 sacks of mace, 700 *piculs* of Japanese copper together with the entire amount of sugar, ginger, porcelain, Chinese beaten gold thread and steel. The sale value of this cargo in Persia should be around f.370,000.

The following was to be sent on to Mocha: 15,000 ponds of cloves, 15,000 ponds of nutmeg and 20 sacks mace. Given the prices of spices there, these should sell in Mocha for not less than around f.60,000.

The remaining goods were for Surat, Cambay and Agra and should fetch around f.170,000, making a total sum of around f.600,000. Taking into account the cargo that Mocha would receive from Governor Van Speult worth a total sale value of around f.50,000, the cargo sent from Surat to Agra in April 1626 by a *kafila* with a sale value of around f.150,000 and finally the cargo sent to Persia with Kistjens of a sale value of around f.500,000, the total amount of capital available with Surat, Persia and Mocha would amount to as much as f.1.3 million.

If the mace could be sold more profitably in Surat and the sorrounding areas itself, it was not to be sent on to Persia or Mocha. According to Batavia's information, Japanese copper did very well in Persia, almost as well as the rials. It was likely to sell in Persia at f.60 per 100 Dutch ponds. If the price in Surat was lower and if Surat could manage without the proceeds from the sale of copper, all of it was to be sent on to Persia, depending upon the resources available at Surat. Persia was to be provided with whatever textiles and other goods it might ask for.

Batavia realized fully that unless additional funds were made available to Surat by Holland, it would be difficult for Van den Broecke to meet Batavia's orders for textiles in full. But considering that the heavy costs of maintenance in the Indies were met mainly by the profit from the sale of textiles from Surat and Coromandel in the region, it was critically important to provide as many clothes for the Indies as possible. If shortage of resources necessitated an under-fulfilling of the orders, the pruning was always to be done in respect of the orders from Holland rather than those for the Indies. As much funds were to be borrowed on interest as necessary. In brief, Van den Broecke was to use all his energy and resources to meet the textile orders from Batavia and only then procure goods for Holland.

The English had already sent a large amount of indigo to Europe. The Danes and the Dutch would be sending further amounts from the Coromandel coast creating a pressure on the sale price. Therefore, Surat was to buy little or no indigo for Europe. The amounts already contracted for at Agra were, of course, to be bought.

If rice could be provided without cutting into orders for other goods, as much as 50 to 100 *lasts* could be sent. Similarly, 20 to 50 *lasts* of wheat could be sent because it was in great demand by the free burghers at Batavia. As many as 100 *lasts* of wheat could be sold annually.

Since both Van den Broecke and Van Speult had strongly advised against the capture of ships from Dabhol, Daman, Chaul and other places under the jurisdiction of the great Mughal, Commander Kistjens had been ordered not to do so.[2] More specifically, the persons and the goods of the Indian merchants were not to be harmed under any circumstances. The only goods that he was authorized to confiscate from such ships were those, if any, belonging to the Portuguese. All the Company ships were to be issued similar instructions. If the Portuguese were found to be operating under the names of Indian merchants, they were to be tolerated.

Batavia approved of the decision to refuse passage to the nominee of the Mughal emperor to Europe or Batavia because it would have been prejudicial to the Company's interests.

* An exact copy is available in the *Bataviaasch Uitgaande Brievenboek*, V.O.C. 853, ff.117-21vo.

1. For Van den Broecke's letters of 4 December 1625 and 6 April 1626, see document nos. 73 and 84. His letter of 8 March 1626 is not available in the Company's archives.
2. Frederik Kistjens had been sent to Surat and Persia in August 1625, see document no. 63. He had left Surat for Persia on 3 December 1625, see document no. 99.

94. Governor-General De Carpentier at Batavia to Governor Van Speult at Surat, 5 August 1626. V.O.C. 1089, ff.118-21 (Copy).*

Batavia had received with the *Heusden* Van Speult's letter of 5 April[1] and had learnt of his safe arrival at Surat.

This letter was being sent with the *Zierikzee* and the *Wapen van Zeeland* under the command of Frederik Kistjens. On arrival at Surat he would be under Van Speult's jurisdiction as had been the case during his earlier voyage.[2]

* An exact copy is available in the *Bataviaasch Uitgaande Brievenboek*, V.O.C. 853, ff.115-17.

1. See document nos. 83 and 84.
2. See document no. 83.

95. Procedures prescribed by the Directors at Amsterdam to be followed by the Governor-General and Council at Batavia in order to ensure the safety of the Company's men and materials, 26 August 1626. V.O.C. 314 (Copy).*

Surat

The Directors trust that while sending Cornelis Arentsz. Vapour[1] to Agra, the Governor-General had satisfied himself regarding Vapour's ability to deal with the Mughal emperor. A regular supply of curiosities for the emperor and his noblemen was to be ensured in order to earn their goodwill.

The troubles faced by the Company at Surat since the time of Van Deynsen[2] had been caused by the machinations of the Portuguese and other enemies of the Dutch. Alternatively, troubles were the result of the supposed alliance that the Indians thought existed between the Dutch and the English. That might be the reason for implicating the Dutch Company for the excesses recently committed by the English at Surat. It was to be clearly explained to the Indians that the Dutch and the English were two distinct nations and resources of each of the two companies were separate and distinct as were their respective directors.

Efforts were to be made to improve relations with the Indians so that more freight cargo from the Gujarati merchants for Persia, Arabia and other neighbouring areas came to the Company. However, the Gujarati merchants were not to be allowed to travel to Batavia along with their cargo in the Company's ships.

Efforts were to be made to extend the Company's trade in the region but without causing offence to our friends or using violence to hinder their trade. The Gujaratis as well as other subjects of the Mughal emperor had for ages been important merchants in the region. Although it might be profitable for us to do so, it would not be fair to try to get all the trade to ourselves except through dexterity and without causing offence. Any damage we caused them in other countries or at sea would be reciprocated by similar damage to us in their country which might even ruin such an important branch of our trade.

The Indian merchants' trade with third parties who were both their friends and ours was, of course, not to be hindered at all. As for their trade with third parties who were their friends but our enemies, again there was nothing that the Company could do anything about. However, in accordance with the usage in Europe and the common rights of nations, we could prevent their supplying our enemies with provisions and war materials.

As for the ships and goods belonging to our enemies, these were to be attacked and captured. The factors were to find out from the Mughal officials the practice regarding the treatment to be meted out to the captured goods.

Particular attention was to be paid to ensuring the security and safety of the Surat port. Consultations might be held in this regard with the government of Surat.

The factors were to provide reliable information regarding the garrison at Diu,[3] together with its situation and fortification. Information was also to be provided as to the best means to inflict the maximum possible damage on the Portuguese there. Also, the factors were to try and identify a suitable port or island which could be used as a retreat for our ships and effects and where a fortification could be erected. These two last matters were to be treated as confidential.

Coromandel

The trade at Pulicat, Tirupapaliyur and adjoining areas can be promoted only after peace had been restored in the area.

The affairs at Masulipatnam were to be clearly investigated. The trade there was very important and a mission might be sent to the king of Golconda and an accomodation reached. The factors' complaints were principally against the *havaldar* of Masulipatnam, who had taken his office on farm from the king of Golconda, and who imposed monopolies, concessions and exactions of various kinds in order to maximize the income from his farm. The Governor-General was to investigate whether it would be in the best interests of the Company to escape the vexations at the hands of the *havaldar* by trying and getting the office on farm for itself.

* The volume is not foliated but this document covers 10 single folios. Instructions only in respect of the establishments at Surat and Coromandel have been incorporated here.

1. The correct name of this man was Hendrick Arentsz. Vapour.
2. The first contacts with Gujarat on behalf of the Company were made by two ships of the fleet of Admiral Matelief that called at Cambay probably in 1606. But David van Deynsen, the Dutch factor, was reportedly harassed so much by the local authorities at the instigation of the Portuguese that towards the end of 1607 he committed suicide at Burhanpur.
3. Diu is situated at a latitude of 20°.42′N and a longitude of 71°.01′E.

96. The Directors at Amsterdam to Van den Broecke at Surat, 29 August 1626. V.O.C. 314 (Copy).*

This letter was being sent with the *Dordrecht*, the *Bommel* and the *Weesp*. A copy of the Directors' letter of December 1624 sent with the *Gouden Leeuw*, the *Walcheren* and the *Heusden* was enclosed.[1] Information regarding the safe arrival of these ships at Surat was received from an English yacht which had left Surat in November 1625 and had reached England in a period of five months. This vessel also informed the Directors of the safe arrival of the *Goede Fortuin*, the *Nieuw Bantam* and the *Bear* at Surat from Batavia.

The late departure of the *Dordrecht* and the *Weesp* from Surat had resulted in their being held up at Mauritius for three months.[2] In the meantime, the *Leeuwin* from Coromandel had joined them there. On their passage from the Cape of Good Hope, these vessels had run into a severe storm. While the *Dordrecht* had reached Texel on 11 February 1626, the *Weesp* and the *Leeuwin* had found it necessary to call at Plymouth where they were detained by the English Company. They, however, were released later and arrived at Texel on the 19th and the 21st of March 1626 respectively. In future, Surat was to instruct all vessels not to call at English ports on the way except in an emergency. All this had happened because the departure of the ships from Surat had been delayed because of the late arrival of the cargo from Persia. Ships leaving Surat for Holland must do so latest by the middle of December and cargo received at Surat after this date ought to be sent on to Batavia.

The cotton sent from Surat with the *Dordrecht* as a sample was not of very good quality. Given the fine quality of Surat textiles, obviously much better quality cotton would be available there.

The Directors had learnt that the late Wouter Heuten was in the good books of Emperor Jahangir. They hoped that Vapour would also be able to establish a good rapport with the Mughal court.

The details provided by Batavia regarding the availability of funds at Surat and Persia were as follows:

The amount remaining in Cambay and Hindustan at the time of the departure of the *Dordrecht* and the *Weesp*		f.120,000
The amount available in Persia		f.355,000
The amount sent from Holland with the *Gouden Leeuw*, the *Walcheren* and the *Heusden* (approximately)		f.635,000
The amount sent from Batavia with the *Goede Fortuin*, *Nieuw Bantam* and the *Bear*		f.390,000
The value of the goods and cash sent from Batavia with the *Hollandia*, the *Oranje* and the *Mauritius*		f.116,000
	Total	f.1,616,000

The following amount would have been used up in:

Meeting the orders from Batavia for 1625		f.230,000
Meeting the orders from Holland for 1625		f.770,000
	Total	f.1,000,000
	Balance	f.616,000
Surat would get from Batavia an excess of about f.150,000 to f.200,000 (sale value) over the amount needed to meet their orders for 1626		f.200,000
The amount available for investment in the return cargo for Holland		f.816,000

With the *Dordrecht*, the *Weesp* and the *Bommel*, specie worth f.600,000 in gold and silver was being sent from Holland. This amount as also the sum received from Batavia in excess of the amount needed for the Indies was to be invested in procuring the return cargo for Holland. The following items were to constitute the return cargo:

1. Persian silk	600 to 800 bales or even more provided the cost price was the same as earlier.
2. Indigo Lahore	As much as possible. Indigo Sarkhej was to be sent only if indigo Lahore could not be procured.
3. Refined saltpetre	A good quantity be sent in square wooden boxes.
4. Cotton yarn	400 to 500 bales.

In addition, some sealing wax, red coral, mark stones and ambergris was also to be sent.

Surat was to keep Persia well provided with cash and goods. The Directors hoped that Persia would be able to procure six hundred bales of silk.

The coarse clothes received from Surat and Coromandel with the *Schoonhoven* had been sold at 13 Flemish *groots* and 3 *pennings* per *ell* at 15 months' credit. The buyers did not find the lot from Surat as good as the one from Coromandel. So Surat was not to send any more coarse clothes. Only 500 to 600 bales of these clothes ought to be sent from Coromandel.

The coarse white broad *baftas* were sold at an open auction at an average price of f.7:14:0 per piece. The fine white *baftas* from Broach were sold at . . . per piece.[3] The blue *baftas* were sold at f.9:2:8 per piece against cash. These were not to be sent until further orders.

The indigo Sarkhej was sold at 6 *schellings* and 10 *groots* per pond at 24 months' credit. The quality was found to be better than that of the lot received with the *Dordrecht* and the *Weesp*. Indigo Bayana was sold at 9 *schellings* and 9 *stuivers* per pond at 24 months' credit.

The Bengal *khasas* were sold at an auction between f.13:5:0 and f.14:5:0 per piece. The *muris* were sold at a public auction at f.9½ to f.10 per piece. The *salampuris* were sold at 7 to 8½ guilders per piece. A good amount of this item was to be sent to Holland.

The Coromandel indigo was found to be of reasonable quality and was sold at f.7:0:3 per pond.

The pepper received with the *Hollandia* had been sold but the nutmeg and the mace were still to be sold. Similarly, the diamonds and the porcelain received with this vessel were sold but the musk had not yet been sold. The Chinese silk was sold at 34 *schellings* and 4 *groots* per pond at 15 months' credit.

* The volume is not foliated but this letter covers 14 single folios.
1. See document no. 45.
2. The *Dordrecht* had left Surat for Holland in April 1625, see document no. 53.
3. The price is not specified in the document.

97. Governor-General De Carpentier at Batavia to Ysbrantsz. at Pulicat, 28 October 1626. V.O.C. 1089, ff.147vo-51vo (Copy).*

Batavia had received Ysbrantsz.'s letter of 4 June 1626 from Pulicat[1] and Maerten van Rossen and Barent Pietersz.'s letter from Masulipatnam dated 15 June 1626.[2]

The Directors were planning to send to the Indies in the spring of 1626 the *Hollandia* together with four other ships of 200 to 250 *lasts* each in addition to four yachts of 50 to 60 *lasts* each to be used against the Portuguese on the Coromandel coast and at other places. The aforementioned ships had been sent to Coromandel with some Hungarian ducats, gold and some goods. Batavia was well aware that Coromandel would get this assistance rather late. Batavia itself had practically run out of rials, silver and gold and was not certain when it would be possible to send the next shipment to Coromandel. Since the Chinese trade had not yet been opened to the Company, Taiwan had been asked to send back to Batavia some of the rials together with the Japanese silver. If Batavia got this, it would be possible for it to send a ship to Coromandel by February 1627. Until then the spices sent to Coromandel with the *Mauritius* would have to suffice.

An English ship, the *Exchange*, had arrived at Batavia from England on 19 October 1626. The English President at Batavia had complained to the Governor-General regarding the hindrances being placed by the Dutch factors in the way of their establishing a factory at Armagon. De Carpentier had replied that according to his information, the English had already established a factory at Armagon and that they had sent both factors and funds there. Ysbrantsz. was to make sure that no direct or indirect injury was inflicted on the English. Batavia was aware of the fact that the English were trying to procure textiles at Armagon just as the Dutch did at Pulicat and that the English would use every means at their disposal to seduce weavers and painters away from Pulicat. Ysbrantsz. was to do his best to prevent this but without giving any cause of complaint to the English. It was possible that the English would find Armagon far too expensive and troublesome as to lose interest in that place. The English were sending to Armagon the *Abigael*, a yacht of about 80 *lasts* with 8,000 rials of eight in cash, some poor quality cloves and some sandalwood bought in Makassar. The yacht was carrying as much on private English accounts as on that of their Company. They had received in May last from Makassar with their ship the *Reformation* about 125 *bahars* of extremely poor quality cloves bought last year at the very high price of 130 rials per *bahar*. It seemed that they would not get any cloves from there this year. This was because on its way to Makassar via Batavia their junk had been wrecked and the upper-merchant aboard together with most of the crew drowned. The English had not sent any ships to Surat this year but four of their ships were reportedly on their way from England to Surat.

The Danes had gone to Makassar with two of their ships which had since returned to Coromandel via the Sunda straits. They had bought 80 *bahars* of cloves there and visited Sukadana[3] on the way. They were thinking of establishing a factory there as also in Banjermasin[4] where they might be able to procure a good amount of pepper.

In the event of a shortage of capital, Ysbrantsz. was to ensure that the fulfilment of the orders from Batavia was affected the least in order to ensure that the intra-Asian trade of the Company did not suffer. The underfulfilment of the orders for the Indies would be much more damaging than in the case of the orders from Holland.

Batavia strongly recommends the procurement of slaves. If they were not available in Coromandel, they were to be procured in Arakan or elsewhere.

Till such time as the position of the Company improved and as long as it continued functioning in Masulipatnam, the authorities there were not to be annoyed.

* An exact copy is available in the *Bataviaasch Uitgaande Brievenboek*, V.O.C. 853, ff.139-41vo.

1. See document no. 89.
2. See document no. 90.
3. Sukadana is in the south-west of Borneo.
4. Banjermasin is on the island of Borneo.

98. The Directors at Amsterdam to Ysbrantsz. at Pulicat, 31 October 1626 or 12 November 1626*. V.O.C. 314# (Copy).

The Directors' last letter to Coromandel had been sent with the *Delfshaven* which had since returned from Batavia. This letter was being sent with the ship *Leeuwin* and the yacht *Kemphaen* with cash and goods as per the invoice.[1]

The Directors had earlier written to Batavia that all ships from the Coromandel coast with return cargo for Holland would come via Batavia and not directly as was the case until then. An exception had, however, been made in the case of the *Leeuwin*, which was to be sent back directly to Amsterdam. The yacht *Kemphaen* was to be used in the Bay of Bengal either for purposes of trade or for inflicting damage on the Portuguese.

Coromandel had written that if Amsterdam provided each

year as much sulphur as had been sent with the *Leeuwin*, the entire gunpowder requirements of the Company for the East Indies could be met by Coromandel. The quality of the sample received was found to be better than that of the European gunpowder. The cost was at most to be 4 *stuivers* per pond. Amsterdam would supply enough sulphur each year.

The cloves had been sold in Coromandel at a very low price. The current price of cloves in Holland was 96 *stuivers* per pond. If the Company continued to sell cloves so cheap in Coromandel, the English and the Danes were likely to buy them there and make a profit of 100 to 200 per cent in Europe. Therefore, if the cloves could not be sold in Coromandel at a higher price, they were either to be sent on to Holland or sold in other places in the East Indies at a price high enough to ensure that the English and the Danes did not find it profitable to buy them there and sell in Europe.

The trade with Bengal was to be promoted in general and in sugar in particular which was doing very well in Persia.

Holland had adequate stocks of fine textiles to last another 4 to 5 years. Therefore, only coarse Guinea cotton cloth including both the raw unbleached as well as the bleached varieties were to be provided by Coromandel. The unbleached variety fetched ½ *stuiver* per *ell* less than the bleached one.

Coromandel was to regularly send to Holland copies of its diary as well of the books of the factory and the garrison. The books of the ships as well as details of the assets left by factors deceased in Coromandel were also to be sent.

* The document is undated but the likely date is one of these two.

\# The volume is not foliated but this letter covers 6 single folios.

1. The invoices of these vessels are not available in the Company's archives.

99. General letter from Governor-General De Carpentier at Batavia to the Directors at Amsterdam, 13 December 1626. V.O.C. 1090, ff.108-46 (Original).*

Since Batavia's last letter to the Directors,[1] the following ships had arrived from Surat: the *Heusden* on 25 June, the *Nieuw Bantam* on 7 July and the captured ship the *Jacinto* on 3 October 1626. All these ships had left Surat together on 10 April. With these ships, Batavia had received a cargo worth f.218,033, consisting of 533 packets of Gujarat clothes, and some wheat, rice and other sundries. On 10 April, Governor Van Speult had also left Surat with 7 ships for Holland with a total cargo worth f.881,075.

Commander Kistjens had left Surat for Persia on 3 December 1625 with a cargo worth f.304,159 consisting of 76,000 rials of eight in cash, a good lot of spices, Dutch broadcloth, different Gujarat clothes and other goods whose total sale value is likely to be around f.500,000.

Surat was completely devoid of cash. In fact they had borrowed funds to the extent of around f.100,000. Spices were not selling very well there because the English had glutted the market with cloves from Makassar. Besides, some Dutch factors had taken cloves there. Strict orders had been issued about this to the Surat Council.

On 5 August 1626, Batavia had sent the *Zierikzee* and the *Wapen van Zeeland* to Surat under the command of Commander Kistjens with a cargo worth f.177,398 consisting of 16,000 rials of eight in cash, 4,000 bags of pepper, 60,000 ponds of cloves, 90,000 ponds of nutmeg, 60 bags of mace, 950 *piculs* of Japanese copper and 1,000 *piculs* of Chinese powder sugar. The total sale value was likely to be around f.640,000. Of this, Persia would get around f.370,000 so that between themselves Surat and Mocha would be left with around f.270,000.

The financial position of the factories at Surat, Persia, Mocha, etc., would thus be as follows:

Capital sent with the *Zierikzee* and the *Wapen van Zeeland* (sale value)	f.640,000
Cargo taken to Persia by six ships last year	f.500,000
Capital sent from Surat to Agra last year (sale value)	f.150,000
Capital sent to Mocha with Governor Van Speult (sale value)	f.50,000
Total	f.1,340,000
As against this, Surat had borrowed on interest Rupees 100,000 (at 22 *stuivers* per rupee)	f.110,000
Balance	f.1,230,000

The Company's affairs at Persia were in good order. As the Directors would have been advised by Vissnich via Aleppo, the Shah held the Dutch there in great esteem. Batavia was only worried that the resumption of hostilities between the Persians and the Turks might cause a stoppage of the Company's trade there, particularly the sale of spices as routes became unsafe.

The English, who were equally interested in the trade at Surat and Persia, had not kept a single ship back at Surat. The *James* and the *Jonas* had been sent to England, the *Anne* without cargo to Batavia, and the *Falcon* to Coromandel. All these ships had left Surat on 10 April. They had as much reason as the Dutch not to keep back any ships at Surat. Three of their ships, the *Dolphin*, the *Palsgrave* and the *Lion* had been engaged by the Portuguese near Bombay while on their way from England causing them to flee. The *Lion* had fled to Persia where it was burnt by the Portuguese frigates between Gombroon and Hormuz. All its personnel numbering 43 were beheaded in a cold-blooded manner. The *Palsgrave* and the *Dolphin* had not yet arrived at Surat.

Since Batavia's last letter to the Directors, the *Arend* and the *Medemblik* had arrived from Coromandel on 8 March and 8 October respectively. Of the cargo brought by these two ships, the following was being sent to Holland: 21,975 ponds of indigo, 13,725 ponds of white cotton yarn, 480 ponds of cotton as a sample, 27,137 ponds of Aceh pepper and 10 packets of clothes. In addition, the following goods were brought by these two ships for Batavia: 630 packets of various kinds of clothes, 98 male and female slaves, 90 *lasts* of rice, 7,600 ponds of gunpowder,

463 ponds of opium and 2,463 ponds of wax. The total value of the cargo for Holland and Batavia was f.245,604.

In 1626, Batavia had been able to send only one ship, the *Mauritius*, to Coromandel on 27 June. It had a cargo worth f.122,577 consisting of 40,000 guilders in rials of eight, 10,000 guilders in unminted silver, 18,000 guilders in unminted gold, 16,000 ponds of cloves, 50,000 ponds of nutmeg, 20,000 ponds of unripe nutmeg (*rompen*), 150 sacks of mace and 900 *piculs* of Japanese copper.

According to the books closed in Coromandel on the 20th of February 1626, the financial situation there was as follows:

Total effects as on 20 February		f.535,595
Capital sent with the *Mauritius* (sale value)		f.250,000
	Total	f.785,595
As against this, one would have to adjust the 16,000 *pagodas* extorted during the time of Van Uffelen		f.78,646
Bad debts at Pulicat		f.7,105
War ammunition and furniture, etc. (illiquid effects)		f.13,451
Cost of maintenance between 1.2.1626 and 1.2.1627 based on the preceding year's experience		f.50,000
Cargo sent with the *Coningh David* to Holland		f.128,150
Cargo sent with the *Medemblik* to Batavia		f.178,755
	Total	f.456,107
Value of the remaining effects		f.329,488

The fulfilment of Batavia's orders for the East Indies alone would need more capital than this. Coromandel had, therefore, been instructed to give priority to the orders from the Indies over those from Holland. This was because the intra-Asian trade, particularly trade in Coromandel clothes, could not be made to suffer. The Directors knew this better than Batavia and would, therefore, be well-advised to provide more capital to Coromandel. Of the spices suplied to Coromandel, some were still lying unsold at Masulipatnam.

The English, the Danes and the Portuguese tended to spoil the market with the cloves from Makassar.

Batavia had strongly recommended to Coromandel to give priority to the procurement of slaves.

The English had established a factory at Armagon, which was about 8 miles to the north of Pulicat. They were trying to attract the producers of painted clothes for the East Indies to this place. In that case, they would not have to share the cost of maintenance of the Pulicat fort with the Dutch.[2]

An English yacht, the *Falcon* had arrived at Batavia from Coromandel on 5 October with about 175 packets of clothes. This was all that the English had been able to buy there over a period of two years.

* Summarized in W.Ph. Coolhaas (ed.), *Generale Missiven*, I, pp. 204-34.

1. See document no. 78.
2. See Om Prakash (ed.), *The Dutch Factories in India 1617-1623*, document no. 122.

100. Van den Broecke, Dirck van der Lee and Jacob Christiaensz. Grijph[1] from the ships the *Walcheren* and the *Dordrecht* in the harbour of Swally to the Directors at Amsterdam, 20 December 1626. V.O.C. 1093, ff.63-5 (Copy).

Given the non-availability of funds at Surat, there was little to do there. Even before the departure of the present shipment, the Surat factory had taken a loan of f.100,000 on interest at 1 per cent per month.

On the 4th of October 1626, six of the Company's ships had arrived at Surat from Mocha together with six English vessels. The *Goede Fortuin* had been lost near Socotra on its way back from Mocha. Of the six English ships, four had come from England.

On the 18th of October, a fleet of Dutch and English ships had been sent to the open sea to escort our ships expected from Europe and Batavia against possible attacks by the Portuguese.

The factors at Mocha were being treated well and regarded with friendship. This was evident from the enclosed copies of the letters from the *badshah*.[2] Governor Van Speult had died at Mocha and had been buried there in style. *Koopman* De Milde was first released but then fearing that we might again attack and capture Muslim ships, he was put back in detention. Before the departure of the ships, he was granted an allowance of 12 rials per month for two years in the form of spices. Surat hoped that this would meet with the approval of the Directors.

The invoices of the goods and cash received from Batavia with the *Zierikzee* and the *Wapen van Zeeland* were enclosed.[3] The goods and cash received for Surat and Persia were rather inadequate and might not be enough even to repay the debts at Surat. The creditors of the Surat factory were demanding their money back which might force the factors at Surat to sell the spices at prices as much as 30 per cent lower than those of last year.

If the Surat factory did not get funds from Europe this year, its creditworthiness would be severely affected. It was important that adequate funds were received and on time. That alone would ensure the timely departure of the ships. Also, if goods were bought at the proper time, a saving of 20 to 30 per cent could be made. After two or three months of the proper season, only left over goods could be procured. Ideally, ships ought to reach Surat by 1 October and be dispatched to Europe, Batavia and Persia as early as possible. Textiles would then be available at Batavia for being dispatched to the Moluccas, Sumatra and other places at the proper time.

Pieter van den Broecke had earlier requested the Directors that a sum of 3,135 guilders, 11 *stuivers* and 8 *pennings* be given to his brother Guilliame van den Broecke, a sugar baker in Amsterdam, for the maintenance of his sisters. He now requests that this sum be increased to 4,500 guilders. The balance of 9,469 guilders, 19 *stuivers* and 8 *pennings* might be kept with the Directors and returned to him on his return to Holland together with interest.[4]

1. Jacob Christiaensz. Grijph had been in the service of the Company since October 1616 as upper-merchant. Between August 1618 and June 1621, he was the director of the factory of Ternate. Thereafter, he was a bailiff at Batavia. In 1622, he repatriated as commander of the return fleet. Between November 1627 and April 1628, he was vice-commander of the fleet under Willem Jansz. in the western quarters. He was present at the funeral ceremony of Coen but, thereafter, not much is known about him.
2. These letters are not available in the Company's archives.
3. These invoices are not available in the Company's archives.
4. If these figures are correct, there was a total of 13,969 guilders, 19 *stuivers* and 8 *pennings* owed to Van den Broecke by the Directors.

1627

101. Van Rossen and Pietersz. at Masulipatnam to the Directors at Amsterdam, 16 January 1627. V.O.C. 1092, ff.374-6vo (Copy).

Maerten van Rossen and Barent Pietersz. who had jointly been incharge of the factory at Masulipatnam for the last 16 months had intended to write to the directors with the *Coningh David* which had left Masulipatnam on 7 March 1626 with a cargo worth f.128,150. They, however, had refrained from doing so because they did not yet have enough experience.

The yacht *Medemblik* had been sent to Batavia on 24 June 1626 where it had arrived on 8 October with a cargo worth f.178,756.

The *Mauritius* had arrived at Masulipatnam from Batavia via Pulicat on 20 October 1626 with a cargo of f.122,577 consisting mostly of spices. Governor Ysbrantsz. had sent the *Jager* from Pulicat to Masulipatnam with a cargo worth f.15,693 which had been taken out of the *Mauritius*. The *Jager* had, however, sunk on the way near Armagon on 8 October in a tornado.

The *Mauritius* had been sent to Batavia on 24 November 1626 via Pulicat from where it departed on 8 December with a total cargo worth f.188,754.

A Danish ship, the *Christiaanshaven*, had arrived at Masulipatnam from Bengal on 14 November 1626. Their yacht, the *Nightingale*, had, however, been lost. Another ship that they had bought in Bengal last year and which had been sent to Tenasserim had not yet returned and it seems that it had been lost. The *Christiaanshaven* had left for Trancquebar on 9 December with textiles, indigo and diamonds worth a total of 24,000 rials bought at Masulipatnam. Most of the textiles were for the southern quarters. The Danes had procured some 70 *lasts* of saltpetre and some indigo at Trancquebar, Porto Novo and Puleceri. From Bengal, they had brought 4,000-4,500 rials worth of ginger, long pepper, sugar and some *taffechelas*. They had sent to Bengal about 8,000 ponds of cloves and 8,000 ponds of sandalwood. But all this was still lying unsold there and their trade at Bengal was not much. They were earlier planning to send the *Christiaanshaven* to Denmark but lately they had been saying that it would instead be sent to Makassar to sell textiles and buy cloves and sandalwood there. At the moment, they had only the *Christiaanshaven* and the *Waterhond* in the Indies, and were very short of both cash and personnel.

An English yacht, the *Abigael*, had arrived at Masulipatnam from Batavia on 30 December 1626 with a cargo worth about 18,000 rials in cash, Japanese silver, lead, 11 *maunds* of nutmeg, 35¾ *bahars* of cloves, 11 *maunds* of mace and so on. Within five days, the yacht had left for Armagon where they had established a factory last year. They intended to persuade the *nayak* to let them construct a fort there which in Van Rossen's opinion was unlikely. Armagon was quite close to Pulicat and they planned to shift their trade and personnel there.

The spices and the copper received with the *Mauritius* at Pulicat had already been sold. The cloves had been sold at 10½ *pagodas* per *maund* and mace at 13 *pagodas* per *maund* of 24 ponds each. A *pagoda* was worth 4 guilders and 5 *stuivers*. Nutmeg were sold at 110 *pagodas* and the unripe variety (*rompen*) at 78 *pagodas* per *bahar* of 480 ponds. Copper was sold at 50 *pagodas* per *bahar*. The factors at Masulipatnam had nothing else to sell or do and were not expecting any assistance from Batavia who only had spices to provide. If cash had been available, all kinds of good textiles, a good amount of indigo and saltpetre could have been bought at Masulipatnam and Palicol.

Masulipatnam hoped to sell annually the following: scarlets—mostly red, some parrot green—10 to 12 cases, lead—200 *bahars*, quicksilver—5-6 *bahars*, vermilion—5-6 *bahars*, spelter—50-60 *bahars*.

The enclosed daily register[1] would highlight the nature of the Company's relations with *havaldar* Muhammad Taqi. The Company had no alternative but to deal with the private merchants to whom the right to trade with the Company had been farmed out.

Commander Anthony Caen[2] had come to Masulipatnam with two of his yachts, the *Pearl* and the *Revenge*. On the way, he had captured a Portuguese fust which had, however, been lost at Arakan. He had captured yet another Portuguese small ship near Pipli, but that too had been lost.

The diamond mine was open again and it was hoped that diamonds would now be available at a reasonable price, probably as cheaply as in the time of Andries Soury.[3]

1. See document no. 102.
2. Anthony Caen came to Bantam aboard the *Middelburg* in November 1614 as an assistant. In May 1619, he took part in the capture of Jacatra in the rank of an under-merchant. He was later sent to Palembang as an envoy. In December 1620, he was sent as an envoy to Mataram to work on the release of the captured Dutchmen there. In March 1632, he was sent as an envoy to the king of Makassar. He repatriated on 27 December 1634. In February 1636, he again left for the Indies with nine ships in the rank of an extraordinary member of the Council of the Indies. He accompanied Van Diemen in his travels to Amboina in 1637 and 1638. In 1638, he captured Trincomalee in Ceylon. He was again in Ceylon between 24 September 1639 and 21 February 1640. Between 31 March 1640 and 11 February 1642, he was the governor of the Moluccas. Thereafter, until 11 September 1642, he was the governor of Amboina. In May 1648, he returned to the Moluccas as an inspector. He returned to Batavia on 6 July where he died on 11 August 1648.
3. See Om Prakash (ed.), *The Dutch Factories in India 1617-1623*, document nos. 116 and 117.

102. Daily Register kept at Masulipatnam between 28 January 1627[1] and 12 November 1627. V.O.C. 1092, ff.383-90vo (Copy).

6 February

The English yacht, the *Abigael*, left Masulipatnam for Armagon. The vessel is reported to have taken many gifts for the *nayak* and other important people at Armagon. The English Company would like to construct a fort there.

8 February

Two small ships arrived from Bengal with sugar, some *taffechelas*, *gingams*, rice, butter, oil and other goods. The Danish *Waterhond* was due to leave within a day or two for Trancquebar with provisions.

10 February

The *cannacappel*[2] of the Danes left for the indigo lands without cash intending to buy indigo against credit. He is unlikely to have much success.

15 February

It was learnt that Captain Vermeer,[3] free merchant from Batavia, had entered Vizagapatnam[4] with his yacht *Pulicat* and a captured yacht. At Bimilipatnam,[5] he had captured a Portuguese *sampan* laden with provisions and some iron.

17 February

We were summoned by *havaldar* Muhammad Taqi to the *bankzall*.[6] He brought up the capture of the Portuguese *sampan* and its goods by Captain Vermeer. According to him, the goods belonged to Mansur Khan and that a *farman* had come from Golconda from the king requiring the restitution of the goods. Maerten van Rossen claimed that it was not in his power to do so because Captain Vermeer was a free merchant and had the permission of the Governor-General to attack Portuguese ships and goods. It was unlikely that the goods belonged to Mansur Khan because he was at war with the Portuguese and would not have risked his goods with them. When the Portuguese were questioned about this, they claimed that the goods belonged to them.

18 February

Two *sampans* laden with provisions and a large amount of cinnamon arrived from Vizagapatnam. They brought the news that Captain Vermeer had left Vizagapatnam 10 days earlier and had presumably gone back to the straits of Malacca and further on to Batavia.

22 February

Barent Pieterz. left for Doelapondy,[7] Wattepoel[8] and Petapuli[9] via Gandasael[10] to collect the goods lying ready there, namely red *bethilles*, *parcallas*, *chavonis* and other varieties of textiles.

24 February

Havaldar Muhammad Taqi ordered that a Hindu thief be cut into four pieces and each piece be hung in each of the four corners of the city as a lesson to others.

25 February

The English yacht, the *Abigael*, arrived from Armagon with eight guns, 36 soldiers and some officers.

26 February

The *Abigael* left for Narsapur. It was leaking and was able to stay above the water with difficulty.

1 March

The Danish *Waterhond* arrived from Bengal due to contrary winds and shortage of water. It carried only some rice.

18 March

Two ships, one belonging to Mir Kasim and the other to Mir Murad,[11] arrived from Pegu with long pepper, lac, rice and a large amount of rubies worth a total of more than 30,000 *pagodas*. Some of the free merchants who had finished their business in Pegu also returned with these ships. The king was still unwilling to release the free merchants in detention there.

22 March

Pietersz. returned from Petapuli. Since all the textiles there were not yet ready, he left the entire lot there after having the ready pieces duly packed.

7 May

The *Medemblik* arrived from Batavia via Pulicat with a cargo worth f.111,123 consisting mainly of gold, some broad cloth and other goods.

18 June

Van Rossen went to Gandasael to see if the Company's suppliers would accept goods in settlement of the amounts we owed them. Some of the suppliers agreed. Lead was delivered at 17½ and tin at 53 *pagodas* per *bahar*.

24 June

A bag of cloves and a big piece of sandalwood belonging to the Danes were found to have been stolen from the customs warehouse. Van der Molen[12] complained to the *havaldar* about it who promised to investigate the matter himself since the employees of the warehouse were his people. But later Van der Molen was instead arrested and released only after gifts of spices had been given.

14 July

In the evening, *Havalda*r Muhammad Taqi left for Golconda where he had been summoned by the king and Mansur Khan. He carried with him a large amount of gifts including two elephants and some curiosities of the total value of more than 1,000 *pagodas*. Since he expected to return to his post, he designated his brother as the temporary *havaldar*.

24 August

Muhammad Taqi returned from Golconda after obtaining the *havaldarship* of Masulipatnam for another year against a sum of 160,000 *pagodas*. In order to get this, he had to present gifts worth more than 15,000 *pagodas* to the king and Mansur Khan.

10 September

The yacht *Duyf* and the sloop *Cleyn Delft* arrived from Pulicat. They had seized a Portuguese *thony* laden with coarse rice.

The following goods were sold to the merchants who had farmed the right to trade with the Company.

Item	*Price (in pagodas)*
Nutmeg	114 per *bahar* of 480 ponds
Japanese copper	50 per *bahar* "
Sandalwood	85 per *bahar* "
Sappanwood	3½ per *bahar* "
Poutchina[13]	95 per *bahar* "
Mace	13 per *maund* of 24 ponds
Cloves	9½ per *maund* "
Vermilion	19 per *maund* "
Quicksilver	21 per *maund* "
Scarlet broadcloth	2 per *gaz* (yard)

Half of the payment was in cash while the other half was to be in textiles to be supplied by them.

On being summoned by *Havaldar* Muhammad Taqi, Marten Ysbrantsz. who happened to be here from Pulicat visited him together with Barent Pietersz. The *havaldar* asked to be supplied with 50 *bahars* of nutmeg and 10 *maunds* of mace, ostensibly on behalf of the king, at 100 *pagodas* per *bahar* and 10 *pagodas* per *maund* respectively. He was told that these spices had been sold out but that we could buy some back from the Company's farmers and supply him at 109 *pagodas* and 13 *pagodas* respectively against cash payment. But an agreement regarding the price could not be reached.

12 September

Since the spices had been asked for on behalf of the king, Ysbrantsz., Van Rossen and Pietersz. went to the *havaldar's* home and agreed to provide nutmeg at 105 *pagodas* per *bahar* and mace at 12½ *pagodas* per *maund* against cash payment. Half the loss involved in this transaction would be borne by the Company's farmers.

19 September

Barent Pietersz. returned from Petapuli. He had collected 17 packets of clothes—mainly in red colour at Dulapondy, Wattepoel, Gandasael and Petapuli. An assistant had been asked to transport the goods in a boat.

22 September

Over the current and the last week, several Muslim ships left Masulipatnam reasonably laden with all varieties of textiles. Two of these went to Pegu, two to Aceh, one to Tenasserim and one to Arakan. Most of these would be back by March or April. Only the ones going to Pegu would have to stay there for a year before they were allowed to leave.

23 September

The Danish ship, the *Waterhond*, left for Pipli in Bengal without picking up any cargo at Masulipatnam. It seemed to have carried only some tobacco, copper, spelter and *poutchina* belonging to Muhammad Taqi and some other Muslim merchants of Masulipatnam.

28 September

At the time of his departure from Masulipatnam, Ysbrantsz. went to *Havaldar* Muhammad Taqi to take his leave and to present him with gifts as was customary. The gifts taken were one piece of broadcloth, 40 ponds each of mace, nutmeg and cloves and 80 ponds of sandalwood. The *havaldar* asked for a Persian horse in gift and returned the gifts to our factory.

29 September

Muhammad Taqi sent Mir Kamal-al-Din asking for the gifts back.

13 October

The English yacht *Abigael* returned from Narsapur. This yacht was reportedly of about 70 to 80 *lasts* and bought for 1,400 *pagodas*.

12 November

The brother of Muhammad Taqi arrived from Golconda to take up the office of the *havaldar*. It was learnt that Muhammad Taqi had failed to obtain the office of the *kotwal* and had been asked by Mansur Khan to look after his affairs.

1. There is no entry between 28 January 1627 and 5 February 1627.
2. Probably a broker.
3. Lambert Vermeer had served as captain in the Moluccas. Since 3 May 1622, he was a member of the Daily Council at Batavia where he lived as free burgher. He participated in a number of trading ventures.
4. It is in Andhra Pradesh at the latitude of 17°.42′N and longitude of 83°.20′E.
5. It is in Andhra Pradesh at the latitude of 17°.53′N and longitude of 83°.30′E.
6. The term *bankzaal* was used both for a warehouse as well as the office of the harbour master.
7. Probably Doddapondy in the Eastern Krishna delta near Masulipatnam.
8. Not identified.
9. Petapuli or peddapalle, more generally known as Nizampatnam, is 40 miles south-west of Masulipatnam.
10. Not identified.
11. Mir Murad was a notable merchant at Masulipatnam.
12. Christoffel van der Molen was an upper-merchant in the service of the Dutch East India Company in 1620. In 1622, he went to Trancquebar in the service of the Danish Company and was a factor at Masulipatnam. Later, he became President at Trancquebar.
13. Not identified.

103. Governor-General De Carpentier at Batavia to Ysbrantsz. at Pulicat, 17 March 1627. V.O.C. 1092, ff.62-71 (Copy).*

De Carpentier's last letter to Marten Ysbrantsz. was dated 28 October 1626[1] with the English yacht, the *Abigael.* Since then Batavia had received Ysbrantsz.'s letter of 5 December[2] with the *Mauritius* and one from Masulipatnam dated 24 November.[3] De Carpentier has fully realized that the Company's trade in Coromandel suffered because of the shortage of funds but the blame for this rested squarely on the shoulders of the Directors. In view of continuing uncertain situation in Coromandel, the Directors considered it prudent to wait awhile before committing more funds for that region. The Directors did not seem to realize that in order to keep the trade in the Indies prospering, funds were required on a continuing basis. The Indies seemed to be overflowing with funds until a few years ago but this was because the volume of trade carried on then was so small. Now the trade at Coromandel, Surat and Persia was suffering because of the shortage of funds. When the current year's return cargo from Batavia, Coromandel, Surat and Persia reached Holland, the Directors would realize that they had indeed waited a year too long to send enough capital.

The shortage of capital with Batavia notwithstanding, in view of the fact that Coromandel lacked funds and Batavia simply could not function without the Coromandel textiles, the *Medemblik* was being sent with a cargo worth f.111,123 consisting mainly of gold, some raw silk, radix China, sandalwood, lead, tin, vermilion, quicksilver and broadcloth.

After the last shipment to Holland, Batavia was entirely devoid of spices. In view of the more profitable avenues of investment, Coromandel did not need to provide any pepper for Holland. Similarly, the procurement of diamonds must be deferred. Also, no rice was to be bought for Batavia which was well provided with it and expecting fresh supplies from Siam and Japan. Further, given the profit rate in Bengal and Arakan, it was not advisable to divert the limited amount of capital available to those areas.

Batavia was happy that the English and the Danes in Coromandel were as 'sick' as the Dutch. Whoever recovered first would be able to deny a lot of profit to the others. The trade of the English at Batavia also was very poor. According to the information provided by Coen, only one yacht, the *Aviso* of 50 *lasts*, had been equipped at Hoorn and dispatched to the East by the Danes, so they could not expect any capital.

Batavia was very poorly supplied with textiles from Coromandel and Gujarat. The *Medemblik* was, therefore, to be sent back at the first opportunity so that it reached Batavia by September.

Since Coromandel was well provided with slaves and more were expected from Arakan, as many were to be sent back with the *Medemblik* as possible.

Pulicat was specifically ordered to first meet the textile orders for the Indies before procuring anything else. Capital received from Batavia as well as from Holland could be used for the purpose. The fulfilment of the orders from Holland was to await the receipt of more capital from there.

The king of Siam had been very pleased to learn that Pulicat had prevented the capture of one of his ships by the Portuguese near Sao Tome. Such acts would be helpful in earning the Company the king's esteem.

Clergyman Nicolaes Molinesz. [4] was being sent together with his family to take up the vacant position of priest in Coromandel.

De Carpentier was pleased that his nephew, Roelandt de Carpentier, had been taken in the Company's service at Pulicat. He was to be promoted according to his merit.

Dirck Ment,[5] a brother of the wife of Governor-General Coen, was being sent with the *Medemblik* as assistant. He had worked for a long time with a dyer and had obtained a reasonable experience of indigo. He could be used for procuring indigo in Coromandel, but was to be sent back to Batavia if no vacancy was available.

* An exact copy is available in the *Bataviaasch Uitgaande Brievenboek*, V.O.C. 854, ff.40-4vo.

1. See document no. 97.
2. This letter is not available in the Company's archives.
3. This letter is not available in the Company's archives.
4. Nicholaes Molinesz. had come as a clergyman to the East in 1626 and held the position of priest in Coromandel until 1632. He returned to Batavia in August 1633 and from May 1634 onwards looked after the Portuguese community there. He travelled to Ceylon with the fleet of Philip Lucas as the priest. He died on 25 December 1640 aboard the *Zantvoort* on its trip from Ceylon to Batavia.
5. Dirck Ment had travelled to the East with the *Hollandia* and had been sent to Coromandel as assistant in 1627. On 10 December 1633, he returned to the East aboard the *Schagen* in the capacity of an under-merchant.

104. Dirck Haspelaer[1] and Hendrick Brouwer[2] at Texel to Ysbrantsz. at Pulicat, 18 March 1627, V.O.C. 315 (Copy).*

Because of the shortage of space in the ships on their way to Batavia, some goods (mainly shipping equipment) had been put aboard the *Leeuwin* and the *Kemphaen* being sent to Coromandel. These goods were to be sent on to Batavia at the first opportunity.

1. Not identified.
2. Hendrick Brouwer was the chief of the factory at Firando in Japan between February 1613 and August 1614. Later between 7 September 1632 and 1 January 1636 he was the Governor-General of the Dutch East Indies.

* The volume is not foliated but this letter covers ½ folio.

105. Van Rossen and Pietersz. at Masulipatnam to Batavia, 17 June 1627. V.O.C. 1091, ff. 604-7 (Copy).

The yacht *Medemblik* had left Masulipatnam for Batavia via Pulicat on 10 June 1627 with a cargo worth f.90,845 consisting mostly of Guinea cloth, red, brown, blue and white *bethilles* and *chavonis*, *salampuris*, *parcallas*, some *palang gobars*, blue *balatius*, *madops*, *madafons*, *chelas*, *taffechelas*, coarse *tapis*, sail cloth, cotton blankets of Golconda, red cotton yarn, Siamese *badjoes*, some Bengal clothes, saltpetre and some iron.

It was difficult to sell the Company's goods partly because of the lack of safety on the routes and partly because of the expected replacement of the *havaldar*. Some lead was sold to persons we owed money to at 17½ *pagodas* per *bahar* while tin was sold at 53 *pagodas* per . . .[1] and raw Chinese silk at 40 *pagodas* per *maund*. It had not yet been possible to sell the broadcloth. Five pieces of scarlet were given to the *havaldar* to be adjusted against the tolls to be paid by the Company and another five to Mir

Kamal-al-Din against goods to be supplied by him. The price had not yet been agreed upon. The *havaldar* was offered a price of 3½ *pagodas* per *gaz*[2] but he was not willing to pay more than 2 *pagodas*. The offer made to Mir Kamal-al-Din was 3 *pagodas* per *gaz* but he was not willing to pay more than 2½ *pagodas*.

The Masulipatnam factory was under heavy debts. These could not be liquidated by the sale of goods because it was very difficult to sell against cash. But even if the entire congo received with the *Medemblik* would have been sold against cash, it would still not have been possible to pay off all the debts. Since mainly spices alone were expected from Batavia, it was critically important that Holland sent liquid cash. It would not be possible to sell the spices quickly because a large quantity had been imported by the Muslim merchants during the current year from Aceh and Tenasserim. In addition, the English had imported some from Batavia and the Danes were expecting some from Makassar.

The buyers of tin made no distinction between the fine English tin and the lot that was imported from Pegu and Tenasserim. Copper was unlikely to fetch more than 45 *pagodas* per....[3] while last year it had been sold at 50 *pagodas*.

The sum of 11,000 *pagodas* that had allegedly been extorted by the *havaldar* from Ramanna and Coutour and paid from the Company's funds had in fact been only 5,000 *pagodas* by the *havaldar* in addition to a sum of 1,000 *pagodas* by way of costs making a total of 6,000 *pagodas*. The Company had thus been cheated by the two merchants.

The *salampuris* being sent would be found useful for making shirts and trousers. An attempt would be made to have *bethilles* of 40 or 30 *asta* length, some pieces of which were being sent, to be manufactured in a finer quality. Subject to the availability of funds, a good quantity of these could be procured at Palicol where they were available more cheaply than at Masulipatnam. *Chavonis* and Negro-cloth could also be procured there as also 3,000 pieces of Guinea-cloth per month and a good quantity of *dungarees*. But because of the shortage of cash, the factors had been forced to remain idle.

The Masulipatnam factors had been obliged to accept red cotton yarn, Siamese *badjoes* and *bethilles* of 24 *asta* because contracts for these had been given out earlier. In future, care would be taken that the orders for the Indies were procured before those from Holland.

Some iron was being sent with the present shipment. Steel and wax were not available. An attempt would be made to send some with the next ship.

The diamond mine was still open. A reasonably large number of stones had reportedly been mined but the price remained high. Three or four Portuguese had allegedly bought a large quantity of diamonds which would affect the price in Europe. At the mine, the current price of a diamond of one *mangelin* (in Masulipatnam 1 *mangelin* was considered to be equal to 1 Dutch carat but at the mine it was treated as 25 per cent different[4]) was 9 to 10 *pagodas* (again the *pagoda* was reckoned 15 per cent differently[5] at the mine), that of two *mangelins* 13 to 15 *pagodas* and of that of three *mangelins* between 20 and 24 *pagodas*.

The Danes were sitting idle at Masulipatnam without any trade, money or ships. They had made no progress in Bengal yet. That land was full of wars with a new *subahdar* each month. The cloves and sandalwood carried there last year were still lying unsold at the time of the departure of the *Waterhond* which had returned to Masulipatnam on 1 March 1627. The Danes were at war with both the Muslims as well as the Portuguese. The Muslims were pressing them daily for more gifts. The Muslim authorities had claimed that from a junk which had stayed there for as long as their ship had, they had charged as much as 4,000 rupees in addition to some sandalwood, cloves and curiosities. The value of the cargo the Danes had received from Bengal did not exceed 5,000-6,000 rials.

1. The unit of weight is not indicated.
2. The *gaz* was a measure whose length varied from one region to another between one *hath* or natural cubit and the English yard.
3. The unit of weight is not specified.
4. The document does not specify if it was 25 per cent higher or lower.
5. It is again not stated whether it was 15 per cent higher or lower.

106. Ysbrantsz. at Pulicat to Governor-General De Carpentier at Batavia, 27 June 1627. V.O.C. 1091, ff.597-603 (Copy).

Marten Ysbrantsz. had firm information that in the affair of Director Van Uffelen, a sum of 11,000 *pagodas* had indeed been extorted from Ramanna and Coutour. But of this amount, the *havaldar* had received only 5,000 *pagodas* and his assistants 1,000 *pagodas*. There did not seem to be any possibility of recovering this sum except through the use of force. If the necessary permission and the resources could be made available by Batavia, then the Indian ships returning during the months of February and March could be ransomed. That would definitely produce results.

The *Medemblik* could not call at Pulicat so the cargo to be laden aboard it was sent on to Masulipatnam. The value of the total cargo carried by the *Medemblik* would be f.144,483.

The ambassador of the king of Arakan had been permitted to travel aboard the *Medemblik* to Batavia together with some textiles that he had bought at Pulicat on his private account. He had come to Coromandel with the slaves that we had bought in Arakan. One slave from Arakan was considered as good as two from Coromandel.

A list of clothes being taken by the free merchants aboard this ship was enclosed.[1] Since the factors in any case did not have the cash to buy all the clothes available at Pulicat, they had been rather liberal in allowing the free merchants to do so and take them to Batavia because otherwise the English would have done so.

The saltpetre trade in the south[2] was at a standstill because of the continuous warfare[3] there. Pulicat had purchased only as much saltpetre as was needed for the manufacture of gunpowder.

A part of the gold received with the *Medemblik* hardly deserved to be called gold in so far as it was of only 7⅕ carats. 1948½ rials worth weight was minted at Pulicat and a profit of f.2,680 made. A part of the gold had been sent to Masulipatnam because the factors there had run out of cash. But there the gold rendered a big loss. The free merchants had sent some gold to Pulicat. If bought with care at Batavia, gold ordinarily afforded a profit of 15 to 20 per cent at Pulicat.

An English ship that had come to Masulipatnam from Surat had brought the news that Dutch Company ships had brought 560 bales of silk from Persia which Van den Broecke had gotten unloaded at Surat. Ysbrantsz. considered this to be rather strange.

News had been received from Nagapattinam and Ceylon that 18 Portuguese vessels including 14 galliots had already arrived at Galle and that four more galliots were expected there from Goa. Their intentions were not entirely clear but the Dutch at Coromandel had no cause for worry.

Two letters from the factors in detention at Pegu were enclosed – one to the Governor-General and the other to the Church Council.[4] The only way to obtain the release of these factors seemed to be to send a frigate there and seize some persons. Last year, Pulicat had hoped that the yacht sent by Malaya – who was well known in Pegu – would be able to secure the release of these persons but that did not happen. All that Dirk van Haps and other free merchants visiting Pegu this year had been able to do was to visit the factors in the prison.

Captain Suylesteyn had accepted the salary of f.90 offered by Batavia and had bound himself to serve the Company for three years. Free merchant Commander Balliouw Caen had come to Pulicat from Mauritius with the *Pearl* and the *Revengie*. Since the *Revengie* needed repairs, Commander Caen had proceeded to Galle with the *Pearl*, the frigate *Bonne Remedie* and a sloop. He returned to Pulicat on the 1st of April together with a ship captured near Nagapattinam. This ship had carried rice which was sold to the Danes at Trancquebar. The commander was advised to cruise around Masulipatnam for the entire month of April. The *Revengie* had since been delivered to the commander after repairs. On the 17th of April, he left for the straits of Malacca on his way to Batavia.

Coromandel was totally devoid of cash and funds had to be borrowed at Masulipatnam in order to meet the costs of the garrison at Pulicat.

The Danish yacht, the *Waterhond*, carrying 30 to 40 bags of sugar and some textiles had been attacked by two yachts on its way from Bengal. It seemed that this was the work of Captain

Vermeer who was in the area at that time. The Danes had complained to Pulicat about this. Information received from Orissa suggested that Vermeer was in Vizagapatnam getting his yachts repaired there. The Danish ship had been carrying some Portuguese passengers who had been picked up in Bengal. Ysbrantsz. wished that Vermeer had taken only these passengers along with their goods and had let the Danish ship proceed on its way.

At Pipli, the Danes had a lot of troubles with both the Muslims as well as the Portuguese. The goods they had taken there were still lying unsold and they were indeed thinking of closing the factory. At Masulipatnam, they had bought the following cargo which had been sent to Makassar with the *Christiaanshaven*:

Item	*Quantity*	*Cost (in pagodas)*
Indigo	13 packets	2,382
White *parcallas*	10 packets	1,156
Red *parcallas*	4 packets	643½
Red *bethilles* of 40 *asta*	4 packets	707½
White *bethilles* of 40 *asta*	5 packets	398½
White *bethilles* of 30 *asta*	6 packets	344
Red *bethilles*	8 packets	1,215
Guinea cloth	11 packets	257
Salampuris	19 packets	960
Brown blue[5]	6 packets	445
Brown blue *bethilles* of 30 *asta*	4 packets	400
Chelas	1 packet	70
Cotton yarn	6 packets	78

The total cost of this cargo was 9,051½ *pagodas*[6] plus tolls. 16 packets of canefustel[7] and one packet of ordinary shirts had also been sent with this ship. The *Christiaanshaven* returned from Makassar on the 17th of June with 100 *bahars* of cloves and 50 *bahars* of sandalwood.

The *Pegel* belonging to Malaya had returned to Pulicat from Arakan on the 2nd of February 1627. A *sampan* freighted by our factors had also arrived with 308 big Bengali slaves bought in Arakan. Twelve of these slaves had died on the way. This number included the three who had been killed by the crew and thrown overboard. Because there were only two Dutchmen among the crew, the slaves had nearly taken over the ship and could have killed the Dutch crew.

Because of a high flood, the island of Manar was mostly under water in late February. The Portuguese castle had been washed away. In Jaffanapatnam also, many houses and gardens had been washed away. Besides, many ships, *sampans* and *thonys* had been wrecked. In Tranquemale, two galliots had been destroyed. Lots of people and animals had died. Of the more than 200 *sampans* going towards Ceylon from Nagapattinam, Sao Tome, Covelan,[8] Porto Novo, Trimelaras,[9] Karikal, etc., no more than 10 could be salvaged.

The complaint lodged by the English with the Governor-General that the Coromandel factors were hindering the establishment of their trade at Armagon was simply to preempt us from complaining against them. They had indeed succeeded in obtaining a *kaul* from Venkatapa Nayak[10] in which he had promised that the Dutch would not be allowed to trade at Armagon. The Company had even been prevented from trading at Cottepatnam where we had been getting textiles manufactured for long. Everybody else was being allowed to trade there freely. One Chinappa, who owed the Company 100 *pagodas,* had given out advances on our account to weavers and painters there but the recovery of this sum now seemed difficult. The English were using all available means to seduce the Company's weavers and painters from Pulicat. It seemed that the costs incurred by the English would be no smaller than they had been at Pulicat and in all probability would go on increasing each year.

1. This list is not available in the Company's archives.
2. The reference is evidently to the kingdom of Carnatic.
3. The reference seems to be to the fights among the local *nayaks* of the kingdom.
4. These letters are not available in the Company's archives.
5. The variety of the textile is not specified.
6. The total in fact works out at 9,056½ *pagodas*.
7. Not identified.
8. This was probably Kobelom to the south of Sao Tome.
9. Trimelaras is to the south of Porto Novo and to the north of Trancquebar.

10. Venkatapa Nayak was one of the feudatory chiefs in southern Coromandel. It was well known that he was a sworn enemy of the Dutch. The English complaint, therefore, was obviously unjustified.

107. Van Rossen and Pietersz. at Masulipatnam to Governor-General De Carpentier at Batavia, 9 July 1627. V.O.C. 1091, ff.608-10 (Copy).

The English ship, the *Abigael*, was still at Narsapur and was expected at Masulipatnam soon to take in the porcelain as also some packets of clothes which would have been readied in the meantime. It was due to leave Masulipatnam by the middle of September[1] or the beginning of October. They had received a letter from Surat saying that a fleet of six Portuguese galleons under the command of Dom Nuno Alvarez Botelho had left Ceylon with the intention of coming to the Coromandel coast and then proceed to the west coast of Sumatra.

The Danish ship, the *Christiaanshaven*, had arrived at Masulipatnam from Makassar because due to westerly winds it could not reach Trancquebar. Its cargo included 60 to 65 Moluccan *bahars* cloves of 600 ponds each, 65-70 *bahars* of sandalwood, some nutmeg and *poutchina*. They claimed that the ship had also brought 90 ponds of gold which seemed unlikely in so far as the cost of this would exceed the total capital that they had taken to Makassar. They planned to take the gold to Trancquebar because the market at Pulicat was very bad. They had offered to sell at Masulipatnam cloves at 9 *pagodas* per *maund* and sandalwood at 85 *pagodas* per *bahar* against the supply of cloth provided the buyer made a part of the payment in cash.

The goods received with the *Medemblik* had mostly been sold to the Company's creditors at the following prices:

Item	*Price (in pagodas)*
Red scarlets	3 per *gaz*
Crab red scarlets	2½ per *gaz*
Green and yellow scarlets	2 per *gaz*
Vermilion	19 per *maund*
Quicksilver	21 per *maund*
Spelter	70 per *bahar*
Poutchina	95 per *bahar*

On the gold received from Pulicat where it had been melted down, the Company lost 744¾ heavy rials or f.1,580.

The current price of rials at Masulipatnam was 8½ to 8¾ *pagodas* per piece but was expected to go up after the departure of the Muslim ships. The ducats had fetched one *pagoda* per piece which still afforded a small profit.

1. In the text, by mistake the month given is December.

108. Governor-General De Carpentier at Batavia to Ysbrantsz. at Pulicat, 11 July 1627. V.O.C. 1092, ff.130-4. (Not stated whether original or copy.)*

The Directors were planning to send the *Leeuwin* to Coromandel with f.250,000 in cash and goods. As a result of its earnest pleas for more capital and ships, the Directors had made a good beginning with the recent shipment that had arrived from Holland. Batavia had thus been enabled to send to Pulicat the *Brouwershaven* and the *Grootenbroek* with a cargo worth f.281,000 including f.225,000 worth of minted and unminted gold. According to Batavia's calculations, Pulicat would thus have a total capital of f.880,000 as follows:

Real effects		f.200,000
Cargo sent with the *Brouwershaven* and the *Grootenbroek* (sale value)		f.380,000
Cargo that Pulicat would get from Holland with the *Leeuwin* (sale value)		f.300,000
	Total	f.880,000

The investment in the return cargo for Holland was not to exceed the proceeds from the sale of the cargo received with the *Leeuwin*. The remaining funds were to be invested in the procurement of clothes for the Indies for 1627 and 1628. The perennial shortage of cash faced by Coromandel leading to missed opportunities of profit in intra-Asian trade should now be a thing of the past. Till such time as Batavia received funds for 1628 from Holland and the spices from the Spice Islands, it would not be possible to send any more capital to Coromandel.

The *Medemblik* and the other two ships ought to be sufficient for the transportation of the slaves and the textiles. The Amsterdam Chamber wanted the *Leeuwin* sent back directly to Amsterdam and not via Batavia.

Batavia considered the Directors' suggestion to take Masulipatnam on farm as both impractical as well as unprofitable. The Company simply could not adopt coercive and tyrannical measures against the merchants the way the Muslim *havaldar* could, quite apart from the fact that such measures were against both Godly laws as well as Christian conscience. Pulicat's advice had been solicited because they alone would be familiar with the local situation.

The direction to attach priority to the textiles orders for the Indies was reiterated.

Only a small quantity of spices was being sent because Surat had informed Batavia that the prices in Surat and Agra had gone down by a third and the sales had declined as a result of the imports from Coromandel via Barhampur.[1] Batavia was, therefore, wondering if too large is quantity of spices had not been sent to Coromandel. Besides, the quantities received at Batavia were rather moderate and spices were doing extremely well in Holland.

* An exact copy is available in the *Bataviaasch Uitgaande Brievenboek*, V.O.C. 854, ff.104vo-109vo.

1. Barhampur or Burhanpur is on the banks of the Tapti river in Madhya Pradesh. It served as the capital of the Faruqi dynasty of Khandesh. Later it was the headquarters of Mughal operations in the south. Throughout the seventeenth century it was headed by either a major member of the royal family or a noble closely related by marriage.

109. Van den Broecke at Surat to Ysbrantsz. at Pulicat, 19 July 1627. V.O.C. 1092, f.368 (Copy).

Since his letter of 15 April 1627,[1] Van den Broecke had not received any communication from Pulicat. The factors at Surat were under heavy debt and were sitting idle. A sum of more than f.200,000 had been borrowed on interest. Surat had been glutted with cloves, nutmeg and mace imported from Coromandel leading to a sharp fall in both sales and prices. The price of cloves had come down from 210 *mahmudis* to 140 *mahmudis*, that of nutmeg from 100 *mahmudis* to 60 *mahmudis* and of mace from 300 *mahmudis* to 120 *mahmudis* per *maund* of 30 Dutch ponds. Once the prices fell, it was very difficult to take them up again.

This letter was being sent with the son of Khoja Nizam named Muhammad Hadoek who had requested Van den Broecke for a letter of recommendation that Pulicat would show him all favours which could be extended without prejudice to the Company's interests. He would try to reciprocate such help.

1. This letter is not available in the Company's archives.

110. Governor-General De Carpentier at Batavia to Van den Broecke at Surat, 3 August 1627. V.O.C. 1092, ff. 149-56 (Copy).*

Van den Broecke's letters dated 24 April and 23 December 1626 and of 9 April 1627 had been duly received.

A cargo worth f.930,116 for Surat and Persia consisting of the following was being sent.

Minted and unminted gold and silver worth	f.618,298
Pepper	7,190 *piculs*
Cloves	30,000 ponds
Nutmeg	65,000 ponds
Mace	40 sacks
Sandalwood	150 *piculs*
Sappanwood	47 *piculs*
Japanese copper	996 *piculs*
Radix china	5,249 ponds
Japanese camphor	121 *piculs*
Sugar	461 *piculs*
Galiga[1]	5,354 ponds
Broadcloth in red carmosyn and other colours	540 pieces
Carsayen[2]	77 pieces
Quicksilver	2,686 ponds
Vermilion	2,894 ponds
Tin	8,767 ponds
Lead	73,880 ponds

The sale value of this cargo was likely to be more than f.1.4 million shared between Surat and Persia as follows:

For Surat	
Goods (sale value)	f.200,000
Cash	f.418,000
Sub-total	f.618,000
For Persia	
Goods (sale value)	f.600,000
Cash	f.200,000
Sub-total	f.800,000
Total	f.1,418,000

The Directors had ordered the following cargo from Surat:

Refined saltpetre	As much as could be sent
Cotton yarn	400-500 bales[3] yearly
Red coral and fine clothes	None till further orders
Indigo Bayana	f.300,000 worth
Guinea cloth	Nil. Will order from Coromandel
Sealing lac and marking stones	Quantity not specified

If enough indigo Bayana was not available and there was space left in the ships, some *baftas* and other clothes could be sent to Holland provided these were available in good quality and at a reasonable price.

The value of the cargo for Holland was not to exceed f.200,000 to f.250,000. The usual orders for the Indies were for goods worth around f.220,000 per annum but considering that so few clothes had been received from Surat last year, this amount was to be increased during the current year to f.250,000.

The sum thus needed for meeting the orders from Holland and the Indies would be around f.500,000. Half of the remaining amount was to be used for procuring goods for Holland (indigo Bayana and refined saltpetre) and the other half for textiles for the Indies. Batavia approved of the policy of borrowing funds locally on interest rather than wait for the arrival of the ships. The cost of interest was likely to be only half of the saving made by procuring the goods on time.

In their letter of 8 December 1625, the Directors had suggested that one or two ships might be kept permanently at Surat to be used to freight the Indian merchants' goods. In addition to increasing the Company's popularity there, this would also be an economically profitable proposition. From Surat's letters it appeared that double the cost of maintaining the ships could be recovered from the freight charges. Also the presence of these ships would enable a reduction in the cost of equipping the Company's ships calling there with guns, etc. But considering that the resource position of the Company at Surat did not permit the investment of much capital in intra-Asian trade with Mocha and Persia, this might not be such a good idea. Besides, the freight cargo carried might compete with the Company's own sales and the freight earnings were probably not going to be too large. The whole idea might, therefore, be dropped. Since carrying freight cargo might be prejudicial to the interests of the Company, the factors were to refrain from doing so provided it could be done without incurring the wrath of important persons who might be in a position to hinder the trade of the Company. No trader was in any case to be allowed to travel to Batavia with his goods in the Company's ships.

Unless Surat decided to keep two ships for the transportation of the silk from Persia and these could make a trip to Mocha in the meantime without jeopardizing the trip to Persia, a ship was not to be sent to Mocha because the amount of spices sent there would not justify that.

It had been decided to make peace with Dabhol whose trade with Surat would no longer be hindered. The Company interests dictated that a policy of peace rather than confrontation be followed with Asian princes.

Two special commissioners were being deputed to inspect the various establishments of the Company. Dirck van der Lee, who had been designated special commissioner for Surat and Persia, was to be provided all assistance.

* An exact copy is available in the *Bataviaasch Uitgaande Brievenboek*, V.O.C. 854, ff.125-31vo.

1. *Galiga*—a red stuff derived from a shrub called galoega in Malay.
2. Not identified.
3. It is not clear whether the unit was bales or ponds. The usual unit was the bale.

111. Instructions for Willem Jansz.,[1] member of the Council of the Indies and ex-governor of Banda, going as commander of the fleet to Surat, 3 August 1627. V.O.C. 1092, ff.142-5vo (Copy).*

In order to facilitate the vigorous conduct and the defence of the Company's trade in Surat and Persia and in order to inflict damage on the Portuguese, it had been decided to send the following fully armed and provisioned ships, namely the *Mauritius*, the *Dordrecht*, the *Noord Holland*, the *Gulden Zeepaard*, the *'s lants' Mauritius*, the *Bommel*, the *Weesp* and the sloop the *Nieuwicheyt* under the command of Willem Jansz.

The fleet was to inflict all possible damage on the Portuguese, the Spaniards and their subjects by capturing their ships and men which were to be brought back to Batavia.

No damage was to be inflicted on the ships from Surat and other places in the Mughal empire, from Persia and Mocha, from Masulipatnam as also from other places where the Company had its trading establishments. Similarly, no damage was to be inflicted on the ships of the French, the Danes and other European nations which were presently in alliance with the United Netherlands.

Special Commissioner for Surat and Persia, Dirck van der Lee, would be travelling with these ships.

The fleet would stay in Persia only as long as necessary for trading purposes and would not prolong its stay in order to provide protection to Persian ships going out to the sea.

Since the English had been laying claims earlier to levy half the toll at Hormuz, the Company's cargo was to be unloaded only at Gombroon and other convenient places.

* An exact copy is available in the *Bataviaasch Uitgaande Brievenboek*, V.O.C. 854, ff.118-21.

1. Willem Jansz. of Amsterdam was the skipper of the *Luyfken Australia* at the end of 1605 or the beginning of 1606. In 1614, he was appointed governor of the Fort Henrius at Solor which he was obliged to surrender on 18 December 1615 on the orders of Van Reynst. On

23 March 1619, he was named a member of the Council of the Indies by Coen. In 1620, he was appointed vice-admiral and later the admiral of the Dutch-English defence fleet. Between October 1623 and February 1627, he was the governor of Banda. In 1628, he returned home for good.

112. Secret instructions by Batavia to Willem Jansz., commander of the fleet going to Surat and Persia, 3 August 1627. V.O.C. 1092, ff.146-6vo (Not stated whether original or copy.)*

Jansz. would give top priority to taking steps towards strengthening the port at Swally with the assistance of the *mutasaddi* of Surat and even the Mughal emperor Jahangir himself. He was also to try and obtain information about the strength of the Portuguese and the best means to inflict the maximum possible damage on them.

Jansz. was also to find out if there was a suitable harbour or island around Surat which could be used as a retreat for the Company's ships and effects and where fortification could be done. This could be useful to protect the Company's effects in the event of an attack.

Both these projects were to be kept secret. If the latter project succeeded, the Company would have a randezvous where its effects concerned with the trade with Surat, Persia, Arabia and Mocha could be kept safely.

Batavia would also like to know the precise way in which the authorities in Surat and Persia ought to be informed of the fact that the English and the Dutch were separate nations and only had an alliance to help each other in the event of an attack by a third party. Also that the English and the Dutch companies were two separate entities with independent funds and directors and did not share in each other's profits or losses.

* An exact copy is available in the *Bataviaasch Uitgaande Brievenboek*, V.O.C. 854, ff.121vo-2.

113. Instructions by Batavia for Upper-merchant Van der Lee going with the fleet as commissioner to visit the Company's factories in Surat and Persia, 3 August 1627. V.O.C. 1092, ff.147vo-148vo (Copy).*

The instructions sent by the Directors for Van der Lee along with their letter of 15 April 1626 were enclosed.[1] Van der Lee would show the instructions to Willem Jansz., the commander of the fleet which will first call at Surat. From Surat, Van der Lee would go to Persia but no further than Gombroon because if he proceeded to Isfahan and then returned to Gombroon, he would be too late to return to Surat.

* An exact copy is available in the *Bataviaasch Uitgaande Brievenboek*, V.O.C. 854, ff.123-4.

1. These documents are not available in the Company's archives.

114. Governor-General De Carpentier at Batavia to Ysbrantsz. at Pulicat, 28 August 1627. V.O.C. 1092, ff.161-2vo (Copy).*

Batavia hoped that Pulicat had already sent the *Medemblik* back because the warehouses at Batavia were empty causing a great deal of loss for the Company's intra-Asian trade and profits. Batavia also hoped that in a few years' time, a situation would have been reached where the Indies no longer had to look to the Netherlands for funds.

This letter was being sent with the *Batavia* (of about 150 *lasts*) which had been captured in the waters of Malacca. A sum of 8,000 rials of eight but no goods were being sent with this vessel. If the *Medemblik* and the other two ships sent to Pulicat earlier were not found adequate to transport the goods to Batavia, the *Batavia* could be kept back at Coromandel. Alternatively, the

Grootenbroek which was somewhat smaller but more capable of defending itself could be kept back.

Pulicat was to keep on buying slaves in accordance with Batavia's earlier orders. These could be purchased in Coromandel or Arakan depending on where they were available cheaper and of better quality. This process was to be continued till the Company's colonies had been well provided with slaves.

As intimated earlier, Pulicat was to send as much rice as possible without cutting into the orders for clothes.

* An exact copy is available in the *Bataviaasch Uitgaande Brievenboek*, V.O.C. 854, ff.146-7vo.

115. The Directors at Amsterdam to Ysbrantsz. at Pulicat, 21 September 1627. V.O.C. 315 (Copy).*

The Directors' last letter dated 19 March 1627[1] had been sent with the ship the *Leeuwin* and the yacht the *Kemphaen*. A copy of that letter was enclosed.[2]

The Directors' orders for fine cotton textiles as communicated through that letter had been modified as per the new orders list enclosed.[3]

The two yachts being sent to Coromandel were to be used there and in the Bay of Bengal both for purposes of trade as well as for inflicting damage on the Portuguese. These two yachts along with the ship the *Vliegende Draeck* were carrying f.250,000 in cash besides goods as per the invoice. The *Vliegende Draeck* was to be sent back to Batavia with the return cargo for onward dispatch to Holland.

As per the calculations in the general letters from Batavia, Coromandel, after the arrival there of the *Mauritius* would have been provided with a capital of approximately f.330,000. Little cargo is likely to be sent from Coromandel for Holland during the year 1627. The first lot would be received by Amsterdam with the ship the *Leeuwin* and the yacht the *Kemphaen*.

As instructed in the last letter, Coromandel was not to sell cloves at a low price but instead to send them on to Holland.

Trade was to be carried on discreetly and any conflict with the Indians, the English and the Danes avoided without, of course, surrendering any of the Company's rights.

Due care was to be taken while buying goods both with regard to quality as well as weight and size. Many discrepancies in the matter of the length and the width of the textiles had been detected. The textiles received with the *Wapen van Hoorn* were extremely poor in quality.

* The volume is not foliated, but this letter covers two single folios.
1. This letter is not available in the Company's archives.
2. This enclosure is not available in the Company's archives.
3. This enclosure is not available in the Company's archives.

116. Van Rossen and Pietersz. at Masulipatnam to Governor-General De Carpentier at Batavia, 10 October 1627. V.O.C. 1094, ff.97-9vo. (Not stated whether original or copy but the signatures would suggest that it is original.)*

Marten Ysbrantsz. had arrived at Masulipatnam on 6 September 1627 with the *Brouwershaven*. This vessel had then been sent on to Arakan on the 21st of September with a cargo worth f.7,892.

The following goods had been sold to the merchants to whom the right to trade with the Company had been farmed out.

Item	*Price in pagodas*
Nutmeg	114 per *bahar*
Japanese copper	50 per *bahar*
Sandalwood	85 per *bahar*
Sappanwood	3¼ per *bahar*
Poutchina	95 per *bahar*
Spelter	65 per *bahar*
Mace	13 per *maund*

Cloves	9½ per *maund*
Vermilion	19 per *maund*
Quicksilver	21 per *maund*
Coloured broadcloth	2 per *gaz*.

Half of the payment was to be in cash and the other half in goods in conformity with the contract. Later the factors had been obliged to provide to *havaldar* Muhammad Taqi against cash 50 *bahars* of nutmeg at 105 *pagodas* per *bahar*, 5 *bahars* of mace at 12½ *pagodas* per *maund* and 14 pieces of broadcloth at 1¾ *pagodas* per *gaz*.

Muhammad Taqi had been summoned to Golconda and he had left for that place on 29 September 1627. It was rumoured that he would serve there as the *kotwal* while continuing to hold the office of the *havaldar* at Masulipatnam. He had left an agent and a brahmin to look after the affairs at Masulipatnam in his absence. One of Taqi's brothers was expected to replace him at Masulipatnam any day. Taqi owed 2,400 *pagodas* for the goods he had bought from the Company.[1] Lingayya, Ramanna and Coutour[2] had stood surety for Taqi. The goods bought by Taqi from us had been left with these three persons who had been instructed to sell the nutmeg at 130 *pagodas* per *bahar* and the mace at 13 *pagodas* per *maund*.

The goods received with the *Medemblik* had not been adequate even to pay back the debts at Masulipatnam. These currently amounted to 16,000 *pagodas*. Some of the goods had been sold to the Company's farmers against the promised supply of textiles.

Funds had been sent to Palicol but because of the high price of yarn not a single piece of cloth had yet been received from there. It was unlikely that any significant amount of clothes would be received from there until after the next harvest of cotton which was expected to be good. De Witt had written from Palicol that the weavers there were not willing to make Guinea cloth and were sitting without work.

The bulk of the ducats had been given to the Company's creditors at Masulipatnam at 16 *fanums* and 13½ *fanums*. If these had been sold against cash, they could not have fetched more than a *pagoda* per piece. At Masulipatnam, ducats were sold at a profit while gold had to be sold at a loss. At the time of the departure of the Indian merchants' ships, the rials were worth 9 *fanums* per piece.

The recent decline in the sales of the Company's goods at Masulipatnam was because of the heavy tolls imposed by the authorities there on goods coming into or going out of the city and the insecurity on the roads leading to the plunder of many caravans and involving the killing of many persons. But both these problems had since been sorted out.

The fact that the factors had not always been able to provide the return cargo pro rata to the availability of resources had been the result of the willingness of the Company's farmers to supply only what was most profitable for them. No improvement in the situation was expected in the near future unless tough measures were adopted.

It was not possible for the Company to take Masulipatnam on farm which had currently been farmed out for 160,000 *pagodas* per annum. Petapuli had similarly been farmed out for 65,000 *pagodas* per annum. Even with their oppressive measures, the farmers found it difficult to raise these sums. If the Company took Masulipatnam on farm, it would only add to its problems.

The diamond mine had again been farmed to the same person who held the farm earlier. The fact that the Dutch, the English and the Danes had not bought any diamonds notwithstanding, they continued to be expensive.

* Printed in H.T Colenbrander (ed.), *Jan Pietersz. Coen, Beschieden Omtrent Zijn Bedrijf in Indie*, The Hague, 1919-53, vol. VII.2, pp. 1174-9.

1. This must have been an earlier lot because the payment for the lot mentioned earlier in this letter had been made in cash.
2. Lingayya, Ramanna and Coutour were the lessees or farmers of the Company's trade. The *havaldar* repeatedly extorted money from them by imprisoning them where they were tortured. Ramanna died of torture in 1629 when the Company had blockaded Masulipatnam.

117. Governor-General De Carpentier at Batavia to Ysbrantsz. at Pulicat, 11 October 1627, V.O.C. 1095, ff.110-12vo (Copy).*

Since Batavia's last letter dated 28 August 1627[1] with the *Batavia*, the yacht *Medemblik* had arrived from Coromandel on 1 September 1627.

With the safe arrival in Coromandel of the *Brouwershaven*, the *Grootenbroek* and the *Batavia* from Batavia and of the *Leeuwin* and the *Kemphaen* from Holland, it was hoped that Pulicat would no longer be short of funds as it had been for sometime in the past.

The *Medemblik* was being sent with f.105,284 in cash besides 100,000 ponds of cloves, 14,000 ponds of nutmeg, 36,000 ponds of broken nutmeg, 60 bags of mace and 50 packets of sandalwood, etc., which together with the cost would be worth a sale value of f.180,000.

In Batavia's letter of 11 June it was estimated that Pulicat would have	f.880,000
Cash sent with the *Batavia*	f.200,400
Total	f.1,080,400
As against this, Batavia had received with the *Medemblik* from Masulipatnam and Pulicat cargo worth	f.144,000
Thus Pulicat would be left with	f.936,400

Priority was to be attached to the textile orders from the southern quarters. Only after meeting these in full or at least in good measure, were the goods for Holland to be procured in accordance with the availability of resources. This was important so as to ensure the continuance of intra-Asian trade. The Company's survival in the Indies was dependent on the profits earned from this trade. Pulicat would have received with the *Leeuwin* and the *Kemphaen* provisions meant for Batavia. These together with the cargo from Pulicat were to be sent to Batavia at the earliest.

The Persian ambassador had arrived at Batavia from Holland with the *Utrecht*. He was going to Coromandel on his way home.

No funds were to be spent on his maintenance, etc. He was, however, to be shown all courtesy. He was a difficult man and had not behaved well with the Directors and even his Princely Excellency.[2] His visit had cost the Company around f.100,000.

Batavia had now been without Coromandel and Surat textiles for quite some time. So an attempt was to be made to send as many textiles as possible.

An open letter for Surat was enclosed. A copy of this was to be sent to Surat overland with at least two *pattamars*.[3]

* An exact copy is available in the *Bataviaasch Uitgaande Brievenboek*, V.O.C. 854, ff.152-4.

1. See document no. 114.
2. This would evidently refer to the *stadhouder*.
3. A *pattamar* was a carrier of letters.

118. Governor-General De Carpentier at Batavia to Ysbrantsz. at Pulicat, 11 October 1627. V.O.C. 1095, ff.112vo-13 (Copy).*

Jan Pietersz. Coen had again been appointed Governor-General of the East Indies by the Directors. He had arrived at Batavia with his family on 27 September 1627. De Carpentier had handed over charge to Coen on 30 September 1627.

* An exact copy is available in the *Bataviaasch Uitgaande Brievenboek*, V.O.C. 854, f.154vo.

119. Governor-General Jan Pietersz. Coen at Batavia to Ysbrantsz. at Pulicat, 11 October 1627. V.O.C. 1095, f.113 (Copy).*

The enclosed letter would show that Jan Pietersz. Coen had taken charge on 28 September 1627[1] from Pieter de Carpentier as Governor-General of the East Indies for a second time. A proclamation to this effect was to be made at Pulicat.

* Printed in H.T Colenbrander (ed.), *Jan Pietersz. Coen*, V, p. 175. An exact copy is available in the *Bataviaasch Uitgaande Brievenboek*, V.O.C. 854, f.155.
1. The date mentioned in document no. 118 was 30 September 1627.

120. Governor-General De Carpentier at Batavia to Van den Broecke at Surat, 11 October 1627. V.O.C. 1095, ff.113vo-114vo (Copy).*

Since De Carpentier's last letter dated 3 August 1627, Governor-General Coen had arrived at Batavia on 27 September along with his family.

In accordance with De Carpentier's earlier orders, Surat was to meet Batavia's orders for clothes in full. If there was a shortage of funds, they were to be borrowed on interest.

* An exact copy is available in the *Bataviaasch Uitgaande Brievenboek*, V.O.C. 854, ff.155-6.

121. Ysbrantsz. at Pulicat to Governor-General De Carpentier at Batavia, 20 October 1627. V.O.C. 1092, ff.377-81vo (Copy).

Ysbrantsz.'s last letter had been dated 28 June[1] which had been sent with the *Medemblik*.

While the *Brouwershaven* and the *Grootenbroek* had arrived at Pulicat on 15 August, the *Batavia* had arrived only on 1 October. This letter was being sent with the *Batavia* carrying a cargo worth f.72,887. The invoice was enclosed.[2] Funds had reached rather late, and in the rainy season it was not possible to procure the textiles, particularly the Pulicat varieties. Besides, the cotton crop had been poor resulting in a rise in the price of cotton to a level not witnessed during Ysbrantsz.'s long stay on the Coromandel coast. Since the crop now standing in the fields was no better, Pulicat expected to be able to procure only a small quantity of textiles. Besides, the Company would not be allowed to make purchases till after the Indian ships had left Coromandel. The persons who sent out ships were important and took precedence in the procurement of goods over the merchants to whom the right to trade with the Company had been farmed out and who procured goods for the Company. Ysbrantsz. had himself been at Palicol during the preceding month and had found that not a single piece of Guinea cloth or any other variety of textiles had been procured there. Because of the shortage of cotton yarn, the weavers were sitting idle without work.

Regarding the suggestion by the Directors to take Masulipatnam on farm, Ysbrantsz. agreed with Batavia[3] that it was not practicable to take on farm the large area which fell under the jurisdiction of the government of Masulipatnam and Petapuli. Thousands of Muslims who lived in the area were religious fanatics and treated the Dutch like dogs and would not like to be governed by Christians. Also, it would in any case be impossible to get the farm. The person who held it currently was one Mansur Khan who was very close to the king of Golconda. The *havaldar* could murder, hang or burn as long as he brought in the money. The Company would not be allowed to do any of this.

Ysbrantsz. had been to Masulipatnam. The factors there had been forced by *Havaldar* Muhammad Taqi to supply him 50 *bahars* of nutmeg at 105 *pagodas* per *bahar* while this item had been sold earlier at 114 *pagodas* per *bahar*. The *havaldar* then forced the farmers of the Company to buy some of the same from him at 130 *pagodas* per *bahar*. Similarly, 5 *bahars* of mace which the factors had sold earlier at 13 *pagodas* per *maund* had to be supplied to Taqi at 12½ *pagodas* per *maund*. If the Company had enjoyed the freedom to sell to any one, the nutmeg would have fetched a price of 125 *pagodas* per *bahar*. The *havaldar* had since asked for two iron canons for his ship. In order to keep friendly relations with this man, the factors would have to accede to this demand. The only remedy was to attack the Muslim ships, seize some influential merchants with friends in Golconda and carry them to Batavia. These people would get a more friendly hearing at the king's court than the Company could ever expect to get in spite of all the gifts that it gave. A new accord would then be possible allowing the Company to function better. The textile trade was unlikely to be particularly adversely affected either. Once the Indian ships were rendered subject to attack, they would not carry any textiles bringing their prices down. The Company might as well forget about sending a mission to the king of Golconda.

The English President, Brown,[4] had told Ysbrantsz. that the excesses they were being subjected to at Masulipatnam were becoming intolerable. When told that the Dutch were in no better a position, he suggested that the two companies could perhaps do something about this together. At the time of Ysbrantsz.'s departure from Masulipatnam, Brown came aboard the ship and asked him to write to Batavia about the problems and that he would do the same to his President at Batavia. The Danes would also be interested in joining in. In the meantime, trade would be carried on as well as possible.

20 *ells* of broadcloth had been presented to Muhammad Taqi along with 86 ponds of sandalwood and 40 ponds each of mace, nutmeg and cloves. But he returned the gifts apparently because they were not enough. But as Ysbrantsz. was arranging for these gifts to be brought back to the Company's warehouse, Taqi sent a message through the *kotwal* that he would arrange to have them collected later.

Malaya had held out good prospects regarding the availability of saltpetre both in Pulicat as well as further south. But since the south was full of wars, it was not possible to say with certainty that the Company would get enough saltpetre even for the production of gunpowder. The present yacht was carrying 20,618 ponds of saltpetre and 22,070 ponds of gunpowder. If enough sulphur were available, as much gunpowder could be manufactured here as required.

Rice and other provisions were available in Masulipatnam only at a record high price. Some rice was being sent as ballast.

The free merchants were a source of nuisance in Coromandel.

They expected that as soon as they landed, ready stocks of textiles ought to be available. They used all kinds of sinister techniques to get hold of textiles from the Company's suppliers. This led to a rise in the prices of the textiles. The free merchants ought to be banned from buying textiles outside the fort at Pulicat. Ysbrantsz. had permitted these merchants to give advances the way the Company did and to receive the textiles with his knowledge. This was an arrangement that the free merchants ought to be fully satisfied with. In view of the overall shortage of textiles, Ysbrantsz. suggests that in respect of the varieties that the Company itself procured, procurement by the free merchants ought to be licensed.

The 922⅝ rials worth of gold received had been found to be 2⅜ rials overweight as follows:

	302¼ rials worth was of 16 carats 2 grains
	396¾ rials worth was of 15 carats 10 grains
	84 rials worth was of 14 carats 2 grains
	142 rials worth was of 13½ carats 0 grains
Total	925 rials worth

The quality was rather poor and the whole lot had to be disposed off at a profit of only f.1,496. Guinea gold afforded a profit of 10½ per cent at Pulicat.

The yacht *Brouwershaven* had been sent from Masulipatnam to Arakan with a cargo of f.7,900 (sale value). Together with the f.3,000 that the factors there already had, this amount should suffice to buy as many slaves as could conveniently be transported by this vessel. If the slaves were not enough to fill the yacht, the remaining space could be filled with rice. The *Brouwershaven* had been instructed to return to Masulipatnam by mid-December.

Weavers and painters in Masulipatnam had been asked to concentrate on the manufacturing of clothes for Java and Malaya until May. Thereafter, they were to prepare the varieties for Arakan, Pegu, Siam and Aceh before they undertook to manufacture anything for other buyers. Malaya had promised that he would ensure that these instructions were duly followed.

The English were seeking to do the same at Armagon. But they were not yet going ahead with the building of a fort there.

Armagon was as convenient for the English as Pulicat was for the Dutch. The English chief, Thomas Johnson,[5] had travelled from Masulipatnam with Ysbrantsz. and had mentioned the troubles they were facing at the hands of the raja.

The Danes had sent the *Waterhond* to Bengal in September. They were unlikely to send any cargo to Denmark till more funds were received from there. Besides, their ships had been eaten away by worms because of their long stay in Coromandel. They had procured some textiles at Trancquebar and the *Christiaanshaven* was likely to be sent to Makassar. Their principal factors received regular salary but their real status was like that of the Dutch free merchants at Batavia.

The situation in respect of the local wars remained unchanged. The *nayaks* of Madura, Gingi and Tanjore were apparently friendly but in reality did not trust each other. The *nayak* of Gingi was interested in recovering the territory that he had lost.

Some Muslim merchants returning from Ceylon had informed that the Portuguese were planning to seize Muscat and that a large force had been sent there from Goa.

1. See document no. 106 where the date is given as 27 June.
2. This invoice is not available in the Company's archives.
3. See document no. 108.
4. George Brown was a merchant at Batavia in 1623 and a factor at Tanjore in March 1624. He returned to Batavia with the *Heart* on 20 November 1624. He was a factor at Masulipatnam in October 1626. Because of extortion, the Masulipatnam factory of the English was closed down on 27 September 1628. Brown left for Armagon and from there for Bantam on 25 June 1629. He returned to England in 1631.
5. Thomas Johnson came to the East in the beginning of 1625 with the ship *Lion* as a pursur. He was a factor at Aceh and in 1627 was at Armagon where he was second in command until February 1629. He returned to England in October 1630 with the *London*.

122. Memorandum from Vapour at Agra to Governor-General Coen at Batavia, 26 October 1627. V.O.C. 1097, ff.421-4 (Copy)*.[1]

In 1626 Agra had written to Batavia[2] about the adverse effect of the import of spices from Masulipatnam into Hindustan on the sale of spices at the Company's factory at Agra as well as on the rate of profit earned there.

A reference to the ledgers suggested that in 1625, mace had been sold at 475 rupees per *maund*, cloves at 180-90 and nutmeg at 100 rupees per *maund*. The current prices of these spices were no more than 200, 125 and 75 rupees per *maund* respectively. Even at these prices, it was very difficult to sell these spices. Unless the sale of spices in Coromandel was properly regulated, the Company's trade both at Coromandel and in Gujarat (including Agra) might be damaged.

During the year 1627, between 300 and 800 bullock carts had come to Agra with spices. News regarding spices coming in from Burhanpur would lead to a decline in the local prices by 10 to 20 rupees per *maund*. This would also make the merchants from Agra, Delhi and Lahore rather cautious in their purchases. While ordinarily they would buy 20 to 30 packets of spices at a time, they were now buying no more than 2 packets at a time. The spices were thus lying unsold.

The indigo trade had also been spoiled and the price of indigo gone up. This is because the merchants coming in with the spices ordinarily invested their sales proceeds in indigo. Having sold the spices, these merchants travelled in groups of 10 to 15 to the indigo villages to buy indigo. Since both the sale of spices and the buying of indigo was done in a hurry, the price of the former went down and of the latter up. This also resulted in a significant increase in the fares for bullock-carts and camels. The cost per *maund* which used to be between 1½ and 1¾ rupees had been pushed up to 2½ rupees per *maund*. Even after the departure of these merchants from Agra the ill effects of their visit continued. For example, their hurry arising out of their anxiety to catch the departing ships for Persia as also their lack of familiarity with the local language and usages, resulted in their being made to pay tolls by the rajas or their revenue farmers at rates up to seven rupees per cart or camel instead of the usual three.

Vapour was of the opinion that the amount of spices the Company imported into Surat was adequate to meet the demand there and in Hindustan. Assume that the only two outlets in the Indies for the substantial quantity of spices produced in the islands of the Moluccas and Banda were Coromandel and Surat (including Hindustan). Assume further that the Company's treasury at Batavia was ill-provided with funds to be able to buy the Coromandel textiles which afforded a very high profit. So clearly the funds must be raised by the sale of spices. But the point was where should these spices be sold—Coromandel or Surat. They were indeed best sold in Surat and Hindustan. If the Indian merchants found it profitable to buy them from the Company in Coromandel and sell in Surat or Agra, clearly it would be more profitable for the Company itself to sell at Surat or Agra. When this matter was discussed with the local bania merchants, they also made the same point. Besides, the situation at Coromandel in any case was not very favourable because we were obliged to deal with only a few merchants to whom the right to trade with the Company had been farmed out. Governor-General De Carpentier had even been planning to close the Masulipatnam factory down. The total amount of spices consumed at Burhanpur, Agra, Delhi, Lahore, Kashmir and Kabul did not justify sales at both Coromandel and Surat. It would, therefore, be best to suspend the sales at Coromandel for two years. If this was not possible, the chiefs of the establishments at Surat and Masulipatnam ought to coordinate with each other regarding the sale of spices.

Postscript

In 1626, the English had imported 50 packets of cloves which had hindered the Company's sales considerably. During the current year, they had again imported 60 *piculs* of cloves which had been bought at 50 to 60 rials per *picul* from some Dutch free merchants at Batavia. They had bribed Captain Simon Jansen who had allowed them to smuggle them out without paying the duties to the Company. That had done a lot of damage to the Company at Agra.

* Printed in H.T. Colenbrander (ed.), *Jan Pietersz. Coen*, VII.2, pp. 1193-1200.

1. It was unusual for anybody other than the head of a regional establishment to write to Batavia. Vapour was only the chief of the factory at Agra, which was under the administrative jurisdiction of the chief factory at Surat. This exception was made because this letter deals mainly with a description of the Company's sale of spices in India.
2. This letter is not available in the Company's archives.

123. Daily register for the period between 6 November 1627 and 21 April 1628 by Commissioner Van der Lee visiting the establishments in Gujarat, Hindustan and Persia. V.O.C. 1094, ff.386-407. (Not stated whether original or copy.)

1627

6 November

Van der Lee arrived at Surat.

8 November

A meeting of the Councils, both of the fleet as well as that of the Surat factory, was called. Van der Lee's commission, instructions and orders were read out at the meeting.

10 November

Van der Lee wrote to Vapour at Agra instructing him to write back immediately concerning the state of the affairs there, particularly because it had been learnt that most of the goods were lying unsold there. He was asked to let Van der Lee know what steps could be taken to improve the state of the trade at Agra.

11 November

While going through the trade books of Surat, it was found that they had not been kept in accordance with the instructions issued by the Director-General.

12 November

Director Van den Broecke had been told that in keeping with the Directors' orders, he ought to send to Batavia each year, along with the trade books, the books of the factory,[1] the resolutions and the sentence books[2] as well as the journal of each factory. These were to be signed by two or three trustworthy persons. Besides, letters to and from Surat were also to be sent to Batavia. Van den Broecke had been asked not to live outside the factory any longer because of reasons of security at night.

14 November

As Director Van den Broecke was getting ready to ship on the *Dordrecht* goods for Europe, a dispute arose between the *mutasaddi* of Surat named Jan Quli Beg and the governor of the lands around Swally, including the beach, named Pahalwan Safid. The Pahalwan was trying to impose a new duty on goods passing through his lands which was opposed by the *mutasaddi* of Surat. As a result, the Company's goods were lying at Surat to its great detriment. The Council finally decided to present a gift of 400 rials of eight to the Pahalwan besides half a piece of red cloth costing f.130 to make him desist from his claim so that the *Dordrecht* could leave at the proper time. The gift having been given, the Pahalwan promised to let the goods be stamped and to issue as many authorizations as were necessary for sending these goods.

18 November

It was found that the spices had a very poor market and were being sold at a very low price. It was to be feared that with the arrival of the new supplies, the situation was not likely to improve in the near future. The English had brought to Surat a large amount of cloves and other spices from Batavia this year. Because of the shortage of resources with them, they would be obliged to sell these spices because the expected ships from England had not yet arrived.

According to the information provided by Vapour, the prices of spices in Agra were lower than they had been in many years. This was because of the large import of these spices overland from Masulipatnam. As a result, the spice trade would be rather poorly off this year.

20 November

For the last 14 days, there had been a rumour here that while sailing out of Goa, three out of the six Portuguese ships had been lost in a storm. Very few people could be saved from the lost ships.

25 November

Van der Lee had been told that Vapour wanted to go back home next year by which time he would have served his contracted term. He had, therefore, written to him to confirm this because if Vapour intended to leave, a replacement ought to be found in time so that he could get to know the important people, learn the language and in general understand the intricacies of the Company's trade at Agra.

30 November

Van der Lee learnt from the books that a rupee was treated as equivalent of 24 *stuivers* in Surat and Broach and of 25 *stuivers* in Agra, Ahmedabad and Cambay. Since this caused confusion in accounts, Van der Lee had ordered that throughout this directorate, a rupee be treated as equivalent of 24 *stuivers*.

4 December

News had arrived at Surat that the great Mughal, Shah Salim, had died.[3] It was greatly to be feared that this might cause a tumult here by persons who would be on the look out to plunder the city. Till such time as a new emperor took over, Van der Lee, on the advice of Van den Broecke, had decided to write to Willem Jansz. to deploy six soldiers to guard the factory till the time he returned from Persia. By the time Van der Lee returned from Persia, a new emperor would hopefully have taken over.

9 December

News had been received from the factors at Agra that on the morning of 19 November they had received three pieces of news. The first was that the emperor was ill, the second that he was dying and the third that he had already been dead for eight days. The last piece of news had been believed the most (and had since turned out to be true). Some of the important persons had fled from the city with their costly belongings to castles: others had employed guards to secure their houses as best they could. The shopkeepers had closed their establishments. The provisions had become extremely expensive. The roads had been rendered unsafe. The boors and the thieves had become active. It was said that Queen Noormahal[4] had arranged for the arrest of her brother, Asaf Khan, because she suspected that he was on the side of Prince Khurram. Prince Khurram was now the eldest son of the late emperor (but he had rebelled against his father) but the queen wanted to see Sultan Bulaqi become the new emperor. This man is the son of the eldest son of the late emperor who had been killed by Prince Khurram.[5]

The Muslim merchants coming from Mocha this year had brought the news that the Arabs of Yemen, which was under the jurisdiction of the great lord of Constantinople, had nearly won it back from him. They had taken back the capital where the *badshah* held his court as also Suble Sybytt and Aden. The *badshah* and many of the important men had been murdered. The city of Teys was under siege and was likely to fall soon. The only city that was holding on was Mocha but was unlikely to do so for long. It was, therefore, likely that the Arabs would get the whole of Yemen back.

The governor (*qilledar*) of the Surat castle, Jan Quli Beg,[6] had been arrested by four persons who had come into the castle in a friendly manner to visit him. They had sat with him for a while but then threatened him with a dagger asking that the castle be handed over by him to Sultan Khurram in the name of Sayyid Khan, the *subahdar* of Gujarat. Beg's men were then turned out of the castle and their own men brought in. Shortly thereafter, guns had been fired as a token that the castle had been taken over. The *kotwal* had been removed and another man appointed in his place. The customs-house had been closed. A public announcement had been made in the city that no one was to provide any assistance to Jan Quli Beg and that the castle had been secured for the new emperor, Khurram (Shah Jahan).

10 December

Together with Director Van den Broecke, Van der Lee met with merchants of the city. They were told that now that it was time to send the *Dordrecht* to Holland and the fleet to Persia, the Company could no longer wait for the goods from them because the customs-house was closed and their goods could not pass through it. The merchants asked for four days within which they would arrange for the goods to be taken to the ship. This request was acceded to because the *Dordrecht* was not yet ready to leave because of the shortage of cargo.

13 December

Firm news had arrived at Surat that Sultan Khurram was only six miles from Surat with an army of 8,000 cavalry. The following day he had reached within two miles of the city. He had been greeted there with gifts by the principal Muslim merchants of the city accompanied by the heads of the Dutch and the English factories. Their services had been offered to him. The Prince had received them in a friendly manner and had issued a new *farman* for free trade and made other handsome promises. The gifts presented on behalf of the Company were worth around 800 rials of eight.

Sultan Khurram continued to stay at the same place but had sent his people into the city desiring that the castle be handed over to them. The new *qilledar* refused to do this saying that he was holding it for the new emperor. Since the prince did not have many guns with him and it was uncertain whether he would be able to conquer the castle, he directed his men into the city and replaced all the senior officers. He took the charge of the customs-house himself. All this proceeded without any trouble and the prince left for Cambay. The representative of the customs-house came to the Dutch factory and asked for 10,000 rupees for Sultan Khurram in payment of tolls allegedly due from us. When we pointed out that only 5,000 rupees were due from us which we duly paid, the man was not satisfied and stayed on in the factory all day asking for the balance.

Five English ships, the *Marie*, the *Heart*, the *Star*, the *Hope* and the *Refus* arrived at Surat four days ago. His Majesty's ambassador to the king of Persia named Milord Cotton had travelled with these ships. An ex-English ambassador to Persia, Robert Charles, as also the ambassador of Persia who had gone to England in 1625, also travelled on these ships.

In Van der Lee's opinion, it was injurious rather than profitable to carry the Muslim merchants' goods in the Company's ships on freight from Surat to Persia. The trip was often delayed in the process and pressure put on us to carry more goods than what the ships could take in. The profit made in the process was not worth the effort. The total earning this year from carrying freight to Persia had been only f.7,301:8:0.

The term of Adam Verhoeven,[7] the upper-merchant at Ahmedabad had expired. But since all reports received about him had been favourable and he had a good knowledge of indigo, his appointment had been renewed by Admiral Willem Jansz. for a period of three years at a monthly salary of f.110.

18 December

Van der Lee had strongly recommended to Director Van den Broecke to ensure that the textile orders from the Indies were supplied in full.

19 December

Van der Lee left Swally.

1628

8 January

The English ships that had left Surat eight days after us met us on the sea and brought letters from Director Van den Broecke. He had advised that the castle at Surat had been delivered to Prince Khurram. The Prince had been declared emperor at Ahmedabad with great pomp.

Van der Lee arrived at Gombroon with the fleet and found that the English had reached there three days earlier. Vissnich had returned from Isfahan with 350 bales of silk more than a month earlier. Many Persian merchants had travelled from the north because they knew that many Muslim merchants came each year with their goods in Dutch and English ships. These goods are either bartered or sold against cash. It was absolutely certain that the Dutch and the English brought a lot of trade to Persia and that because of our transportation of the Muslims goods we were thought of highly. Because of the conquest of Hormuz, Persia had been rendered completely without trade which was now being brought back to them by the Dutch and the English.

23 January

Given the nature of the issues that the Directors had asked him to investigate, Van der Lee had put to Vissnich the following questions:

a. What means ought to be adopted to improve the Company's trade?
b. What were the likely problems that could lead to a reduction in trade and in what way could these be solved?
c. Were the prospects of trade in the current year good?
d. What were the prospects of trade for the coming years?

Huybert Vissnich provided the following answers:

a. What was needed for an increase in the trade with Persia was general peace among the kings and princes of the neighbouring areas so that the merchants could travel safely and carry the goods to the places where they were most in demand.
b. The expected wars of the king of Persia might cause hindrances to trade.
c. There was little prospect of an improvement in the situation as long as the present war lasted. But the accord reached with Mulaim Beg last year ought to prove profitable for the Company. The Persian merchants would be encouraged if Dutch ships were to come over twice annually. If the merchants had an opportunity to go to India every six months (which was the case when the Portuguese were at Hormuz), Surat could derive a lot of profit from this trade.

d. Regarding the sale of goods in Persia, the factors were obliged to deal with the king's men. A large amount of clothes from Hindustan, Coromandel and Sindh could be sold here. A good amount of coarse and not fine Japanese copper could also be sent which ought, however, to be absolutely pure and refined to the maximum extent possible.

Silk was the only profitable return cargo unless the tapestries afforded a profit in Europe. Some gold and silk textiles, pearls, alum, fruits, sulphur, etc., were usually carried from Persia to India. But on the last-mentioned item, the profit had been very poor over the last few years.

26 January

The term of Vissnich had been renewed by Jansz. for a period of two years at a salary of f.160 per month beginning from the date his current term expired.

2 February

In Persia, trade was conducted with the king or his nominees because all the silk had to pass through the king. It was true that some amount of silk could be bought against cash from the merchants in Gilan and Farrabad where it was produced provided one paid 12 tomans (=185 rials of eight) per 2 bales of silk as the king's duties and took it to Aleppo and other areas in Turkey or to Moscow. If this silk was brought to Isfahan, the cost would be only marginally less than the price paid to the king. As against this, the price the Company received from the king for the goods sold to him was higher than what the Company could get from the smaller merchants. This made for a good and profitable trade. If the Company traded with merchants other than the king, it would not have been able to sell as many goods in three years. This was because of the shortage of cash and the general poverty in the population because of the continuous ongoing war with Turkey. The goods that the king took from the Dutch and the English sometimes remained in the warehouses for years. On the basis of the estimates regarding the possible sales in various cities, the goods were distributed all over the kingdom and sold to the traders who took up to a year to make the payment. The Company could not deal with them on this kind of basis.

The spices were brought to Persia not simply by the Dutch and the English but also by the Portuguese and the Indian merchants. The spices brought were mainly pepper together with some cloves, cinnamon, cardamom and ginger. Other goods brought in were indigo Sarkhej, coarse clothes, tobacco, sugar, tin, steel, borax, sal ammoniac and Hindustan confectionary. The traders carried these goods to Shiraz, Isfahan and other places to be sold at a profit. They were allowed to sell to anyone they chose to.

In Van der Lee's opinion, it would be advisable to ask Director Van den Broecke to invest 12,000-13,000 rials of the cash intended for Persia in Gujarat coarse goods such as rice, tobacco, gumlac, cotton, indigo and similar items. On arrival in Gombroon, these goods could be sold against cash at a profit of 50 to 100 per cent. These profits would help to offset the costs of the gifts that had to be given in Persia.

In case the Company planned to engage in as much trade in Persia as had been the case during the current year, it would be desirable to request the king to arrange for the silk to be sent from Isfahan to Gombroon at the Company's expense to be stocked there so that as soon as the Dutch ships arrived, the silk could be loaded on to them in proportion to the value of the goods brought in by them. This would enable the Company to save on the cost of the interest for one year as also not to run the risk of non-availability. As against this, in the event of the Shah's death, who was now 60 years old, there would be the possibility of a tumult subjecting the Company's effects to plunder. Since these people did not engage in maritime trade, the Company would not even be in a position to take reprisals. In Van der Lee's opinion, if the Company brought in one-fourth of its capital in cash, the Shah could be persuaded to keep an adequate quantity of silk in stock in Gombroon.

Admiral Jansz. and the Council had decided to ask Vissnich to procure the silk in good time to ensure that it arrived in Gombroon by July or August so that it could be sent to Europe by November or December.

It had been learnt that the Shah of Persia had ordered that the eyes of his youngest son, Iman Quli Mirza, who had allegedly been carrying on a secret correspondence with the Turks and had been trying to flee there, be taken out and he be sent to Isfahan from Sultaniyeh. When this man arrived at Isfahan, he heard his son crying bitterly over the tragedy. He said that the child was unlucky to be born in this world and that when he grew old, he had nothing to look forward to but what befell himself. Then he took opium and died. The Shah called his grandson to him and kept him there.

The personnel in Persia consisted of the following:

Huybert Vissnich—chief One upper-merchant 2 under-merchants 4 assistants	A total staff of eight persons

The English had brought this year from Persia about 850 bales of silk but had very little cargo there. The Dutch factors collected 350 bales of silk. They had also carried some Muslim goods on freight. It was much better to carry these goods from Persia to Surat rather than the other way round. They expected to earn by way of freight charges a sum of about f.10,000.

In a memorandum left for Vissnich dated 17 February, Van der Lee asked him to cut the costs at Persia, which were much higher than in other factories, to the maximum extent possible.

[Other administrative details in the memorandum have been left out.]

17 February

Left Persia on 17 February and arrived at Swally on 7 March.

10 March

Accompanied by Director Van den Broecke, Van der Lee arrived at Surat. The Mughal emperor's death notwithstanding, the Company's trade at Surat had been proceeding smoothly.

12 March

Van der Lee left Surat to visit the factories at Ahmedabad, Cambay and Broach.

17 March

Van der Lee arrived at Ahmedabad. He first visited the warehouses and found them empty. The news was that Prince Khurram [Shah Jahan] was the new emperor.

18 March

The chief factor at Ahmedabad was asked to answer the following questions:

a. What were the means by which the Company's trade could be improved?
b. Was there any danger of the trade being reduced and if so how could it be remedied?
c. What were the prospects of trade in the current year and in the coming years?
d. What were the goods available in Ahmedabad for export to Europe and to Batavia and what were the quantities available thereof?
e. What were the goods similarly available in Cambay?
f. What goods from Europe and Batavia could be sold in Ahmedabad with details of the quantities and the expected prices?

The chief was also asked to mention anything else of importance for the Company's trade in Ahmedabad. The chief at Ahmedabad replied as follows:

a. If the Directors were willing to believe what the factors had learnt by long experience and from other merchants including the English, there were goods by the sale of which a treasure could be earned in Hindustan and Gujarat. For example, more than 2,000 *maunds* or 60,000 Dutch ponds of quicksilver could be sold each year; of vermilion, 1,500 *maunds*; of elephant tusks, 100 *bahars*; of tortoise horn, 400-500 *maunds*; of alum, 50-60 *maunds*; of sandalwood, 200-300 *maunds*; of agilwood, 40-50 *maunds*; of benzoin, 100-200 *maunds*; of the best quality Borneo camphor, 50 ponds; of poor quality camphor, 100 *maunds* and of radix China, 100 *maunds*. About cloves, nutmeg and mace, Batavia already had the necessary information. A large amount of profit could be made by the sale of these goods.
b. Regarding the circumstances that might lead to a reduction in trade, the most important was the non-availability of adequate cash and goods. It was to the great detriment of the Company that when the ships departed from Surat, the

Gujarat factories were ordinarily under debt to the extent of f.100,000 to f.200,000.

Goods bought in a hurry had to be paid at a rate 15 to 20 per cent higher. Besides, the quality is not as good and the quantity not as large. All goods produced in Cambay must be contracted for in advance as also a part of those produced in Ahmedabad and Broach. To prevent buying in haste, the Directors must keep the factors in Gujarat well provided with cash and goods. Otherwise one could imagine how much of interest will have to be paid on a loan of f.100,000. The spices had gone down in price because of the import from Masulipatnam via Burhanpur. Only if the sale of spices in Coromandel was confined to the quantities consumed locally, could the spices do better in Gujarat. Also, the price of the spices sold at Coromandel ought to be increased. Since the Company competed with the English in buying indigo Sarkhej, it became very difficult to procure it if the factors did not have enough cash at the right time. The merchants of Ahmedabad as well as the indigo farmers of Sarkhej knew very well that once the ships arrived, the factors would be obliged to buy because the ships could not be sent back empty. Therefore, they increased the price at that time and the factors had to dance to their tune. On the other hand, if they had cash available at the right time, they would have bought indigo Sarkhej cheaper by 10 to 15 per cent.

c. Regarding whether the Company would have a good trade during the current and the coming years, nothing could be said with certainty. Things would become clear only during the rainy season. If in the beginning of the rainy season, that is in June and July, it rained very hard, the crops of both indigo and cotton standing in the fields would be adversely affected. On the other hand, if it rained too little, the crops would be lost due to the shortage of water. A hard wind after the rains does no good to the crops either. Besides, in view of the troubles created by Prince Khurram before he became king, some of the farmers might have fled and to that extent, the crops sown would be that much smaller.

Regarding the quantity of clothes and other goods that could be procured annually in Ahmedabad for Holland and the southern quarters, the factors had the following information:

Indigo Sarkhej: In a good year, 15,000-20,000 *maunds*: in a normal or a slack year, 8,000-10,000 *maunds*. Indigo was bought by the Dutch, the English and many other merchants. Foreign merchants carried a large amount of it to Mocha. Besides, a large amount was sold within the country. A large amount of indigo could be procured currently at Ahmedabad and Sarkhej. Over the last two years, the English and the Dutch had bought no indigo Sarkhej and stocks had built up. The price of both indigo Sarkhej as well as of indigo Bayana at Agra, however, continued to be high.

Saltpetre: 6,000-7,000 *maunds* and even more could be procured each year. But it must be done in time because otherwise the English purchased it. One could also purchase per annum 300-400 *maunds* of sal ammoniac, 200-50 *maunds* of spiconardi, 1,500-2,000 *maunds* of gumlac, 100 *maunds* of white cuminseed, and 300-400 *maunds* of lignum vitae.

Textiles: Around Ahmedabad, and mainly in Cambay and Broach, textiles were manufactured in black and other colours. Ten times the amount ordered by Batavia could be bought. These varieties included a large amount of red and black *chelas*, black and white *berams*, black *cannekins*, *baftas* of 28 yards, black and white *chelas*, broad and small *dhoti dholka,* both coarse and fine. The broad ones were available at about 50 rupees per 20 pieces. Then one could get *armosins*, poor-quality *alcatifs*, some gold *alcatifs* and bright *orhnis* of gold and silver worn by women around their necks and heads in place of veils. Then there were the golden *kamarbands* and many other varieties with gold and silver work.

Of these varieties of textiles, one could buy as many as one wanted. After the ships had left Surat for Batavia, the factors ought to gradually put out contracts for these textiles. The Company could then get them 10 to 20 per cent cheaper than if they were bought in a hurry. When the factors were short of cash, they had to buy from the banias who got their stock manufactured during the rainy season and which they sold to the Dutch. Some other varieties of clothes which were produced in

Patan, which was about 14 *kos*[8] from Ahmedabad, were silk *patolas* of different lengths and prices and eight varieties of *alachas* of 27-8 yards length and 1 yard width. The price ranged between 40 and 100 rupees per 20 pieces. Other varieties available included *kamarbands* and some *rumals*. But these varieties had to be specially ordered.

As far as Cambay was concerned, the potential for sales was rather limited. It was true that the Portuguese brought in from Goa goods such as elephant tusks, tortoise horn, quicksilver, vermilion, agilwood, porcelain, lignum vitae, tin, lead and small quantities of cloves and other things. The goods they bought there were mainly clothes which they carried to Goa, Chaul, Mozambique, Malacca and other places. Since the time at the disposal of the Portuguese at Cambay was limited, they sold the goods at a low profit. They made the bulk of their profit on the goods they bought there.

A large variety of textiles manufactured in Cambay were exported to Mocha and Jeddah. The varieties that the Muslims took there included *cannekins*, *mossaffyzery*,[9] *minatashis*, *siadder corgia*,[9] *Cadia*,[9] *sounzou*,[9] *siadder sampwaly*,[9] *allegias*, fine *berams*, *sikandari cadia rissemy*[9] and many other similar varieties. A large variety of textiles was available in Cambay. One had to go about procuring them on time because all these had to be contracted for in advance, particularly the varieties that the Dutch exported to the southern quarters.

Items	*Prices*
Saltpetre	2 rupees per *maund* of 30½ ponds
Indigo Sarkhej	12 to 15 rupees per *maund*. The price varies with the crop and with the demand
Spiconardy	4 rupees per *maund* of 30½ Dutch ponds
Sal ammoniac	6 rupees per *maund* of 30½ Dutch ponds
Powder sugar	3 to 4 rupees per *maund* of 30½ Dutch ponds
Sugar candy	6 to 7 rupees per *maund* of 30½ Dutch ponds

White cumin	2 to 2½ rupees per *maund* of 30½ Dutch ponds
Ligna vitae	4 rupees per *maund* of 30½ Dutch ponds
Walnuts	7 to 7½ rupees per *maund* of 30½ Dutch ponds
Asafoetida	15 to 40 rupees per *maund* of 30½ Dutch ponds
Opium (bought second hand)	70-80 rupees per *maund* of 30½ Dutch ponds

Prices of goods that could be sold in Ahmedabad

Quicksilver	100 rupees per *maund*
Vermilion	90 to 100 rupees per *maund*
Elephant tusks	400-500 rupees per *bahar*
Tortois horn	100 to 110 rupees per *maund*
Alamber[9]	4, 7, and 10 rupees respectively for the three qualities per *ceer* of ¾ ponds
Sandalwood	25 to 40 rupees per *maund*
Benzoin	25 to 30 rupees per *maund*
Borneo camphor	1 rupee per *tola* or 1/43 ponds
Poor quality camphor	15 to 18 rupees per *maund*
Poutchina	15 to 17 rupees per *maund*
Tin	15 to 16 rupees per *maund*
Lead	3¾ to 4 rupees per *maund*

The local market for cloves, nutmeg and mace was quite small. These spices could only be sold in the city and the sorrounding areas.

While Van der Lee was in Ahmedabad, the English sold in one lot quicksilver worth 80,000 rupees (or 40,000 rials of eight) on which they had made no smaller than 100 per cent profit. The English had almost monopolized the trade in quicksilver and vermilion and made a large profit on it. Van der Lee hoped that the Company would also participate in this trade.

Since Cambay fell under the jurisdiction of Ahmedabad, it was not necessary to maintain a separate factory there. The contracts of textiles for the southern quarters could be put out at Cambay through a broker. As soon as they were ready, the incharge at Ahmedabad could go there to examine them and to have them packed. Because in Hindustan even small transactions of selling or buying could not be carried out without the bania brokers, it was to be presumed that they made a lot for themselves.

The personnel at the Ahmedabad factory (which had jurisdiction over Cambay as well), was as follows:

One upper-merchant
Two under-merchants
Two assistants

In addition, there were 13 or 14 persons including messengers, servants, a cartman incharge of the cart and two oxen and one horse. Given the Indian norm, this was not a large number.

20 March

Van der Lee left Ahmedabad and arrived at Cambay the following day where various kinds of clothes for the southern quarters were procured. This city was on the River Indus which at this point was about 2 miles wide. The Portuguese ordinarily came to Cambay twice a year. They came here with an armada and bought and sold goods mentioned in the section on Ahmedabad above.

25 March

Van der Lee left Cambay and arrived at Broach on 27 March. The Company's factors there were busy in collecting and packing the textiles for the southern quarters. This city was populated mainly by weavers who were engaged in weaving fine and coarse *baftas* of all varieties. These were available here in better quality and lower price than in any other place. Besides, various other varieties of clothes useful for the southern quarters were manufactured here.

Van der Lee summoned the factor and asked him about the trade at Broach putting to him the same questions as at Ahmedabad.

The factor's replies were as follows:

In the first place, Broach was a city where little trade was carried on. This trade was only in clothes which were mainly *baftas*, broad and small. Besides, very fine small *baftas* of 30 to 45 guilders a piece were also manufactured here which were consumed by the rich people of this area. Besides, Negro clothes, *niquanias*,[10] *soffel*,[10] *tcharolia*[10] *hosema*[10] and other similar varieties were manufactured here. They also produced *chelas*, *trikandia*, *berams*, *alachas* of yarn and silk which were also called *taffechelas*. *Guinees* of 52 *ells* length and *cangans*—both black and white—were also manufactured here. But the latter had to be contracted for and the money given in advance, because no one else bought these clothes here. If contracts were given, other clothes could also be made in sufficient quantities. This was because the whole of this city along with its suburbs was populated mainly by weavers who did nothing but weave.

Many varieties of clothes were bought in this city for Mocha, Jeddah, Persia and Aceh. In addition, the Dutch and the English bought for the southern quarters. The ships left in the months of December to April during which period the textiles were at their most expensive. Usually, our factors received cash only in October or November to buy clothes for the southern quarters and for Holland. That meant that the factors had to buy the clothes at a high price. Mostly the weavers were very poor and lived on a day-to-day basis by weaving. What they prepared during the day and the night, they were obliged to sell the next day itself so that the factors could not buy anything without cash. Very few contracts were put out so that they simply could not do without enough cash here. The goods were much cheaper during the rainy season than during the dry season. This was because during the rainy season there were few merchants around while the weavers were obliged to continue selling their clothes because they did not have the means to store their goods for 2 to 3 months. Also since the weavers were not pressed for time during the rainy season, one could have any kind of textiles made during that period. The rainy season began mostly at the end of April or at the beginning of May and ended at the beginning of October. During these five months, one could get the clothes 15 to 20 per cent cheaper than in the other 5 or 6 months. The result was that the bania merchants who had the resources to do so bought up these clothes during the rainy season and held on until October when ships from all places including those of the Dutch and the English arrived here. They then made a profit of 15 to 20 per cent. The Company could make this profit in the same way as the bania merchants if it had resources to buy in time for the southern quarters and Holland. During the last three years, it had never happened that the factors had sufficient cash in stock to buy the textiles at the right time. It would be even better if the factors were allowed to borrow at 1 to 1¼ per cent per month during the rainy season because even then the Company would gain by about 10 per cent. Besides, the quality of the clothes procured then would be better as had been their experience during the last three years.

Regarding the prospects of trade during the current year, nothing could be said with certainty. But the general opinion among the populace and the merchants was that the trade this year would be as good as last year which was very reasonable.

No goods could be sold here because there were no local merchants of any standing. The only merchants of standing were the ones who bought the clothes during the rainy season and then sold them from October onwards to merchants who sent their ships to Hormuz, Mocha and Aceh and to the Dutch and the English at a good profit.

The only item this place could provide for Europe and the southern quarters was clothes—black and white and of different colours which were useful for the southern quarters. The factors, therefore, must buy here against cash. The only other items bought and sold here were cotton, cotton yarn and similar goods all against cash.

The personnel at Broach consisted of one upper-merchant and three assistants. Following the custom of the land, they kept one cart, two oxen and one horse besides messengers and servants and a cartman, in all 12 to 13 persons.

29 March

Van der Lee left Broach.

1 April

Van der Lee received letters from Agra. They described how Emperor Khurram, now called Shah Jahan Badshah Ghazi, had ascended the throne on 14 February. This was after Prince Bulaqi (son of Khurram's eldest brother Khusrau killed earlier) who had been installed as emperor had been beheaded along with certain other important men.[11] As a result, people were very unhappy at the beginning of Shah Jahan's reign.

In Agra, the factors had bought 2,500 *maunds* of old and new indigo and 1,600 *maunds* of saltpetre, each of 60 Dutch ponds. Some of it had already been dispatched on camels. But the rest could not yet leave because some money was still due on it.

The factors at Agra had complained seriously about the spice trade. The spices sold by the Dutch in Masulipatnam cheaply were brought overland to Agra. This led to a reduction in both the price and the amount sold. It was clear that of the spices sold by the Company in Coromandel, not even half were consumed within that area. The bulk of the spices were transported at great cost to Agra, Delhi, Lahore and Kashmir where they were consumed. The good price and market for these spices that had been there in Agra two to three years ago was no longer there. It seemed that the spices were sold very cheap at Masulipatnam because otherwise they could not be carried to Agra involving great cost and yet affording a profit there in spite of a slack market. As a result, the merchants at Agra did not buy a large amount from the Dutch because they were worried that a large amount might arrive via Burhanpur.

If the Dutch sold in Masulipatnam only as many spices as could be consumed within the neighbouring areas, they could sell in Gujarat and Hindustan annually 50,000 ponds of cloves, 60,000 ponds of nutmeg and 50 sacks of mace. The Agra factory alone might sell 35,000 ponds of cloves, 30,000 ponds of nutmeg and 30 sacks of mace at a good price. This was, of course, subject to the condition that the English did not import a large amount there and spoil the market.

Vapour had written from Agra that since he had been promoted and given a good salary, he was willing to continue serving the Company after the expiry of his current term.

At Surat, Van der Lee asked Van den Broecke the relevant questions (same as at Ahmedabad).

Van den Broecke's response was as follows:

The way to improve the trade was to keep the factories in Gujarat always well provided. In that case the factors could get the cargoes for Europe and the southern quarters prepared properly and profitably.

The experienced persons ought to be continued in their positions.

If Dutch ships damaged ships belonging to Surat or neighbouring areas, it was likely to cause a tremendous amount of problems and often ten times the damage. The factors would like to keep the stocks ready by the time the ships arrived from Batavia. But they needed funds for that.

It was certain that they could meet in full the annual orders both from Europe and the southern quarters provided they had enough cash.

About the possibilities of sales in Surat, nothing could be said with absolute certainty. Because of the large import of spices from Masulipatnam, they could no longer be certain about their prices in Surat.

6 April

A ship from Arabia arrived at Surat with the news that the kingdom of Yemen had been completely taken over by the Arabs and the Turks had been expelled.

Surat was the chief factory for the trade in Gujarat and Hindustan and only a few varieties of clothes were manufactured there, namely *baftas* and *berams*. Most of the other varieties came from the nearby villages of Navsari and Gandevi. All kinds of goods could be sold here such as cloves, nutmeg and mace, sandalwood, quicksilver, vermilion, lead and many other goods. These were carried from Surat to other areas.

The personnel at Surat consisted of the following:

1 Director
1 Upper-merchant
1 Book-keeper-general
3 Under-merchants
1 Secretary to the Director
1 Doctor
3 Assistants
1 Bottler
1 Barber
1 Interpreter
6 marksmen
2 boys

These persons were not always stationed in Surat but often

travelled with caravans to wherever they were needed. Also in the present troubled times, following the death of Emperor Jahangir, it was necessary to keep enough men in the factory for reasons of security.

15 April

The following memorandum was left for Director Van den Broecke. The costs in this factory were excessive. They ought to be cut to the extent possible. Some of the horses which were very expensive to maintain ought to be sold off. Borrowing of funds at Agra to be repaid at Surat needed to be stopped.

The books were to be maintained in the manner that Van der Lee had recommended to the book-keeper.

Van der Lee left for Swally in the company of Van den Broecke and other friends.

21 April

Van der Lee left Swally aboard the *Gulden Zeepaard.* He reached Batavia in June 1628.

[The summary of the daily register on ff.404vo-407 has not been translated because the points mentioned there have already been covered in the daily register.]

[This daily register was submitted by Van der Lee to the authorities at Batavia on 12 June 1628.]

1. These were the so-called *logie-boeken.*
2. These were the so-called *sententie boeken.*
3. This, of course, was emperor Jahangir who died on 28 October 1627.
4. Queen Nur Jahan was also known as Noormahal.
5. Prince Dawar Bakhsh, the son of late Prince Khusrau, was also known as Prince Bulaqi. Following the death of Emperor Jahangir on 28 October 1627 in Rajauri on the outskirts of the city of Lahore, several rival claimants to the throne emerged. The contest centered essentially on the rivalry between Shahryar, the youngest son of Jahangir, who was married to a daughter of Nur Jahan and Prince Khurram. While Nur Jahan's candidate was Shahryar, that of her brother Asaf Khan, the *wazir* of the empire, was Khurram. Considering that Khurram was in the Deccan and would need time to reach Lahore, Asaf Khan was anxious to neutralize Shahryar in the meantime. With the support

of several Mughal nobles, he organized the crowning of Dawar Bakhsh. At the same time, Shahryar also declared himself emperor and took over the imperial treasury at Lahore. The battle between the two princes look place near Lahore itself and Asaf Khan managed to capture Shahryar alive, obliging him to submit formally to Dawar Bakhsh. Immediately on hearing the news of the death of Jahangir, Khurram left for Agra after sending a *farman* to Asaf Khan ordering him to eliminate both Shahryar and Dawar Bakhsh. On 19 January 1628, Dawar Bakhsh was made prisoner at the same time that the Friday prayers were read in the name of Khurram, who was now proclaimed emperor with the title of Shah Jahan. Some days later, Shahryar, Dawar Bakhsh and his brother Gurshasp were all executed. Shah Jahan was formally crowned emperor at Agra on 14 February 1628. But a rumour soon spread that Dawar Bakhsh had in fact been spared and had escaped to Iran and eventually Istanbul. But in fact the person who had done this was a cousin of Dawar Bakhsh who had tried to pass himself off as Dawar Bakhsh. He was so identified and sent to India on the request of Shah Jahan and executed in 1636.

6. Jan Quli Beg, also known as Mirza Quli Beg, in fact continued to be the *qilledar* of the Surat castle for many years.
7. Adam Claessen Verhoeven had come to Surat in 1617 as an assistant aboard the *Middelburg*. He served in the directorate of Surat until 1629 when Coen recalled him to Batavia.
8. The *kos* was a common measure of distance in India. Though there were significant regional variations, it might roughly be regarded as equal to two miles.
9. Not identified.
10. Not identified.
11. See note 5 above.

124. General Letter from Governor-General Coen at Batavia to the Directors at Amsterdam, 9 November 1627. V.O.C. 1091, ff.1-25 (Original).*

The *Zierikzee*, the *Bear*, the *Mauritius* and the *Lands Hollandia* had arrived at Batavia from Surat on 6 July 1627 with 450 bales of Persian silk. For the intra-Asian trade, Batavia had received only 249 packets of clothes and 11 packets of drugs costing a total of around f.100,000 against Batavia's annual orders for a minimum of f.220,000 worth of goods. This would adversely affect the intra-Asian trade of the Company during the year.

According to the books received from Surat, the value of the remaining effects with them was very small. Once the *kafila* from Agra had reached Surat, it would have collected for Europe a total cargo worth about f.150,000 consisting mostly of indigo, some saltpetre, some *alcatifs* and fine clothes besides about 150 bales of Persian silk. This entire cargo would be sent on to Holland by November 1627.

According to Batavia's calculations, once out of the funds left over from last year at Surat, Cambay, Ahmedabad and Agra, a sum of f.150,000 was invested in the procurement of goods for Holland, the sum of nearly f.200,000 taken on interest at Surat and Agra repaid, the costs at these factories met and allowances made for the bad debts, etc., little funds would be left with these factories. All this assumes that the sale of spices at these factories had been reasonable during the year. But in fact the sale of spices had not been very good and their prices at Agra had come down by a third. This was the result of the Company taking spices to Persia and Coromandel. Besides, spices were also imported by the English, the Portuguese and the Danes. This had persuaded the Armenian and Indian merchants who used to buy spices at Agra for overland transportation to Persia and neighbouring areas no longer to engage in this trade. That, in turn, had resulted in a drop in the sale of spices at Agra. It was, therefore, important that the Company imported spices into Coromandel, Surat, Persia and Mocha in a co-ordinated fashion and proportion so that a good sale of spices at all these places was ensured.

For the conduct of the trade at Surat and Persia, Batavia had sent on 4 August 1627, the ships, the *Groot Mauritius*, the *Noord Hollandia*, the *S'Lands Mauritius*, the *Gulden Zeepaard*, the *Dort*, the *Bommel* and the *Weesp* under the charge of Willem Jansz., the former governor of Banda. These ships had been manned with 700 soldiers and properly provided with victuals. They had carried the following cargo: minted and unminted gold and silver worth f.618,000, 7,000 *piculs* of pepper, 30,000 ponds of cloves, 65,000 ponds of nutmeg, 40 sacks of mace, 150 *piculs* of sandalwood, 47 *piculs* of sappanwood, 996 *piculs* of Japanese copper, 5,000 ponds of radix china, 5,000 ponds of *galiga*, 120 *piculs* of Japanese camphor, 460 *piculs* of sugar, 540 pieces of broadcloth in red and other colours, 2,686 ponds of quicksilver, 2,894 ponds of vermilion, 8,767 ponds of tin and 73,880 ponds of lead.

The sales proceeds from this cargo were likely to be around f.1.4 million. The regional breakdown was likely to be as follows:

a. For Surat, Cambay and Agra	
a. Cash	f.418,000
b. Sales proceeds of goods	f.200,000
Total	f.618,000
b. For Persia	
a. Cash	f.200,000
b. Sales proceeds of goods at the prices agreed upon with the king's factor there	f.600,000
Total	f.800,000

Once this capital reached Surat safely, the trade there would be revived and that at Persia, which until now had been rather sober, register an increase.

In addition to goods worth f.150,000 procured from last year's funds and 150 bales of Persian silk, Surat ought to be able to supply goods worth over f.100,000 out of the funds sent to them by Batavia this year. For the Indies, textile orders worth f.250,000 had also been placed with Surat. These two amounts would add up to f.350,000. Deducting this amount from the total of f.618,000 worth of cash and goods sent to Surat, the factors there would be left with f.268,000. Further deducting the establishment costs, etc., the net amount left with them would be around f.250,000. Surat had been instructed to invest half of this amount in the goods for Europe and the other half in goods for the Indies. By November 1628, Surat ought to be able to procure for Holland a cargo worth around f.120,000, but no more.

In order to facilitate the timely procurement of textiles for Batavia, Van den Broecke had been instructed to borrow whatever funds were needed for two to four months rather than keeping the orders under-fulfilled like last year. A timely procurement of textiles would save twice the cost of interest. If Van den Broecke had done the same last year as we had instructed him to do, a profit of f.150,000 could have been made in intra-Asian trade. That profit had instead been earned by our declared enemies as well as rival friends.

The Directors' observations as well as orders regarding the return cargo for Holland had been communicated to Surat. Batavia had only added that in view of the orders for indigo Sarkhej having been duly supplied with the *Gouden Leeuw*, the *Oranje* and the *Walcheren*, this item might be excluded. In the event of an adequate quantity of indigo Bayana not being available for the *Dort*, the shortfall was to be made up with *baftas* and other textiles rather than sending a smaller ship.

The Directors had suggested that one or two ships could be kept permanently in the seas of Surat, Persia and Mocha both to facilitate the freight traffic which would be appreciated by the Muslim traders and improve the Company's relations with the authorities as well as to enhance the Company's security in the region. This was, however, to be done only if there was no great risk involved and there was a prospect of making a profit. Given the Company's current resources and the potential problems involved, this did not seem advisable for the time being.

Commander Willem Jansz. had been instructed to keep one or two strong vessels ready to transport the expected large amount of silk from Persia in 1628. This silk could then be sent from Surat on to Holland in November 1628 together with the other cargo originating at Surat. An early receipt of this silk at Surat would avoid the necessity of keeping it there for another year as happened with the 600 bales last season. The only problem in implementing this plan would arise if the Portuguese ships decided to spend the winter at Muscat. But if they conserved their power at Goa the way they did last year, this project could be put into effect.

Surat had been instructed to send the silk received from Persia this year for Holland on to Batavia rather than keeping it there and expose it to risk at the hands of the Muslims. It will reach Holland via Batavia at least as early as directly from Surat, if not earlier.

In view of the small amount of spices sent this year to Surat and Persia, it would not be advisable to send a ship to Mocha unless it could be done without jeopardising a trip to Persia and ensuring that a cargo which could be sold at Mocha quickly at a good profit was available.

Batavia had instructed Surat that a permanent factory was not to be established at Mocha until express orders to that effect were received from the Directors and a new mandate obtained from the *badshah* of Mocha. In the meantime, it would be advisable to trade there only from the ships or even to neglect the trade if the profits were no more than what the late Van der Speult had been able to earn there. He had been able to sell spices there worth no more than f.26,000 in all.

According to the books closed at Surat on 31 December 1626, the costs over one year in the factories at Surat, Ahmedabad, Broach and of the voyage to Mocha amounted to f.79,000. This amount included f.59,000 most of which was towards the costs on the ships of the fleet of late Van Speult. The general profits in these factories had amounted to f.123,000. This, however, did not include the costs and the profits at the Agra factory because the books from there had not yet been received at Surat.

The total costs at the factory at Persia between 1 October 1625 and 1 October 1626 amounted to f.17,000 including f.2,000 spent on ships and f.9,000 on gifts. The net profit amounted to f.234,000 which had been earned on the following:

	f.80,000 on 215,000 ponds of pepper
	f.70,000 on 50,000 ponds of nutmeg
	f.70,000 on 25,000 ponds of cloves
	f.5,000 on 30 bags of mace
	f.9,000 on miscellaneous goods
Total	f.234,000

Persia could thus provide additional funds for the intra-Asian trade. The Directors could also hope to sell 2,000-3,000 bales of Persian silk annually without cutting into the sales of the Chinese silk.

The *Medemblik* had arrived at Batavia from Coromandel on 1 September 1627 with a cargo of f.144,000 consisting of 422 packets of clothes, 27,135 ponds of raw and refined saltpetre, 30,605 ponds of iron, 12,700 ponds of gunpowder and 173 slaves.

Batavia had sent to Coromandel on 28 August 1627 the yacht *Batavia* of about 150 *lasts* with f.20,000 in cash. The *Medemblik* had been sent there on 13 October with a cargo worth f.120,885 consisting mainly of cash and some spices whose total sales proceeds were likely to amount to f.180,000. Earlier, the *Brouwershaven* and the *Grootenbroeck* had been sent there with a cargo estimated to be worth f.280,000 there. Holland had sent to Coromandel cargo worth f.300,000 with the *Leeuwin*. After the *Medemblik* had left Coromandel, they still had with them f.50,000. All this together amounted to a total of f.830,000.

For a long time now, things had gone poorly on the Coromandel coast. They had not been able to meet Batavia's orders for intra-Asian trade anywhere near the amounts asked for, causing a great amount of lost profit for the Company. This was partly because the Directors had sent no funds whatever to Coromandel last year. The best the Directors could do was to expect a return cargo from there worth the amount sent by them with the *Leeuwin*.

The proposal to take Masulipatnam on farm was neither practical nor profitable. The tyrannical measures the Muslim *havaldar* could adopt in relation to the merchants could never be adopted by the Company. Nor would the Company like to do that given the Dutch nature, the Godly laws and its Christian conscience. Considering that the adoption of extortionate measures notwithstanding, the Muslim *havaldars* had found it difficult to raise the resources they had committed towards the farm, the proposal was likely to involve losses for the Company. In addition, it would involve further problems with the other Europeans as well as Asians operating there.

As desired by the Directors, Batavia had obtained a reasonable amount of gunpowder from Coromandel. If adequate sulpher was made available to them from Holland, they could provide enough gunpowder for the whole of the Indies. But Batavia would still need some gunpowder from Holland because while the Dutch lot remained good for two years and more, the lot from Coromandel did not for more than a year.

The extorted sum of 16,000 pagodas could be recovered with interest only if the Company took retaliatory steps. Coromandel had been suggesting that reprisals against Muslim ships could be taken in the months of February and March. This would be the only means to get the money back because the royal treasury at Golconda would never agree to reimburse the amount. Coromandel was certain of success if the requisite force were made available. A further postponement of this would only make matters worse.

The Company was not likely to do any profitable trade as yet in Bengal. The Danes would have closed their factory there but were not allowed to do so by the Muslim governors and merchants because they wanted the continuance of the Danish factory as a security against Danish attacks on the sea. Bengal was full of wars and troubles so that everything there was out of order. The governor there was changed each month and his only interest was to extort money.

The Danes had troubles with the *havaldar* of Masulipatnam, Muhammad Taqi, who had already extorted 500 *pagodas* from them.

An envoy of the king of Arakan had arrived at Batavia from Coromandel with the *Medemblik*. In his letter, the king had offered the Company all friendship, good treatment and peaceful trade in his country.

Since the Company was no longer permitted to trade in Cottapaten, its debtors had shifted there and there was nothing the Company could do about it.

According to the books closed at Coromandel on 31 January 1627, the profit earned amounted to f.80,000 and the general costs to f.50,000, so that the net profit earned was no more than f.30,000. This happened partly because of the loss of the *Jager* which had put the profits back by about f.50,000.

As desired by the Directors, Upper-merchant Dirck van der Lee had been deputed to visit the Surat factories and sent there with the latest fleet.

* Printed in H.T. Colenbrander (ed.), *Jan Pietersz. Coen*, V, pp. 16-62.

125. The Directors at Amsterdam* to Ysbrantsz. at Pulicat, 3 December 1627. V.O.C. 315# (Copy).

The Directors' last letter to Coromandel had been dated 21 September 1627,[1] but the vessels that carried it had sailed together with the fleet to Batavia only on 12 October 1627. The *Vliegende Draek* together with another vessel had, however, wrecked soon after. The cash carried by the *Vliegende Draek* had been transferred to the *Prins Willem*. The *Schiedam* with f.200,000 worth of gold was being sent to compensate for the *Vliegende Draek*.

The three Surat ships were still under arrest at Porsmuyden under the pretext of the Amboina affair.[2] The Directors hoped that these vessels would be released soon. In the meantime, Van den Broecke was to make a public announcement to the captains of the Company's ships not to call at English ports.

* This letter had been written on behalf of the Directors.
\# The volume is not foliated but the letter covers three single folios.
1. See document no. 115.
2. The reference is to the notorious 'massacre of Amboina' in February 1623.

126. Van den Broecke, Van der Lee and Grijph at Surat to the Amsterdam Chamber, 15 December 1627. V.O.C. 1093, ff. 65vo-68. (Copy).*

Nothing much had happened at Surat since their last letter dated 20 December 1626. The factors had been sitting idle because of the non-availability of cash. The fact that the *Dordrecht*, the *Weesp* and the *Bommel* sent by Amsterdam had gone on to Batavia last year had put back the trade here considerably. Van den Broecke was surprised that the gold and the ducats intended for Surat and which would have rendered a very handsome profit here had instead been sent to Coromandel. Considering that the merchants of Surat and Coromandel were in close contact, this might lead to a fall in the price of gold and ducats at Surat.

The only way to ensure that the ships were able to leave Surat for Holland by 1 December each year was to provide it with one year's requirement of funds in advance.

Admiral Willem Jansz. had arrived from Batavia on 4 November 1627 with seven ships and a sloop with cargo for Surat and Persia. More than half of the proceeds from this cargo would go towards the repayment of the loans at Surat, leaving little cash for the procurement of goods for Batavia and Holland. These ships took more than three months to get to Surat from Batavia. The proper season for the procurement of goods had thus been missed.

Surat would await the Directors' evaluation of the manner in which the 150 bales of Persian silk carried by the present shipment had been packed. Efforts would be made to procure as much of indigo Bayana as possible. The crop had been bad for two years in succession and the Armenians had bought a large amount. The price would, therefore, be somewhat high. Things were no better with indigo Sarkhej. Attempts would also be made to procure a good quantity of saltpetre.

It was not possible to improve the quality of the Guinea-cloth manufactured here. No more of these would, therefore, be sent till further orders. Similarly, fine textiles such as *minatashis*, *cannikens*, painted clothes, and Persian and Hindustan *tapis* would not be sent till further orders. Whatever of these varieties had been put in the *Dordrecht* was already in the Company's warehouses. If these had been sent back, the Company would have suffered a considerable amount of loss.

As much cotton had been put in the *Dordrecht* as it could take. This was the best quality available. Surat had noted that the Directors were surprised that a finer quality was not produced at Surat.

The resources available at Surat would hardly suffice for the procurement of the textiles for the Indies in the quantities asked for unless the spices could be sold. There was, however, little likelihood of that happening because Surat had been glutted by the English imports as well as by the imports from Coromandel.

In order to procure Holland's orders for indigo, saltpetre and other items by December next year, funds would have to be borrowed on interest.

The English had sent two ships, the *Palsgrave* and the *Blessing*, to England laden mostly with Malabarese pepper bought at Surat at 15 to 16 *mahmudis* per 30 Dutch ponds. Besides, they had sent 200 bales of silk bought at Surat last year, some indigo Bayana and Sarkhej, some saltpetre and a large amount of *dhoti-dholkas* or sail-cloth. They had also sent some broad *baftas* costing 8 to 14 *mahmudis* per piece.

Another three English ships had gone to Hormuz and the *Exchange* to Batavia with a cargo of clothes. They spoiled the Company's trade at Batavia in no small measure. Besides, they carried a large amount of freight cargo to Batavia. They thus spoiled the Company's trade in any manner they could.

Six English ships which had gone out last year with a considerable amount of textiles on private account returned to Surat on 11 October 1627.[1] They had brought cargoes on private account of spices – cloves, nutmeg and mace – , sandalwood, tortoise horn, radix china and other goods. This would spoil the Company's trade at Surat. The prices of spices will fall. They were selling cloves at 110 *mahmudis* per 30 Dutch ponds while the Dutch factors had sold them earlier at 210 *mahmudis*. If the English continued in this manner and the Coromandel coast continued to be provided with spices in quantities greater than what they could sell, the trade in spices will give losses rather than profits for the Company.

Five English ships arrived at Surat from England on 11 December 1627 with a large cargo for Surat and Persia. This would lead to a rise in the prices of return goods here by 15 to 20 per cent. These ships had brought along the Persian ambassador. An English ambassador, Robert Shirley, going to the Persian king, Shah Abbas, also arrived with these ships. In all probability, the English would now revive their Persian trade.

If the news that four Portuguese galleons had stayed on in Persia was found to be correct, two strong ships would be retained here. These would be sent to Mocha with spices with orders to go on from there in September to Hormuz to collect the silk which would be lying ready there by that time.

Van den Broecke had noted the disapproval of the Directors in allowing the Persian ambassador to travel on a Company ship and hoped that he would be excused. The king of Persia was expected to disapprove of the impertinence of his ambassador. It might even cost him his neck. The great Mughal had also desired that one of his men be permitted to travel to Holland in one of the Company ships in order to be able to buy some rarities. Van den Broecke had excused himself by claiming that he did not have the authority to accede to such a request.

The late Upper-merchant Wouter Heuten had a good reputation at the Mughal court at Agra. The same was true of Upper-merchant Hendrick Arentsz. Vapour. He had gone to the king with the gift of a *casuwaris* bird to seek a new *farman*. The *farmans* he procured were good but cost a lot of money. The expenses were probably unnecessary because in any case gifts had always to be given to the governor of the place where the Company traded.

News had been received of the death of the great Mughal.[2] A chronicle containing details of the important events in the empire since the time of Jahangir's grandfather was enclosed.

Definitive news had been received on the 12th of December 1627 that Prince Khurram, son of the late king, was only seven miles from Surat with an army of 8,000 horsemen. Merchants of Surat were worried that the town might be plundered because the castle was being held for Prince Bulaqi,[3] nephew of Prince Khurram.

Upper-merchant Francisco Pelsaert's term had expired and he had expressed a desire to return home. He had done a good job as the chief at Agra and Van den Broecke would have liked him to stay on. But since he had so desired, he was being allowed to return with this shipment. He would make a detailed report to the Directors.[4]

Van den Broecke's own term in office had expired and he would have liked to return by the present shipment. But since no replacement had arrived, he was obliged to stay on.

Admiral Jansz. was planning to go to Persia on the 17th of December with the remaining ships of the fleet.

The *Dordrecht* was carrying a cargo worth f.380,953.

* This letter was signed by Van der Lee and Christaensz. Grijph only because Van den Broecke had returned to Surat before the ships could sail. However, a copy of this letter dated 16 December 1627 (V.O.C. 1092, f.372vo) was signed by Van den Broecke.

1. The cargo brought back by these ships suggests that they had returned from Batavia or somewhere else in the Indonesian archipelago.
2. This was Emperor Jahangir who died on 28 October 1627 in Rajauri on the outskirts of Lahore.
3. See note 5 in document no. 123.
4. The well-known account of Pelsaert edited by Moreland and Geyl as *Jahangir's India* (Cambridge, 1925) probably originated in this report. An authentic Dutch version was provided in 1979 by D.H.A. Kolff and H.W. van Santen as *De Geschriften van Francisco Pelsaert over Mughal Indie, 1627, Kroniek en Remonstrantie*, The Hague, 1979.

127. The Directors[1] at Amsterdam to Ysbrantsz. at Pulicat, 23 December 1627. V.O.C. 315 (Copy).*

The invoice of the *Schiedam* carrying cash and cargo worth f.258,446:6:8 was enclosed.[2]

* The volume is not foliated but this letter covers half a folio.

1. The letter was written on behalf of the Directors.
2. The enclosure is not available in the Company's archives.

128. Van den Broecke at Surat to Governor-General De Carpentier at Batavia, 25 December 1627. V.O.C. 1094, ff.53-4vo (Copy)*.

[The contents of this letter are covered by Van den Broecke et al.'s letter to the Directors dated 15 December 1627, document no. 126.]

* This letter had been addressed to De Carpentier because Surat was not yet aware of the return of Coen as Governor-General. Printed in H.T. Colenbrander (ed.), *Jan Pietersz. Coen*, VII.2, pp. 1208-11.

129. Ysbrantsz.'s instructions for Jan Jansz.[1] and Captain Frederick Ryksen[2] going with the yacht the *Grootenbroeck*, the frigate the *Bonne Remedie* and the sloop the *Leeuw Jong* from Pulicat to Point de Galle, 26 December 1627. V.O.C. 1094, ff.110-11 (Not stated whether original or copy).

They would go to Ceylon and cruise 10 to 20 miles east of the Point de Galle. All possible damage was to be inflicted on the Portuguese vessels that they might come across. They were to remain to the east of Galle rather than go very near it because the big Portuguese ships mostly passed east of Galle.

They would jointly decide on a randezvous where all their ships could meet. If they were able to get some prizes, no packets, bales or cases found inside were to be opened or plundered. All the Portuguese men who might be captured were to be well protected and brought to Pulicat. Others found aboard Christians, Muslims or Hindus—were not to be allowed to leave either.

No Muslim or Hindu ship carrying a Dutch pass was to be damaged. If such a ship needed help, it was to be duly provided. But if such a ship was found to be carrying Portuguese men or goods, these were to be brought to Pulicat without causing them any damage. If the *Leeuwin* was met near Ceylon, it was to be asked to return to Pulicat immediately.

English and Danish ships encountered were to be shown all friendship but they were not to be boarded. The cruise was to continue as long as the northern monsoon lasted which was usually the end of February or early March.

The ship of the king of Tenasserim and some ships from Arakan were awaited in March. If they were met, they were to be escorted safely to Pulicat.

1. The reference is to Admiral Willem Jansz. who arrived from Batavia on 4 November 1627. See document no. 126.
2. Lying in the Surat river, Ryksen had damaged more than 180 Portuguese fusts and accompanying Muslim vessels. In recognition of his faithful services, the Company presented him with a token gift worth f.400. In 1629, Ryksen served as the captain of the *Weesp* in the fleet to Surat and Persia.

130. An extract from the invoice of the *Macht van Dort* from Surat to Holland, December 1627, V.O.C. 1093, ff.77-87. (Not stated whether original or copy.)

Cotton yarn, textiles, etc., of a total value of f.380,952:12:13.[1]

1. The details have not been taken down because of the length of the invoice.

APPENDIX I

Documents not included

The following is the list of the documents also consulted but not included in this volume either because they did not contain any particularly useful information or because they did not pertain to India.

1. Governor-General Pieter de Carpentier at Batavia to Pieter van den Broecke at Surat, 24 July 1624. V.O.C. 1082, ff.289-90 (Copy). An exact copy is available in the *Bataviaasch Uitgaande Brievenboek*, V.O.C. 851, ff.85-6.
2. Private (*particuliere*) letter from Van den Broecke at Surat to the Directors at Amsterdam, 22 April 1625. V.O.C. 1084, f.6 (Original).
3. Instructions from Governor-General De Carpentier at Batavia for the persons incharge of the ships the *Arend* and the *Coningh David* going to Arakan and Coromandel respectively, 24 September 1625. V.O.C. 1085, ff.163vo-4vo (Copy). An exact copy is available in the *Bataviaasch Uitgaande Brievenboek*, V.O.C. 852, ff.148-9.
4. Jan Van der Burch at Pulicat to Governor-General De Carpentier at Batavia, 5 December 1625. V.O.C. 1087, ff.170-2vo (Copy).
5. Instructions from Governor-General De Carpentier at Batavia to Commander Frederik Kistjens going to Surat, 5 August 1626. V.O.C. 1089, ff.132-3vo. (Not stated whether original or copy).
6. Commission for Kistjens going to Surat, 5 August 1626. V.O.C. 1089, ff.133vo-4. (Not stated whether original or copy.)
7. Private (*particuliere*) letter from Governor-General De Carpentier at Batavia to Governor Herman van Speult at Surat, 5 August 1626. V.O.C. 1089, ff.129-9vo (Copy). An exact copy is available in *Bataviaasch Uitgaande Brievenboek*, V.O.C. 853, ff.123-3vo.

8. Governor-General De Carpentier at Batavia to the Directors at Amsterdam, 15 December 1626. V.O.C. 1090, ff.151-5. (Not stated whether original or copy.)
9. Van den Broecke at Surat to the Directors at Amsterdam, 31 December 1627. V.O.C. 1093, f.73 (Original).

APPENDIX II

Names of the ships that carried the documents from and to India

Information regarding the names of the ships that carried the letters and other documents to and from India as well as those relating to India is available only in respect of the following documents. It will be seen that letters written in different dates were often carried by the same ship. This was because the ship did not actually leave until after more letters were ready for dispatch:

Document No.	*Date*	*From*	*To*	*Name of the Ship*
1	*2*	*3*	*4*	*5*
2	3 January 1624	Batavia	Amsterdam	The *Haas*
17	29 January 1624	Surat	Batavia	The *Reformation*
22	26 March 1624	Batavia	Masulipatnam	The *Wapen van Rotterdam*
23	26 March 1624	Batavia	Masulipatnam	"
24	26 March 1624	Batavia	Pulicat	"
25	26 March 1624	Batavia	Surat	"
26	26 March 1624	Batavia	Masulipatnam	"
27	26 March 1624	Batavia	Masulipatnam	"
31	25 June 1624	Batavia	Masulipatnam	The *Schoonhoven*
32	25 June 1624	Batavia	Pulicat	"
33	25 June 1624	Batavia	Coromandel	"

34	25 June 1624	Batavia	Coromandel	"
35	2 July 1624	Masulipatnam	Batavia	The *Wapen van Enkhuizen*
37	9 August 1624	Batavia	Surat	The *Zuid Holland*, the *Bantam* and the *Weesp*
39	25 August 1624	Masulipatnam	Arakan	The *Vrede* and the *Medemblik*
41	4 October 1624	Masulipatnam	Amsterdam	The *Schoonhoven*
42	12 October 1624	Pulicat	Amsterdam	"
43	12 October 1624	Pulicat	Amsterdam	"
44	29 December 1624	Masulipatnam	Batavia	The *Wapen van Rotterdam*
45	December 1624	Amsterdam	Surat	The *Gouden Leeuw*, the *Walcheren* and the *Heusden*
46	December 1624	Amsterdam	Masulipatnam	"
47	21 January 1625	Pulicat	Batavia	The *Wapen van Rotterdam*
51	24 April 1625	Surat	Amsterdam	The *Dordrecht*
59	14 June 1625	Pulicat	Batavia	The *Vrede*
60	26 June 1625	Masulipatnam	Batavia	"
61	26 July 1625	Batavia	Masulipatnam	The *Edam*
62	28 July 1625	Batavia	Coromandel	"
64	14 August 1625	Batavia	Surat	The *Goede Fortuin*, the *Bear* and the *Nieuw Bantam*

65	14 August 1625	Batavia	Surat	"
66	12 September 1625	Batavia	Surat	The *Hollandia*, the *Oranje* and the *Mauritius*
67	12 September 1625	Batavia	Surat	"
68	24 September 1625	Batavia	Masulipatnam	The *Coningh David*
69	16 October 1625	Pulicat	Batavia	The *Edam*
73	4 December 1625	Surat	Batavia	The *Arend*
75	1625	Amsterdam	Surat	The *Haas*
77	27 January 1626	Pulicat	Batavia	The *Arend*
81	8 March 1626	Masuli-patnam	Amsterdam	The *Coningh David*
82	8 March 1626	Masuli-patnam	Amsterdam	"
83	5 April 1626	Surat	Batavia	The *Heusden*
89	4 June 1626	Pulicat	Batavia	The *Medemblik*
90	15 June 1626	Masuli-patnam	Batavia	"
91	27 June 1626	Batavia	Pulicat	The *Mauritius*
92	27 June 1626	Batavia	Pulicat	"
93	5 August 1626	Batavia	Surat	The *Zierikzee* and the *Wapen van Zeeland*
94	5 August 1626	Batavia	Surat	"
96	29 August 1626	Amsterdam	Surat	The *Dordrecht*, the *Bommel* and the *Weesp*

97	28 October 1626	Batavia	Pulicat	The *Abigael*
98	31 October 1626 or 12 November 1626	Amsterdam	Pulicat	The *Leeuwin* and the *Kemphaen*
100	20 December 1626	Swally	Amsterdam	The *Gouden Leeuw*, the *Walcheren* and the *Oranje*
103	17 March 1627	Batavia	Pulicat	The *Medemblik*
108	11 July 1627	Batavia	Pulicat	The *Brouwershaven* and the *Grootenbroek*
110	3 August 1627	Batavia	Surat	The *Mauritius*, the *Dordrecht*, the *Noord Hollandt*, the *Gulden Zeepard*, *'s Lants' Mauritius*, the *Bommel*, the *Weesp* and the *Nieuwicheyt*
111	3 August 1627	Batavia	Surat	"
112	3 August 1627	Batavia	Surat	"
113	3 August 1627	Batavia	Surat	"
114	28 August 1627	Batavia	Pulicat	The *Batavia*
116	10 October 1627	Masulipatnam	Batavia	The yacht *Grootenbroek*
117	11 October 1627	Batavia	Pulicat	The yacht *Medemblik*

118	11 October 1627	Batavia	Pulicat	"
119	11 October 1627	Batavia	Pulicat	"
120	11 October 1627	Batavia	Surat	"
121	20 October 1627	Pulicat	Batavia	The *Batavia*
126	15 December 1627	Swally	Amsterdam	The *Dordrecht*
129	26 December 1627	Pulicat	Point de Galle	The yacht *Grootenbroek*, the frigate *Bonne Remedie*, and the sloop *Leeuw Jong*

APPENDIX III

Additional copies of the documents

In respect of many documents, the Company's archives contain multiple copies within the *Overgekomen Brieven en Papieren* series. The following lists the archival information relating to the additional copies in this series. Additional copies available in the *Bataviaasch Uitgaande Brievenboek* series have already been mentioned in the notes to the relevant documents.

Document No.	*Source where the additional copy or copies available*
2	V.O.C. 1080, ff.1-34vo
6	V.O.C. 1082, ff.1-6vo
7	V.O.C. 1082, ff.7-8vo
10	V.O.C. 1082, ff.8vo-9
21	V.O.C. 1083, ff.209-12vo
40	V.O.C. 1083, ff.219-221vo
41	(1) V.O.C. 1083, ff.222-4
	(2) V.O.C. 1084, ff.169-71
42	V.O.C. 1084, ff.172-4vo
43	(1) V.O.C. 1084, ff.55-7
	(2) V.O.C. 1084, f.191
49	V.O.C. 1085, ff.174-82vo
51	(1) V.O.C. 1084, ff.132-5vo
	(2) V.O.C. 1090, ff.90-2vo
53	V.O.C. 1085, f.187
54	V.O.C. 1085, f.186
59	V.O.C. 1086, ff.161-4
71	V.O.C. 1086, ff.7-7vo
77	V.O.C. 1090, ff.26-30vo
78	V.O.C. 1089, ff.1-25
81	V.O.C. 1090, ff.237-44
100	V.O.C. 1093, ff.53-5
121	V.O.C. 1094, ff.100-4vo
124	(1) V.O.C. 1092, ff.1-25
	(2) V.O.C. 1095, ff.133-67
126	(1) V.O.C. 1092, ff.370-2vo
	(2) V.O.C. 1093, ff.55vo-58vo

APPENDIX IV

The old numbers of The V.O.C. volumes

The *Verenigde Oostindische Compagnie* (V.O.C.) volumes were earlier designated and numbered as *Koloniaal Archief* (K.A.) volumes. The following lists the V.O.C. numbers and the corresponding K.A. numbers of the volumes used in the present work.

V.O.C. No.	*K.A. No.*
314	452
315	453
851	755
852	756
853	757
854	758
1079	991
1080	992
1081	993
1082	994
1083	995
1084	996
1085	997
1086	998
1087	999
1088	1000
1089	1001
1090	1002
1091	1003
1092	1004
1093	1005
1094	1006
1095	1007
1096	1008
1097	1009

Bibliography

PRINTED RECORDS, SELECTIONS

Jan Pietersz. Coen, Bescheiden Omtrent Zijn Bedriff in Indie, ed. H.T. Colenbrander, vols. 1-6, W. Ph. Coolhaas, vol. 7 in 2 parts, The Hague, 1919-53.

Generale Missiven Van Governeurs-Generaal en Raden Aan Heren XVII Der Verenigde Oost-Indische Compagnie, ed. W. Ph. Coolhaas, vol. 1, 1610-38, The Hague, 1960.

The English Factories in India 1618-1669, ed. W. Foster, 13 vols., Oxford, 1906-27.

The English Factories in India (New Series) 1670-1685, ed. C. Fawcett, 4 vols., Oxford, 1936-53.

Corpus-Diplomaticum Neerlando Indicum, ed. J.E. Heeres, vols. 1-2, F.W. Stapel, vols. 3-6, The Hague, 1907-53.

Dagh-Register gehouden in 't Casteel Batavia, 1624-1682, ed. J.E. Heeres et al., 31 vols., The Hague and Batavia, 1887-1931.

The Early Annals of the English in Bengal, ed. C.R. Wilson, 3 vols., London, 1845-1917.

CONTEMPORANEOUS WORKS

Bernier, Francois, *Travels in the Mogul Empire, AD 1656-1668*, ed. A. Constable, New Delhi, 1984.

Bowrey, Thomas, *A Geographical Account of Countries Round the Bay of Bengal, 1669 to 1679*, ed. R.C. Temple, Cambridge, 1905.

Dam, Pieter van, *Beschryvinge van de Oost-Indische Compagnie*, ed. F.W. Stapel, et al., 4 books in 7 parts, The Hague, 1927-39.

Hamilton, Alexander, *A New Account of the East Indies*, ed. W. Foster, 2 vols., London, 1930.

Havart, Daniel, *Op-en Ondergang van Coromandel*, Amsterdam, 1693.

Jonge, J.K.J. De, *De Opkomst van het Nederlandsch Gezag in Oost Indie*, 1595-1844, 17 vols. in 18 parts and 2 registers. The Hague and Amsterdam, 1862-1909.

Travels of Fray Sebastien Manrique, 1629-1643, ed. C.E. Luard, 2 vols., Oxford, 1927.

De geschriften van Francisco Pelsaert over Mughal Indie, 1627: Kroniek en Remonstrantie, eds. D.H.A. Kolff and H.W. van Santen, The Hague, 1979.

The Suma Oriental of Tome Pires: An Account of the East, from the Red Sea to Japan, written in Malacca and India in 1512-1515, ed. Armando Cortesao, 2 vols., London, 1944.

Roe, Thomas, *The Embassy of Sir Thomas Roe to the Court of the Great Mogul, 1615-1619*, ed. W. Foster, London, 1926, reprinted 1970.

Tavernier, Jean Baptiste, *Travels in India, 1640-1667*, 2 vols., trans. V. Ball, revised and ed. W. Crooke, London, 1925, reprinted New Delhi, 1977.

Valentijn, Francois, *Oud en Nieuwe Oost Indien*, Amsterdam, 1724-26.

Secondary Works

Arasaratnam, S., *Merchants, Companies and Commerce on the Coromandel Coast 1650-1740*, Delhi, 1986.

Boxer, C.R. *The Dutch Sea-Borne Empire*, New York, 1965.

Bruijn, J.R., Gaastra, F.S. and Schoffer, I., *Dutch-Asiatic Shipping*, 2 vols., The Hague, 1979.

Chaudhuri, K.N., *The Trading World of Asia and the English East India Company, 1660-1760*, Cambridge, 1978.

Coolhaas, W. Ph., *Pieter van den Broecke in Azie*, 2 vols., The Hague, 1962.

Furber, Holden, *Rival Empires of Trade in the Orient, 1600-1800*, Minneapolis & Oxford, 1976.

Glamann, K., *Dutch-Asiatic Trade 1620-1740*, Copenhagen/The Hague, 1958.

Irwin, John and Schwartz, P.R., *Studies in Indo-European Textile History*, Ahmedabad, 1966.

Macleod, N., *De Oost-Indische Compagnie als Zeemogenheid in Azie, 1602-1605*, 2 vols., Rijswijk, 1927.

Meilink-Roelofsz., M.A.P., *De VOC in Azie, Bussum*, 1976.

———, *Asian Trade and European Influence in the Indonesian Archipelago between 1500 and about 1630*, The Hague, 1962.

Moreland, W.H., *India at the Death of Akbar*, New Delhi, 1983.

———, *From Akbar to Aurangzeb: A Study in Indian Economic History*, New Delhi, 1972.

Prakash, Om, *The Dutch East India Company and the Economy of Bengal 1630-1720*, Princeton, 1985.

———, *European Commercial Enterprise in Pre-colonial India*, vol. II.5 in the *New Cambridge History of India* series, Cambridge, 1998.

———, ed., *The Dutch Factories in India, 1617-1623*, Delhi, 1984.

Raychaudhuri, Tapan, *Jan Company in Coromandel, 1605-1690*, The Hague, 1962.

———, and Habib, Irfan, eds., *The Cambridge Economic History of India*, vol. 1, Cambridge, 1982.

Santen, H.W. van, *De Verenigde Oost-Indische Compagnie in Gujarat en Hindustan, 1620-1660*, Leiden, 1982.

Steensgaard, Niels, *The Asian Trade Revolution of the Seventeenth Century: The East India Companies and the Decline of Cavavan Trade*, Chicago, 1974.

Subrahmanyam, Sanjay, *The Political Economy of Commerce , Southern India, 1500-1650*, Cambridge, 1990.

Terpstra, H., *De Nederlanders in Voor Indie*, Amsterdam, 1947.

———, *De Opkomst der Westerkwartieren van de Oost-Indische Compagnie, Suratte, Arabie, Perzie*, The Hague, 1918.

———, *De Vestiging van de Nederlanders aan de Kust van Koromandel*, Groningen, 1911.

General Index

Index of Textiles

(B) Bengal, (C) Coromandel, (G) Gujarat

Geographical Index

Index of Persons' Names

Index of Ships' Names

EurIndia

A few words on EURINDIA...

EurIndia will focus specifically on the history of the economic and cultural relations between both regions through their documentary aspects, in particular the large textual and iconographic collections preserved in India and Europe in the fields of map drawing and textile trade.

EurIndia Partnership consists of European (University of Gent—Belgium; Universita Cattolica di Piacenza—Italie; Archives d'Outre-Mer—France; Centre de Conservation du Livre—France) and Indian (University of Delhi; Punjab State Archives) organizations with specific expertise on EurIndia fields of action.

EurIndia's website *www.eurindia.org,* available in several languages, shows a large presentation of the project, the partners, news & events, as well as 'Public Results' section frequently updated and dedicated to the results obtained by the actions developed.

CONTACT: EurIndia Coordinator, Stephane Ipert, Centre de Conservation du Livre, France.

ECCP

The overall objective of the ECCP is to strengthen and enhance civil society links and cross-cultural cooperation between India and the European Union through increased dialogue, information exchange and networking. This will help raise awareness of India in the European Union and of the European Union in India.